Books by Ernest Hemingway

THE ENDURING HEMINGWAY

THE NICK ADAMS STORIES

ISLANDS IN THE STREAM

THE FIFTH COLUMN AND FOUR STORIES
   OF THE SPANISH CIVIL WAR

BY-LINE: ERNEST HEMINGWAY

A MOVEABLE FEAST

THREE NOVELS

THE SNOWS OF KILIMANJARO AND OTHER STORIES

THE HEMINGWAY READER

THE OLD MAN AND THE SEA

ACROSS THE RIVER AND INTO THE TREES

FOR WHOM THE BELL TOLLS

THE SHORT STORIES OF ERNEST HEMINGWAY

TO HAVE AND HAVE NOT

GREEN HILLS OF AFRICA

WINNER TAKE NOTHING

DEATH IN THE AFTERNOON

IN OUR TIME

A FAREWELL TO ARMS

MEN WITHOUT WOMEN

THE SUN ALSO RISES

THE TORRENTS OF SPRING

BY-LINE: ERNEST HEMINGWAY

BY-LINE:
ERNEST HEMINGWAY

Selected Articles and Dispatches of Four Decades

EDITED BY **WILLIAM WHITE**

CHARLES SCRIBNER'S SONS · NEW YORK

THIS BOOK PUBLISHED SIMULTANEOUSLY IN
THE UNITED STATES OF AMERICA AND IN CANADA—
COPYRIGHT UNDER THE BERNE CONVENTION.

ALL RIGHTS RESERVED. NO PART OF THIS BOOK
MAY BE REPRODUCED IN ANY FORM WITHOUT
THE PERMISSION OF CHARLES SCRIBNER'S SONS

7 9 11 13 15 17 19   F/P   20 18 16 14 12 10 8 6

PRINTED IN THE UNITED STATES OF AMERICA

Library of Congress Catalog Card Number 67-15483

ISBN 0-684-10233-1 (cloth)
ISBN 0-684-13685-6 (paper)

Contents

CONTENTS

CONTENTS

II. *Esquire, 1933–1936*

CONTENTS

III. *Spanish Civil War, 1937–1939*

CONTENTS

IV. *World War II*

CONTENTS

Hemingway needs no introduction . . .

ERNEST HEMINGWAY, the best-known writer of his generation, needs no introduction to readers today. But this volume, made up of less than one third of the identifiable prose he wrote for newspapers and magazines between 1920 and 1956, does need a few words of explanation. Early in his career, some time before 1931, Hemingway wrote to his bibliographer, Louis Henry Cohn, that the "newspaper stuff I have written . . . has nothing to do with the other writing which is entirely apart. . . . The first right that a man writing has is the choice of what he will publish. If you have made your living as a newspaperman, learning your trade, writing against deadlines, writing to make stuff timely rather than permanent, no one has any right to dig this stuff up and use it against the stuff you have written to write the best you can."

This is a perfectly reasonable attitude for a novelist or creative writer to take in distinguishing between his fiction and his newspaper reporting. Yet in his more than forty years of writing, not only did Hemingway use the very same material for both news accounts and short stories: he took pieces he first filed with magazines and newspapers and published them with virtually no change in his own books as short stories. For example, two pieces, "A Silent, Ghastly Procession" and "Refugees from Thrace" are news reports (for *The Toronto Daily Star*) based on experiences he was later to use in *In Our Time* (1930), where he wrote:

"The Greeks were nice chaps too. When they evacuated they had all their baggage animals they couldn't take off with them so they just broke their forelegs and dumped them into the shallow water. All those mules with their forelegs broken and pushed over into the shallow water. It was all a pleasant business. My word yes a most pleasant business."

The same material turns up again in "On the Quai at Smyrna" in *The Fifth Column and the First Forty-Nine Stories* (1938) and a few other places. Another Toronto *Star* "news story," "Christmas on the Roof of the World," which is included in the present collection, was privately printed (not by Hemingway) as *Two Christmas Tales* (1959). But the blurring of the distinction between his news writing and his imaginative writing is most evident in these three instances: "Italy, 1927," a factual account of a motor trip through Spezia, Genoa and Fascist Italy, first published in *The New Republic* (May 18, 1927) as journalism, then used as a short story in *Men Without Women* (1927) with a new title, "Che Ti Dice La Patria," and in *The Fifth Column and the First Forty-Nine Stories* (1938); "Old Man at the Bridge," cabled as a news dispatch from Barcelona and published in *Ken* (May 19, 1938) and also put into the *First Forty-Nine Stories* without even a new title; and "The Chauffeurs of Madrid," originally sent on May 22, 1937, by the North American Newspaper Alliance (NANA) to subscribers of its foreign service as part of Hemingway's coverage of the Spanish Civil War, and which was included by Hemingway in *Men at War* (1942), which he edited and subtitled "The Best War Stories of All Time." (What did he mean by "stories"?) Hemingway also used in the same collection the Caporetto passages from *A Farewell to Arms* and the El Sordo sequence from *For Whom the Bell Tolls.* As Chaucer liked to say, "What nedeth wordes mo?"

As a reporter and foreign correspondent in Kansas City (before World War I), Chicago, Toronto, Paris among the expatriates, the Near East, in Europe with the diplomats and statesmen, in Germany and Spain, Hemingway soaked up persons and places and life like a sponge: these were to become matter for his short stories and novels. His use of this material, however, sets him apart from other creative writers who, as he himself says, made their living as journalists, learning their trade, writing against deadlines, writing to make stuff timely rather than permanent. Hemingway, no matter what he wrote or why he was writing, or for whom, was always the creative writer: he used his material to suit his imaginative purposes. This does not mean that he was not a good reporter, for he showed a grasp of politics and economics, was an amazing observer, and knew how to dig for information. But his craft was the craft of fiction, not factual reporting. And though he wrote as he saw things, his writing shows most vividly how he *felt* about what he saw. If the details were sometimes slighted, the picture as a whole—full of the emotional impact of the events on the people—was clear, lucid and full. For the picture as a whole was what Hemingway the artist cared about.

In selecting the 77 articles in the present volume, I have not limited myself to "uncollected" material, for many of the Toronto *Star* pieces appear in *Hemingway: The Wild Years* (1962), edited by Gene Z. Hanrahan; "Marlin off the Morro" (*Esquire*) in *American Big Game Fishing* (1935), edited by Eugene V. Connett; "A. D. in Africa" (*Esquire*) in *Fun in Bed: Just What the Doctor Ordered* (1938), edited by Frank Scully; "Remembering Shooting-Flying" (*Esquire*) in *Esquire's First Sports Reader* (1945), edited by Herbert Graffis; "On the Blue Water" (*Esquire*) in *Blow the Man Down* (1937), edited by Eric Devine; "Notes on the Next War" and "The Malady of Power" (*Esquire*) as outstanding essays in American magazines in *American Points of View 1934–1935* (1936) and *American Points of View 1936* (1937), edited by William H. and Kathryn Coe Cordell; "The Clark's Fork Valley, Wyoming" (*Vogue*) in *Vogue's First Reader* (1942), with an introduction by Frank Crowninshield; "A New Kind of War" (NANA) in *A Treasury of Great Reporting* (1949), edited by Louis L. Snyder and Richard B. Morris; and "London Fights the Robots," (*Collier's*) in *Masterpieces of War Reporting: The Great Moments of World War II* (1962), edited by Louis L. Snyder.

The 29 selections (in Section I) from Hemingway's 154 in the Toronto *Daily Star* and *Star Weekly* represent his first contribution and the best of his work for those papers. The last piece in the section was written in Paris after he left journalism and launched his career as a short-story writer. By the time he was writing his "letters" almost every month in the 1930's for *Esquire*—which make up the second section—this career was at its height. Of Hemingway's 31 contributions to *Esquire* I have chosen 17; however, of the remaining 14, six are fiction, outside the scope of my collection.

The NANA dispatches, nine of which I have chosen from the 28 he cabled from Europe, represent Hemingway's return to professional newspaper reporting during the Spanish war. In this third section I also have two articles (out of 14) he wrote for *Ken,* an anti-Fascist magazine edited by Arnold Gingrich; they are not up to the quality of "Old Man at the Bridge," but they are examples of the sort of thing he wrote for almost every issue of this periodical. Although "The Clark's Fork Valley, Wyoming," from *Vogue,* has nothing to do with the Spanish war, it is in this section because of its 1939 date. It is clearly a change-of-pace item and represents Hemingway's continuing interest in fishing, hunting, and the out-of-doors. Every section in the book—except for the one on World War II—has such an article by Hemingway the naturalist, the hunter, the fisherman.

Section IV is made up of eight articles from the short-lived ad-less New York newspaper *PM,* written in 1941, and six reports he wrote for *Collier's* in 1944 as the chief of their European Bureau —"only enough to keep from being sent home." These *PM* dispatches, the work of a mature observer on his first Oriental trip, six months before the bombing of Pearl Harbor, show Hemingway's grasp of things to come; for he predicted that Japan's attack on British and American bases in the Pacific and southeast Asia would force us into the war. Datelined Hong Kong, Rangoon, and Manila, they were all written from notes made abroad after his return to New York. His seven by-lined news stories and the interview by Ralph Ingersoll, which Hemingway edited, are an excellent analysis of the military situation, but they contrast somewhat with his other war correspondence, for the Toronto *Star,* NANA, and *Collier's,* which emphasizes people and places instead of politics. When Hemingway finally got back to Europe for *Collier's,* his escapades led to his being investigated and cleared by army authorities—for violating the Geneva Convention. Of more significance from a journalism standpoint is the fact that his second *Collier's* article, "London Fights the Robots," was chosen in 1962 as one of the "masterpieces of war reporting" by history professor Louis L. Snyder.

For the last section of *By-Line: Ernest Hemingway* I have a fishing article from *Holiday* and a hunting article from a men's magazine, *True;* Hemingway's own account in *Look* of what happened in his near-fatal plane crashes in Africa in 1954; and more about the author himself and his writing in a later *Look* article of 1956.

The texts in the collection follow those of the printed versions in their original newspaper and magazine appearances. I have mainly used the original titles, except for certain newspaper headlines which are too long for an anthology of this kind and which are certainly not Hemingway's in any case. In each instance where a change was made I have included in the table of contents the original headline. (To do otherwise would have caused bibliographical confusion and difficulties for literary historians.) But I have deleted subheads, which were written by newspaper copyreaders purely for typographical purposes to break up long columns of type, and I have quietly (without the use of the academic "sic") corrected obvious misspellings and typographical errors, regularized capitalization and some punctuation. These are accepted practices for a reading text. For the Toronto selections, a considerable debt is due to W. L. McGeary, librarian of the Toronto *Star.*

Hemingway's literary apprenticeship was served in journalism, and his later work in the field earned him money and sent him to places where he wished to be. Yet his enthusiasm, his compassion, and his imagination made such writing far more than just timely stuff. Some readers will no doubt view the material as rounding out the Hemingway record; others, it is to be hoped, will regard it simply as among the best newspaper and magazine reporting available in our troubled times.

WILLIAM WHITE

FRANKLIN VILLAGE, MICHIGAN
February 16, 1967

BY-LINE: ERNEST HEMINGWAY

ONE

> *Reporting, 1920-1924*

Circulating Pictures

➤ *The Toronto Star Weekly* · FEBRUARY 14, 1920

HAVE you a coming Corot, a modern Millet, a potential Paul Potter or a Toronto Titian temporarily adding whatever the new art adds to your home? If not it is possible to obtain one of the finest works of the moderns for a limited time for a mere fraction of its value.

The Circulating Pictures movement had its genesis in Toronto with Mrs. W. Gordon Mills of 63 Farnham Avenue, who last spring approached one of the foremost Canadian artists with the proposition that she might borrow a picture or two for the summer months. The artist, who is one of those that have introduced anger into art, readily consented and together they discussed the possibility of starting a circulating picture gallery. A number of young married women of Toronto enthusiastically took up the idea and now a gallery of circulating pictures is in full swing, or rather circulation.

According to Mrs. Kenneth T. Young, of 152 Bloor Street West, the circulating gallery is at present a very close corporation. After being asked by a writer for The Star Weekly for a story on the new application of Harvey's principle of circulation, she talked it over with the other circulatees and they decided that the publication of their names or the names of the artists would give a taint of commercialism to the entire scheme which would quite spoil it. It wouldn't be nearly so enjoyable to have one or two colorful joyous pictures in your home if you knew that any other responsible person might have them too. Imagine the élan to be derived from the public library if only a dozen or so persons were allowed to make use of it!

The reporter learned, however, that the principle under which the circulating gallery is operating is this: the young matrons select the pictures they wish from the rich, semi-starving or impecunious artists, depending upon the degree of the artist's modernity and his faculty for advertising, and pay ten per cent of the picture's assessed value. They then have possession of it for six months. The present scheme has been for each of the young women to have two pictures and after their kick—to use a slang phrase—has worn off, or after it has become so intensified as to make an exchange advisable, to trade with her nearest fellow member of the gallery.

For example, a picture by one of the artists, who, to quote Mrs. Mills, "has introduced anger into art," might be so potent if hung in the living-room that it might be exchanged after only a few days, perhaps at the husband's request.

Another might be so powerfully pastoral in motif that the husband might be as easily controlled by it as the cobra by the fakir's pipes. Such a picture might remain in a home indefinitely, doing yeoman service on the occasion of such domestic incidents as teething, the purchase of spring hats or the discovery of an overdrawn account.

Then there is the painter's side of it. By this arrangement he receives something at least. His pictures are viewed by many more people and at the end of six months he receives them back ready for sale. But commercialism must not enter in.

A Free Shave

➤ *The Toronto Star Weekly* · MARCH 6, 1920

THE land of the free and the home of the brave is the modest phrase used by certain citizens of the republic to the south of us to designate the country they live in. They may be brave— but there is nothing free. Free lunch passed some time ago and on attempting to join the Free Masons you are informed it will cost you seventy-five dollars.

The true home of the free and the brave is the barber college. Everything is free there. And you have to be brave. If you want to save $5.60 a month on shaves and hair cuts go to the barber college, but take your courage with you.

For a visit to the barber college requires the cold, naked, valor of the man who walks clear-eyed to death. If you don't believe it, go to the beginner's department of the barber's college and offer yourself for a free shave. I did.

As you enter the building you come into a well-appointed barber shop on the main floor. This is where the students who will soon graduate work. Shaves cost five cents, haircuts fifteen.

"Next," called one of the students. The others looked expectant.

"I'm sorry," I said. "I'm going upstairs."

Upstairs is where the free work is done by the beginners.

A hush fell over the shop. The young barbers looked at one another significantly. One made an expressive gesture with his forefinger across his throat.

"He's going upstairs," said a barber in a hushed voice.

"He's going upstairs," the other echoed him and they looked at one another.

I went upstairs.

Upstairs there was a crowd of young fellows standing around in white jackets and a line of chairs ran down the wall. As I entered the room two or three went over and stood by their chairs. The others remained where they were.

"Come on you fellows, here's another one," called one of the white coats by the chairs.

"Let those work that want to," replied one of the group.

"You wouldn't talk that way if you were paying for your course," returned the industrious one.

"Shut up. The Government sends me here," replied the non-worker and the group went on with their talking.

I seated myself in the chair attended by a red haired young fellow.

"Been here long?" I asked to keep from thinking about the ordeal.

"Not very," he grinned.

"How long before you will go downstairs?" I asked.

"Oh, I've been downstairs," he said, lathering my face.

"Why did you come back up here?" said I.

"I had an accident," he said, going on with the lathering.

Just then one of the non-workers came over and looked down at me.

"Say, do you want to have your throat cut?" he enquired pleasantly.

"No," said I.

"Haw! Haw!" said the non-worker.

Just then I noticed that my barber had his left hand bandaged.

"How did you do that?" I asked.

"Darn near sliced my thumb off with the razor this morning," he replied amiably.

The shave wasn't so bad. Scientists say that hanging is really a very pleasant death. The pressure of the rope on the nerves and arteries of the neck produces a sort of anesthesia. It is waiting to be hanged that bothers a man.

According to the red haired barber there are sometimes as many as one hundred men on some days who come for free shaves.

"They are not all 'bums' either. A lot of them take a chance just to get something for nothing."

Free barbering is not the only free service to be obtained in Toronto. The Royal College of Dental Surgeons does dental work for all who come to the college at Huron and College streets. The only charge made is for materials used.

Approximately one thousand patients are treated, according to Dr. F. S. Jarman, D.D.S., head of the examination department of the clinic. All the work is done by the senior students under the direction of dental specialists.

Teeth are extracted free if only a local anesthetic is used, but a charge of two dollars is made for gas. According to Dr. Jarman dentists in general practice charge three dollars to extract a single tooth. At the Dental College you can have twenty-five teeth extracted for two dollars! That should appeal to the bargain hunters.

Prophylaxis, or thorough cleaning of the teeth, is done at the college for from fifty cents to a dollar. In private practice this would cost from a dollar to ten dollars.

Teeth are filled if the patient defrays the cost of the gold. Usually from a dollar to two dollars. Bridge work is done under the same system.

No patients are refused at the Dental College. If they are unable to defray the cost of the materials used they are cared for just the same. The person who is willing to take a chance can surely save money on dentistry.

At Grace Hospital across Huron street from the Dental College, there is a free dispensary for the needy poor that gives free medical attention to an average of 1,241 patients a month.

This service is only for the "needy" poor. Those of us who are poor and are not adjudged needy by the social service nurse in charge have to pay for the medical service. According to the figures at the Grace Hospital, over half of the cases treated last

7

month were of Jewish nationality. The others were a conglomeration of English, Scotch, Italian, Macedonian and people of unknown origin.

Free meals were formerly served at the Fred Victor Mission, Queen and Jarvis streets. But the authorities at the mission state that there is almost no demand now. Prohibition and the war solved the "bum" problem and where formerly there was a long queue of "down-and-outs" lined up to receive free meal tickets, there is now only an occasional supplicant.

If you wish to secure free board, free room, and free medical attention there is one infallible way of obtaining it. Walk up to the biggest policeman you can find and hit him in the face.

The length of your period of free board and room will depend on how Colonel [George Taylor] Denison [police magistrate] is feeling. And the amount of your free medical attention will depend on the size of the policeman.

The Best Rainbow Trout Fishing

➤ *The Toronto Star Weekly* · AUGUST 28, 1920

RAINBOW trout fishing is as different from brook fishing as prize fighting is from boxing. The rainbow is called *Salmo iridescens* by those mysterious people who name the fish we catch and has recently been introduced into Canadian waters. At present the best rainbow trout fishing in the world is in the rapids of the Canadian Soo.

There the rainbow have been taken as large as fourteen pounds from canoes that are guided through the rapids and halted at the pools by Ojibway and Chippewa boatmen. It is a wild and nerve-frazzling sport and the odds are in favor of the big trout who tear off thirty or forty yards of line at a rush and then will sulk at the base of a big rock and refuse to be stirred into action by the pumping of a stout fly rod aided by a fluent monologue of Ojibwayian profanity. Sometimes it takes two hours to land a really big rainbow under those circumstances.

The Soo affords great fishing. But it is a wild nightmare kind of fishing that is second only in strenuousness to angling for tuna off Catalina Island. Most of the trout too take a spinner and refuse a fly and to the 99 per cent pure fly fisherman, there are no one hundred per centers, that is a big drawback.

Of course the rainbow trout of the Soo will take a fly but it is rough handling them in that tremendous volume of water on the light tackle a fly fisherman loves. It is dangerous wading in the spots that can be waded, too, for a mis-step will take the angler over his head in the rapids. A canoe is a necessity to fish the very best water.

Altogether it is a rough, tough, mauling game, lacking in the meditative qualities of the Izaak Walton school of angling. What would make a fitting Valhalla for the good fisherman when he dies would be a regular trout river with plenty of rainbow trout in it jumping crazy for the fly.

There is such a one not forty miles from the Soo called the— well, called the river. It is about as wide as a river should be and a little deeper than a river ought to be and to get the proper picture you want to imagine in rapid succession the following fade-ins:

A high pine covered bluff that rises steep up out of the shadows. A short sand slope down to the river and a quick elbow turn with a little flood wood jammed in the bend and then a pool.

A pool where the moselle colored water sweeps into a dark swirl and expanse that is blue-brown with depth and fifty feet across.

There is the setting.

The action is supplied by two figures that slog into the picture up the trail along the river bank with loads on their backs that would tire a pack horse. These loads are pitched over the heads onto the patch of ferns by the edge of the deep pool. That is incorrect. Really the figures lurch a little forward and the tump line loosens and the pack slumps onto the ground. Men don't pitch loads at the end of an eight mile hike.

One of the figures looks up and notes the bluff is flattened on top and that there is a good place to put a tent. The other is lying on his back and looking straight up in the air. The first reaches over and picks up a grasshopper that is stiff with the fall of the evening dew and tosses him into the pool.

The hopper floats spraddle legged on the water of the pool an instant, an eddy catches him and then there is a yard long flash of flame, and a trout as long as your forearm has shot into the air and the hopper has disappeared.

"Did you see that?" gasped the man who had tossed in the grasshopper.

It was a useless question, for the other, who a moment before, would have served as a model for a study entitled "Utter Fatigue," was jerking his fly rod out of the case and holding a leader in his mouth.

We decided on a McGinty and a Royal Coachman for the flies and at the second cast there was a swirl like the explosion of a depth bomb, the line went taut and the rainbow shot two feet out of water. He tore down the pool and the line went out until the core of the reel showed. He jumped and each time he shot into the air we lowered the tip and prayed. Finally he jumped and the line went slack and Jacques reeled in. We thought he was gone and then he jumped right under our faces. He had shot upstream towards us so fast that it looked as though he were off.

When I finally netted him and rushed him up the bank and could feel his huge strength in the tremendous muscular jerks he made when I held him flat against the bank, it was almost dark. He measured twenty-six inches and weighed nine pounds and seven ounces.

That is rainbow trout fishing.

The rainbow takes the fly more willingly than he does bait. The McGinty, a fly that looks like a yellow jacket, is the best. It should be tied on a number eight or ten hook.

The smaller flies get more strikes but are too small to hold the really big fish. The rainbow trout will live in the same streams with brook trout but they are found in different kinds of places. Brook trout will be forced into the shady holes under the bank and where alders hang over the banks, and the rainbow will dominate the clear pools and the fast shallows.

Magazine writers and magazine covers to the contrary the brook or speckled trout does not leap out of water after he has been hooked. Given plenty of line he will fight a deep rushing fight. Of course if you hold the fish too tight he will be forced by the rush of the current to flop on top of the water.

But the rainbow always leaps on a slack or tight line. His leaps are not mere flops, either, but actual jumps out of and parallel with the water of from a foot to five feet. A five-foot jump by any fish sounds improbable, but it is true.

If you don't believe it tie onto one in fast water and try and force him. Maybe if he is a five-pounder he will throw me down and only jump four feet eleven inches.

Plain and Fancy Killings, $400 Up

➤ *The Toronto Star Weekly* · DECEMBER 11, 1920

CHICAGO.—Gunmen from the United States are being imported to do killings in Ireland. That is an established fact from Associated Press dispatches.

According to underworld gossip in New York and Chicago, every ship that leaves for England carries its one or two of these weasels of death bound for where the hunting is good. The underworld says that the gunmen are first shipped to England where they lose themselves in the waterfronts of cities like Liverpool and then slip over to Ireland.

In the Red Island they do their job of killing, collect their contract price and slip back to England. It is said that the price for a simple killing, such as a marked policeman or member of the Black and Tans, is four hundred dollars. It may seem exorbitant when you remember that the old pre-war price in New York was one hundred dollars, but the gunman is a specialist and his prices, like those demanded by prize-fighters, have advanced.

For killing a well-guarded magistrate or other official as much as one thousand dollars is demanded. Such a price for even a fancy killing is ridiculous, according to an ex-gunman I talked with in Chicago.

"Some of those birds are sure grabbing off the soft dough in Ireland. It's mush to pull a job in that country but trust the boys to get theirs. One job means a trip to Paris."

It is a fact that there have been more American underworld characters in Paris this summer and fall than ever before. They say that if you throw a stone into a crowd in front of one of the

13

mutuel booths at the famous Longchamps race course outside of Paris, you would hit an American gunman, pickpocket or strong-arm artist.

Most of the blood money from Ireland went to back some pony or other. For the gunman believes in taking a chance. He believes that if he can make enough of a stake he can settle down and quit the business. But it is hard for him to quit, for there are very few professions outside of prize-fighting that pay so well.

The retired shuffler off of mortal coils who honors me with his acquaintance is about thirty-eight. Perhaps it were better not to describe him too closely, because he might run on to a Toronto paper. But he is about as handsome as a ferret, has fine hands, and looks like a jockey a little overweight.

He quit gunning when the quitting was good—when the country went dry and liquor running became the best paying outdoor occupation.

After his principal customers discovered that it was altogether better and cheaper to ship whiskey up from the big warehouses in Kentucky than to take the chance of running it across the imaginary line that separates the U.S. and Canada he retired.

Now he is a man about town and bond salesmen call on him. When I talked with him he kept steering the subject away from gunning and the Irish situation to ask my honest opinion on some Japanese government bonds that will pay eleven per cent interest.

In the course of an afternoon I learned a number of things about the trade. Yes, there were American "bump-off" artists in Ireland. Yes, he knew some that were there personally. Well, he didn't know who was in the right in Ireland. No, it didn't matter to him. He understood it was all managed out of New York. Then you worked out of Liverpool. No, he wouldn't care particularly about killing Englishmen. But, then, they gotta die sometime.

He's heard that most of the guns were Wops—Dagoes, that is. Most gunmen were Wops, anyway. A Wop made a good gun. They usually worked in pairs. In the U.S.A. they nearly always worked out of a motor car, because that made the getaway much easier. That was the big thing about doing a job. The getaways. Anybody can do a job. It's the getaway that counts. A car made it much easier. But there was always the chauffeur.

Had I noticed, he went on, that most of the jobs that fell through were the fault of the chauffeur? The police traced the car and then got the chauffeur and he squealed. That was what was bad about a car, he said. "You can't trust any of them.".

That's the type of mercenary that is doing the Irishmen's killings for them. He isn't a heroic or even a dramatic figure. He just sits hunched over his whiskey glass, worries about how to invest his money, lets his weasel mind run on and wishes the boys luck. The boys seem to be having it.

Tuna Fishing in Spain

➤ *The Toronto Star Weekly* · FEBRUARY 18, 1922

VIGO, SPAIN.—Vigo is a pasteboard looking village, cobble streeted, white and orange plastered, set up on one side of a big, almost landlocked harbor that is large enough to hold the entire British navy. Sun-baked brown mountains slump down to the sea like tired old dinosaurs, and the color of the water is as blue as a chromo of the bay at Naples.

A grey pasteboard church with twin towers and a flat, sullen fort that tops the hill where the town is set up look out on the blue bay, where the good fishermen will go when snow drifts along the northern streams and trout lie nose to nose in deep pools under a scum of ice. For the bright, blue chromo of a bay is alive with fish.

It holds schools of strange, flat, rainbow-colored fish, hunting-packs of long, narrow Spanish mackerel, and big, heavy-shouldered sea-bass with odd, soft-sounding names. But principally it holds the king of all fish, the ruler of the Valhalla of fishermen.

The fisherman goes out on the bay in a brown lateen sailed boat that lists drunkenly and determinedly and sails with a skimming pull. He baits with a silvery sort of a mullet and lets his line out to troll. As the boat moves along, close hauled to keep the bait under water, there is a silver splatter in the sea as though a bushel full of buckshot had been tossed in. It is a school of sardines jumping out of water, forced out by the swell of a big tuna who breaks water with a boiling crash and shoots his entire length six feet into the air. It is then that the fisherman's heart lodges against his palate, to sink to his heels when the tuna falls back into the water with the noise of a horse diving off a dock.

A big tuna is silver and slate blue, and when he shoots up into the air from close beside the boat it is like a blinding flash of quicksilver. He may weigh 300 pounds and he jumps with the eagerness and ferocity of a mammoth rainbow trout. Sometimes five and six tuna will be in the air at once in Vigo Bay, shouldering out of the water like porpoises as they herd the sardines, then leaping in a towering jump that is as clean and beautiful as the first leap of a well-hooked rainbow.

The Spanish boatmen will take you out to fish for them for a dollar a day. There are plenty of tuna and they take the bait. It is a back-sickening, sinew-straining, man-sized job even with a rod that looks like a hoe handle. But if you land a big tuna after a six-hour fight, fight him man against fish when your muscles are nauseated with the unceasing strain, and finally bring him up alongside the boat, green-blue and silver in the lazy ocean, you will be purified and be able to enter unabashed into the presence of the very elder gods and they will make you welcome.

For the cheerful, brown-faced gods that judge over the happy hunting grounds live up in the old, crumbly mountains that wall the bright, blue bay of Vigo. They live there wondering why the good, dead fishermen don't come down to Vigo where the happy hunting grounds are waiting.

The Hotels in Switzerland

➤ *The Toronto Star Weekly* · MARCH 4, 1922

LES AVANTS, SWITZERLAND.—Switzerland is a small, steep country, much more up and down than sideways, and is all stuck over with large brown hotels built on the cuckoo clock style of architecture. Every place that the land goes sufficiently sideways a hotel is planted, and all the hotels look as though they had been cut out by the same man with the same scroll saw.

You walk along a wild-looking road through a sweep of dark forest that spreads over the side of a mountain. There are deer tracks in the snow and a big raven teeters back and forth on the high branch of a pine tree, watching you examine the tracks. Down below there is a snow softened valley that climbs into white, jagged peaks with more splashes of pine forest on their flanks. It is as wild as the Canadian Rockies. Then you round a bend in the road and see four monstrous hotels looking like mammoth children's playhouses of the iron-dog-on-the-front-lawn period of Canadian architecture, squatting on the side of the mountain. It does something to you.

The fashionable hotels of Switzerland are scattered over the country, like bill-boards along the right of way of a railroad and in winter are filled with utterly charming young men, with rolling white sweaters and smoothly brushed hair, who make a good living playing bridge. These young men do not play bridge with each other, not in working hours at least. They are usually playing with women who are old enough to be their mothers and who deal the cards with a flashing of platinum rings on plump fingers. I do not know just how it all is worked, but the young men look quite contented and the women can evidently afford to lose.

Then there are the French aristocracy. These are not the splendid aristocracy of toothless old women and white mustached old men that are making a final stand in the Faubourg St. Honore in Paris against ever increasing prices. The French aristocracy that comes to Switzerland consists of very young men who wear very old names and very tight in the knees riding breeches with equal grace. They are the few that have the great names of France who, through some holdings or other in iron or coal, were enriched by the war and are able to stop at the same hotels with the men who sold blankets and wine to the army. When the young men with the old names come into a room full of profiteers, sitting with their pre-money wives and post-money daughters, it is like seeing a slim wolf walk into a pen of fat sheep. It seems to puncture the value of the profiteers' titles. No matter what their nationality, they have a heavy, ill-at-ease look.

Beside the bridge-men who were the dancing men and will be again, and the old and the new aristocracy, the big hotels house ruddy English families who are out all day on the ski slopes and bob-sled runs; pale-faced men who are living in the hotel because they know that when they leave it they will be a long time in the sanitarium, elderly women who fill a loneliness with the movement of the hotel life, and a good sprinkling of Americans and Canadians who are travelling for pleasure.

The Swiss make no distinction between Canadians and citizens of the United States. I wondered about this, and asked a hotelkeeper if he didn't notice any difference between the people from the two countries.

"Monsieur," he said, "Canadians speak English and always stay two days longer at any place than Americans do." So there you are.

Hotelkeepers, they say, are very wise. But all the Americans I have seen so far were very busy learning to talk English. Harvard was founded for that purpose, it is sometimes rumored, so if the people from the States ever slow up, the hotelkeepers may have to find some new tests.

The Swiss Luge

➤ *The Toronto Star Weekly* · MARCH 18, 1922

CHAMBY SUR MONTREUX, SWITZERLAND.—The luge is the Swiss flivver. It is also the Swiss canoe, the Swiss horse and buggy, the Swiss pram and the Swiss combination riding horse and taxi. Luge is pronounced looge, and is a short, stout sled of hickory built on the pattern of little girls' sleds in Canada.

You realize the omnipotence of the luge when on a bright Sunday you see all of Switzerland, from old grandmothers to street children, coasting solemnly down the steep mountain roads, sitting on these little elevated pancakes with the same tense expression on all their faces. They steer with their feet stuck straight out in front and come down a twelve mile run at a speed of from twelve to thirty miles an hour.

Swiss railroads run special trains for lugeurs between Montreux, at the edge of Lake Geneva, and the top of Col du Sonloup, a mountain 4,000 feet above sea level. Twelve trains a day are packed on Sunday, with families and their sleds. They put up their lunch, buy an all-day ticket, good for any number of rides on the winding, climbing, Bernese Oberland railway, and then spend the day sliding gloriously down the long, icy mountain road.

Steering a luge takes about as long to learn as riding a bicycle. You get on the sled, lean far back and the luge commences to move down the icy road. If it starts to sheer off to the right you drop your left leg and if it goes too far to the left you let your right foot drag. Your feet are sticking straight out before you. That is all there is to steering, but there is a great deal more to keeping your nerve.

You go down a long, steep stretch of road flanked by a six hundred foot drop-off on the left and bordered by a line of trees on the right. The sled goes fast from the start and soon it is rushing faster than anything you have ever felt. You are sitting absolutely unsupported, only ten inches above the ice, and the road is feeding past you like a movie film. The sled you are sitting on is only just large enough to make a seat and is rushing at motor car speed towards a sharp curve. If you lean your body away from the curve and drop the right foot the luge will swing around the curve in a slither of ice and drop shooting down the next slope. If you upset on a turn you are hurled into a snow bank or go shooting down the road, lugeing along on various plane surfaces of your anatomy.

Additional hazards are provided for the lugeurs by hay sleds and wood sleds. These have long, curved-up runners, and are used to haul the hay down from the mountain meadows where it was cut and cured in the summer, or to bring down great loads of firewood and faggots cut in the forests. They are big, slow-moving sledges and are pulled by their drivers, who haul them by the long curved-up runners and pull themselves up in front of their loads to coast down the steepest slopes.

Because there are many lugeurs, the men with the hay and wood sleds get tired of pulling their loads to one side when they hear a lugeur come shooting down, shouting for the right of way. A lugeur at thirty miles an hour, with no brakes but his feet, has the option of hitting the sleds ahead of him or shooting off the road. It is considered a very bad omen to hit a wood sled.

There is a British colony at Bellaria, near Vevey, in the canton of Vaud, on Lake Geneva. The two apartment buildings they live in are at the foot of the mountains and the British are nearly all quite rapid lugeurs. They can leave Bellaria, where there will be no snow and a mild, springlike breeze, and in half an hour by the train be up in the mountain where there are fast, frozen roads and thirty inches of snow on the level. Yet the air is so dry and crisp and the sun shines so brightly that while the Bellarians are waiting for a train at Chamby, half way up the mountain to Sonloup, they have tea out of doors in the afternoon in perfect comfort clad in nothing heavier than sports clothes.

The road from Chamby to Montreux is very steep and fairly dangerous for lugeing. It is, however, one of the favorite runs of the Britons from Bellaria, who take it nightly on their way home to their comfortable apartment buildings just above the lake. This makes some very interesting pictures, as the road is only used by the most daring lugeurs.

One wonderful sight is to see the ex-military governor of Khartoum seated on a sled that looks about the size of a postage stamp, his feet stuck straight out at the sides, his hands in back of him, charging a smother of ice dust down the steep, high-walled road with his muffler straight out behind him in the wind and a cherubic smile on his face while all the street urchins of Montreux spread against the walls and cheer him wildly as he passes.

It is easy to understand how the British have such a great Empire after you have seen them luge.

American Bohemians in Paris

➤ *The Toronto Star Weekly* · MARCH 25, 1922

PARIS, FRANCE.—The scum of Greenwich Village, New York, has been skimmed off and deposited in large ladlesful on that section of Paris adjacent to the Cafe Rotonde. New scum, of course, has risen to take the place of the old, but the oldest scum, the thickest scum and the scummiest scum has come across the ocean, somehow, and with its afternoon and evening levees has made the Rotonde the leading Latin Quarter show place for tourists in search of atmosphere.

It is a strange-acting and strange-looking breed that crowd the tables of the Cafe Rotonde. They have all striven so hard for a careless individuality of clothing that they have achieved a sort of uniformity of eccentricity. A first look into the smoky, high-ceilinged, table-crammed interior of the Rotonde gives the same feeling that hits you as you step into the bird house at the zoo. There seems to be a tremendous, raucous, many-pitched squawking going on broken up by many waiters who fly around through the smoke like so many black and white magpies. The tables are full—they are always full—someone is moved down and crowded together, something is knocked over, more people come in at the swinging door, another black and white waiter pivots between tables toward the door and, having shouted your order at his disappearing back, you look around you at individual people.

You can only see a certain number of individuals at the Rotonde at one night. When you have reached your quota you are quite aware that you must go. There is a perfectly definite moment when you know you have seen enough of the Rotonde

23

inmates and must leave. If you want to know how definite it is, try and eat your way through a jug of soured molasses. To some people the feeling that you cannot go on will come at the first mouthful. Others are hardier. But there is a limit for all normal people. For the people who crowd together around the tables of the Cafe Rotonde do something very definite to that premier seat of the emotions, the stomach.

For the first dose of Rotonde individuals you might observe a short, dumpy woman with newly-blonde hair, cut Old Dutch Cleanser fashion, a face like a pink enameled ham and fat fingers that reach out of the long blue silk sleeves of a Chinese-looking smock. She is sitting hunched forward over the table, smoking a cigaret in a two-foot holder, and her flat face is absolutely devoid of any expression.

She is looking flatly at her masterpiece that is hung on the white plaster wall of the cafe, along with some 3,000 others, as part of the Rotonde's salon for customers only. Her masterpiece looks like a red mince pie descending the stairs, and the adoring, though expressionless, painter spends every afternoon and evening seated at the table before it in a devout attitude.

After you have finished looking at the painter and her work you can turn your head a little and see a big, light-haired woman sitting at a table with three young men. The big woman is wearing a picture hat of the Merry Widow period and is making jokes and laughing hysterically. The three young men laugh whenever she does. The waiter brings the bill, the big woman pays it, settles her hat on her head with slightly unsteady hands, and she and the three young men go out together. She is laughing again as she goes out of the door. Three years ago she came to Paris with her husband from a little town in Connecticut, where they had lived and he had painted with increasing success for ten years. Last year he went back to America alone.

Those are two of the twelve hundred people who jam the Rotonde. You can find anything you are looking for at the Rotonde—except serious artists. The trouble is that people who go on a tour of the Latin Quarter look in at the Rotonde and think

24

they are seeing an assembly of the real artists of Paris. I want to correct that in a very public manner, for the artists of Paris who are turning out creditable work resent and loathe the Rotonde crowd.

The fact that there are twelve francs for a dollar brought over the Rotonders, along with a good many other people, and if the exchange ever gets back to normal they will have to go back to America. They are nearly all loafers expending the energy that an artist puts into his creative work in talking about what they are going to do and condemning the work of all artists who have gained any degree of recognition. By talking about art they obtain the same satisfaction that the real artist does in his work. That is very pleasant, of course, but they insist upon posing as artists.

Since the good old days when Charles Baudelaire led a purple lobster on a leash through the same old Latin Quarter, there has not been much good poetry written in cafes. Even then I suspect that Baudelaire parked the lobster with the concierge down on the first floor, put the chloroform bottle corked on the washstand and sweated and carved at the Fleurs du Mal alone with his ideas and his paper as all artists have worked before and since. But the gang that congregates at the corner of the Boulevard Montparnasse and the Boulevard Raspail have no time to work at anything else; they put in a full day at the Rotonde.

Genoa Conference

➤ *The Toronto Daily Star* · APRIL 13, 1922

GENOA, ITALY.—Italy realizes the danger of inviting the Soviet delegation to the Genoa conference, and has brought fifteen hundred picked military policemen from other parts of Italy into Genoa to crush any Red or anti-Red disturbance as soon as it starts.

This is a far-sighted move, for the Italian government remembers the hundreds of fatal clashes between the fascisti and the Reds in the past two years, and is anxious that there should be as little civil war as possible while the conference is in progress.

They face a very real danger. Sections of Italy, principally Tuscany and in the north, have seen bloody fighting, murders, reprisals and pitched battles in the last few months over communism. The Italian authorities accordingly fear the effect on the Reds of Genoa when they see the delegation of eighty representatives from Soviet Russia, amicably received and treated with respect.

There is no doubt but that the Reds of Genoa—and they are about one-third of the population—when they see the Russian Reds, will be moved to tears, cheers, gesticulations, offers of wines, liqueurs, bad cigars, parades, vivas, proclamations to one another and the wide world and other kindred Italian symptoms of enthusiasm. There will also be kissings on both cheeks, gatherings in cafes, toasts to Lenin, shouts for Trotsky, attempts by three and four highly illuminated Reds to form a parade at intervals of two and three minutes, enormous quantities of chianti drunk and general shouts of "Death to the Fascisti!"

That is the way all Italian Red outbreaks start. Closing the cafes usually stops them. Uninspired by the vinous products of their native land, the Italian communist cannot keep his enthusiasm up to the demonstration point for any length of time. The cafes close, the "Vivas" grow softer and less enthusiastic, the paraders put it off till another day and the Reds who reached the highest pitch of patriotism too soon roll under the tables of the cafes and sleep until the bar-tender opens up in the morning.

Some of the Reds going home in a gentle glow chalk up on a wall in straggling letters, VIVA LENIN! VIVA TROTSKY! and the political crisis is over, unless of course they meet some fascisti. If they happen to meet some fascisti, things are very different again.

The fascisti are a brood of dragons' teeth that were sown in 1920 when it looked as though Italy might go bolshevik. The name means organization, a unit of fascisti is a fascio, and they are young ex-veterans formed to protect the existing government of Italy against any sort of bolshevik plot or aggression. In short, they are counter-revolutionists, and in 1920 they crushed the Red uprising with bombs, machine guns, knives and the liberal use of kerosene cans to set the Red meeting places afire, and heavy iron-bound clubs to hammer the Reds over the head when they came out.

The fascisti served a very definite purpose and they crushed what looked like a coming revolution. They were under the tacit protection of the government, if not its active support, and there is no question but that they crushed the Reds. But they had a taste of unpenalized lawlessness, unpunished murder, and the right to riot when and where they pleased. So now they have become almost as great a danger to the peace of Italy as the Reds ever were.

When the fascisti hear that there is a Red demonstration on, and I have tried to indicate the casual and childish nature of ninety-seven out of every hundred Red demonstrations in Italy, they feel in honor bound as the ex-preservers of their country in time of peril to go out and put the Reds to the sword. Now the North Italian Red is father of a family and a good workman six days out of seven, on the seventh he talks politics. His leaders have formally rejected Russian communism and he is Red as some Canadians are Liberal. He does not want to fight for it, or convert the world to it, he merely wants to talk about it, as he has from time immemorial.

The fascisti make no distinction between socialists, communists, republicans or members of co-operative societies. They are all Reds and dangerous. So the fascisti hear of the Reds meeting, put on their long, black, tasseled caps, strap on their trench knives, load up with bombs and ammunition at the fascio and march toward the Red meeting singing the fascist hymn, "Youth" ["Giovanezza"]. The fascisti are young, tough, ardent, intensely patriotic, generally good looking with the youthful beauty of the southern races, and firmly convinced that they are in the right. They have an abundance of the valor and intolerance of youth.

Marching down the street, the fascisti, marching as a platoon, come on three of the Reds chalking a manifesto on one of the high walls of the narrow street. Four of the young men in the black fezzes seize the Reds and in the scuffle one of the fascisti gets stabbed. They kill the three prisoners and spread out in three and fours through the streets looking for Reds.

A sobered Red snipes a fascisto from an upper window. The fascisti burn down the house.

You can read the reports in the papers every two or three weeks. The casualties given are usually from ten to fifteen Reds killed and twenty to fifty wounded. There are usually two or three fascisti killed and wounded. It is a sort of desultory guerrilla warfare that has been going on in Italy for well over a year. The last big battle was in Florence some months ago, but there have been minor outbreaks since.

To prevent any fascisti-Red rows happening in Genoa, the fifteen hundred military police have been brought in. They are none of them natives of Genoa, so they can shoot either side without fear or favor. Italy is determined on order during the conference, and the carabiniere, as the military police are called, wearing their three-cornered Napoleon hats, with carbines slung across their backs, with their fierce upturned mustaches and their record as the bravest troops and the best marksmen in the Italian army, stalk the streets in pairs, determined that there shall be order. And, as the fascisti fear the carabiniere, when they have orders to shoot, as much as the Reds fear the fascisti, there is a pretty good chance that order will be kept.

Russian Girls at Genoa

➤ *The Toronto Daily Star* · APRIL 24, 1922

GENOA, ITALY.—The great hall of the Palazzo San Giorgio, where the sessions of the Genoa conference are held, is about half the size of Massey Hall [Toronto] and is overlooked by a marble statue of Columbus sitting on a pale marble throne sunk deep into the wall.

Columbus, and the press gallery at the other end of the hall, look down on a rectangle of green-covered tables arranged in the familiar shape of tables at banquets, lodges, Y.M.C.A. dinners and college reunions. There is a white pad of paper at each table that, from the press gallery, looks like a tablecloth, and for two hours before the conference opened a woman in a salmon-covered hat arranged and re-arranged the ink-wells at the long rectangle of tables.

At the left of the statue of Columbus, a marble plaque twelve feet high is set into the wall bearing a quotation from Machiavelli's history, telling of the founding of the Banco San Giorgio, site of the present palace, the oldest bank in the world. Machiavelli, in his day, wrote a book that could be used as a text-book by all conferences, and, from all results, is diligently studied.

To the left of the rather pompous marble Columbus is another plaque similar in size to the quotation from Machiavelli, on which is carved two letters from Columbus to the Queen of Spain and the Commune of Genoa. Both letters are highly optimistic in tone.

Delegates began to come into the hall in groups. They cannot find their place at the table, and stand talking. The rows of camp chairs that are to hold the invited guests begin to be filled with the top-hatted, white-mustached senators and women in

Paris hats and wonderful, wealth-reeking fur coats. The fur coats are the most beautiful things in the hall.

There is an enormous chandelier, with globes as big as association [soccer] footballs, hanging above the tables. It is made up of a tangled mass of griffons and unidentified beasts and when it switches on everyone in the press gallery is temporarily blinded. All around the wall of the hall are the pale marble effigies of the fine, swash-buckling pirates and traders that made Genoa a power in the old days when all the cities of Italy were at one another's throats.

The press gallery fills up and the British and American correspondents light cigarets and identify for one another the various bowing delegates as they enter the hall at the far end. The Poles and Serbs are the first in; then they come in crowds carrying their eight-quart silk hats. Marcel Cachin, editor of Humanité, circulation 250,000, and leader of the French communist party, comes in and sits behind me. He has a drooping face, frayed red mustache and his black ˙tortoise shell spectacles are constantly on the point of sliding off the tip of his nose. He has a very rich wife and can afford to be a communist.

Next to him sits Max Eastman, editor of The Masses, who is doing a series of special articles for a New York paper and who looks like a big, jolly, middle-western college professor. He and Cachin converse with difficulty.

Movie men set up a camera under the nose of one of the niched-in Genoese heroes who look down at it with a frozen marble expression of disapproval. The Archbishop of Genoa in wine colored robes and a red skull cap stands talking with an old Italian general with a withered apple of a face and five wound stripes. The old general is General Gonzaga, commander of the cavalry corps; he looks a sunken faced, kind eyed Attila with his sweeps of mustaches.

The hall is as noisy as a tea party. Journalists have filled the gallery, there is only room for 200 and there are 750 applicants and many late comers sit on the floor.

When the hall is nearly full, the British delegation enters. They have come in motor cars through the troop-lined streets and enter with élan. They are the best dressed delegation. Sir Charles Blair Gordon, head of the Canadian delegation, is blonde, ruddy-faced and a little ill at ease. He is seated fourth from Lloyd George's left at the long table.

Walter Rathenau, with the baldest bald head at the conference and a scientist's face, comes in accompanied by Dr. Wirth, German chancellor, who looks like a tuba player in a German band. They are half way down one of the long tables. Rathenau is another wealthy socialist and considered the ablest man in Germany.

Prime Minister Facta of Italy takes the chair. So obscure has been his political career, until he came into light as a compromise premier when it looked as though Italy would be unable to form a cabinet, that biographies of him were issued to all the newspaper men by the Italian government.

Everyone is in the room but the Russians. The hall is crowded and sweltering and the four empty chairs of the Soviet delegation are the four emptiest looking chairs I have ever seen. Everyone is wondering whether they will not appear. Finally they come through the door and start making their way through the crowd. Lloyd George looks at them intently, fingering his glasses.

Litvinoff, with a big ham-like face, is in the lead. He is wearing the rectangular red insignia. After him comes Tchitcherin with his indeterminate face, his indefinite beard and his nervous hands. They blink at the light from the chandelier. Krassin is next. He has a mean face and a carefully tailored Van Dyke beard and looks like a prosperous dentist. Joffe is last. He has a long, narrow, spade beard, and wears gold rimmed glasses.

A mass of secretaries follow the Russian delegates, including two girls with fresh faces, hair bobbed in the fashion started by Irene Castle, and modish tailored suits. They are far and away the best looking girls in the conference hall.

The Russians are seated. Some one hisses for silence, and Signor Facta starts the dreary round of speeches that sends the conference under way.

Fishing the Rhone Canal

➤ *The Toronto Daily Star* · JUNE 10, 1922

GENEVA, SWITZERLAND.—In the afternoon a breeze blows up the Rhone valley from Lake Geneva. Then you fish up-stream with the breeze at your back, the sun on the back of your neck, the tall white mountains on both sides of the green valley and the fly dropping very fine and far off on the surface and under the edge of the banks of the little stream, called the Rhone canal, that is barely a yard wide, and flows swift and still.

Once I caught a trout that way. He must have been surprised at the strange fly and he probably struck from bravado, but the hook set and he jumped into the air twice and zigged nobly back and forth toward every patch of weed at the current bottom until I slid him up the side of the bank.

He was such a fine trout that I had to keep unwrapping him to take a look and finally the day got so hot that I sat under a pine tree on the back of the stream and unwrapped the trout entirely and ate a paper-bag full of cherries I had and read the trout-dampened Daily Mail. It was a hot day, but I could look out across the green, slow valley past the line of trees that marked the course of the Rhone and watch a waterfall coming down the brown face of the mountain. The fall came out of a glacier that reached down toward a little town with four grey houses and three grey churches that was planted on the side of the mountain and looked solid, the waterfall, that is, until you saw it was moving. Then it looked cool and flickering, and I wondered who lived in the four houses and who went to the three churches with the sharp stone spires.

Now if you wait until the sun gets down behind the big

33

shoulder of the Savoie Alps where France joins on to Switzerland, the wind changes in the Rhone valley and a cool breeze comes down from the mountains and blows down stream toward the Lake of Geneva. When this breeze comes and the sun is going down, great shadows come out from the mountains, the cows with their manypitched bells begin to be driven along the road, and you fish down the stream.

There are a few flies over the water and every little while some big trout rises and goes "plop" where a tree hangs over the water. You can hear the "plop" and look back of you up the stream and see the circles on the water where the fish jumped. Then is the time to rewrap the trout in Lord Northcliffe's latest speech reported verbatim, the reported imminent demise of the coalition, the thrilling story of the joking earl and the serious widow, and, saving the [Horatio] Bottomley [fraud] case to read on the train going home, put the trout filled paper in your jacket pocket. There are great trout in the Canal du Rhone, and it is when the sun has dropped back of the mountains and you can fish down the stream with the evening breeze that they can be taken.

Fishing slowly down the edge of the stream, avoiding the willow trees near the water and the pines that run along the upper edge of what was once the old canal bank with your back cast, you drop the fly on to the water at every likely looking spot. If you are lucky, sooner or later there will be a swirl or a double swirl where the trout strikes and misses and strikes again, and then the old, deathless thrill of the plunge of the rod and the irregular plunging, circling, cutting up stream and shooting into the air fight the big trout puts up, no matter what country he may be in. It is a clear stream and there is no excuse for losing him when he is once hooked, so you tire him by working him against the current and then, when he shows a flash of white belly, slide him up against the bank and snake him up with a hand on the leader.

It is a good walk in to Aigle. There are horse chestnut trees along the road with their flowers that look like wax candles and the air is warm from the heat the earth absorbed from the sun. The road is white and dusty, and I thought of Napoleon's grand army, marching along it through the white dust on the way to the St. Bernard pass and Italy. Napoleon's batman may have gotten up at sun up before the camp and sneaked a trout or two out of the Rhone canal for the Little Corporal's breakfast. And before Napoleon, the Romans came along the valley and built this road and some Helvetian in the road gang probably used to sneak away from the camp in the evening to try for a big one in one of the pools under the willows. In the Roman days the trout perhaps weren't as shy.

So I went along the straight white road to Aigle through the evening and wondered about the grand army and the Romans and the Huns that traveled light and fast, and yet must have had time to try the stream along towards daylight, and very soon I was in Aigle, which is a very good place to be. I have never seen the town of Aigle, it straggles up the hillside, but there is a cafe across the station that has a galloping gold horse on top, a great wisteria vine as thick through as a young tree that branches out and shades the porch with hanging bunches of purple flowers that bees go in and out of all day long and that glisten after a rain; green tables with green chairs, and seventeen per cent dark beer. The beer comes foaming out in great glass mugs that hold a quart and cost forty centimes, and the barmaid smiles and asks about your luck.

Trains are always at least two hours apart in Aigle, and those waiting in the station buffet, this cafe with the golden horse and the wisteria hung porch is a station buffet, mind you, wish they would never come.

German Inn-Keepers

➤ *The Toronto Daily Star* · SEPTEMBER 5, 1922

OBERPRECHTAL-IN-THE-BLACK-FOREST.—We came slipping and sliding down the steep, rocky trail through the shadowed light of the pine trees and out into a glaring clearing where a saw mill and a white plastered gasthaus baked in the sun.

A German police dog barked at us, a man stuck his head out of the door of the gasthaus and looked at us. We were not sure this was the place we had been sent to, so we walked a little way down the road that ran through the clearing to see if there was another inn in sight. There was nothing but the valley, the white road, the river and the steep wooded hills. We had been walking since early in the morning and we were hungry.

Inside the inn Bill Bird and I found the proprietor and his wife sitting at a table eating soup.

"Please can we get two double rooms?" Bill asked.

The proprietor's wife started to answer and the proprietor glared at her while onion soup dribbled through his mustache.

"You can't get rooms here to-day or to-morrow or any other time, Auslanders," he snarled.

"Herr Trinckler in Triberg recommended us to come here for the fishing," Bill said trying to mollify him.

"Trinckler?" His lower lip reached up and swept a ration of onion soup out of the mustache. "Trinckler, eh? Trinckler is not the man who runs this place." He went back to the soup.

Bill and I each had a wife out in the clearing. Said wives had begun to be hungry about four miles back on the trail over the mountain. I, myself, was so hungry that my stomach was beginning to rumble and turn over on itself. Bill is built on the lean and graceful lines of an early Italian primitive. Any food he eats shows up on him at once like an ostrich swallowing a baseball. He looked leaner than ever. So we were very polite.

"We are very hungry," Bill said, and I can state he looked it. "How far is it to the next gasthaus?"

The proprietor pounded on the table. "You'll have to find that out for yourselves."

We found it at the end of four miles of hot, white road and it wasn't much to look at. Like most Schwarzwald inns it was named Gasthaus zum Roessle or Inn of the Pony. The pony is the favorite symbol of the Black Forest inn keeper but there are plenty of Adlers (Eagles) and Sonnes (Suns).

All these inns are white plastered and clean looking outside and uniformly neat and dirty inside. The sheets are short, the feather beds are lumpy and the mattresses are bright red, the beer is good, the wine is bad, dinner is at noon, you have to select your piece of black bread carefully to make sure you are missing a sour one, the proprietor never understands what you say, his wife twists her apron strings and shakes her head, there are workmen with their suspenders over their undershirts eating hunks of black bread they carve off the loaf with a pocket knife and wash down with sour wine, the beams of the ceiling are dark and smoky, chickens scratch in the front yard and the manure pile smokes below the bedroom windows.

The particular pony inn we stopped at had all these attributes and a few more. It had a good meal of fried veal, potatoes, lettuce salad and apple pie, served by the proprietor who looked as stolid as an ox and sometimes stopped with a plate of soup in his hand to stare vacantly out of the window. His wife had a face like a camel. That particular lift of the head and look of utter stupidity that belongs only to the bactrian and the South German peasant woman.

It was a hot day outside but the inn was cool and dim and we ate a big dinner with our rucksacks piled in a corner. A table of Germans in the corner kept glancing over at us. When we were on the second bottle of beer and the last of the washbowl full of salad, a tall, dark-haired woman came over to our table and asked us if we were not speaking English.

That was not very hard to answer and it developed that she was an American singer studying opera in Berlin. She looked about forty-five, but like all good singers she had at last discovered that all her life she had been on the wrong track, had been the victim of bad teachers and now she was at last on the right track. Elsa Sembry was teaching her and she was really teaching her. It was Sembry's great secret. Something about the glottis or the epiglottis. I could not make out quite which. But it makes all the difference in the world. You depress one and elevate the other and that is all there is to it.

Mrs. Hemingway and Mrs. Bird went upstairs into one of the little white-washed rooms to go to sleep on the squeaky beds after their 15-mile walk, Mrs. Hemingway's and Mrs. Bird's walk, not the bed's walk; and Bill and I went on down the road to find the town of Oberprechtal and try to get fishing licenses. We were sitting in front of the Gasthaus zur Sonne engaged in an intense conversation with the proprietor, which was proceeding very well as long as I kept my German out of it, when the singer appeared. She was carrying a notebook under her arm. She was in a confiding mood.

Her voice, it seemed—you understand she was telling us all this in the absolutely impersonal manner with which all singers discuss their voices—was a coloratura soprano that had been favorably compared with Melba's and Patti's.

"Gatti-Casazza said I needed just a little more seasoning," she explained. "That's why I'm here. But you ought to hear me trill"—she trilled softly and through her nose. "I never thought much of Galli-Curci. She's not really a singer, you know. Listen to this." She trilled again, a little louder and a little more through her nose. I was impressed. I had never heard anyone trill so softly through their nose or so loudly and clearly through their nose. It was an experience.

She then told us that Mary Garden could not sing, that Yvonne Gall was a bum, that Tetrazzini was a washout, that

Mabel Garrison was a flat tire. After demolishing these impostors she again spoke in a cool impersonal manner of her own indistinguishability from Patti and Melba. We then went back up the road to our inn.

At dinner that night we ran into our second example of German nastiness—and there have only been two examples encountered in two weeks in the Black Forest. The trip isn't over yet but those are plenty.

Our table was set for five, the singer had joined us, and when we came into the dining-room of the inn to sit down we found there were two blonde-haired Germans sitting at the end of the table placed very close to ours. To avoid disturbing them my wife walked all the way around the table. They then changed their seats and Mrs. Bird had to walk all the way around the other side of the table. While we were eating they kept up a fire of comment in German on us auslanders. Then they got up to go. They started to come past our end of the table and I stood up and moved my chair forward to let them by. The space was too narrow. There was a perfectly clear way for them to get out around the other end of the table. Instead, they grabbed my chair and pushed it. I stood up and let them through, and have regretted it ever since.

Early in married life I discovered that the secret of marital happiness did not lie in engaging in brawls in a public house.

"We are Germans," announced one of the two sneeringly.

"Du bist ein schweinhund," which was undoubtedly ungrammatical but seemed understandable. Bill grabbed a bottle by the neck. It looked like the beginning of an international incident.

They stood in the door a minute, but the odds evidently looked too even and workingmen at the next table seemed to be siding with us.

"Schieber!" one of them said, looking up at the two sportclothed, round heads in the door. "Schieber" means profiteer.

The door closed. They went out.

"If only I could speak German," I lamented. "It is bad to

possess a fairly extensive vocabulary and to have a feeling of being dumb when someone is cursing you out."

"Do you know what you ought to have said to them?" said the singer, in an instructive manner. "You ought to have asked them, 'Who won the war?' Or have said, 'Yes, it is easy to see that you are Germans.' I wish that I had thought to say the things I thought of."

That continued for some time. Then she began to trill. She trilled a great many operas while we sat in the smoky inn. However, that night we all went out walking up the road between the black pine hills with a thin finger-nail paring of a moon in the sky, and the singer stepped in a puddle. The next morning the singer had a hoarse voice and she couldn't sing very well. But she did the best she could at demonstrating the use of glottis to Mrs. Bird and the rest of us all went fishing.

A Paris-to-Strasbourg Flight

➤ *The Toronto Daily Star* · SEPTEMBER 9, 1922

STRASBOURG, FRANCE.—We were sitting in the cheapest of all the cheap restaurants that cheapen that very cheap and noisy street, the Rue des Petits Champs in Paris.

We were Mrs. Hemingway, William E. Nash, Mr. Nash's little brother, and myself. Mr. Nash announced, somewhere between the lobster and the fried sole, that he was going to Munich the next day and was planning to fly from Paris to Strasbourg. Mrs. Hemingway pondered this until the appearance of the rognons sautés aux champignons, when she asked, "Why don't we ever fly anywhere? Why is everybody else always flying and we always staying home?"

That being one of those questions that cannot be answered by words, I went with Mr. Nash to the office of the Franco-Rumanian Aero Company and bought two tickets, half price for journalists, for 120 francs, good for one flight from Paris to Strasbourg. The trip is ten hours and a half by best express train, and takes two hours and a half by plane.

My natural gloom at the prospect of flying, having flown once, was deepened when I learned that we flew over the Vosges mountains and would have to be at the office of the company, just off the Avenue de l'Opera, at five o'clock in the morning. The name Rumanian in the title of the firm was not encouraging, but the clerk behind the counter assured me there were no Rumanian pilots.

At five o'clock the next morning we were at the office. We had to get up at four, pack and dress and wake up the proprietor of the only taxi in the neighborhood by pounding on his door in the dark, to make it. The proprietor augments his income by doubling at nights as an accordion player in a bal musette and it took a stiff pounding to wake him.

While he changed a tire we waited in the street and joked with the boy who runs the charcuterie at the corner and who had gotten up to meet the milkman. The grocery boy made us a couple of sandwiches, told us he had been a pilot during the war, and asked me about the first race at Enghien. The taxi driver asked us into his house to have a drink of coffee, being careful to enquire if we preferred white wine, and with the coffee warming us and munching the paté sandwiches, we drove in state down the empty, grey, early morning streets of Paris.

The Nashes were waiting at the office for us, having lugged two heavy suitcases a couple of miles on foot because they did not know any taxi drivers personally. The four of us rode out to Le Bourget, the ugliest ride in Paris, in a big limousine and had some more coffee in a shed there outside the flying field. A Frenchman in an oily jumper took our tickets, tore them in two and told us that we were going in two different planes. Out of the window of the shed we could see them standing, small, silver-painted, taut and shining in the early morning sun in front of the airdrome. We were the only passengers.

Our suitcase was stowed aboard under a seat beside the pilot's place. We climbed up a couple of steps into a stuffy little cabin and the mechanic handed us some cotton for our ears and locked the door. The pilot climbed into his seat back of the enclosed cock-pit where we sat, a mechanic pulled down on the propeller and the engine began to roar. I looked around at the pilot. He was a short little man, his cap backwards on his head, wearing an oil stained sheep-skin coat and big gloves. Then the plane began to move along the ground, bumping like a motorcycle, and then slowly rose into the air.

We headed almost straight east of Paris, rising in the air as though we were sitting inside a boat that was being lifted slowly by some giant, and the ground began to flatten out beneath us. It looked cut into brown squares, yellow squares, green squares and big, flat blotches of green where there was a forest. I began to understand cubist painting.

Sometimes we came down quite low and could see bicyclists on the road looking like pennies rolling along a narrow white strip. At other times we would lift up and the whole landscape would contract. Always we were bounded by a smoky, purple horizon that made all the earth look flat and uninteresting. And always there was the strong, plugged-out roaring, the port-hole windows to look out of, and back of us the open cock-pit with the bridge of the pilot's broad nose and his sheep-skin coat visible with his dirty glove moving the joy stick from side to side or up and down.

We went over great forests, that looked as soft as velvet, passed over Bar le Duc and Nancy, grey red-roofed towns, over St. Mihiel and the front and in an open field I could see the old trenches zig-zagging through a field pocked with shell holes. I shouted to Mrs. Hemingway to look out but she didn't seem to hear me. Her chin was sunk forward into the collar of her new fur coat that she had wanted to christen with a plane trip. She was sound asleep. Five o'clock had been too much.

Beyond the old 1918 front we ran into a storm that made the pilot fly close down to the ground and we followed a canal that we could see below us through the rain. Then after a long stretch of flat, dull looking country we crossed the foot hills of the Vosges that seemed to swell up to meet us and moved over the forest covered mountains that looked as though they rose up and fell away under the plane in the misty rain.

The plane headed high out of the storm into the bright sunlight and we saw the flat, treelined, muddy ribbon of the Rhine off on our right. We climbed higher, made a long, left turn and a fine long swoop down that brought our hearts up into our mouths like falling in an elevator and then just as we were above the ground zoomed up again, then settled in another swoop and our wheels touched, bumped, and then we were roaring along the smooth flying field up to the hangar like any motorcycle.

There was a limousine to meet us to take us in to Strasbourg and we went in to the passenger shed to wait for the other plane. The man at the bar asked us if we were going to Warsaw. It was all very casual and very pleasant. An annoying smell of castor oil from the engine had been the only drawback. Because the plane was small and fast and because we were flying early in the morning, there had been no airsickness.

"When did you have your last accident?" I asked the man back of the refreshment bar.

"The middle of last July," he said. "Three killed."

But that very morning in the south of France a slow moving pilgrim train had slipped back from the top of a steep grade and telescoped itself on another train climbing the grade, making matchwood of two coaches and killing over thirty people. There had been a big falling off in business on the Paris-Strasbourg line after the July accident. But the same number of people seem to ride on railway trains.

German Inflation

➤ *The Toronto Daily Star* · SEPTEMBER 19, 1922

KEHL, GERMANY—The boy in a Strasbourg motor agency where we went to make some enquiries about crossing the frontier, said, "Oh yes. It is easy to get over into Germany. All you have to do is go across the bridge."

"Don't you need any visa?" I said.

"No. Just a permit stamp to go from the French." He took his passport out of his pocket and showed the back covered with rubber stamps. "See? I live there now because it is so much cheaper. It's the way to make money."

It is all right.

It is a three-mile street car ride from the centre of Strasbourg out to the Rhine and when you get to the end of the line the car stops and everyone piles out to herd into a long picket-fenced pen that leads to the bridge. A French soldier with a fixed bayonet loafs back and forth across the road and watches the girls in the passport pen from under his steel blue helmet. There is an ugly brick custom house at the left of the bridge and a wooden shed at the right where the French official sits behind a counter and stamps passports.

The Rhine is swift, yellow and muddy, runs between low, green banks, and swirls and sucks at the concrete abutments of the long, iron bridge. At the other end of the bridge you see the ugly little town of Kehl looking like some dreary section of Dundas [Toronto].

If you are a French citizen with a French passport the man back of the counter simply stamps your passport "sortie Pont de Kehl" and you go across the bridge into occupied Germany.

45

If you are a citizen of some other of the allied countries the
official looks at you suspiciously, asks you where you are from,
what you are going to Kehl for, how long you are going to stay,
and then stamps your passport with the same sortie. If you
should happen to be a citizen of Kehl who has been in Strasbourg on business and is returning to dinner—and as Kehl's
interests are bound up in Strasbourg's as all suburbs are to the
city they are attached to, you would be bound to have to go to
Strasbourg on business if you had any kind of business at all—
you are held in line for fifteen to twenty minutes, your name
is looked up in a card index to see if you have ever spoken
against the French regime, your pedigree taken, questions put
to you and finally you too are given the same old sortie. Everyone can cross the bridge but the French make it very nasty for
the Germans.

Once across the muddy Rhine you are in Germany, and the
German end of the bridge is guarded by a couple of the meek-
est and most discouraged looking German soldiers you have
ever seen. Two French soldiers with fixed bayonets walk up
and down and the two German soldiers, unarmed, lean against
a wall and look on. The French soldiers are in full equipment
and steel helmets, but the Germans wear the old loose tunics
and high peaked, peace-time caps.

I asked a Frenchman the functions and duties of the German
guard.

"They stand there," he answered.

There were no marks to be had in Strasbourg, the mounting
exchange had cleaned the bankers out days ago, so we changed
some French money in the railway station at Kehl. For ten
francs I received 670 marks. Ten francs amounted to about
ninety cents in Canadian money. That ninety cents lasted Mrs.
Hemingway and me for a day of heavy spending and at the
end of the day we had one hundred and twenty marks left!

Our first purchase was from a fruit stand beside the main
street of Kehl where an old woman was selling apples, peaches
and plums. We picked out five very good looking apples and

gave the old woman a fifty mark note. She gave us back thirty-eight marks in change. A very nice looking, white bearded old gentleman saw us buy the apples and raised his hat.

"Pardon me, sir," he said, rather timidly, in German, "how much were the apples?"

I counted the change and told him twelve marks.

He smiled and shook his head. "I can't pay it. It is too much."

He went up the street walking very much as white bearded old gentlemen of the old regime walk in all countries, but he had looked very longingly at the apples. I wish I had offered him some. Twelve marks, on that day, amounted to a little under two cents. The old man, whose life's savings were probably, as most of the non-profiteer classes are, invested in German pre-war and war bonds, could not afford a twelve-mark expenditure. He is a type of the people whose incomes do not increase with the falling purchasing value of the mark and the krone.

With marks at 800 to the dollar, or eight to a cent, we priced articles in the windows of the different Kehl shops. Peas were 18 marks a pound, beans 16 marks; a pound of Kaiser coffee, there are still many "Kaiser" brands in the German republic, could be had for 34 marks. Gersten coffee, which is not coffee at all but roasted grain, sold for 14 marks a pound. Fly paper was 150 marks a package. A scythe blade cost 150 marks, too, or eighteen and three-quarters cents! Beer was ten marks a stein or one cent and a quarter.

Kehl's best hotel, which is a very well turned out place, served a five-course table d'hote meal for 120 marks, which amounts to fifteen cents in our money. The same meal could not be duplicated in Strasbourg, three miles away, for a dollar.

Because of the customs regulations, which are very strict on persons returning from Germany, the French cannot come over to Kehl and buy up all the cheap goods they would like to. But they can come over and eat. It is a sight every afternoon to see the mob that storms the German pastry shops and tea places. The Germans make very good pastries, wonderful pastries, in fact, that, at the present tumbling mark rate, the French of

Strasbourg can buy for a less amount apiece than the smallest French coin, the one sou piece. This miracle of exchange makes a swinish spectacle where the youth of the town of Strasbourg crowd into the German pastry shop to eat themselves sick and gorge on fluffy, cream-filled slices of German cake at five marks the slice. The contents of a pastry shop are swept clear in half an hour.

In a pastry shop we visited, a man in an apron, wearing blue glasses, appeared to be the proprietor. He was assisted by a typical "boche" looking German with close cropped head. The place was jammed with French people of all ages and descriptions, all gorging cakes, while a young girl in a pink dress, silk stockings, with a pretty, weak face and pearl earrings in her ears took as many of their orders for fruit and vanilla ices as she could fill.

She didn't seem to care very much whether she filled the orders or not. There were soldiers in town and she kept going over to look out of the window.

The proprietor and his helper were surly and didn't seem particularly happy when all the cakes were sold. The mark was falling faster than they could bake.

Meanwhile out in the street a funny little train jolted by, carrying the workmen with their dinner-pails home to the outskirts of the town, profiteers' motor cars tore by raising a cloud of dust that settled over the trees and the fronts of all the buildings, and inside the pastry shop young French hoodlums swallowed their last cakes and French mothers wiped the sticky mouths of their children. It gave you a new aspect on exchange.

As the last of the afternoon tea-ers and pastry eaters went Strasbourg-wards across the bridge the first of the exchange pirates coming over to raid Kehl for cheap dinners began to arrive. The two streams passed each other on the bridge and the two disconsolate looking German soldiers looked on. As the boy in the motor agency said, "It's the way to make money."

Hamid Bey

➤ *The Toronto Daily Star* · OCTOBER 9, 1922

CONSTANTINOPLE.—Bismarck said all men in the Balkans who tuck their shirts into their trousers are crooks. The shirts of the peasants, of course, hang outside. At any rate, when I found Hamid Bey—next to Kemal, perhaps the most powerful man in the Angora government—in his Stamboul office where he directs the Kemalist government in Europe, while drawing a large salary as administrator of the Imperial Ottoman Bank, a French capitalized concern—his shirt was tucked in, for he was dressed in a grey business suit.

Hamid Bey's office is at the top of a steep hill beyond an old seraglio and houses the Red Crescent—equivalent to our Red Cross—of which Hamid Bey is one of the leaders and where attendants in Red Crescent khaki carry out the orders of the Angora government.

"Canada is anxious about the possibility of a massacre of Christians when Kemal enters Constantinople," I said.

Hamid Bey, big and bulky, with grey moustaches, wing-collared and with a porcupine hair-cut, looked over his glasses and spoke French.

"What have the Christians to fear?" he asked. "They are armed and the Turks have been disarmed. There will be no massacre. It is the Greek Christians who are massacring the Turks now in Thrace. That's why we must occupy Thrace now—to protect our people."

That is the only guarantee of protection Constantinople Christians have, except the Allied police force, while toughs from the Crimea to Cairo are gathered in Constantinople hop-

49

ing that the patriotic orgy of Kemal's triumphant entry will bring a chance to start a fire in the tinder-dry, wooden tenements and begin killing and looting. The allied police force is compact and efficient, but Constantinople is a great sprawling city of a million and a half, crowded with a desperate element.

The man who raises a thirst somewhere east of Suez is going to be unable to slake it in Constantinople once Kemal enters the city. A member of the Anatolian government tells me that Constantinople will be as dry as Asiatic Turkey where alcohol is not allowed to be imported, manufactured or sold. Kemal has also forbidden card playing and backgammon and the cafes of Brusa are dark at eight o'clock.

This devotion to the laws of the prophet does not prevent Kemal himself and his staff from liking their liquor, as the American, who went to Smyrna to protect American tobacco, found when his eight bottles of cognac made him the most popular man in Asia Minor at Kemalist headquarters.

Kemal's edict will halt the great importation of American raw alcohol shipped to Constantinople in drums and marked "medicinal." This is made into an absinthe-like drink and is sipped by the Turks as they sit in the coffee shops, puffing their bubble-bubble pipes.

A Silent, Ghastly Procession

➤ *The Toronto Daily Star* · OCTOBER 20, 1922

ADRIANOPLE.—In a never-ending, staggering march the Christian population of Eastern Thrace is jamming the roads towards Macedonia. The main column crossing the Maritza River at Adrianople is twenty miles long. Twenty miles of carts drawn by cows, bullocks and muddy-flanked water buffalo, with exhausted, staggering men, women and children, blankets over their heads, walking blindly along in the rain beside their worldly goods.

This main stream is being swelled from all the back country. They don't know where they are going. They left their farms, villages and ripe, brown fields and joined the main stream of refugees when they heard the Turk was coming. Now they can only keep their places in the ghastly procession while mud-splashed Greek cavalry herd them along like cow-punchers driving steers.

It is a silent procession. Nobody even grunts. It is all they can do to keep moving. Their brilliant peasant costumes are soaked and draggled. Chickens dangle by their feet from the carts. Calves nuzzle at the draught cattle wherever a jam halts the stream. An old man marches bent under a young pig, a scythe and a gun, with a chicken tied to his scythe. A husband spreads a blanket over a woman in labor in one of the carts to keep off the driving rain. She is the only person making a sound. Her little daughter looks at her in horror and begins to cry. And the procession keeps moving.

At Adrianople where the main stream moves through, there

is no Near East relief at all. They are doing very good work at Rodosto on the coast, but can only touch the fringe.

There are 250,000 Christian refugees to be evacuated from Eastern Thrace alone. The Bulgarian frontier is shut against them. There is only Macedonia and Western Thrace to receive the fruit of the Turk's return to Europe. Nearly half a million refugees are in Macedonia now. How they are to be fed nobody knows, but in the next month all the Christian world will hear the cry: "Come over into Macedonia and help us!"

"Old Constan"

➤ *The Toronto Daily Star* · OCTOBER 28, 1922

CONSTANTINOPLE.—In the morning when you wake and see a mist over the Golden Horn with the minarets rising out of it slim and clean towards the sun and the muezzin calling the faithful to prayer in a voice that soars and dips like an aria from a Russian opera, you have the magic of the East.

When you look from the window into the mirror and discover your face is covered with a mass of minute red speckles from the latest insect that discovered you last night, you have the East.

There may be a happy medium between the East of Pierre Loti's stories and the East of everyday life, but it could only be found by a man who always looked with his eyes half shut, didn't care what he ate, and was immune to the bites of insects.

No one knows how many people there are in Constan. Old timers always call it Constan, just as you are a tenderfoot if you call Gibraltar anything but Gib. There has never been a census. Estimates of the population give a million and a half inhabitants. This does not include hundreds of battered Fords, forty thousand Russian refugees in every uniform of the Czar's army in all stages of dilapidation, and about an equal number of Kemalist troops in civilian clothes who have filtered into the city in order to make sure that Constantinople will go to Kemal no matter how the peace negotiations come out. All these have entered since the last estimate.

If it doesn't rain in Constan the dust is so thick that a dog trotting along the road that parallels the Pera hillside kicks up a puff like a bullet striking every time his paws hit the ground. It is almost ankle deep on a man and the wind swirls it in clouds.

If it rains this is all mud. The sidewalks are so narrow that everyone has to walk in the street and the streets are like rivers. There are no traffic rules and motor cars, street cars, horse cabs and porters with enormous loads on their backs all jam up together. There are only two main streets and the others are alleys. The main streets are not much better than alleys.

Turkey is the national dish of Turkey. These birds live a strenuous life chasing grasshoppers over the sun-baked hills of Asia Minor and are about as tough as a race horse.

All the beef is bad because the Turk has practically no cattle. A sirloin steak may be either the last appearance of one of the black, muddy, sad-eyed buffalo with the turned back horns who sidle along the streets drawing carts or the last charge of Kemal's cavalry. My jaw muscles are beginning to bulge like a bull-dog's from chewing, or chawing, Turkish meat.

The fish is good, but fish is a brain-food and any one taking about three good doses of a brain-food would leave Constan at once—even if he had to swim to do it.

There are one hundred and sixty-eight legal holidays in Constan. Every Friday is a Mohammedan holiday, every Saturday is a Jewish holiday, and every Sunday is a Christian holiday. In addition there are Catholic, Mohammedan and Greek holidays during the week, not to mention Yom Kippur and other Jewish holidays. As a result, every young Constaner's life ambition is to go to work for a bank.

No one who makes any pretence of conforming to custom dines in Constantinople before nine o'clock at night. The theatres open at ten. The night clubs open at two, the more respectable night clubs, that is. The disreputable night clubs open at four in the morning.

All night hot sausage, fried potato and roast chestnut stands run their charcoal braziers on the sidewalk to cater to the long lines of cab men who stay up all night to solicit fares from the revellers. Constantinople is doing a sort of dance of death before the entry of Kemal Pasha, who has sworn to stop all booze, gambling, dancing and night clubs.

Galata, half way up the hill from the port, has a district that is more unspeakably horrible than the foulest heydey of the old Barbary Coast. It festers there, trapping the soldiers and sailors of all the allies and of all nations.

Turks sit in front of the little coffee houses in the narrow blind-alley streets at all hours, puffing on their bubble-bubble pipes and drinking deusico, the tremendously poisonous, stomach rotting drink that has a greater kick than absinthe and is so strong that it is never consumed except with an hors d'oeuvre of some sort.

Before the sun rises in the morning you can walk through the black, smooth worn streets of Constan and rats will scuttle out of your way, a few stray dogs nose at the garbage in the gutters, and a bar of light comes through the crack in a shutter letting out a streak of light and the sound of drunken laughing. That drunken laughing is the contrast to the muezzin's beautiful, minor, soaring, swaying call to prayer, and the black, slippery, smelly offal-strewn streets of Constantinople in the early morning are the reality of the Magic of the East.

Refugees from Thrace

➤ *The Toronto Daily Star* · NOVEMBER 14, 1922

SOFIA, BULGARIA.—In a comfortable train with the horror of the Thracian evacuation behind me, it is already beginning to seem unreal. That is the boon of our memories.

I have described that evacuation in a cable to The Star from Adrianople. It does no good to go over it again. The evacuation still keeps up. No matter how long it takes this letter to get to Toronto, as you read this in The Star you may be sure that the same ghastly, shambling procession of people being driven from their homes is filing in unbroken line along the muddy road to Macedonia. A quarter of a million people take a long time to move.

Adrianople itself is not a pleasant place. Dropping off the train at 11 o'clock at night, I found the station a mud-hole crowded with soldiers, bundles, bed-springs, bedding, sewing machines, babies, broken carts, all in the mud and the drizzling rain. Kerosene flares lit up the scene. The station master told me he had shipped fifty-seven cars of retreating troops to Western Thrace that day. The telegraph wires were all cut. There were more troops piling up and no means to evacuate them.

Madame Marie's, the station master said, was the only place in town where a man could sleep. A soldier guided me to Madame Marie's down the dark side streets. We walked through mud puddles and waded around sloughs that were too deep to go through. Madame Marie's was dark.

I banged on the door and a Frenchman in bare feet and trousers opened it. He had no room but I could sleep on the floor if I had my own blankets. It looked bad.

Then a car rolled up outside, and two moving picture operators, with their chauffeur, came in. They had three cots and asked me to spread my blankets on one. The chauffeur slept in the car. We all turned in on the cots and the taller of the movie men who was called "Shorty" told me they had had an awful trip coming up from Rodosto on the Sea of Marmora.

"Got some swell shots of a burning village to-day." Shorty pulled off a boot. "Good show—a burning village. Like kickin' over an ant hill." Shorty pulled off the other boot. "Shoot it from two or three directions and it looks like a regular town on fire. Gee I'm tired. This refugee business is hell all right. Man sure sees awful things in this country." In two minutes he was snoring.

I woke up about one o'clock in the morning with a bad chill, part of my Constantinople-acquired malaria, killed the mosquitoes who had supped too heavily to fly away from my face, waited out the chill, took a big dose of aspirin and quinine and went back to sleep. Repeated the process along toward morning. Then Shorty woke me.

"Say boy, look at this film box." I looked at it. It was crawling with lice. "Sure are hungry. Going after my film. Sure are hungry little fellows."

The cots were alive with them. I have been lousy during the war, but I have never seen anything like Thrace. If you looked at any article of furniture, or any space on the wall steadily for a moment you saw it crawl, not literally crawl, but move in greasy, minute specks.

"They wouldn't hurt a man," Shorty said. "They're just little fellows."

"These fellows are nothing. You ought to see the real grown-up variety at Lule Burgas."

Madame Marie, a big, slovenly Croatian woman, gave us some coffee and sour black bread in the bare room that served as dining room, salon, hotel office and parlor.

"Our room was lousy, madame," I said cheerfully, to make table talk.

57

She spread out her hands. "It is better than sleeping in the road? Eh, monsieur? It is better than that?"

I agreed that it was, and we went out with madame standing looking after us.

Outside it was drizzling. At the end of the muddy side street we were on I could see the eternal procession of humanity moving slowly along the great stone road that runs from Adrianople across the Maritza valley to Karagatch and then divides into other roads that cross the rolling country into Western Thrace and Macedonia.

Shorty and Company were going a stretch along the road in their motor car en route back to Rodosto and Constantinople and gave me a lift along the stone road past the procession of refugees into Adrianople. All the stream of slow big-wheeled bullock and buffalo carts, bobbing camel trains and sodden, fleeing peasantry were moving west on the road, but there was a thin counter stream of empty carts driven by Turks in ragged, rain-soaked clothes and dirty fezzes which was working back against the main current. Each Turk cart had a Greek soldier in it, sitting behind the driver with his rifle between his knees and his cape up around his neck to keep the rain out. These carts had been commandeered by the Greeks to go back country in Thrace, load up with the goods of refugees and help the evacuation. The Turks looked sullen and very frightened. They had reason to be.

At the fork of the stone road in Adrianople all the traffic was being routed to the left by a lone Greek cavalry man who sat on his horse with his carbine slung over his back and accomplished the routing by slashing dispassionately across the face with his quirt any horse or bullock that turned toward the right. He motioned one of the empty carts driven by a Turk to turn off to the right. The Turk turned his cart and prodded his bullocks into a shamble. This awoke the Greek soldier guard riding with him, and seeing the Turk turning off the main road, he stood up and smashed him in the small of the back with his rifle butt.

The Turk, he was a ragged, hungry-looking Turk farmer, fell out of the cart on to his face, picked himself up in terror and ran down the road like a rabbit. A Greek cavalryman saw him running, kicked spurs into his horse and rode the Turk down. Two Greek soldiers and the cavalryman picked him up, smashed him in the face a couple of times, he shouting at the top of his voice all the time, and he was led, bloody-faced and wild eyed, not understanding what it was all about, back to his cart and told to drive on. Nobody in the line of march had paid any attention to the incident.

I walked five miles with the refugee procession along the road, dodging camels that swayed and grunted along, past flat wheeled ox carts piled high with bedding, mirrors, furniture, pigs tied flat, mothers huddled under blankets with their babies, old men and women leaning on the back of the buffalo carts and just keeping their feet moving, their eyes on the road and their heads sunken; ammunition mules, mules loaded with stacks of rifles, tied together like wheat sheaves, and an occasional battered Ford car with Greek staff officers, red eyes grubby from lack of sleep, and always the slow, rain soaked, shambling, trudging Thracian peasantry, plodding along in the rain, leaving their homes behind.

When I had crossed the bridge over the Maritza, running a brick-red quarter mile wide flood, where yesterday had been a dry river bed covered with refugee carts, I turned off to the right and cut up side roads to Madame Marie's to write a cable to The Star. All the wires were cut and I finally got an Italian colonel, who was returning to Constantinople with an Allied commission, to promise to file it for me at the telegraph office there the next day.

The fever was going strong and Madame Marie brought me a bottle of sickly sweet Thracian wine to take my quinine with.

"I won't care when the Turks come," Madame Marie said, sitting her great bulk down at the table and scratching her chin.

"Why not?"

"They're all the same. The Greeks and Turks and the Bulgars. They're all the same." She accepted a glass of the wine. "I've seem them all. They've all had Karagatch."

"Who are the best?" I asked.

"Nobody. They're all the same. The Greek officers sleep here and then will come the Turk officers. Some day the Greek officers will come back again. They all pay me." I filled up her glass.

"But the poor people that are out there in the road." I couldn't get the horror of that twenty mile long procession out of my mind, and I had seen some dreadful things that day.

"Oh well." Madame Marie shrugged. "It is always that way with the people. Toujours la meme chose. The Turk has a proverb, you know. He has many good proverbs. 'It is not only the fault of the axe but of the tree as well.' That is his proverb."

That is his proverb all right.

"I'm sorry about the lice, Monsieur." Madame Marie had forgiven me under the influence of the bottle. "But what do you expect? This is not Paris." She stood up, big and slovenly, and wise as people get wisdom in the Balkans. "Good-bye, Monsieur. Yes, I know 100 drachmas is too much for the bill. But I have the only hotel here. It is better than the street? Eh?"

Mussolini:
Biggest Bluff in Europe

➤ *The Toronto Daily Star* · JANUARY 27, 1923

LAUSANNE, SWITZERLAND.—In the Château de Ouchy, which is
so ugly that it makes the Odd Fellows' Hall of Petoskey, Michigan, look like the Parthenon, are held the sessions of the
Lausanne Conference.

Ouchy is pronounced Ooshy, not Ouchy, and about sixty
years ago was a little fishing village of weather-stained houses,
a white painted, pleasant inn with a shady front porch where
Byron used to sit resting his bad leg on a chair while he looked
out across the blue of Lake Geneva and waited for the supper
bell to ring, and an old ruined tower that rose out of the reeds
at the edge of the lake.

The Swiss have torn down the fishing buildings, nailed up a
tablet on the inn front porch, hustled Byron's chair into a
museum, filled in the reedy shore with dirt from the excavations
for the enormous, empty hotels that cover the slope up the hill
to Lausanne, and built the ugliest building in Europe around
the old tower. This building, of pressed grey stone, resembles
one of the love nests that sauerkraut kings used to build along
the Rhine before the war as dream-homes for their sauerkraut
queens and embodies all the worst phases of the iron-dog-on-
the-lawn school of architecture. A steep hill runs up from the
lake side to the town of Lausanne itself on the hill.

You can tell when the conference is in session by the rows of
limousines parked along the Château facing the lake. These
limousines each bear the flag of their delegation. The Bulgarian
and Russian flags are missing. Premier Stambuliski, of Bulgaria,
bulks out of the swinging doors of the Château, looks suspi-

61

ciously at the two helmeted Swiss policemen, scowls at the crowd and walks off up the hill to his hotel. Stambuliski cannot afford to ride in a limousine, even if he had the money. It would be reported to Sofia and his peasant government would demand an explanation. A few weeks ago he made an impassioned defense in the Bulgarian assembly to a charge by a group of his sheepskin-coated electors that he had been wearing silk socks, not getting up until 9 o'clock in the morning, drinking wine, and becoming corrupted by the slothful life of the city.

The Russian delegation never know when they are going to be invited to the conference and when excluded and decided early, in one of their midnight family councils at the Hotel Savoy, that to keep a limousine all the time would be too expensive. A taxi comes up to the door and Arrens, the Cheka man and Bolshevist press agent, comes out, his heavy, dark facing sneering and his one roving eye shooting away out of control; he is followed by Rakovsky and Tchitcherin. Rakovsky, the Ukrainian, has the pale face, wonderfully modeled features, hawk-nosed and tight-lipped, of an old Florentine nobleman.

Tchitcherin is not as he was at Genoa when he seemed to blink at the world as a man who has come out of darkness into too strong sunlight. He is more confident now, has a new overcoat, and a better groomed look, he has been living well in Berlin, and his face is fuller, although he looks the same as ever in profile with his wispy red beard and mustache and his furtive old clothes man slouch.

Everyone wants to see Ismet Pasha but once they have seen him they have no desire to see him again. He is a little dark man, absolutely without magnetism, looking as small and uninteresting as a man can look. He looks more like an Armenian lace seller than a Turkish general. There is something mouselike about him. He seems to have a genius for being unrecognized. Mustapha Kemal has a face that no one can forget, and Ismet has a face no one can remember.

I think the solution is that Ismet has a good movie face. I have seen him, in pictures, look stern, commanding, forceful and, in a way, handsome. Anyone who has seen in real life the weak, petulant face of any one of a dozen movie stars who look beautiful on the screen, knows what I mean. Ismet's face is not weak or petulant, it is simply plain and characterless. I remember seeing Ismet in the first days of the conference come in to the Hotel Savoy as a crowd of newspaper correspondents were coming out from one of Tchitcherin's famous "mass interviews." Ismet, waiting for the lift, stood in the midst of this crowd of men who had been trying to get appointments to speak with him for days, and not one of them recognized him. He was too unobtrusive.

It was too good to spoil, but I stepped up and greeted him.

"It is very funny, this, Excellency," I said as a couple of correspondents crowded him away from the door of the lift.

He smiled like a school girl, shrugged his shoulders and raised his hands to his face in a mock gesture of shame. He giggled.

"Get an appointment to come and talk with me," he said, shook hands, stepped into the lift and grinned at me. The interview was over.

When I did interview him we got along very well, as we both spoke such bad French. Ismet conceals his defective knowledge of French, which is a disgrace to an educated Turk, as in Turkey a knowledge of French is as much a social necessity as it is in Russia, by pretending to be deaf. He appreciates a joke, Ismet does, and he smiles delightedly to himself as he curls back in his chair and has the remarks of the great shouted into his ear in Turkish by his secretary.

The next time I saw Ismet, after I had interviewed him, he was sitting at a table in a jazz dancing palace in Montreux smiling delightedly at the dancers, a pair of large, grey haired Turks sitting at his table with him and looking morosely on while he ate quantities of cakes, drank three cups of tea and made countless jokes in bad French with the waitress who brought the tea. The waitress seemed delighted with Ismet and Ismet with her, they were having a wonderful time. Not a soul in the place had recognized him.

In contrast to Ismet there was Mussolini. Mussolini is the biggest bluff in Europe. If Mussolini would have me taken out and shot tomorrow morning I would still regard him as a bluff. The shooting would be a bluff. Get hold of a good photo of Signor Mussolini some time and study it. You will see the weakness in his mouth which forces him to scowl the famous Mussolini scowl that is imitated by every 19 year old Fascisto in Italy. Study his past record. Study the coalition that Fascismo is between capital and labor and consider the history of past coalitions. Study his genius for clothing small ideas in big words. Study his propensity for dueling. Really brave men do not have to fight duels, and many cowards duel constantly to make themselves believe they are brave. And then look at his black shirt and his white spats. There is something wrong, even histrionically, with a man who wears white spats with a black shirt.

There is not space here to go into the question of Mussolini as a bluff or as a great and lasting force. Mussolini may last fifteen years or he may be overthrown next spring by Gabriele D'Annunzio, who hates him. But let me give two true pictures of Mussolini at Lausanne.

The Fascist dictator had announced he would receive the press. Everybody came. We all crowded into the room. Mussolini sat at his desk reading a book. His face was contorted into the famous frown. He was registering Dictator. Being an ex-newspaper man himself he knew how many readers would be reached by the accounts the men in the room would write of the interview he was about to give. And he remained absorbed in his book. Mentally he was already reading the lines of the two thousand papers served by the two hundred correspondents. "As we entered the room the Black Shirt Dictator did not look up from the book he was reading, so intense was his concentration, etc."

I tip-toed over behind him to see what the book was he was reading with such avid interest. It was a French-English dictionary—held upside down.

The other picture of Mussolini as Dictator was on the same

day when a group of Italian women living in Lausanne came to the suite of rooms at the Beau Rivage Hotel to present him with a bouquet of roses. There were six women of the peasant class, wives of workmen living in Lausanne, and they stood outside the door waiting to do honor to Italy's new national hero who was their hero. Mussolini came out of the door in his frock coat, his gray trousers and his white spats. One of the women stepped forward and commenced her speech. Mussolini scowled at her, sneered, let his big-whited African eyes roll over the other five women and went back into the room. The unattractive peasant women in their Sunday clothes were left holding their roses. Mussolini had registered Dictator.

Half an hour later he met Clare Sheridan, who has smiled her way into many interviews, and had time for half an hour's talk with her.

Of course the newspaper correspondents of Napoleon's time may have seen the same things in Napoleon, and the men who worked on the Giornale D'Italia in Caesar's day may have found the same discrepancies in Julius, but after an intimate study of the subject there seems to be a good deal more of Bottomley, an enormous, war-like, duel fighting, successful Italian Horatio Bottomley, in Mussolini than there does of Napoleon.

It isn't really Bottomley though. Bottomley was a fool. Mussolini isn't a fool and he is a great organizer. But it is a very dangerous thing to organize the patriotism of a nation if you are not sincere, especially when you work their patriotism to such a pitch that they offer to loan money to the government without interest. Once the Latin has sunk his money in a business he wants results and he is going to show Signor Mussolini that it is much easier to be the opposition to a government than to run the government yourself.

A new opposition will rise, it is forming already, and it will be led by that old, bald-headed, perhaps a little insane but thoroughly sincere, divinely brave swashbuckler, Gabriele D'Annunzio.

A Russian Toy Soldier

➤ *The Toronto Daily Star* · FEBRUARY 10, 1923

LAUSANNE, SWITZERLAND.—Georgi Tchitcherin comes from a noble Russian family. He has a wispy red beard and mustache, big eyes, a high forehead and walks with a slouch like an old clothes man. He has plump, cold hands that lie in yours like a dead man's and he talks both English and French with the same accent in a hissing, grating whisper.

Tchitcherin was an old Czarist diplomat and if Lenin is the Napoleon that made a dictatorship out of the Russian revolution, Tchitcherin is his Talleyrand. Their careers are both very similar. Both Tchitcherin and Talleyrand were diplomats under the monarchy that preceded their revolution, both were sent abroad as ambassadors under the revolution, both were refused by the countries they were sent to, both were in exile and both became the director of foreign affairs of the dictatorship that followed their revolution.

"We came to Lausanne with one program," Tchitcherin said to me one afternoon. "And we will leave it with the same program. The straits, both the Dardanelles and the Bosporus, must be closed to warships."

He spoke with the tired intensity of a man who is saying a thing for the hundredth time, who believes it and is as impassioned about it as the first time, but has become wearied from not being understood.

"As long as the straits are open to warships," he went on, "Russia is at the mercy of any nation that sends a fleet into the Black Sea. We can have no safety, no freedom to develop, no security from invasion as long as battleships and dreadnoughts

66

can enter the Black Sea. There is only one thing for Russia to do if warships are allowed to enter, and that is to arm. She must build battleships in order to have a great fleet in the Black Sea. That means the crippling of her productive power by diverting it to build a great navy. But she must do it."

"How about naval disarmament?" I asked.

"Russia was not invited to the Washington conference," Tchitcherin shrugged his shoulders. "And what has come of that conference? How near are we to naval disarmament now? We are dealing with facts, with conditions as they exist. Russia would be the first to accept an invitation to a naval disarmament conference, but until we have complete naval disarmament, we can only keep warships out of the Black Sea in one way. That way is to have the straits closed to all warships and fortified by the Turks so they can enforce the closing."

Tchitcherin was on his best ground now. He is an old Russian diplomat and he is soundest when he is fighting for the national aims of Russia. He sees that the problems of Soviet Russia, the territorial and national problems, are the same as they were under the Russian Empire. The world revolution did not come off and Russia faces the same problems she always faced. Tchitcherin knows those problems. He knows the rivalry between Russia and Great Britain in the east and he knows that as long as Russia is a nation, no matter who governs, and as long as there is a British Empire, their interests will conflict. Now he is trying to gain by treaties advantages and securities that later would have to be gained or lost by wars.

Tchitcherin knows that a Russian invasion of India through Afghanistan would be impossible as long as the Crimea was open to a counter invasion by the British Fleet. Lord Curzon knows that too. Tchitcherin knows that the Black Sea coast is the great thousand-mile Achilles tendon of Russia. Lord Curzon knows that too.

It was this daily, bitter struggle between the British Empire and the future Russian empire with Curzon, a tall, cold, icicle of a man holding the whip hand with the British fleet, and

Tchitcherin fighting, fighting, with arguments, historical instances, facts, statistics and impassioned pleas and finally, seeing it was hopeless, simply talking for history, registering his objections for future generations to read, that made the Lausanne conference so interesting. It is this same unreconcilable difference between Russia and Great Britain that will run like a crack through any Near East treaty that is made in Lausanne and keep it from having permanence.

With his cold hands and his cold brain and his red wispy beard, his inhuman capacity for work, his dislike and distrust of women, his indifference to publicity, public opinion, money or anything except his work and Russia, Tchitcherin looked like a man without a weakness. Then came the pictures that accompany this article.

Tchitcherin, you must know, has never been a soldier. He is timid, personally. He does not fear assassination, but he would turn pale if you shook your fist under his nose. Until he was twelve years old his mother kept him in dresses. He is all brain and he simply feeds his body because it is a supporting part of his brain.

Several of us knew all this about him. Then one Sunday morning as the churches were emptying in Lausanne and the mountain goers were hiking down the streets with their skis and packs, to catch the train to Aigle or the Diablerets, a group of correspondents stopped in front of a photographer's window. It was displaying the photographs you see here.

"They're faked," one man said. "Why he's never had a uniform on in his life."

We all looked closely at the photographs.

"Nope. They're not faked." Some one said: "I can tell. They're not faked. Let's go and ask Slocombe."

We found George Slocombe, the correspondent of the London Daily Herald who is Tchitcherin's very good friend and sometimes his mouthpiece. George was sitting in the press room of the Lausanne Palace Hotel, his big black sombrero back on his head, his curling red beard sticking out at an angle, his pipe in his mouth.

"Yes," he said, looking at the picture I showed him, "Aren't they awful? I couldn't believe it when I saw them. He had them taken himself, and now the photographer is selling them."

"But where does he get that awful uniform, George?" I asked. "He looks like a combination of the headkeeper at Sing Sing and the concierge at the Crillon."

"Isn't it horrible?" George sucked his pipe. "All the commissars are automatically generals in the Red army, and Tchitcherin is commissar for foreign affairs, you know. He got that uniform made in Berlin. He took it off the hanger last night in the closet in his room and showed it to me. He is dreadfully proud of it. You ought to see him in it."

So that is Tchitcherin's weakness. The boy who was kept in dresses until he was twelve years old always wanted to be a soldier. And soldiers make empires and empires make wars.

Getting into Germany

➤ *The Toronto Daily Star* · MAY 2, 1923

OFFENBURG, BADEN.—In Paris they said it was very difficult to get into Germany. No tourists allowed. No newspaper men wanted. The German consulate will not visa a passport without a letter from a consulate or chamber of commerce in Germany saying, under seal, it is necessary for the traveller to come to Germany for a definite business transaction. The day I called at the consulate it had been instructed to amend the rules to permit invalids to enter for the "cure" if they produced a certificate from the doctor of the health resort they were to visit showing the nature of their ailment.

"We must preserve the utmost strictness," said the German consul and reluctantly and suspiciously after much consultation of files gave me a visa good for three weeks.

"How do we know you will not write lies about Germany?" he said before he handed me back the passport.

"Oh, cheer up," I said.

To get the visa I had given him a letter from our embassy, printed on stiff crackling paper and bearing an enormous red seal which informed "whom it may concern" that Mr. Hemingway, the bearer, was well and favorably known to the embassy and had been directed by his newspaper, The Toronto Star, to proceed to Germany and report on the situation there. These letters do not take long to get, commit the embassy to nothing, and are as good as diplomatic passports.

The very gloomy German consular attache was folding the letter and putting it away.

"But you cannot have the letter. It must be retained to show cause why the visa was given."

"But I must have the letter."

"You cannot have the letter."

A small gift was given and received.

The German, slightly less gloomy but still not happy: "But tell me why was it you wanted the letter so?"

Me, ticket in pocket, passport in pocket, baggage packed, train not leaving till midnight, some articles mailed, generally elated. "It is a letter of introduction from Sarah Bernhardt, whose funeral you perhaps witnessed to-day, to the Pope. I value it."

German, sadly and slightly confused: "But the Pope is not in Germany."

Me, mysteriously, going out the door: "One can never tell."

In the cold, grey, street-washing, milk-delivering, shutters-coming-off-the-shops, early morning, the midnight train from Paris arrived in Strasbourg. There was no train from Strasbourg into Germany. The Munich Express, the Orient Express, the Direct for Prague? They had all gone. According to the porter I might get a tram across Strasbourg to the Rhine and then walk across into Germany and there at Kehl get a military train for Offenburg. There would be a train for Kehl sooner or later, no one quite knew, but the tram was much better.

On the front platform of the street car, with a little ticket window opening into the car through which the conductor accepted a franc for myself and two bags, we clanged along through the winding streets of Strasbourg and the early morning. There were sharp peaked plastered houses criss-crossed with great wooden beams, the river wound and rewound through the town and each time we crossed it there were fishermen on the banks, there was the wide modern street with modern German shops with big glass show windows and new French names over their doors, butchers were unshuttering their shops and with their assistants hanging the big carcasses of beeves and horses outside the doors, a long stream of carts were coming into market from the country, streets were being flushed and washed. I caught a glimpse down a side street of the great red stone cathedral. There was a sign in French and another in German forbidding anyone to talk to the motorman and the motorman chatted in French and German to his friends who got on the car as he swung his levers and checked or speeded our progress along the narrow streets and out of the town.

In the stretch of country that lies between Strasbourg and the Rhine the tram track runs along a canal and a big blunt nosed barge with LUSITANIA painted on its stern was being dragged smoothly along by two horses ridden by the bargeman's two children while breakfast smoke came out of the galley chimney and the bargeman leaned against the sweep. It was a nice morning.

At the ugly iron bridge that runs across the Rhine into Germany the tram stopped. We all piled out. Where last July at every tram there had formed a line like the queue outside an arena hockey match there were only four of us. A gendarme looked at the passports. He did not even open mine. A dozen or so French gendarmes were loafing about. One of these came up to me as I started to carry my bags across the long bridge over the yellow, flooded, ugly, swirling Rhine and asked: "How much money have you?"

I told him one hundred and twenty-five dollars "Americain" and in the neighborhood of one hundred francs.

"Let me see your pocket book."

He looked in it, grunted and handed it back. The twenty-five five-dollar bills I had obtained in Paris for mark-buying made an impressive roll.

"No gold money?"

"Mais non, monsieur."

He grunted again and I walked, with the two bags, across the long iron bridge, past the barbed wire entanglement with its two French sentries in their blue tin hats and their long needle bayonets, into Germany.

Germany did not look very cheerful. A herd of beef cattle were being loaded into a box car on the track that ran down to the bridge. They were entering reluctantly with much tail-twisting and whacking of their legs. A long wooden customs shed with two entrances, one marked, "Nach Frankreich" and one "Nach Deutschland," stood next to the track. A German soldier was sitting on an empty gasoline tin smoking a cigaret. A woman in an enormous black hat with plumes and an appalling collection of hat boxes, parcels and bags, was stalled opposite the cattle-loading process. I carried three of the bundles for her into the shed marked "towards Germany."

"You are going to Munich, too?" she asked, powdering her nose.

"No. Only Offenburg."

"Oh, what a pity. There is no place like Munich. You have never been there?"

"No, not yet."

"Let me tell you. Do not go anywhere else. Anywhere else in Germany is a waste of time. There is only Munich."

A grey-headed German customs inspector asked me where I was going, whether I had anything dutiable, and waved my passport away.

"You go down the road to the regular station."

The regular station had been the important customs junction on the direct line between Paris and Munich. It was deserted. All the ticket windows closed. Everything covered with dust. I wandered through it to the track and found four French soldiers of the 170th Infantry Regiment, with full kit and fixed bayonets.

One of them told me there would be a train at 11.15 for Offenburg, a military train: it was about half an hour to Offenburg, but this droll train would get there about two o'clock. He grinned. Monsieur was from Paris? What did monsieur think about the match Criqui-Zjawnny Kilbane? Ah. He had thought very much the same. He had always had the idea that he was no fool, this Kilbane. The military service? Well, it was all the same. It made no difference where one did it. In two months now he would be through. It was a shame he was not free, perhaps we could have a talk together. Monsieur had seen this Kilbane box? The new wine was not bad at the buffet. But after all he was on guard. The buffet is straight down the corridor. If monsieur leaves the baggage here it will be all right.

In the buffet was a sad-looking waiter in a dirty shirt and soup and beer stained evening clothes, a long bar and two forty-year-old French second lieutenants sitting at a table in the corner. I bowed as I entered and they both saluted.

"No," the waiter said. "There is no milk. You can have black coffee, but it is ersatz coffee. The beer is good."

The waiter sat down at the table. "No, there is no one here now," he said. "All the people you say you saw in July cannot come now. The French will not give them passports to come into Germany."

"All the people that came over here to eat don't come now?" I asked.

"Nobody. The merchants and restaurant keepers in Strasbourg got angry and went to the police because everybody was coming over here to eat so much cheaper and now nobody in Strasbourg can get a passport to come here."

"How about all the Germans who worked in Strasbourg?" Kehl was a suburb of Strasbourg before the peace treaty, and all their interests and industries were the same.

"That is all finished. Now no Germans can get passports to go across the river. They could work cheaper than the French, so that is what happened to them. All our factories here are shut down. No coal. No trains. This was one of the biggest and busiest stations in Germany. Now nix. No trains, except the military trains, and they run when they please."

Four poilus came in and stood up to the bar. The waiter greeted them cheerfully in French. He poured out their new wine, cloudy and golden in their glasses, and came back and sat down.

"How do they get along with the French here in town?"

74

"No trouble. They are good people. Just like us. Some of them are nasty sometimes, but they are good people. Nobody hates, except profiteers. They had something to lose. We haven't had any fun since 1914. If you made any money it gets no good, and there is only to spend it. That is what we do. Some day it will be over. I don't know how. Last year I had enough money saved up to buy a gasthaus in Hernberg; now that money wouldn't buy four bottles of champagne."

I looked up at the wall where the prices were:

Beer,	350 marks a glass.
Red wine,	500 marks a glass.
Sandwich,	900 marks.
Lunch,	3,500 marks.
Champagne,	38,000 marks.

I remembered that last July I stayed at a de luxe hotel with Mrs. Hemingway for 600 marks a day.

"Sure," the waiter went on. "I read the French papers. Germany debases her money to cheat the allies. But what do I get out of it?"

There was a shrill peep of a whistle outside. I paid and shook hands with the waiter, saluted the two forty-year-old second lieutenants, who were now playing checkers at their table, and went out to take the military train to Offenburg.

King Business in Europe

The Toronto Star Weekly · SEPTEMBER 15, 1923

THE other day in Paris I ran into my old pal Shorty. Shorty is a film service movie operator. He takes the news films you see at the movies. Shorty was just back from Greece.

"Say," said Shorty, "that George is a fine kid."

"What George?" I asked.

"Why, the king," said Shorty. "Didn't you meet him? You know who I mean. The new one."

"I never met him," I said.

"Oh, he's a white man," Shorty said, signaling the waiter. "He's a prince, that boy. Look at this."

I looked at it. It was a sheet of note paper embossed with the royal arms of Greece, and written in English.

> *The King would be very pleased if Mr. Wornall would call either in the morning or in the afternoon. He will be expected all day. If he will be so good as to answer by the bearer a carriage will be sent to bring him to the royal palace.*
>
> —*(Signed) GEORGE.*

"Oh, he's a wonderful kid," said Shorty, folding the letter carefully and putting it back into his wallet.

"Why, you know I went out there in the afternoon with my camera. We drove into the palace grounds past a lot of these big tall babies in ballet skirts with their rifles held at salute. I got out and he came walking down the drive and shook hands and said: 'Hello. How have you been, Mr. Wornall?'

"We went for a walk around the grounds and there was the

76

queen clipping a rose bush. 'This is the queen,' said George. 'How do you do?' she said."

"How long did you stay?" I asked.

"Oh, a couple of hours," Shorty said. "The king was glad to have somebody to talk to. We had whiskey and soda at a table under a big tree. The king said it was no fun being shut up there. They hadn't given him any money since the revolution and wouldn't let any of the Greek aristocracy visit him. They wouldn't let him go outside the grounds.

" 'It's frightfully dull, you know,' he said. 'Andrew was the lucky one. They banished him, you know, and now he can live in London or Paris or wherever he wants.' "

"What language did you talk with him?" I said.

"English, of course," Shorty answered. "That's what all the Greek royal family speak. Mrs. Leeds, you know. I ran off a lot of film of him and the queen all around the palace and out in the field. He wanted me to take him with an old binder they had out in one of the big fields inside the walls. 'This will look fine in America, won't it?' he said."

"What's the queen like?" I said.

"Oh, I didn't get to know her very well," Shorty answered. "I only stayed a couple of hours. I never like to stick around with them too long. Some Americans just abuse them. They get an invitation out to the palace and then the king can't get rid of them. But the queen's nice, all right. When I left the king said: 'Well, maybe we'll meet in the States sometime.' Like all the Greeks, he wants to get over to the States."

George of Greece is the newest king in Europe, and probably the most uncomfortable. As Shorty says, he is a very nice boy, and he isn't having any fun at all. He was put into the job by a revolutionary committee last fall, and he stays in just as long as they let him.

George is married to a Rumanian princess, daughter of Queen Marie and King Ferdinand of Rumania and just now his mother-in-law is making a tour of the capitals of Europe to get George recognized—and, incidentally, her daughter recognized as queen.

Which brings us to Rumania, where the king business isn't flourishing so well either.

King Ferdinand looks as worried as any man who hides his true expression behind a crop of choice upper Danube whiskers can look. Rumania is the one country that no one in Europe takes seriously. When the statesmen and their friends were living in the best hotels of Paris during the year 1919 and making the treaty that was designed to Europeanize the Balkans, and succeeded in Balkanizing Europe, the Rumanians had a choice collection of rapid talkers and historical precedent-quoters massed for action.

When these talkers had finished and the treaties were signed it developed that Rumania had been given all the land of her neighbors in every direction that any Rumanian had mentioned. The treaty makers probably considered this a cheap price to pay to free themselves from the presence of the ardent Rumanian patriots. At any rate, Rumania now has to maintain one of the largest standing armies in Europe to keep down revolts of her new Rumanians whose one desire is to cease to be Rumanians.

Sooner or later large chunks of Rumania are going to break off and drift away like an ice floe when it hits the Gulf Stream. Queen Marie, who is a first-rate bridge player, a second-rate poetess, a very high-grade puller of European political strings, and who uses more make-up than all the rest of the European royal families combined, is making every effort to form such European alliances that this coming disintegration will be stopped. On the other side, Prince Carol, who is a most charming, oh, most charming young man and president of the Prince Carol Film Company, which had the exclusive filming of the especially staged Rumanian coronation, does not appear to be greatly interested.

Meanwhile the officers of the Rumanian army, which will bear the brunt of Hungarian and Russian attacks sometime within the next ten years, use lip stick, rouge their faces, and wear corsets. This is no exaggeration. I have, with my own eyes, seen Rumanian officers, infantry officers, using lip sticks in a cafe. I have seen cavalry officers rouged like chorus men. I would not swear to the corsets. Appearances may be deceptive.

Working back from Rumania, we enter the realm of King Boris of Bulgaria. Boris is the son of Ferdinand the Fox. When the near-eastern front crumbled in 1918, and the Bulgarian troops came home with revolutionary committees at their heads, they released a large, rough, foul-mouthed ex-farmer named Stambuliski from the jail where he had been ever since he had tried to get Bulgaria into the war on the side of the allies. Stambuliski came out of jail like a bull coming from his dark pen into the bright glare of the bull ring. His first charge was toward King Ferdinand. Ferdinand left the country. Boris, his son, wished to go, too. "If you attempt to leave the country I'll have you shot," Stambuliski roared.

Boris stayed. Stambuliski used to keep him in an ante-room and call him in when he wanted an interpreter to talk to people he wished to be especially polite to. Newspaper correspondents, for example.

Boris is blond, pleasant and talkative. He heartily dislikes Bulgaria and wants to live in Paris. Now Stambuliski has been overthrown by the old pro-German army officers, grafters, intriguing politicians and Bulgarian intellectuals, which means in Bulgaria people who have absorbed sufficient learning so as to be no longer honest, and killed like an escaping convict by the people who ruined the country he has been trying to save. Boris is still the king, but he is now controlled by the will of his father Ferdinand and the old fox's advisors.

I have not seen him for over a year, but they say he is still as blond, but not as pleasant nor talkative. He is not married, but Queen Marie, the matchmaker, is grooming a daughter.

Next in line is Alexander of Yugo-Slavia, or as the Yugo-Slavs insist it is, the Kingdom of the Serbs, Croats and Slovenes. Alexander is the son of King Peter of Serbia. He is no relation to the Croats and Slovenes. I saw him one night in a Montmartre resort in Paris, where he had come incognito for a last visit to the capital before his marriage. There were a number of Serbs and several Frenchmen with him, all in evening dress. Various girls were at the table. It was a big night for the wine growers. Alexander was quite drunk and very happy.

Shortly after this trip the marriage was postponed, but eventually took place.

Victor Emanuel of Italy is a very short, serious little man with a grey, goat-like beard and tiny hands and feet. His legs looked as thin but as sturdy as a jockey's when he used to wear roll puttees with his uniform. His queen is almost a head taller than himself. The Italian king's lack of stature is a characteristic of the ancient house of Savoy, the greatest of whose long heritage of rulers have been little taller than bantam-weight boxers.

Just at present the king of Italy is probably the most popular king in Europe. He has handed over his kingdom, his army and his navy to Mussolini. Mussolini handed them politely back with many protestations of loyalty to the house of Savoy. Then he decided to keep the army and navy himself. When he will ask for the kingdom no one knows.

I have talked to many Fascisti, the old original nucleus of the party, who have all sworn that they were republicans. "But we trust Mussolini," they said. "Mussolini will know when the time is ripe."

There is a chance, of course, that Mussolini will renounce his old republicanism just as Garibaldi did. He has done so temporarily, and he has a genius for making something that he is doing temporarily appear to be permanent.

But the Fascist party to exist must have action. It is getting a little satisfaction now out of Corfu and the Adriatic. If it needed a republic to hold it together it would get a republic.

As a man and a human being, there is probably no finer father or more democratic ruler on the continent than Victor Emanuel.

The King of Spain has been king ever since he can remember. He was born king, and you can trace the evolution of his familiarly photographed under-jaw on the five-peseta pieces since

1886. It's no treat for him to be king. He's never been anything else. He was much handsomer as a baby, if the peseta pieces are accurate, but then we all were.

Alfonso is another king whose throne rests on a volcano. But it doesn't seem to worry him much. He is an excellent polo player and the best amateur motor car driver in Spain.

Recently the king drove his car from Santander, a summer watering place in the north of Spain, to Madrid, over mountains, hills, and along precipices at an average speed of sixty miles an hour. There was a good deal of criticism in many of the Spanish papers. "If we have responsibilities to a king does not a king have responsibilities to us to keep himself intact, etc." The trip was not well received. But two weeks later the king opened the new motor racing track at San Sebastian by turning off two laps himself at well over one hundred kilometers an hour. His time was only four kilometers an hour behind the winner of the Grand Prix.

The day of the Grand Prix at San Sebastian there was another Spanish military disaster in Morocco in which the Spanish lost over 500 killed, there was a revolt in the barracks at Malaga, and two regiments of troops mutinied, refusing to leave Spain for the Moorish front. The desultory guerrilla warfare that has been going on in Barcelona between the labor men and the government, and which has resulted in over two hundred assassinations in less than a year continues. But there are no attempts on the life of the king. The people don't take Alfonso too seriously. They have had him for a long time.

In the north live the respectable kings—Haakon of Norway, Gustaf of Sweden and Christian of Denmark. They are so well situated that no one ever hears much about them. Except the king of Sweden, who is an ardent and very good tennis player and plays regularly with Suzanne Lenglen as his partner every winter at Cannes.

Albert of Belgium and his wife, Queen Elizabeth, everyone knows.

John II of Liechtenstein is a ruler who has had little pub-

licity. Prince John has ruled over the Principality of Liechtenstein since 1858. He is eighty-three years old this year.

I have always thought of Liechtenstein as a manager of prize
fighters that used to live in Chicago, but it seems there is a very
prosperous country of that name ruled over by John the second.
John the first was his father. They've kept the country very much
in the family for over a hundred years. Liechtenstein is all of
sixty-five square miles and lies on the border between Switzerland and Austria. It had been a dependency of Austria but announced its independence on November 7th, 1918. Two years
ago the gallant Liechtensteiners made a treaty with the Swiss
to run their post and telegraph system for them. All of the 10,876
inhabitants were doing well at the last report except Prince John
who is having a little trouble with his teeth.

So far I have only mentioned the European kings who are
still holding down their jobs. Ex-kings would take an article in
themselves. I have never seen the kaiser nor Harry K. Thaw
nor Landru. A good many of my best friends, though, have
climbed up the wall of the garden at Doorn or attempted to gain
admission disguised as bales of hay, cases of lager beer or Ba-
varian diplomats. Even when they have seen the kaiser, however, they report the result as unsatisfactory.

Japanese Earthquake

➤ *The Toronto Daily Star* · SEPTEMBER 25, 1923

THERE are no names in this story.

The characters in it are a reporter, a girl reporter, a quite beautiful daughter in a Japanese kimono, and a mother. There is a small chorus of friends who spend some time talking in the next room, and get up as the reporter and the girl reporter go through the room and out of the door.

At four o'clock in the afternoon the reporter and the girl reporter stood on the front porch. The front door bell had just rung.

"They'll never let us in," said the girl reporter.

Inside the house they heard someone moving around and then a voice said, "I'll go down. I'll attend to them, Mother."

The door opened one narrow crack. The crack ran from the top of the door to the bottom, and about half way up it was a very dark, very beautiful face, the hair soft and parted in the middle.

"She is beautiful, after all," thought the reporter. He had been sent on so many assignments in which beautiful girls figured, and so few of the girls had ever turned out to be beautiful.

"Who do you want?" said the girl at the door.

"We're from The Star," the reporter said. "This is Miss So and So."

"We don't want to have anything to do with you. You can't come in," the girl said.

"But—" said the reporter and commenced to talk. He had a very strong feeling that if he stopped talking at any time, the door would slam. So he kept on talking. Finally the girl opened

83

the door. "Well, I'll let you in," she said. "I'll go upstairs and ask my mother."

She went upstairs, quick and lithe, wearing a Japanese kimono. It ought to have some other name. Kimono has a messy, early morning sound. There was nothing kimonoey about this kimono. The colors were vivid and the stuff had body to it, and it was cut. It looked almost as though it might be worn with two swords in the belt.

The girl reporter and the reporter sat on a couch in the parlor. "I'm sorry to have done all the talking," whispered the reporter.

"No. Go on. Keep it up. I never thought we'd get in at all," said the girl reporter. "She is good-looking, isn't she?" The reporter had thought she was beautiful. "And didn't she know what she was doing when she got that kimono!"

"Sh—. Here they come."

Down the stairs came the girl in the Japanese kimono. With her was her mother. Her mother's face was very firm.

"What I want to know," she said, "is where you got those pictures?"

"They were lovely pictures, weren't they?" said the girl reporter.

Both the girl reporter and the reporter denied any knowledge of the pictures. They didn't know. Really, they didn't know. It was a fact. Eventually they were believed.

"We won't say anything. We don't want to be in the newspapers. We've had too much already. There are plenty of people that suffered much worse than we did in the earthquake. We don't want to talk about it at all."

"But I let them in, mother," said the daughter. She turned to the reporter. "Just exactly what is it you want to know from us?"

"We just want you to tell us as you remember it just what happened," the reporter said.

"If we talk to you and tell you what you want to know will you promise that you won't use our names?" asked the daughter.

"Why not just use the names," suggested the reporter.

"We won't say a word unless you promise not to use the names," said the daughter.

"Oh, you know newspaper reporters," the mother said. "They'll promise it and then they'll use them anyway." It looked as though there wasn't going to be any story. The remark had made the reporter violently angry. It is the one unmerited insult. There are enough merited ones.

"Mrs. So and So," he said, "the president of the United States tells reporters things in confidence which if known would cost him his job. Every week in Paris the prime minister of France tells fifteen newspaper reporters facts that if they were quoted again would overthrow the French government. I'm talking about newspaper reporters, not cheap news tipsters."

"All right," said the mother. "Yes, I guess it's true about newspaper reporters."

Then the daughter began the story and the mother took it up.

"The boat [the Canadian Pacific's *Empress of Australia*] was all ready to sail," said the daughter. "If mother and father hadn't been down at the dock, I don't believe they would have escaped!"

"The Empress boats always sail at noon on Saturday," said the mother.

"Just before twelve o'clock, there was a great rumbling sound and then everything commenced to rock back and forth. The dock rolled and bucked. My brother and I were on board the boat leaning against the rail. Everybody had been throwing streamers. It only lasted about thirty seconds," said the daughter.

"We were thrown flat on the dock," said the mother. "It was a big concrete dock and it rolled back and forth. My husband and I hung on to each other and were thrown around by it. Many people were thrown off. I remember seeing a rickshaw driver clambering back up out of the water. Cars and everything else went in, except our car. It stayed on the dock right alongside the Prince de Bearn's, the French consul's car, till the fire."

"What did you do when the shock was over?" asked the reporter.

"We went ashore. We had to climb. The dock was crumbled in places and great chunks of concrete broken off. We started up the Bund along the shore and could see that the big go-downs, the storage houses, were all caved in. You know the Bund. The driveway straight along the waterfront. We got as far as the British consulate and it was all caved in. Just fallen in on itself like a funnel. Just crumbled. All the walls were down and we could look straight through from the front of the building to the open compound at the back. Then there was another shock and we knew it wasn't any use going on or trying to get up to our house. My husband heard that the people had been out of the office and there was nothing you could do about the men that had been working in the go-downs. There was a big cloud of dust all over everything from the buildings that had caved in. You could hardly see through it, and fires were breaking out all over."

"What were the people doing? How were they acting?" asked the reporter.

"There wasn't any panic. That was the strange thing. I didn't see anyone even hysterical. There was one woman at the Russian consulate though. It stood right next to the British consulate and it hadn't fallen in yet but was badly shaken. She came out to the front gate crying and there were a bunch of coolies sitting against the iron fence in front of the consulate yard. She begged them to help her get her daughter out of the building. 'She's just a little fellow,' she said in Japanese. But they just sat there. They wouldn't move. It seemed as though they couldn't move. Of course nobody was going around helping anybody else then. Everybody had themselves to look after."

"How did you get back to the boat?" asked the girl reporter.

"There were some sampans, native boats, and finally my husband found one and we started back. But the fire was going so badly then and the wind was offshore. There was an awful wind for a while. We got to the dock finally and, of course, they couldn't get a gangplank out, but they put out a rope for us and we got on board."

The mother didn't need any prompting or questions now. That day and the following days and nights in Yokohama harbor had her in their grip again. Now the reporter saw why she didn't want to be interviewed and why no one had any right to interview her and stir it all up afresh. Her hands were very quietly nervous.

"The Prince's boy [son of the Prince de Bearn, French consul] was left in their house. He had been sick. They had just come down to the dock to see the boat off. The foreign quarter is up on a bluff where we all lived, and the bluff just slid down into the town. The Prince got ashore and made his way up to the wreck of his house. They got the boy out but his back was hurt. They worked hours getting him out. But they couldn't get the French butler out. They had to go away and leave him in there because the fire got too close."

"They had to leave him in there alive with the fire coming on?" asked the girl reporter.

"Yes, they had to leave the French butler in there," said the mother. "He was married to the housemaid so they had to tell her they had gotten him out."

The mother went on, in a dull, tired voice.

"There was a woman on the [liner] Jefferson coming home that had lost her husband. I didn't recognize her. There was a young couple, too, that had been only out a short time. They'd just been married. His wife was down in the town shopping when it happened. He couldn't get to where she was on account of the fire. They got the head doctor out all right from the American Hospital. They couldn't get out the assistant doctor and his wife, though. The fire came so quick. The whole town was solid fire.

"We were on the boat of course. Part of the time you couldn't see the shore on account of the smoke. When it was bad was when the submarine oil tanks burst and the oil caught on fire. It moved down the harbor and toward the dock. When it got to the dock we wondered if we'd been saved on board the Empress just to get burned. The captain had all the boats launched on the far side away from the fire and was all ready to put us into them. We couldn't go on the side toward the fire of course. It was too hot. They were playing the hoses on it to drive it away. It kept coming on though.

"All the time they were working to cut through the anchor chain that had fouled in the propeller. Just to cut it away from the boat. Finally they got the Empress away from the dock. It was wonderful the way they got her away without any tug. It was something you wouldn't have believed it was possible to do in Yokohama harbor. It was wonderful.

"Of course they were bringing wounded people and refugees on all day and all night. They came out in sampans or anything. They took them all on. We slept on the deck.

"My husband said he was relieved when we'd got outside the breakwater," the mother said. "There're supposed to be two old [volcanic] craters in the harbor itself, and he was worried that something was going to happen from them."

"Was there no tidal wave?" asked the reporter.

"No. There wasn't any at all. When we were on our way to Kobe, after we had left Yokohama finally, there were three or four small shocks that you could feel in the boat. But there weren't any tidal waves."

Her mind was going back to Yokohama harbor. "Some of the people that had stood up all night in the water were very tired," she offered.

"Oh, the people that had stood up all night in the water," said the reporter softly.

"Yes. To keep out of the fire. There was one old woman who must have been seventy-six years old. She was in the water all night. There were lots of people in the canals, too. Yokohama's all cut up with canals, you know."

"Didn't that make it more confused in the earthquake?" asked the girl reporter.

"Oh, no. They were very good things to have in a fire," said the mother quite seriously.

"What did you think when it started?" asked the reporter.

88

"Oh, we knew it was an earthquake," said the mother. "It was just that nobody knew it was going to be so bad. There's been lots of earthquakes there. Once, nine years ago, we'd have five shocks in one day. We just wanted to get into the town to see if everything was all right. But when we saw it was so bad, we knew then it didn't matter about things. I hadn't intended to come home. Just my daughter and son were sailing. My husband is still in Kobe. He has a lot of work to do now re-organizing."

Just then the telephone rang. "My mother is busy just now interviewing the reporters," the daughter said in the next room. She was talking with some friends that had come in. It was something about music. The reporter listened with his odd ear for a moment to see if it was anything about the earthquake. But it wasn't.

The mother was very tired. The girl reporter stood up. The reporter got up.

"You understand. No names," said the mother.

"You're sure? They wouldn't do any harm, you know."

"You said you wouldn't use the names," the mother said wearily. The reporters went out. The friends stood up as they went through the room.

The reporter took a look at the Japanese kimono as the door was shut.

"Who's going to write the story. You or me?" asked the girl reporter.

"I don't know," said the reporter.

Bull Fighting a Tragedy

➤ *The Toronto Star Weekly* · OCTOBER 20, 1923

IT was spring in Paris and everything looked just a little too beautiful. Mike and I decided to go to Spain. Strater drew us a fine map of Spain on the back of a menu of the Strix restaurant. On the same menu he wrote the name of a restaurant in Madrid where the specialty is young suckling pig roasted, the name of a pension on the Via San Jerónimó where the bull fighters live, and sketched a plan showing where the Grecos are hung in the Prado.

Fully equipped with this menu and our old clothes, we started for Spain. We had one objective—to see bull fights.

We left Paris one morning and got off the train at Madrid the next noon. We saw our first bull fight at 4.30 that afternoon. It took about two hours to get tickets. We finally got them from scalpers for twenty-five pesetas apiece. The bull ring was entirely sold out. We had barrera seats. These the scalper explained in Spanish and broken French were the first row of the ringside, directly under the royal box, and immediately opposite where the bulls would come out.

We asked him if he didn't have any less distinguished seats for somewhere around twelve pesetas, but he was sold out. So we paid the fifty pesetas for the two tickets, and with the tickets in our pockets sat out on the sidewalk in front of a big cafe near the Puerta del Sol. It was very exciting, sitting out in front of a cafe your first day in Spain with a ticket in your pocket that meant that rain or shine you were going to see a bull fight in an hour and a half. In fact, it was so exciting that we started out for the bull ring on the outskirts of the city in about half an hour.

The bull ring or Plaza de Toros was a big, tawny brick amphitheatre standing at the end of a street in an open field. The yellow and red Spanish flag was floating over it. Carriages were driving up and people getting out of buses. There was a great crowd of beggars around the entrance. Men were selling water out of big terra cotta water bottles. Kids sold fans, canes, roasted salted almonds in paper spills, fruit and slabs of ice cream. The crowd was gay and cheerful but all intent on pushing toward the entrance. Mounted civil guards with patent leather cocked hats and carbines slung over their backs sat their horses like statues, and the crowd flowed through.

Inside they all stood around in the bull ring, talking and looking up in the grandstand at the girls in the boxes. Some of the men had field glasses in order to look better. We found our seats and the crowd began to leave the ring and get into the rows of concrete seats. The ring was circular—that sounds foolish, but a boxing ring is square—with a sand floor. Around it was a red board fence—just high enough for a man to be able to vault over it. Between the board fence, which is called the barrera, and the first row of seats ran a narrow alley way. Then came the seats which were just like a football stadium except that around the top ran a double circle of boxes.

Every seat in the amphitheatre was full. The arena was cleared. Then on the far side of the arena out of the crowd, four heralds in medieval costume stood up and blew a blast on their trumpets. The band crashed out, and from the entrance on the far side of the ring four horsemen in black velvet with ruffs around their necks rode out into the white glare of the arena. The people on the sunny side were baking in the heat and fanning themselves. The whole sol side was a flicker of fans.

Behind the four horsemen came the procession of the bull fighters. They had been all formed in ranks in the entrance way ready to march out, and as the music started they came. In the front rank walked the three espadas or toreros, who would have charge of the killing of the six bulls of the afternoon.

They came walking out in heavily brocaded yellow and black

costumes, the familiar "toreador" suit, heavy with gold embroidery, cape, jacket, shirt and collar, knee breeches, pink stockings, and low pumps. Always at bull fights afterwards the incongruity of those pink stockings used to strike me. Just behind the three principals—and after your first bull fight you do not look at their costumes but their faces—marched the teams or cuadrillas. They are dressed in the same way but not as gorgeously as the matadors.

Back of the teams ride the picadors. Big, heavy, brown-faced men in wide flat hats, carrying lances like long window poles. They are astride horses that make Spark Plug look as trim and sleek as a King's Plate winner. Back of the pics come the gaily harnessed mule teams and the red-shirted monos or bull ring servants.

The bull fighters march in across the sand to the president's box. They march with easy professional stride, swinging along, not in the least theatrical except for their clothes. They all have the easy grace and slight slouch of the professional athlete. From their faces they might be major league ball players. They salute the president's box and then spread out along the barrera, exchanging their heavy brocaded capes for the fighting capes that have been laid along the red fence by the attendants.

We leaned forward over the barrera. Just below us the three matadors of the afternoon were leaning against the fence talking. One lighted a cigaret. He was a short, clear-skinned gypsy, Gitanillo, in a wonderful gold brocaded jacket, his short pigtail sticking out under his black cocked hat.

"He's not very fancy," a young man in a straw hat, with obviously American shoes, who sat on my left, said.

"But he sure knows bulls, that boy. He's a great killer."

"You're an American, aren't you?" asked Mike.

"Sure," the boy grinned. "But I know this gang. That's Gitanillo. You want to watch him. The kid with the chubby face is Chicuelo. They say he doesn't really like bull fighting, but the town's crazy about him. The next to him is Villalta. He's the great one."

I had noticed Villalta. He was straight as a lance and walked like a young wolf. He was talking and smiling at a friend who leaned over the barrera. Upon his tanned cheekbone was a big patch of gauze held on with adhesive tape.

"He got gored last week at Malaga," said the American.

The American, whom later we were to learn to know and love as the Gin Bottle King, because of a great feat of arms performed at an early hour of the morning with a container of Mr. Gordon's celebrated product as his sole weapon in one of the four most dangerous situations I have ever seen, said: "The show's going to begin."

Out in the arena the picadors had galloped their decrepit horses around the ring, sitting straight and stiff in their rocking chair saddles. Now all but three had ridden out of the ring. These three were huddled against the red painted fence of the barrera. Their horses backed against the fence, one eye bandaged, their lances at rest.

In rode two of the marshals in the velvet jackets and white ruffs. They galloped up to the president's box, swerved and saluted, doffing their hats and bowing low. From the box an object came hurtling down. One of the marshals caught it in his plumed hat.

"The key to the bull pen," said the Gin Bottle King.

The two horsemen whirled and rode across the arena. One of them tossed the key to a man in torero costume, they both saluted with a wave of their plumed hats, and had gone from the ring. The big gate was shut and bolted. There was no more entrance. The ring was complete.

The crowd had been shouting and yelling. Now it was dead silent. The man with the key stepped toward an iron barred, low, red door and unlocked the great sliding bar. He lifted it and stepped back. The door swung open. The man hid behind it. Inside it was dark.

Then, ducking his head as he came up out of the dark pen, a bull came into the arena. He came out all in a rush, big, black and white, weighing over a ton and moving with a soft-gallop. Just as he came out the sun seemed to dazzle him for an instant. He stood as though he were frozen, his great crest of muscle up, firmly planted, his eyes looking around, his horns pointed forward, black and white and sharp as porcupine quills. Then he charged. And as he charged I suddenly saw what bull fighting is all about.

For the bull was absolutely unbelievable. He seemed like some great prehistoric animal, absolutely deadly and absolutely vicious. And he was silent. He charged silently and with a soft galloping rush. When he turned he turned on his four feet like a cat. When he charged the first thing that caught his eye was a picador on one of the wretched horses. The picador dug his spurs into the horse and they galloped away. The bull came on in his rush, refused to be shaken off, and in full gallop crashed into the animal from the side, ignored the horse, drove one of his horns high into the thigh of the picador, and tore him, saddle and all, off the horse's back.

The bull went on without pausing to worry the picador lying on the ground. The next picador was sitting on his horse braced to receive the shock of the charge, his lance ready. The bull hit him sideways on, and horse and rider went high up in the air in a kicking mass and fell across the bull's back. As they came down the bull charged into them. The dough-faced kid, Chicuelo, vaulted over the fence, ran toward the bull and flopped his cape into the bull's face. The bull charged the cape and Chicuelo dodged backwards and had the bull clear in the arena.

Without an instant's hesitation the bull charged Chicuelo. The kid stood his ground, simply swung back on his heels and floated his cape like a ballet dancer's skirt into the bull's face as he passed.

"Olé!"—pronounced Oh-Lay!—roared the crowd.

The bull whirled and charged again. Without moving Chicuelo repeated the performance. His legs rigid, just withdrawing his body from the rush of the bull's horns and floating the cape out with that beautiful swing.

Again the crowd roared. The Kid did this seven times. Each time the bull missed him by inches. Each time he gave the bull a free shot at him. Each time the crowd roared. Then he flopped the cape once at the bull at the finish of a pass, swung it around behind him and walked away from the bull to the barrera.

"He's the boy with the cape all right," said the Gin Bottle King. "That swing he did with the cape's called a Veronica."

The chubby faced Kid who did not like bull fighting and had just done the seven wonderful Veronicas was standing against the fence just below us. His face glistened with sweat in the sun but was almost expressionless. His eyes were looking out across the arena where the bull was standing making up his mind to charge a picador. He was studying the bull because a few minutes later it would be his duty to kill him, and once he went out with his thin, red-hilted sword and his piece of red cloth to kill the bull in the final set it would be him or the bull. There are no drawn battles in bull fighting.

I am not going to describe the rest of that afternoon in detail. It was the first bull fight I ever saw, but it was not the best. The best was in the little town of Pamplona high up in the hills of Navarre, and came weeks later. Up in Pamplona, where they have held six days of bull fighting each year since 1126 A.D., and where the bulls race through the streets of the town each morning at six o'clock with half the town running ahead of them. Pamplona, where every man and boy in town is an amateur bull fighter and where there is an amateur fight each morning that is attended by 20,000 people in which the amateur fighters are all unarmed and there is a casualty list at least equal to a Dublin election. But Pamplona, with the best bull fight and the wild tale of the amateur fights, comes in the second chapter.

I am not going to apologize for bull fighting. It is a survival of the days of the Roman Coliseum. But it does need some explanation. Bull fighting is not a sport. It was never supposed to be. It is a tragedy. A very great tragedy. The tragedy is the death of the bull. It is played in three definite acts.

The Gin Bottle King—who, by the way, does not drink gin—

95

told us a lot of this that first night as we sat in the upstairs room of the little restaurant that made a specialty of roast young suckling pig, roasted on an oak plank and served with a mushroom tortilla and vino rojo. The rest we learned later at the bull fighters' pensione in the Via San Jeronimo, where one of the bull fighters had eyes exactly like a rattlesnake.

Much of it we learned in the sixteen fights we saw in different parts of Spain from San Sebastian to Granada.

At any rate bull fighting is not a sport. It is a tragedy, and it symbolizes the struggle between man and the beasts. There are usually six bulls to a fight. A fight is called a corrida de toros. Fighting bulls are bred like race horses, some of the oldest breeding establishments being several hundred years old. A good bull is worth about $2,000. They are bred for speed, strength and viciousness. In other words a good fighting bull is an absolutely incorrigible bad bull.

Bull fighting is an exceedingly dangerous occupation. In sixteen fights I saw there were only two in which there was no one badly hurt. On the other hand it is very remunerative. A popular espada gets $5,000 for his afternoon's work. An unpopular espada though may not get $500. Both run the same risks. It is a good deal like Grand Opera for the really great matadors except they run the chance of being killed every time they cannot hit high C.

No one at any time in the fight can approach the bull at any time except directly from the front. That is where the danger comes. There are also all sorts of complicated passes that must be done with the cape, each requiring as much technique as a champion billiard player. And underneath it all is the necessity for playing the old tragedy in the absolutely custom bound, law-laid-down way. It must all be done gracefully, seemingly effortlessly and always with dignity. The worst criticism the Spaniards ever make of a bull fighter is that his work is "vulgar."

The three absolute acts of the tragedy are first the entry of the bull when the picadors receive the shock of his attacks and attempt to protect their horses with their lances. Then the horses go out and the second act is the planting of the banderillos. This is one of the most interesting and difficult parts but among the easiest for a new bull fight fan to appreciate in technique. The banderillos are three-foot, gaily colored darts with a small fish hook prong in the end. The man who is going to plant them walks out into the arena alone with the bull. He lifts the banderillos at arm's length and points them toward the bull. Then he calls "Toro! Toro!" The bull charges and the banderillero rises to his toes, bends in a curve forward and just as the bull is about to hit him drops the darts into the bull's hump just back of his horns.

They must go in evenly, one on each side. They must not be shoved, or thrown or stuck in from the side. This is the first time the bull has been completely baffled, there is the prick of the darts that he cannot escape and there are no horses for him to charge into. But he charges the man again and again and each time he gets a pair of the long banderillos that hang from his hump by their tiny barbs and flop like porcupine quills.

Last is the death of the bull, which is in the hands of the matador who has had charge of the bull since his first attack. Each matador has two bulls in the afternoon. The death of the bull is most formal and can only be brought about in one way, directly from the front by the matador who must receive the bull in full charge and kill him with a sword thrust between the shoulders just back of the neck and between the horns. Before killing the bull he must first do a series of passes with the muleta, a piece of red cloth he carries about the size of a large napkin. With the muleta the torero must show his complete mastery of the bull, must make the bull miss him again and again by inches, before he is allowed to kill him. It is in this phase that most of the fatal accidents occur.

The word "toreador" is obsolete Spanish and is never used. The torero is usually called an espada or swordsman. He must be proficient in all three acts of the fight. In the first he uses the cape and does veronicas and protects the picadors by taking the bull out and away from them when they are spilled to the ground. In the second act he plants the banderillos. In the third act he masters the bull with the muleta and kills him.

Few toreros excel in all three departments. Some, like young Chicuelo, are unapproachable in their cape work. Others like the late Joselito are wonderful banderilleros. Only a few are great killers. Most of the greatest killers are gypsies.

Pamplona in July

➤ *The Toronto Star Weekly* · OCTOBER 27, 1923

IN Pamplona, a white-walled, sun-baked town high up in the hills of Navarre, is held in the first two weeks of July each year the World's Series of bull fighting.

Bull fight fans from all Spain jam into the little town. Hotels double their prices and fill every room. The cafes under the wide arcades that run around the Plaza de la Constitucion have every table crowded, the tall Pilgrim Father sombreros of Andalusia sitting over the same table with straw hats from Madrid and the flat blue Basque caps of Navarre and the Basque country.

Really beautiful girls, gorgeous, bright shawls over their shoulders, dark, dark-eyed, black-lace mantillas over their hair, walk with their escorts in the crowds that pass from morning until night along the narrow walk that runs between inner and outer belts of cafe tables under the shade of the arcade out of the white glare of the Plaza de la Constitucion. All day and all night there is dancing in the streets. Bands of blue-shirted peasants whirl and lift and swing behind a drum, fife and reed instruments in the ancient Basque Riau-Riau dances. And at night there is the throb of the big drums and the military band as the whole town dances in the great open square of the Plaza.

We landed at Pamplona at night. The streets were solid with people dancing. Music was pounding and throbbing. Fireworks were being set off from the big public square. All the carnivals I had ever seen paled down in comparison. A rocket exploded over our heads with a blinding burst and the stick came swirling and whishing down. Dancers, snapping their fingers and whirling in perfect time through the crowd, bumped into us before we could get our bags down from the top of the station bus. Finally I got the bags through the crowd to the hotel.

We had wired and written for rooms two weeks ahead. Nothing had been saved. We were offered a single room with a single bed opening on to the kitchen ventilator shaft for seven dollars a day apiece. There was a big row with the landlady, who stood in front of her desk with her hands on her hips, and her broad Indian face perfectly placid, and told us in a few words of French and much Basque Spanish that she had to make all her money for the whole year in the next ten days. That people would come and that people would have to pay what she asked. She could show us a better room for ten dollars apiece. We said it would be preferable to sleep in the streets with the pigs. The landlady agreed that might be possible. We said we preferred it to such a hotel. All perfectly amicable. The landlady considered. We stood our ground. Mrs. Hemingway sat down on our rucksacks.

"I can get you a room in a house in the town. You can eat here," said the landlady.

"How much?"

"Five dollars."

We started off through the dark, narrow, carnival-mad streets with a boy carrying our rucksacks. It was a lovely big room in an old Spanish house with walls thick as a fortress. A cool, pleasant room, with a red tile floor and two big, comfortable beds set back in an alcove. A window opened on to an iron grilled porch out over the street. We were very comfortable.

All night long the wild music kept up in the street below. Several times in the night there was a wild roll of drumming, and I got out of bed and across the tiled floor to the balcony. But it was always the same. Men, blue-shirted, bareheaded, whirling and floating in a wild fantastic dance down the street behind the rolling drums and shrill fifes.

Just at daylight there was a crash of music in the street below. Real military music. Herself was up, dressed, at the window.

"Come on," she said. "They're all going somewhere." Down

below the street was full of people. It was five o'clock in the morning. They were all going in one direction. I dressed in a hurry and we started after them.

The crowd was all going toward the great public square. People were pouring into it from every street and moving out of it toward the open country we could see through the narrow gaps in the high walls.

"Let's get some coffee," said Herself.

"Do you think we've got time? Hey, what's going to happen?" I asked a newsboy.

"Encierro," he said scornfully. "The encierro commences at six o'clock."

"What's the encierro?" I asked him.

"Oh, ask me to-morrow," he said, and started to run. The entire crowd was running now.

"I've got to have my coffee. No matter what it is," Herself said.

The waiter poured two streams of coffee and milk into the glass out of his big kettles. The crowd was still running, coming from all the streets that fed into the Plaza.

"What is this encierro anyway?" Herself asked, gulping the coffee.

"All I know is that they let the bulls out into the streets."

We started out after the crowd. Out of a narrow gate into a great yellow open space of country with the new concrete bull ring standing high and white and black with people. The yellow and red Spanish flag blowing in the early morning breeze. Across the open and once inside the bull ring, we mounted to the top looking toward the town. It cost a peseta to go up to the top. All the other levels were free. There were easily twenty thousand people there. Everyone jammed on the outside of the big concrete amphitheatre, looking toward the yellow town with the bright red roofs, where a long wooden pen ran from the entrance of the city gate across the open, bare ground to the bull ring.

It was really a double wooden fence, making a long entryway from the main street of the town into the bull ring itself. It made a runway about two hundred and fifty yards long. People were jammed solid on each side of it. Looking up it toward the main street.

Then far away there was a dull report.

"They're off," everybody shouted.

"What is it?" I asked a man next to me who was leaning far out over the concrete rail.

"The bulls! They have released them from the corrals on the far side of the city. They are racing through the city."

"Whew," said Herself. "What do they do that for?"

Then down the narrow fenced-in runway came a crowd of men and boys running. Running as hard as they could go. The gate feeding into the bull ring was opened and they all ran pell-mell under the entrance levels into the ring. Then there came another crowd. Running even harder. Straight up the long pen from the town.

"Where are the bulls?" asked Herself.

Then they came in sight. Eight bulls galloping along, full tilt, heavy set, black, glistening, sinister, their horns bare, tossing their heads. And running with them three steers with bells on their necks. They ran in a solid mass, and ahead of them sprinted, tore, ran and bolted the rear guard of the men and boys of Pamplona who had allowed themselves to be chased through the streets for a morning's pleasure.

A boy in his blue shirt, red sash, white canvas shoes with the inevitable leather wine bottle hung from his shoulders, stumbled as he sprinted down the straightaway. The first bull lowered his head and made a jerky, sideways toss. The boy crashed up against the fence and lay there limp, the herd running solidly together passed him up. The crowd roared.

Everybody made a dash for the inside of the ring, and we got into a box just in time to see the bulls come into the ring filled with men. The men ran in a panic to each side. The bulls, still bunched solidly together, ran straight with the trained steers across the ring and into the entrance that led to the pens.

That was the entry. Every morning during the bull fighting

festival of San Fermin at Pamplona the bulls that are to fight in the afternoon are released from their corrals at six o'clock in the morning and race through the main street of the town for a mile and a half to the pen. The men who run ahead of them do it for the fun of the thing. It has been going on each year since a couple of hundred years before Columbus had his historic interview with Queen Isabella in the camp outside of Granada.

There are two things in favor of there being no accidents. First, that fighting bulls are not aroused and vicious when they are together. Second, that the steers are relied upon to keep them moving.

Sometimes things go wrong, a bull will be detached from the herd as they pile through into the pen and with his crest up, a ton of speed and viciousness, his needle-sharp horns lowered, will charge again and again into the packed mass of men and boys in the bull ring. There is no place for the men to get out of the ring. It is too jammed for them to climb over the barrera or red fence that rims the field. They have to stay in and take it. Eventually the steers get the bull out of the ring and into the pen. He may wound or kill thirty men before they can get him out. No armed men are allowed to oppose him. That is the chance the Pamplona bull fight fans take every morning during the Feria. It is the Pamplona tradition of giving the bulls a final shot at everyone in town before they enter the pens. They will not leave until they come out into the glare of the arena to die in the afternoon.

Consequently Pamplona is the toughest bull fight town in the world. The amateur fight that comes immediately after the bulls have entered the pens proves that. Every seat in the great amphitheatre is packed. About three hundred men, with capes, odd pieces of cloth, old shirts, anything that will imitate a bull fighter's cape, are singing and dancing in the arena. There is a shout, and the bull pen opens. Out comes a young bull just as fast as he can come. On his horns are leather knobs to prevent his goring anyone. He charges and hits a man. Tosses him high in the air, and the crowd roars. The man comes down on the ground, and the bull goes for him, bumping him with his head. Worrying him with his horns. Several amateur bull fighters are flopping their capes in his face to make the bull charge and leave the man on the ground. Then the bull charges and bags another man. The crowd roars with delight.

Then the bull will turn like a cat and get somebody who has been acting very brave about ten feet behind him. Then he will toss a man over the fence. Then he picks out one man and follows him in a wild twisting charge through the entire crowd until he bags him. The barrera is packed with men and boys sitting along the top, and the bull decides to clear them all off. He goes along, hooking carefully with his horn and dropping them off with a toss of his horns like a man pitching hay.

Each time the bull bags someone the crowd roars with joy. Most of it is home talent stuff. The braver the man has been or the more elegant pass he has attempted with his cape before the bull gets him the more the crowd roars. No one is armed. No one hurts or plagues the bull in any way. A man who grabbed the bull by the tail and tried to hang on was hissed and booed by the crowd and the next time he tried it was knocked down by another man in the bull ring. No one enjoys it all more than the bull.

As soon as he shows signs of tiring from his charges, the two old steers, one brown and the other looking like a big Holstein, come trotting in and alongside the young bull who falls in behind them like a dog and follows them meekly on a tour of the arena and then out.

Another comes right in, and the charging and tossing, the ineffectual cape waving, and wonderful music are repeated right over again. But always different. Some of the animals in this morning amateur fight are steers. Fighting bulls from the best strain who had some imperfection or other in build so they could never command the high prices paid for combat animals, $2,000 to $3,000 apiece. But there is nothing lacking in their fighting spirit.

The show comes off every morning. Everybody in town turns out at five-thirty when the military bands go through the streets. Many of them stay up all night for it. We didn't miss one, and it is quelque sporting event that will get us both up at five-thirty o'clock in the morning for six days running.

As far as I know we were the only English-speaking people in Pamplona during the Feria of last year [July].

There were three minor earthquakes while we were there. Terrific cloud bursts in the mountains and the Ebro River flooded out Zaragossa. For two days the bull ring was under water and the Corrida had to be suspended for the first time in over a hundred years. That was during the middle of the fair. Everyone was desperate. On the third day it looked gloomier than ever, poured rain all morning, and then at noon the clouds rolled away up across the valley, the sun came out bright and hot and baking and that afternoon there was the greatest bull fight I will perhaps ever see.

There were rockets going up into the air and the arena was nearly full when we got into our regular seats. The sun was hot and baking. Over on the other side we could see the bull fighters standing ready to come in. All wearing their oldest clothes because of the heavy, muddy going in the arena. We picked out the three matadors of the afternoon with our glasses. Only one of them was new. Olmos, a chubby faced, jolly looking man, something like Tris Speaker. The others we had seen often before. Maera, dark, spare and deadly looking, one of the very greatest toreros of all time. The third, young Algabeno, the son of a famous bull fighter, a slim young Andalusian with a charming Indian looking face. All were wearing the suits they had probably started bull fighting with, too tight, old fashioned, outmoded.

There was the procession of entrance, the wild bull fight music played, the preliminaries were quickly over, the picadors retired along the red fence with their horses, the heralds sounded their trumpets and the door of the bull pen swung open. The bull came out in a rush, saw a man standing near the barrera and charged him. The man vaulted over the fence and the bull charged the barrera. He crashed into the fence in full charge and ripped a two by eight plank solidly out in a splinter-ing smash. He broke his horn doing it and the crowd called for a new bull. The trained steers trotted in, the bull fell in meekly behind them, and the three of them trotted out of the arena.

The next bull came in with the same rush. He was Maera's bull and after perfect cape play Maera planted the banderillos. Maera is Herself's favorite bull fighter. And if you want to keep any conception of yourself as a brave, hard, perfectly balanced, thoroughly competent man in your wife's mind never take her to a real bull fight. I used to go into the amateur fights in the morning to try and win back a small amount of her esteem but the more I discovered that bull fighting required a very great quantity of a certain type of courage of which I had an almost complete lack the more it became apparent that any admiration she might ever redevelop for me would have to be simply an antidote to the real admiration for Maera and Villalta. You cannot compete with bull fighters on their own ground. If anywhere. The only way most husbands are able to keep any drag with their wives at all is that, first there are only a limited number of bull fighters, second there are only a limited number of wives who have ever seen bull fights.

Maera planted his first pair of banderillos sitting down on the edge of the little step-up that runs around the barrera. He snarled at the bull and as the animal charged leaned back tight against the fence and as the horns struck on either side of him, swung forward over the brute's head and planted the two darts in his hump. He planted the next pair the same way, so near to us we could have leaned over and touched him. Then he went out to kill the bull and after he had made absolutely unbelievable passes with the little red cloth of the muleta drew up his sword and as the bull charged Maera thrust. The sword shot out of his hand and the bull caught him. He went up in the air on the horns of the bull and then came down. Young Algabeno flopped his cape in the bull's face. The bull charged him and Maera staggered to his feet. But his wrist was sprained.

With his wrist sprained, so that every time he raised it to sight for a thrust it brought beads of sweat out on his face, Maera tried again and again to make his death thrust. He lost his sword again and again, picked it up with his left hand from the mud floor of the arena and transferred it to the right for the thrust. Finally he made it and the bull went over. The bull nearly got him twenty times. As he came in to stand up under us at the barrera side his wrist was swollen to twice normal size. I thought of prize fighters I had seen quit because they had hurt their hands.

There was almost no pause while the mules galloped in and hitched on to the first bull and dragged him out and the second came in with a rush. The picadors took the first shock of him with their bull lances. There was the snort and charge, the shock and the mass against the sky, the wonderful defense by the picador with his lance that held off the bull, and then Rosario Olmos stepped out with his cape.

Once he flopped the cape at the bull and floated it around in an easy graceful swing. Then he tried the same swing, the classic "Veronica," and the bull caught him at the end of it. Instead of stopping at the finish the bull charged on in. He caught Olmos squarely with his horn, hoisted him high in the air. He fell heavily and the bull was on top of him, driving his horns again and again into him. Olmos lay on the sand, his head on his arms. One of his teammates was flopping his cape madly in the bull's face. The bull lifted his head for an instant and charged and got his man. Just one terrific toss. Then he whirled and chased a man just in back of him toward the barrera. The man was running full tilt and as he put his hand on the fence to vault it the bull had him and caught him with his horn, shooting him way up into the crowd. He rushed toward the fallen man he had tossed who was getting to his feet and all alone—Algabeno grabbed him by the tail. He hung on until I thought he or the bull would break. The wounded man got to his feet and started away.

The bull turned like a cat and charged Algabeno and Algabeno met him with the cape. Once, twice, three times he made the perfect, floating, slow swing with the cape, perfectly, graceful, debonair, back on his heels, baffling the bull. And he had command of the situation. There never was such a scene at any world's series game.

There are no substitute matadors allowed. Maera was finished. His wrist could not lift a sword for weeks. Olmos had been gored badly through the body. It was Algabeno's bull. This one and the next five.

He handled them all. Did it all. Cape play easy, graceful, confident. Beautiful work with the muleta. And serious, deadly killing. Five bulls he killed, one after the other, and each one was a separate problem to be worked out with death. At the end there was nothing debonair about him. It was only a question if he would last through or if the bulls would get him. They were all very wonderful bulls.

"He is a very great kid," said Herself. "He is only twenty."

"I wish we knew him," I said.

"Maybe we will some day," she said. Then considered a moment. "He will probably be spoiled by then."

They make twenty thousand a year.

That was just three months ago. It seems in a different century now, working in an office. It is a very long way from the sun baked town of Pamplona, where the men race through the streets in the mornings ahead of the bulls to the morning ride to work on a Bay-Caledonia car. But it is only fourteen days by water to Spain and there is no need for a castle. There is always that room at 5 Calle de Eslava, and a son, if he is to redeem the family reputation as a bull fighter, must start very early.

Trout Fishing in Europe

➤ *The Toronto Star Weekly* · NOVEMBER 17, 1923

BILL JONES went to visit a French financier who lives near Deauville and has a private trout stream. The financier was very fat. His stream was very thin.

"Ah, Monsieur Zshones, I will show you the fishing." The financier purred over the coffee. "You have the trout in Canada, is it not? But here! Here we have the really charming trout fishing of Normandy. I will show you. Rest yourself content. You will see it."

The financier was a very literal man. His idea of showing Bill the fishing was for Bill to watch and the financier to fish. They started out. It was a trying sight.

If undressed and put back on the shelf piece by piece the financier would have stocked a sporting goods store. Placed end to end his collection of flies would have reached from Keokuk, Ill., to Paris, Ont. The price of his rod would have made a substantial dent in the interallied debt or served to foment a central American revolution.

The financier flung a pretty poisonous fly, too. At the end of two hours one trout had been caught. The financier was elated. The trout was a beauty, fully five and a half inches long and perfectly proportioned. The only trouble with him was some funny black spots along his sides and belly.

"I don't believe he's healthy," Bill said doubtfully.

"Healthy? You don't think he's healthy? That lovely trout? Why, he's a wonder. Did you not see the terrific fight he made before I netted him?" The financier was enraged. The beautiful trout lay in his large, fat hand.

"But what are those black spots?" Bill asked.

"Those spots? Oh, absolutely nothing. Perhaps worms. Who can say? All of our trout here have them at this season. But do not be afraid of that, Monsieur Zshones. Wait until you taste this beautiful trout for your breakfast!"

It was probably the proximity to Deauville that spoiled the financier's trout stream. Deauville is supposed to be a sort of combination of Fifth Avenue, Atlantic City, and Sodom and Gomorrah. In reality it is a watering place that has become so famous that the really smart people no longer go to it and the others hold a competitive spending contest and mistake each other for duchesses, dukes, prominent pugilists, Greek millionaires and the Dolly sisters.

The real trout fishing of Europe is in Spain, Germany and Switzerland. Spain has probably the best fishing of all in Galicia. But the Germans and the Swiss are right behind.

In Germany the great difficulty is to get permission to fish. All the fishing water is rented by the year to individuals. If you want to fish you have first to get permission of the man who has rented the fishing. Then you go back to the township and get a permission, and then you finally get the permission of the owner of the land.

If you have only two weeks to fish, it will probably take about all of it to get these different permissions. A much easier way is simply to carry a rod with you and fish when you see a good stream. If anyone complains, begin handing out marks. If the complaints keep up, keep handing out marks. If this policy is pursued far enough the complaints will eventually cease and you will be allowed to continue fishing.

If, on the other hand, your supply of marks runs out before the complaints cease you will probably go either to jail or the hospital. It is a good plan, on this account, to have a dollar bill secreted somewhere in your clothes. Produce the dollar bill. It is ten to one your assailant will fall to his knees in an attitude of extreme thanksgiving and on arising break all existing records to the nearest, deepest and wooliest German hand knitted sock, the south German's savings bank.

Following this method of obtaining fishing permits, we fished all through the Black Forest. With rucksacks and fly-rods, we hiked across country, sticking to the high ridges and the rolling crests of the hills, sometimes through deep pine timber, sometimes coming out into a clearing and farmyards and again going, for miles, without seeing a soul except occasional wild looking berry pickers. We never knew where we were. But we were never lost because at any time we could cut down from the high country into a valley and know we would hit a stream. Sooner or later every stream flowed into a river and a river meant a town.

At night we stopped in little inns or gasthofs. Some of these were so far from civilization that the innkeepers did not know the mark was rapidly becoming worthless and continued to charge the old German prices. At one place, room and board, in Canadian money, were less than ten cents a day.

One day we started from Triberg and toiled up a long, steadily ascending hill road until we were on top of the high country and could look out at the Black Forest rolling away from us in every direction. Away off across country we could see a range of hills, and we figured that at their base must flow a river. We cut across the high, bare country, dipping down into valleys and walking through woods, cool and dim as a cathedral on the hot August day. Finally we hit the upper end of the valley at the foot of the hills we had seen.

In it flowed a lovely trout stream and there was not a farmhouse in sight. I jointed up the rod, and while Mrs. Hemingway sat under a tree on the hillside and kept watch both ways up the valley, caught four real trout. They averaged about three-quarters of a pound apiece. Then we moved down the valley. The stream broadened out and Herself took the rod while I found a look-out post.

She caught six in about an hour, and two of them I had to come down and net for her. She had hooked a big one, and after he was triumphantly netted we looked up to see an old German in peasant clothes watching us from the road.

"Gut tag," I said.

"Tag," he said. "Have you good fishing?"

"Yes. Very good."

"Good," he said. "It is good to have somebody fishing." And went hiking along the road.

In contrast to him were the farmers in Ober-Prechtal, where we had obtained full fishing permits, who came down and chased us away from the stream with pitchforks because we were Auslanders.

In Switzerland I discovered two valuable things about trout fishing. The first was while I was fishing a stream that parallels the Rhone river and that was swollen and grey with snow water. Flies were useless, and I was fishing with a big gob of worms. A fine, juicy-looking bait. But I wasn't getting any trout or even any strikes.

An old Italian who had a farm up the valley was walking behind me while I fished. As there was nothing doing in a stream I knew from experience was full of trout, it got more and more irritating. Somebody just back of you while you are fishing is as bad as someone looking over your shoulder while you write a letter to your girl. Finally I sat down and waited for the Italian to go away. He sat down, too.

He was an old man, with a face like a leather water bottle.

"Well, Papa, no fish to-day," I said.

"Not for you," he said solemnly.

"Why not for me? For you, maybe?" I said.

"Oh yes," he said, not smiling. "For me trout always. Not for you. You don't know how to fish with worms." And spat into the stream.

This touched a tender spot, a boyhood spent within forty miles of the Soo, hoisting out trout with a cane pole and all the worms the hook would hold.

"You're so old you know everything. You are probably a rich man from your knowledge of fishworms," I said.

This bagged him.

"Give me the rod," he said.

He took it from me, cleaned off the fine wriggling gob of trout food, and selected one medium-sized angleworm from my box. This he threaded a little way on the number 10 hook, and let about three-fourths of the worm wave free.

"Now that's a worm," he said with satisfaction.

He reeled the line up till there was only the six feet of leader out and dropped the free swinging worm into a pool where the stream swirled under the bank. There was nothing doing. He pulled it slowly out and dropped it in a little lower down. The tip of the rod twisted. He lowered it just a trifle. Then it shot down in a jerk, and he struck and horsed out a 15-inch trout and sent him back over his head in a telephone pole swing.

I fell on him while he was still flopping.

The old Italian handed me the rod. "There, young one. That is the way to use a worm. Let him be free to move like a worm. The trout will take the free end and then suck him all in, hook and all. I have fished this stream for twenty years and I know. More than one worm scares the fish. It must be natural."

"Come, use the rod and fish now," I urged him.

"No. No. I only fish at night," he smiled. "It is much too expensive to get a permit."

But by my watching for the river guard while he fished and our using the rod alternately until each caught a fish, we fished all day and caught 18 trout. The old Italian knew all the holes, and only fished where there were big ones. We used a free wriggling worm, and the 18 trout averaged a pound and a half apiece.

He also showed me how to use grubs. Grubs are only good in clear water, but are a deadly bait. You can find them in any rotten tree or sawlog, and the Swiss and Swiss-Italians keep them in grub boxes. Flat pieces of wood bored full of auger holes with a sliding metal top. The grub will live as well in his hole in the wood as in the log and is one of the greatest hot weather baits known. Trout will take a grub when they will take nothing else in the low water days of August.

The Swiss, too, have a wonderful way of cooking trout. They boil them in a liquor made of wine vinegar, bay leaves, and a dash of red pepper. Not too much of any of the ingredients in the boiling water, and cook until the trout turns blue. It preserves the true trout flavor better than almost any way of cooking. The meat stays firm and pink and delicate. Then they serve them with drawn butter. They drink the clear Sion wine when they eat them.

It is not a well-known dish at the hotels. You have to go back in the country to get trout cooked that way. You come up from the stream to a chalet and ask them if they know how to cook blue trout. If they don't you walk on a way. If they do, you sit down on the porch with the goats and the children and wait. Your nose will tell you when the trout are boiling. Then after a little while you will hear a pop. That is the Sion being uncorked. Then the woman of the chalet will come to the door and say, "It is prepared, Monsieur."

'Then you can go away and I will do the rest myself.

Inflation and the German Mark

➤ *The Toronto Star Weekly* · DECEMBER 8, 1923

"Now if any gentleman needs his quarter for a meal or a bed—"

The barker stood in a narrow alley opposite Osgoode Hall, Toronto. In front of him was a soap box with a few envelopes of foreign money.

In front of the soap box stood a crowd of out-of-workers, shifting from foot to foot in the mud, and listening dull-eyed to the spellbinder.

"As I say," went on the barker, moistening his lips under his grey mustache, "if a gentleman has an immediate need for his quarter, I don't want it. But if he is prepared to make an investment, I am offering him the chance to make himself rich for life.

"Only a quarter, gentlemen. Just one Canadian quarter, and Russia is bound to come back. A quarter buys this 250,000 Soviet ruble note. Who'll buy one?"

Nobody seemed on the point of buying. But they all listened to him perfectly seriously.

It was the Russian ruble, the Austrian kronen and German mark, not worth the paper they are printed on, making a last stand as serious money in Toronto's Ward.

"In normal times this note I hold here is worth about $125,-000. Suppose it goes up to where the ruble is worth only one cent. You will have $2,500. You can walk right into a bank and get $2,500 for this one note."

One man's eyes shone and he moistened his lips.

The barker lifted the little pink bit of worthless paper up and looked at it lovingly.

115

"And Russia is coming back, gentlemen. Every day her money gets more valuable. Don't let anyone tell you Russia isn't coming back. Once a country gets to be a republic she stays that way, gentlemen. Look at France. She's been a republic a long time."

A man in the front row in an old army coat nodded. Another man scratched his neck.

The barker drew out a big blue-green bill and laid it alongside the Russian ruble note.

No one explained to the listening men that the cheap looking Russian money had been printed in million-ruble denominations as fast as the presses could work in order to wipe out the value of the old imperial money and in consequence the money holding class. Now the Soviet has issued rubles backed by gold. None of these are in the hands of the barkers.

"To the first man that pays a quarter for this 250,000 ruble note I am going to give free this German mark note for 10,000 marks."

The barker held both notes up for inspection.

"Don't ever think that Germany is through. You saw in the paper this morning that Poincare is weakening. He's weakening, and the mark will come back, too."

He was Coue-izing the crowd. A man pulled out a quarter.

"Gimme one."

He took the two bills, folded them and put them in his inside coat pocket. He smiled as the spieler went on. He had a stake in Europe again.

The foreign news would never be dry to him now.

Four or five more men bought a half-million rubles for a quarter. The rubles are not even quoted on the exchange any more—yet they and the worthless German marks have been sold all over Canada as investments.

Then the money seller leaned over and picked up an envelope of thousand mark notes. They were the well printed pre-war notes that were in common use in Germany until the exchange tumbled from 20,000 marks to the dollar this spring down the toboggan where you can almost name the number of billions you want for a dollar and get them. None of these marks are worth any more than any others. Except as pieces of paper for wall papering or soap wrappers.

"These are special," the money seller said. "I'm selling these at a dollar apiece. They used to be fifty cents. Now I've raised the price. Nobody has to buy them that doesn't want them. They're the real pre-war marks."

He fondled them. The real pre-war marks.

Worth 15 cents a trillion before the New York banks refused to quote them any more last week.

"What makes them any better than those marks you gave away?" asked a gaunt man leaning against the wall in the alley. He was one of those who had invested a quarter in Europe and was jealous of this new mark being sprung on him.

"They're all signed for in the treaty of Versailles," the barker said confidentially. "Every one of these is signed for in the peace treaty. Germany has thirty years to redeem them at par."

The men standing in front of the soap box looked respectfully at the marks that were signed for in the treaty. They were obviously out of reach of investors. But it was something to be near them.

On the wall of the one-storey shack that bounded the alley, the tall youth who smoked a pipe and stood in the background while the vendor of money talked had tacked a number of clippings and samples of foreign money.

The clippings were mostly about the economic comeback made by Soviet Russia and various other foreign dispatches of an optimistic tone.

With his forefinger the money vendor traced out the story of a dollar loan to some Austrian bank.

"Now, who wants to buy 10,000 Austrian kronen for a dollar?" he asked the crowd, holding up one of the big purple bills of the old Hapsburg currency.

In the banks to-day the Austrian crown is worth .0014½ cents. In other words, about 14 cents for 10,000 kronen. At one dollar for 10,000, the men in the alley were invited to take a flyer in Austrian currency.

"Now, personally, I only keep enough Canadian money to pay the bills," the spellbinder went on. "You can't tell what is going to happen to Canadian money. Look at these different currencies to-day. A wise plan is to keep a little Russian money, a little German money, a little Austrian money, and a little British money."

Most of the men looked as though even the smallest amount of Canadian money would be exceedingly welcome. But they listened on, and every lot offered, after the spellbinder had talked long enough, found a quarter produced by somebody, and the hope of getting rich quick implanted in some man.

"Take these Austrian bills, for example," the money seller went on. "There's a bill I sold for $2. Now I'm selling it for only a dollar. And I'll give a million-ruble Soviet note away with it."

At this announcement some of those who had bought the rubles for two bits a quarter-million looked sullen.

"Oh, these are a different ruble," the vendor assured them. "There are some of these rubles here I wouldn't take $10 for. Let some gentleman offer me ten dollars and see if he can get them."

No gentleman offered.

"I won't deny I have rivals," the spieler proceeded. "They try and undersell me. They cut prices on me. But now I'm going to cut prices on them. My big rival asks 40 cents for a million-ruble note. I'm going to undercut him to the limit. He's started this competition. Let's see if he can stick in it. Gentlemen, I will give this million-ruble note away with an Austrian note for 10,000 crowns. All for $1."

No one seemed to have a dollar. So the reporter bought.

"There's a gentleman that can size up an investment," the spieler said. "Now, you other gentlemen. You know Austria is coming back. She's got to come back. Say the Austrian crown gets up to only half a cent in value. You have $50 right off the bat."

But a dollar was out of the class of the investors present.

Reluctantly the soap box merchant went back to the more moderate amounts.

"Now if a man wants to invest a quarter," he commenced, and held up one of the pink paper quarter-million ruble notes.

Again his audience was with him. This was all right. There were still a few quarters to be invested. What was just one more meal in the face of a chance for a quarter-million dollars?

War Medals for Sale

➤ *The Toronto Star Weekly* · DECEMBER 8, 1923

WHAT is the market price of valor? In a medal and coin shop on Adelaide street the clerk said: "No, we don't buy them. There isn't any demand."

"Do many men come in to sell medals?" I asked.

"Oh, yes. They come in every day. But we don't buy medals from this war."

"What do they bring in?"

"Victory medals mostly, 1914 stars, a good many M.M.'s, and once in a while a D.C.M., or an M.C. We tell them to go over to the pawnshops where they can get their medal back if they get any money for it."

So the reporter went up to Queen street and walked west past the glittering windows of cheap rings, junk shops, two-bit barber shops, second-hand clothing stores, and street hawkers, in search of the valor mart.

Inside the pawnshop it was the same story.

"No, we don't buy them," a young man with shiny hair said from behind a counter of unredeemed pledges. "There is no market for them at all. Oh, yes. They come in here with all sorts. Yes, M.C.'s. And I had a man in here the other day with a D.S.O. I send them over to the second-hand stores on York street. They buy anything."

"What would you give me for an M.C.?" asked the reporter.

"I'm sorry, Mac. We can't handle it."

Out on to Queen street went the reporter, and into the first second-hand shop he encountered. On the window was a sign, "We Buy and Sell Everything."

The opened door jangled a bell. A woman came in from the

back of the shop. Around the counter were piled broken door
bells, alarm clocks, rusty carpenters' tools, old iron keys, kew-
pies, crap shooters' dice, a broken guitar and other things.

"What do you want?" said the woman.

"Got any medals to sell?" the reporter asked.

"No. We don't keep them things. What do you want to do?
Sell me things?"

"Sure," said the reporter. "What'll you give me for an M.C.?"

"What's that?" asked the woman, suspiciously, tucking her
hands under her apron.

"It's a medal," said the reporter. "It's a silver cross."

"Real silver?" asked the woman.

"I guess so," the reporter said.

"Don't you know?" the woman said. "Ain't you got it with
you?"

"No," answered the reporter.

"Well, you bring it in. If it's real silver maybe I'll make you
a nice offer on it." The woman smiled. "Say," she said, "it ain't
one of them war medals, is it?"

"Sort of," said the reporter.

"Don't you bother with it, then. Them things are no good!"

In succession the reporter visited five more second-hand
stores. None of them handled medals. No demand.

In one store the sign outside said, "We Buy and Sell Everything of Value. Highest Prices Paid."

"What you want to sell?" snapped the bearded man back of
the counter.

"Would you buy any war medals?" the reporter asked.

"Listen, maybe those medals were all right in the war. I ain't
saying they weren't, you understand? But with me business is
business. Why should I buy something I can't sell?"

The merchant was being very gentle and explanatory.

"What will you give me for that watch?" asked the reporter.

The merchant examined it carefully, opened the case and
looked in the works. Turned it over in his hand and listened
to it.

"It's got a good tick," suggested the reporter.

"That watch now," said the heavily bearded merchant judicially, laying it down on the counter. "That watch now, is worth maybe sixty cents."

The reporter went on down York street. There was a second-hand shop every door or so now. The reporter got, in succession, a price on his coat, another offer of seventy cents on his watch, and a handsome offer of 40 cents for his cigaret case. But no one wanted to buy or sell medals.

"Every day they come in to sell those medals. You're the first man ever ask me about buying them for years," a junk dealer said.

Finally, in a dingy shop, the searcher found some medals for sale. The woman in charge brought them out from the cash till.

They were a 1914-15 star, a general service medal and a victory medal. All three were fresh and bright in the boxes they had arrived in. All bore the same name and number. They had belonged to a gunner in a Canadian battery.

The reporter examined them.

"How much are they?" he asked.

"I only sell the whole lot," said the woman, defensively.

"What do you want for the lot?"

"Three dollars."

The reporter continued to examine the medals. They represented the honor and recognition his King had bestowed on a certain Canadian. The name of the Canadian was on the rim of each medal.

"Don't worry about those names, Mister," the woman urged. "You could easy take off the names. Those would make you good medals."

"I'm not sure these are what I'm looking for," the reporter said.

"You won't make no mistake if you buy those medals, Mister," urged the woman, fingering them. "You couldn't want no better medals than them."

"No, I don't think they're what I want," the reporter demurred.

"Well, you make me an offer on them."

"No."

"Just make me an offer. Make me any offer you feel like."

"Not to-day."

"Make me any kind of an offer. Those are good medals, mister. Look at them. Will you give me a dollar for all the lot?"

Outside the shop the reporter looked in the window. You could evidently sell a broken alarm-clock. But you couldn't sell an M.C.

You could dispose of a second-hand mouth-organ. But there was no market for a D.C.M.

You could sell your old military puttees. But you couldn't find a buyer for a 1914 Star.

So the market price of valor remained undetermined.

Christmas on the Roof of the World

➤ *The Toronto Star Weekly* · DECEMBER 22, 1923

WHILE it was still dark, Ida, the little German maid, came in and lit the fire in the big porcelain stove, and the burning pine wood roared up the chimney.

Out the window the lake lay steel gray far down below, with the snow-covered mountains bulking jagged beyond it, and far away beyond it the massive tooth of the Dent du Midi beginning to lighten with the first touch of morning.

It was so cold outside. The air felt like something alive as I drew a deep breath. You could swallow the air like a drink of cold water.

I reached up with a boot and banged on the ceiling.

"Hey, Chink. It's Christmas!"

"Hooray!" came Chink's voice down from the little room under the roof of the chalet.

Herself was up in a warm, woollen dressing-robe, with the heavy goat's wool ski-ing socks.

Chink knocked at the door.

"Merry Christmas, mes enfants," he grinned. He wore the early morning garb of big, woolly dressing-robe and thick socks that made us all look like some monastic order.

In the breakfast-room we could hear the stove roaring and crackling. Herself opened the door.

Against the tall, white porcelain stove hung the three long ski-ing stockings, bulging and swollen with strange lumps and bulges. Around the foot of the stove were piled boxes. Two new shiny pairs of ash skis lay alongside the stove, too tall to stand in the low-ceilinged chalet room.

For a week we had each been making mysterious trips to the Swiss town below on the lake. Hadley and I, Chink and I, and Hadley and Chink, returning after dark with strange boxes and bundles that were concealed in various parts of the chalet. Finally we each had to make a trip alone. That was yesterday. Then last night we had taken turns on the stockings, each pledged not to sleuth.

Chink had spent every Christmas since 1914 in the army. He was our best friend. For the first time in years it seemed like Christmas to all of us.

We ate breakfast in the old, untasting, gulping, early morning Christmas way, unpacked the stockings, down to the candy mouse in the toe, each made a pile of our things for future gloating.

From breakfast we rushed into our clothes and tore down the icy road in the glory of the blue-white glistening alpine morning. The train was just pulling out. Chink and I shot the skis into the baggage car, and we all three swung aboard.

All Switzerland was on the move. Ski-ing parties, men, women, boys and girls, taking the train up the mountain, wearing their tight-fitting blue caps, the girls all in riding-breeches and puttees, and shouting and calling out to one another. Platforms jammed.

Everybody travels third class in Switzerland, and on a big day like Christmas the third class overflows and the overflow is crowded into the sacred red plush first class compartments.

Shouting and cheering the train crawled alongside the mountain, climbing up towards the top of the world.

There was no big Christmas dinner at noon in Switzerland. Everybody was out in the mountain air with a lunch in the rucksack and the prospect of the dinner at night.

When the train reached the highest point it made in the mountains, everybody piled out, the stacks of skis were unsorted from the baggage-car and transferred to an open flat car hooked on to a jerky little train that ran straight up the side of the mountain on cog wheels.

At the top we could look over the whole world, white, glistening in the powder snow, and ranges of mountains stretching off in every direction.

It was the top of a bob sled run that looped and turned in icy windings far below. A bob shot past, all the crew moving in time, and as it rushed at express train speed for the first turn, the crew all cried, "Ga-a-a-r!" and the bob roared in an icy smother around the curve and dropped off down the glassy run below.

No matter how high you are in the mountains there is always a slope going up.

There were long strips of seal-skin harnessed on our skis, running back from the tip to the base in a straight strip with the grain of the hair pointing back, so that you pushed right ahead through the snow going up hill. If your skis had a tendency to slide back the slipping movement would be checked by the seal skin hairs. They would slide smoothly forward, but hold fast at the end of each thrusting stride.

Soon the three of us were high above the shoulder of the mountain that had seemed the top of the world. We kept going up in single file, sliding smoothly up through the snow in a long upward zig-zag.

We passed through the last of the pines and came out on a shelving plateau. Here came the first run-down—a half-mile sweep ahead. At the brow the skis seemed to drop out from under and in a hissing rush we all three swooped down the slope like birds.

On the other side it was thrusting, uphill, steady climbing again. The sun was hot and the sweat poured off us in the steady up-hill drive. There is no place you get so tanned as in the mountains in winter. Nor so hungry. Nor so thirsty.

Finally we hit the lunching place, a snowed-under old log cattle barn where the peasant's cattle would shelter in the summer when this mountain was green with pasture. Everything seemed to drop off sheer below us.

The air at that height, about 6,200 feet, is like wine. We put on our sweaters that had been in our ruck-sacks coming up, unpacked the lunch and the bottle of white wine, and lay back on our ruck-sacks and soaked in the sun. Coming up we had been wearing sun glasses against the glare of the snowfields, and now we took off the amber shaded goggles and looked out on a bright, new world.

"I'm really too hot," Herself said. Her face had burned coming up, even through the last crop of freckles and tan.

"You ought to use lampblack on your face," Chink suggested.

But there is no record of any woman that has ever yet been willing to use that famous mountaineer's specific against snow-blindness and sun-burn.

It was no time after lunch and Herself's daily nap, while Chink and I practised turns and stops on the slope, before the heat was gone out of the sun and it was time to start down. We took off the seal skins and waxed our skis.

Then in one long, dropping, swooping, heart-plucking rush we were off. A seven-mile run down and no sensation in the world that can compare with it. You do not make the seven miles in one run. You go as fast as you believe possible, then you go a good deal faster, then you give up all hope, then you don't know what happened, but the earth came up and over and over and you sat up and untangled yourself from your skis and looked around. Usually all three had spilled together. Sometimes there was no one in sight.

But there is no place to go except down. Down in a rushing, swooping, flying, plunging rush of fast ash blades through the powder snow.

Finally, in a rush we came out on to the road on the shoulder of the mountain where the cog-wheel railway had stopped coming up. Now we were all a shooting stream of ski-ers. All the Swiss were coming down, too. Shooting along the road in a seemingly endless stream.

It was too steep and slippery to stop. There was nothing to do but plunge along down the road as helpless as though you were in a mill race. So we went down. Herself was way ahead somewhere. We could see her blue beret occasionally before it got too dark. Down, down, down the road we went in the dusk, past chalets that were a burst of lights and Christmas merriment in the dark.

Then the long line of ski-ers shot into the black woods, swung to one side to avoid a team and sledge coming up the road, passed more chalets, their windows alight with the candles from the Christmas trees. As we dropped past a chalet, watching nothing but the icy road and the man ahead, we heard a shout from the lighted doorway.

"Captain! Captain! Stop here!"

It was the German-Swiss landlord of our chalet. We were running past it in the dark.

Ahead of us, spilled at the turn, we found Herself and we stopped in a sliding slither, knocked loose our skis, and the three of us hiked up the hill towards the lights of the chalet. The lights looked very cheerful against the dark pines of the hill, and inside was a big Christmas tree and a real Christmas turkey dinner, the table shiny with silver, the glasses tall and thin stemmed, the bottles narrow-necked, the turkey large and brown and beautiful, the side dishes all present, and Ida serving in a new crisp apron.

It was the kind of a Christmas you can only get on top of the world.

A NORTH OF ITALY CHRISTMAS

MILAN, the sprawling, new-old, yellow-brown city of the north, tight frozen in the December cold.

Foxes, deer, pheasants, rabbits, hanging before the butcher shops. Cold troops wandering down the streets, from the Christmas leave trains. All the world drinking hot rum punches inside the cafes.

Officers of every nationality, rank and degree of sobriety crowded into the Cova cafe across from the Scala theatre, wishing they were home for Christmas.

A young lieutenant of Arditi, telling me what Christmas is

like in the Abruzzi, "where they hunt bears and the men are men, and the women are women."

The entry of Chink with the great news.

The great news is that up the Via Manzoni there is a mistletoe shop being run by the youth and beauty of Milan for the benefit of some charity or other.

We sort out a battle patrol as rapidly as possible, eliminating Italians, inebriates and all ranks above that of major.

We bear down on the mistletoe shop. The youth and beauty can be plainly seen through the window. A large bush of mistletoe hangs outside. We all enter. Prodigious sales of mistletoe are made. We observe the position. We depart, bearing large quantities of mistletoe which we give to passing charwomen, beggars, policemen, politicians and cab-drivers.

We re-enter the shop. We buy more mistletoe. It is a great day for charity. We depart, bearing even larger quantities of mistletoe which we present to passing journalists, bar-tenders, street-sweepers and tram conductors.

We re-enter the shop. By this time the youth and beauty of Milan have become interested. We insist that we must purchase the large bush of mistletoe outside the shop, an empty bank building. We pay a large sum for the bush, and then, in plain sight of the shop window, we insist on presenting it to a very formal looking man who is passing along the Via Manzoni wearing a top hat and carrying a stick.

The very formal gentleman refuses the gift. We insist that he take it. He declines. It is too great an honor for him. We inform him that it is a point of honor with us that he accept. It is a little Canadian custom for Christmas. The gentleman wavers.

We call a cab for the gentleman, all this within plain sight of the shop window, and assist him to enter and place the large mistletoe tree beside him on the seat.

He drives off with many thanks and in some embarrassment. Many people stop to stare at him.

By this time the youth and beauty of Milan inside the shop are intrigued.

We re-enter the shop and in lowered voices explain that in Canada there is a certain custom connected with mistletoe.

The youth and beauty take us into the back room and introduce us to the chaperones. They are very estimable ladies, the Contessa di This, very large and cheerful, the Principessa di That, very thin and angular and aristocratic. We are led away from the back room and informed in whispers that the chaperones will be going out for tea in one-half an hour.

We depart bearing vast quantities of mistletoe, which we present, formally, to the head waiter of the Grand d'Italia restaurant. The waiter is touched by this Canadian custom and makes a fitting response.

We leave, chewing cloves, for the mistletoe shop. Under the small remaining quantity of mistletoe we demonstrate the sacred Canadian custom. Eventually the chaperones return. We are warned by a whistle up the street.

Thus the true use of mistletoe was brought to Northern Italy.

CHRISTMAS IN PARIS

Paris with the snow falling. Paris with the big charcoal braziers outside the cafes, glowing red. At the cafe tables, men huddled, their coat collars turned up, while they finger glasses of *grog Americain* and the newsboys shout the evening papers.

The buses rumble like green juggernauts through the snow that sifts down in the dusk. White house walls rise through the dusky snow. Snow is never more beautiful than in the city. It is wonderful in Paris to stand on a bridge across the Seine looking up through the softly curtaining snow past the grey bulk of the Louvre, up the river spanned by many bridges and bordered by the grey houses of old Paris to where Notre Dame squats in the dusk.

It is very beautiful in Paris and very lonely at Christmas time.

The young man and his girl walk up the Rue Bonaparte from the Quai in the shadow of the tall houses to the brightly lighted little Rue Jacob. In a little second floor restaurant, The Veritable Restaurant of the Third Republic, which has two rooms, four tiny tables and a cat, there is a special Christmas dinner being served.

"It isn't much like Christmas," said the girl.

"I miss the cranberries," said the young man.

They attack the special Christmas dinner. The turkey is cut into a peculiar sort of geometrical formation that seems to include a small taste of meat, a great deal of gristle, and a large piece of bone.

"Do you remember turkey at home?" asks the young girl.

"Don't talk about it," says the boy.

They attack the potatoes which are fried with too much grease.

"What do you suppose they're doing at home?" says the girl.

"I don't know," said the boy. "Do you suppose we'll ever get home?"

"I don't know," the girl answered. "Do you suppose we'll ever be successful artists?"

The proprietor entered with the dessert and a small bottle of red wine.

"I had forgotten the wine," he said in French.

The girl began to cry.

"I didn't know Paris was like this," she said. "I thought it was gay and full of light and beautiful."

The boy put his arm around her. At least that was one thing you could do in a Parisian restaurant.

"Never mind, honey," he said. "We've been here only three days. Paris will be different. Just you wait."

They ate the dessert, and neither one mentioned the fact that it was slightly burned. Then they paid the bill and walked downstairs and out into the street. The snow was still falling. And they walked out into the streets of old Paris that had known the prowling of wolves and the hunting of men and the tall old houses that had looked down on it all and were stark and unmoved by Christmas.

The boy and the girl were homesick. It was their first Christmas away from their own land. You do not know what Christmas is until you lose it in some foreign land.

Conrad, Optimist and Moralist

➤ *Transatlantic Review* · OCTOBER, 1924

WHAT is there you can write about him now that he is dead?

The critics will dive into their vocabularies and come up with articles on the death of Conrad. They are diving now, like prairie dogs.

It will not be hard for the editorial writers; Death of John L. Sullivan, Death of Roosevelt, Death of Major Whittlesey, Death of President Coolidge's Son, Death of Honored Citizen, Passing of Pioneer, Death of President Wilson, Great Novelist Passes, it is all the same.

> Admirers of Joseph Conrad, whose sudden death is an occasion for general regret, usually think of him as an artist of the first rank, as a remarkable story teller and as a stylist. But Mr. Conrad was also a deep thinker and serene philosopher. In his novels, as in his essays etc.

It will run like that. All over the country.

And what is there that you can say about him now that he is dead?

It is fashionable among my friends to disparage him. It is even necessary. Living in a world of literary politics where one wrong opinion often proves fatal, one writes carefully. I remember how I was made to feel how easily one might be dropped from the party, and the short period of Coventry that followed my remarking when speaking of George Antheil that I preferred my Stravinsky straight. I have been more careful since.

It is agreed by most of the people I know that Conrad is a bad writer, just as it is agreed that T. S. Eliot is a good writer.

If I knew that by grinding Mr. Eliot into a fine dry powder and sprinkling that powder over Mr. Conrad's grave Mr. Conrad would shortly appear, looking very annoyed at the forced return, and commence writing I would leave for London early tomorrow morning with a sausage grinder.

One should not be funny over the death of a great man, but you cannot couple T. S. Eliot and Joseph Conrad in a sentence seriously any more than you could see, say, André Germain and Manuel Garcia (Maera) walking down the street together and not laugh.

The second book of Conrad's that I read was *Lord Jim*. I was unable to finish it. It is, therefore, all I have left of him. For I cannot re-read them. That may be what my friends mean by saying he is a bad writer. But from nothing else that I have ever read have I gotten what every book of Conrad has given me.

Knowing I could not re-read them I saved up four that I would not read until I needed them badly, when the disgust with writing, writers and everything written of and to write would be too much. Two months in Toronto used up the four books. One after another I borrowed them from a girl who had all of his books on a shelf, bound in blue leather, and had never read any of them. Let us be exact. She had read *The Arrow of Gold* and *Victory*.

In Sudbury, Ontario, I bought three back numbers of the Pictorial Review and read *The Rover,* sitting up in bed in the Nickle Range Hotel. When morning came I had used up all my Conrad like a drunkard, I had hoped it would last me the trip, and felt like a young man who has blown his patrimony. But, I thought, he will write more stories. He has lots of time.

When I read the reviews they all agreed *The Rover* was a bad story.

And now he is dead and I wish to God they would have taken some great, acknowledged technician of a literary figure and left him to write his bad stories.

TWO

Esquire, 1933-1936

Marlin off the Morro:
A Cuban Letter

Esquire · AUTUMN, 1933

THE rooms on the northeast corner of the Ambos Mundos Hotel
in Havana look out, to the north, over the old cathedral, the
entrance to the harbor, and the sea, and to the east to Casablanca
peninsula, the roofs of all houses in between and the width of the
harbor. If you sleep with your feet toward the east, this may be
against the tenets of certain religions, the sun, coming up over
the Casablanca side and into your open window, will shine on
your face and wake you no matter where you were the night
before. If you do not choose to get up you can turn around the
other way in the bed or roll over. That will not help for long
because the sun will be getting stronger and the only thing
to do is close the shutter.

Getting up to close the shutter you look across the harbor
to the flag on the fortress and see it is straightened out toward
you. You look out the north window past the Morro and see
that the smooth morning sheen is rippling over and you know
the trade wind is coming up early. You take a shower, pull on
an old pair of khaki pants and a shirt, take the pair of moccasins
that are dry, put the other pair in the window so they will be
dry next night, walk to the elevator, ride down, get a paper at
the desk, walk across the corner to the cafe and have breakfast.

There are two opposing schools about breakfast. If you knew
you were not going to be into fish for two or three hours, a good
big breakfast would be the thing. Maybe it is a good thing anyway but I do not want to trust it, so drink a glass of vichy, a
glass of cold milk and eat a piece of Cuban bread, read the papers
and walk down to the boat. I have hooked them on a full

stomach in that sun and I do not want to hook any more of
them that way.

We have an ice-box that runs across the stern of the boat with
bait iced down on one side and beer and fruit iced on the other.
The best bait for big marlin is fresh cero mackerel or kingfish
of a pound to three pounds weight. The best beer is Hatuey, the
best fruits, in season, are Filipino mangoes, iced pineapple, and
alligator pears. Ordinarily we eat the alligator pears for lunch
with a sandwich, fixing them with pepper and salt and a freshly
squeezed lime. When we run into the beach to anchor, swim
and cook a hot lunch on days when fish are not running you
can make a French dressing for the pears, adding a little mustard. You can get enough fine, big avocados to feed five people
for fifteen cents.

The boat is the Anita, thirty-four feet long, very able in a sea,
with plenty of speed for these fish, owned and skippered by
Capt. Joe Russell of Key West who brought the first load of
liquor that ever came into that place from Cuba and who knows
more about swordfish than most Keywesters do about grunts.
The other man on board is the best marlin and swordfisherman
around Cuba, Carlos Gutierrez, of Zapata, 31, Havana, 54 years
old, who goes Captain on a fishing smack in the winter and
fishes marlin commercially in the summer. I met him six years
ago in Dry Tortugas and first heard about the big marlin that
run off Cuba from him. He can, literally, gaff a dolphin through
the head back-handed and he has studied the habits of the
marlin since he first went fishing for them as a boy of twelve
with his father.

At the boat leaves the San Francisco wharf, tarpon are rolling
in the slip. Going out of the harbor you see more of them rolling
near the live fish cars that are buoyed alongside the line of
anchored fishing smacks. Off the Morro in the entrance to the
harbor there is a good coral bottom with about twenty fathoms
of water and you pass many small boats bottom fishing for mut-
ton fish and red snappers and jigging for mackerel and occasional kingfish. Outside the breeze freshens and as far as you

can see the small boats of the marlin fishermen are scattered. They are fishing with four to six heavy handlines in from forty to seventy fathoms drifting for the fish that are travelling deep. We troll for the ones that are on the surface feeding, or travelling, or cruising fifteen or twenty fathoms down. They see the two big teasers or the baits and come up with a smash, usually going head and shoulders out of water on the strike.

Marlin travel from east to west against the current of the gulf stream. No one has ever seen them working in the other direction, although the current of the gulf stream is not so stable; sometimes, just before the new moon, being quite slack and at others running strongly to the westward. But the prevailing wind is the northeast trade and when this blows the marlin come to the top and cruise with the wind, the scythe tail, a light, steely lavender, cutting the swells as it projects and goes under; the big fish, yellow looking in the water, swimming two or three feet under the surface, the huge pectoral fins tucked close to the flanks, the dorsal fin down, the fish looking a round, fast-moving log in the water except for the erect curve of that slicing tail.

The heavier the current runs to the eastward the more marlin there are; travelling along the edge of the dark, swirling current from a quarter of a mile to four miles off shore; all going in the same direction like cars along a highway. We have been fighting a fish, on days when they were running well, and seen six others pass close to the boat during a space of half an hour.

As an indication of how plentiful they are, the official report from the Havana markets from the middle of March to the 18th of July this year showed eleven thousand small marlin and one hundred and fifty large marlin were brought into the market by the commercial fishermen of Santa Cruz del Norte, Jaruco, Guanabo, Cojimar, Havana, Chorrera, Marianao, Jaimanitas, Baracoa, Banes, Mariel and Cabañas. Marlin are caught at Matanzas and Cardenas to the east and at Bahai Honda to the west of the towns mentioned but those fish are not shipped to Havana. The big fish had only been running two weeks when this report was compiled.

BY-LINE: ERNEST HEMINGWAY

Fishing with rod and reel from the middle of April through the 18th of July of this season we caught fifty-two marlin and two sailfish. The largest black marlin was 468 pounds, and 12 feet 8 inches long. The largest striped marlin was 343 pounds and 10 feet five inches. The biggest white marlin weighed 87 pounds and was 7 feet 8 inches in length.

The white marlin run first in April and May, then come the immature striped marlin with brilliant stripes which fade after the fish dies. These are most plentiful in May and run into June. Then come the black and striped marlin together. The biggest run of striped marlin is in July and as they get scarce the very big black marlin come through until into September and later. Just before the striped marlin are due to run the smaller marlin drop off altogether and it seems, except for an occasional school of small tuna and bonito, as though the gulf stream were empty. There are so many color variations, some of them caused by feed, others by age, others by the depth of water, in these marlin that anyone seeking notoriety for himself by naming new species could have a field day along the north Cuba coast. For me they are all color and sexual variations of the same fish. This is too complicated a theory to go into a letter.

The marlin hit a trolled bait in four different ways. First, with hunger, again with anger, then simply playfully, last with indifference. Anyone can hook a hungry fish who gives him enough line, doesn't backlash and sets the hook hard enough. What happens then is something else. The main thing is to loosen your drag quickly enough when he starts to jump and make his run, and get the boat after him as he heads out to sea. The hungry marlin smashes at the bait with bill, shoulders, top fin and tail out. If he gets one bait he will turn and charge the other. If you pull the bait out of his mouth he will come for it again as long as there is any bait on the hook.

The angry fish puzzled us for a long time. He would come from below and hit the bait with a smash like a bomb exploding in the water. But as you slacked line to him he has dropped it. Screw down on the drag and race the bait in and he would slam it again without taking it. There is no way to hook a fish acting that way except to strike hard as he smashes. Put the drag on, speed up the boat and sock him as he crashes it. He slams the bait to kill it as long as it seems to be alive.

The playful marlin, probably one who has fed well, will come behind a bait with his fin high, shove his bill clear out of water and take the bait lightly between his bill and pointed lower jaw. When you turn it loose to him he drops it. I am speaking of absolutely fresh bait caught that same day; if the bait were stale you might expect them all to refuse it once they had tasted it. This sort of fish can often be made to hit by speeding the boat up and skipping the bait over the top of the water with the rod. If he does take it, do not give him too much line before you hit him.

The indifferent fish will follow the boat for as many as three or four miles. Looking the baits over, sheering away, coming back to swim deep down below them and follow, indifferent to the bait, yet curious. If such a fish swims with his pectoral fins tucked close to his sides he will not bite. He is cruising and you are on his course. That is all. The minute a marlin sees the bait, if he is going to strike, he raises his dorsal fin and spreads those wide, bright blue pectorals so that he looks like some great, under-sea bird in the water as he follows.

The black marlin is a stupid fish. He is immensely powerful, can jump wonderfully and will break your back sounding but he has not the stamina of the striped marlin, nor his intelligence. I believe they are mostly old, female fish, past their prime and that it is age that gives them that black color. When they are younger they are much bluer and the meat, too, is whiter. If you fight them fast, never letting up, never resting, you can kill them quicker than you could ever kill a striped marlin of the same size. Their great strength makes them very dangerous for the first forty minutes. I mean dangerous to the tackle; no fish is dangerous to a man in a launch. But if you can take what they have to give during that time and keep working on them they will tire much quicker than any striped marlin. The 468 pounder was hooked in the roof of the mouth, was in no way tangled in the leader, jumped eight times completely clear, towed the boat stern first when held tight, sounded four times, but was brought to gaff at the top of the water, fin and tail out, in sixty-five minutes. But if I had not lost a much larger striped marlin the day before after two hours and twenty minutes, and fought a black one the day before for forty-five I would not have been in shape to work him so hard.

Fishing in a five-mile-an-hour current, where a hooked fish will always swim against the current, where the water is from four hundred to seven hundred fathoms deep, there is much to learn about tactics in fighting big fish. But one myth that can be dissipated is the old one that the water pressure at one thousand feet will kill the fish. A marlin dies at the bottom only if he has been hooked in the belly. These fish are used to going to the bottom. They often feed there. They are not built like bottom fish which live always at the same depth but are built to be able to go up and down in any depth. I have had a marlin sound four hundred yards straight down, all the rod under water over the side, bent double with that weight going down, down, down, watching the line go, putting on all pressure possible on the reel to check him, him going down and down until you are sure every inch of line will go. Suddenly he stops sounding and you straighten up, get onto your feet, get the butt in the socket and work him up slowly, finally you have the double line on the reel and think he is coming to gaff and then the line begins to rip out as he hooks up and heads off to sea just under the surface to come out in ten long, clean jumps. This after an hour and a half of fight. Then to sound again. They are a fish all right. The 343 pounder jumped 44 times.

You can fish for them in Cuba from April all through the summer. Big ones will be accidental until the middle of June and we only saw four broadbill all season. But in July and August it is even money any day you go out that you will hook into a fish from three hundred pounds up. Up means a very long way up. The biggest marlin ever brought into the market by the commercial fishermen weighed eleven hundred and seventy-five pounds with head cut off, gutted, tail cut off and flanks cut away; eleven hundred and seventy-five pounds when on the slab, nothing but the saleable meat ready to be cut into steaks. All right. You tell me. What did he weigh in the water and what did he look like when he jumped?

The Friend of Spain:
A Spanish Letter

➤ *Esquire* · JANUARY, 1934

DAY before yesterday the writer of this letter while looking through an open window at the red, fresh-water crayfish, the prawns, the bowls of Russian salad, the boiled goose-barnacles, the hams, the sausages, the trussed up redleg partridges ready for the grill, displayed in the window of the three-floor bar, restaurant and shall we say meeting place that the former waiters of the old Casa Moran have opened in the Calle Arlaban in Madrid, saw an old friend standing at the bar and went in to greet him.

To accomplish this it was necessary to disengage one's self from the attentions of one beggar without hands who smilingly presented the stumps in competition with anything the window showed, while holding his pocket open with his elbow; one Gypsy mother who patted the writer on the back with one arm and gave her child to nurse with the other while urging that one be a good sport and buy the little fellow some solid food; two ambulatory salesmen of neckwear who urged him to discard that old tie on the spot and put on something worthy; a seller of bad fountain pens; a caricaturist who said it was all right to say the hell with caricatures but he had never known prosperity let alone happiness and *he* had to draw caricatures for a living meanwhile; and one old man, very little over five feet tall, with a bright red face and long white mustache who put his arm around the writer and said, very thickly, that he was his pal.

Entering the bar and getting into conversation, I found there was something strange in the manner of the old friend. Where formerly, and in many places, he had tried to dissuade me from drinking this particular beverage he now urged me to have an absinthe. Just one. Why not have one?

No, I told him with some dignity. I was not like that now.

But what about our mutual friend so and so, he asked, mentioning someone we had never been able to agree on. He had always maintained this chap was a charlatan and grafter while I had upheld him as a really noble fellow souled with honor.

He's all right.

He's a good man, said my old Spanish friend. A good man with great inquietude of spirit.

By this time I knew there was something very wrong and thought it must be that my old friend was probably meeting someone in that bar that he would rather I did not see him meet; so I said that I must be off. I had tried to purchase a round but it seemed that everything there was paid for not only by my old friend but by a rather seedy looking new friend who had been gored in the neck and whose name I did not catch.

After three rounds in an uncomfortable atmosphere of mutual esteem and appreciation during which we made several engagements without actually naming a date, I left, very puzzled. I had finally succeeded in paying for a round and I hoped things might be getting back to a normal basis.

Next day I found out what it was all about. It was in the Sunday paper. My old friend had written an article entitled Mister Hemingway, Friend of Spain. Now when you become known as A Friend of France it usually means that you are dead, the French would not commit themselves that far if you were alive, and that you have either spent much money for France, obtained much money for France, or simply sucked after certain people long enough to get the Legion of Honor. In the last case they call you a Friend of France in much smaller type.

A Friend of Soviet Russia is very different. It usually refers to a person who is getting, or expects to get, considerable from Soviet Russia. It may only be one who hopes to get much in or for his own country by the implanting of the system of Soviet

Russia. But it is nothing like a Friend of France. A Friend of France is one who has given his all; or as near his all as he could be persuaded to give. They once said, or rather told us, every man has two countries; his own and France. That might be amended now to: every man has three countries—his own, France and the poor house.

Now I do not know just what constitutes a Friend of Spain, but when they call you that it is time to lay off. Spain is a big country and it is now inhabited by too many politicians for any man to be a friend to all of it with impunity. The spectacle of its governing is at present more comic than tragic; but the tragedy is very close.

The country seems much more prosperous. There is much more money being spent. People are travelling who never travelled before; people go to bull fights who could not afford it before, and many people are swimming who never took a bath before. A good deal more money is coming in in taxes than the royal establishment ever received, but now that money goes to the innumerable functionaries of the republic. These spread all over the country and while the peasants are as bad off as ever, the middle class is being taxed more than ever, and the rich certainly will be wiped out, although there is no sign of it yet; a great new bureaucracy is having more money than it ever had before and going in for much comfort, many vacations and considerable style. Politics is still a lucrative profession and those in the factions on the outside promise to pay their debts as soon as they get their turn in power. So that a good business man might vote a man in as head of the government in order that he might pay his wine bill.

In Santander, one of the most unattractive towns in Spain, dusty, crowded, with a bastard Basque architecture alternating with the best of the late Brighton school, but popularized as a watering place by the King going there for the summer because it was considered safer than San Sebastian, there was not a room to stay the night in any sort of a hotel.

146

San Sebastian, one of the very pleasantest places of Europe, was as crowded but with very different people. The crowd at Santander had gone there because the King had gone there. They were going to go to the seashore because, now, they had the money to. They did not seem to know whether they were having any fun or not. But they had been to the seashore. The people of San Sebastian knew what they had come for-and were having a very good time.

Bull fighting, of course, has been in a bad way for a couple of hundred years and the first Sunday story that any newly arrived correspondent sends back to his paper from Madrid has always been that one about Bullfights on Wane as Football Sweeps Spain. This was first sent, I believe, by Washington Irving who was then writing for the, then, New York Sun under the pen name of Irvin S. Washington. It was a story I always liked to write myself because you finally got so you could do it quicker than most stories; but no one ever improved on Irvin S. Washington's original dispatch.

A sad thing happened, tho, in connection with this story. A correspondent for the, then, New York Times on arriving in Madrid cabled his story instead of sending it by mail. The Times sent him into coventry, I believe, and refused to admit receiving any communications from him over a period of some years. I used to meet him wandering around and ask him how things were going.

"I simply don't hear from them," he said desperately.

"Do you write them?" I asked.

"Yes," he said.

"Do you cable them?"

"As often as I dare."

"Do you send them registered letters?"

"I hadn't thought of that," he said, brightening.

"Try it," I urged.

Later I promised to look them up if I ever got to New York and see if I could do anything about his strange plight. But when I got to New York they had moved. I tried to trace them, but it was no good. Years later I heard that the poor fellow was still in Madrid.

Bull fighting, as usual, is in bad shape.

Marcial Lelanda has two children, over a million pesetas, a good bull ranch—rather a good big ranch for raising bulls; and a firm and sound resolution to take no more chances with horned animals. He knows enough so that he can appear in the ring with them and dispatch them without risk; but it is no fun for the spectators either.

Domingo Ortega, fighting nearly a hundred fights a year for two seasons has, very obviously, learned how to fight bulls. He fights every one that comes into the ring in exactly the same way, punishing them all in the same way; dominating them; showing his domination by stroking the horn; and killing them quickly and trickily. If you see him once you know how he will be a hundred times.

He is desperately monotonous yet he does something, that is he dominates every bull that comes out; while the trashy lot of opposition he usually has need luck to do anything. He was gored, once, in September and so lost the chance of beating Belmonte's record of 112 fights in a season. He will fight around ninety.

Armillita Chico, a young, slim, brown, chinless Mexican with legs that hang from under his shoulders, a handful of crooked teeth, wonderful wrists, and great intelligence and knowledge of bulls is many times a better matador than Ortega, but is held back by his negative personality in the ring. Armillita gets everything out of a bull that bull will give. Ortega makes the same bull conform, and conform quickly, to his own limitations. But the public goes crazy about Ortega's theater, his attitudes, his false tragedy; while Armillita's cold intelligence, his classic perfection and his superlative skill, which seems to eliminate danger, does not stay in their memories. But his merit is being realized and he will fight more fights in Spain this year than any other Mexican has ever fought except the great Gaona.

Victoriano de la Serna after a bad season last year and less than twenty fights, has blossomed out again this season as a phenomenon. He has now completed his medical studies and taken his degree, and his enemies claim that his bursts of extraordinary courage originate in a hypodermic syringe and that if he does not care to fight he knows the secret of producing a high fever and frothing at the mouth. This is nothing but scandal.

He is a strange case. He is not a coward but in the three times I saw him this September he did all the things that a bull fighter usually does only when unable to control himself through fear. He did them cynically, perfectly cool and unworried, to avoid risk and to deliberately insult the public. In the ring he has an overwhelming conceit that is pathological.

His style with the cape is slow, delicate, but, to me, unsound. He makes his passes with the cape by turning his body while keeping his arms out rather than keeping his body still and moving the arms ahead of the bull. It is a way of using the cape as though it were the muleta; and it is a form of using one of the trick passes perfected by Nicanor Villalta. But he does it very gracefully and well.

With the muleta he is more or less at the mercy of the bull. With a bull that charges and re-charges on a straight line he could probably do a better faena than anyone now in the ring. He is very intelligent, but he does not dominate. He is an unsound, enigmatic, interesting, and highly irritating performer.

By irritating I mean this: At Salamanca he was getting fourteen thousand pesetas a fight. That is twice the amount some. of the other matadors were getting. He was paid this because they knew he could do twice as much if he drew a good bull. His first bull was not much but he worked him as well as he could and the public were all with him. His second bull was perfect for the muleta and La Serna made four excellent passes. As he drew away from the bull to rest him looking up into the stands, putting his hand proudly to his chest to indicate "Look at me. The great Victoriano de la Serna!" some spectator, not impressed, whistled. La Serna looked up where the whistle had come from as though to say "All right. I'll show you." Then, with no more passes, no faena, doing nothing he had been paid for, he ran in on the bull and stabbed him in the lungs. The bull choked to death, vomiting his blood.

The next day the public treated him very severely but applauded the little good work he did. La Serna left the ring wrapped in his cape under the jeers of the spectators; then stooped, took off his fighting shoes, and walked in his stocking feet to his motor car. At the car he knocked the shoes together to get the dust off them and then dropped them delicately to the ground.

"I don't want even the dust of Salamanca," he said.

Now this superb gesture was first attributed to Saint Teresa on leaving Avila after disappointments there, later to various bullfighters on leaving Mexico. For Victoriano to employ it, merely because he had cheated the public, showed he was a well-read young fellow. But it did not endear him to the public of Salamanca, even to your correspondent who had also paid his money and traveled some distance to see the young doctor perform.

Of the new fighters, the youngest brother of Gitanillo de Triano, who was killed in Madrid two years ago, is a good looking gypsy with a beautiful style with cape and muleta. But he knows very little about bulls and is already having great trouble dominating his fear. Fernando Dominguez is very good with the muleta but is without personality and is a pitiful killer. Maravilla is ill, gored nearly every time he fights, and is only a shell of himself. Corrochano had one excellent fight in Madrid and has done nothing in the provinces. Chiquito de la Audiencia seems to have lost his nerve.

The annual Messiah appeared in the person of Felix Colomo, a delivery boy at the pelota court, who made two sensational fights in Madrid and received a bad horn wound. Out of the hospital, he fought in Huesca and was very bad, in Gijon and was good; then went back into the hospital with a terrific wound received at La Coruña. He is managed by Torquito, an ex-matador from Bilbao, who will probably have enough sense not to fight him again this season no matter how hungry both may be.

Florentino Ballesteros, son of the matador of the same name killed in the Madrid ring toward the end of the war, seems to be a very competent, workmanlike fighter, skillful, without genius, but an excellent killer. He killed seven bulls in the little ring of Vista Alegre just outside of Madrid in his farewell performance before becoming a full matador, and bored the public with the dullness of his excellence.

Not seeing any fights until the last of August, I cannot report on how the bulls were in early and mid-season but in September the Salamanca bulls were uniformly poor, colorless, without force, bravery or style. Esteban Gonzales sent a splendid lot of bulls to Madrid from Utrera outside of Sevilla, and Miura's sent a novillada the last of September that was braver, bigger and better armed than all the corridas we had seen until then.

The old cafe Fornos is gone, torn down to put up an office building, and the former inmates can be found at the Regina next door. There is a new cafe called the Aquarium which looks like the last phase of Montparnasse except that it is crowded. Out on the Manzanares where we all used to go to swim and cook paellas along the Pardo road they have damned the river and built an artificial beach with very modern bathing installation, real sand, a big lagoon and very cold and, remarkably, clean water. There were a lot of small fish swimming around in it; always a good sign in a public bathing place, and it was really not a bad place to swim. Anyone able to swim across the river and back, possibly two hundred yards, was looked on by the non-swimming bathers with the awe we used to feel for Ederle when taking a good look at the channel from the breakwater at Boulogne; and a native swimmer out of his depth without water-wings was a source of inquietude to all the more serious minded. But the Madrileños whose only exercise used to be walking to the cafe are all going in for sports, for picnics in the country and for walking trips in the Sierras. The characteristic shape of the girls is changing. They seem to be taller and not so far around. Exercise and the example of the American cinema, possibly, is responsible. And what else do you want to know?

Well, we have an ambassador from whom the Spaniards have learned that there are at least two kinds of American newspapermen who can become ambassadors. Their previous experience had been with Alexander Moore. Sometimes it makes you wonder, too, why aside from the desire to honor him, President Roosevelt should send such a very able newspaperman, and such a good Democrat, so far away from the scene of hostilities. Perhaps Mr. Bowers really wanted to be an ambassador. I never asked him.

A Paris Letter

➤ *Esquire* · FEBRUARY, 1934

THIS time last year we were driving home from Cooke City, Montana, in a blizzard. The boys who had tried to drag Bull-Neck Moose-Face, the truck driver, to death the night of the Old Timers' Fish Fry because he was alleged to have hit a lady with a poker, were still in jail. The big trout had dropped back down the river into the deep pools of the canyon. The deer had come down from the high country and had gone down the river to their winter range and the elk had gone into the Park.

We had run into two other outfits when we were hunting sheep up Pilot Creek and lost a shot at two very big rams because some other hunters had spooked them. We felt the country was getting a little crowded. Yet three times I had ridden the twenty-five miles of trail from the ranch up to the camp on Timber Creek and not seen a living soul.

The fourth time, coming back on the road from Crandall, I saw some hunters camped down the river. They waved and I waved back but it was too far away to recognize them. A little further along the road I saw a grouse in some willows. Old Bess, the horse, saw it too and started to tremble. She kept on trembling and breathing hard through her nose while I got down and, holding the reins, shot the grouse. If I would have let go of the reins she would have left the country. But with them held all she did was give a big jerk with her head when the pistol went off, then stopped trembling when she saw me put the pistol away in the holster. I put the grouse in the saddle pocket and mounted.

We kept moving along and then, coming toward us, right

beside the road, at a trot in an open meadow was a moose. It was a bull with a good head and he stopped still when he saw us. He wasn't thirty yards away and he shone black, looked very big, and I could see his bell clearly, and his horns were the color of black walnut meats. He seemed to look at Bess instead of at me. I got down easy and pulled the rifle out of the saddle bucket as I swung down. He stood there looking at us with Bess trembling and blowing.

I looked his head over very carefully. It was a nice head but it was nothing to kill him for. He had plenty of meat and no one would eat moose meat when there is such a thing as elk. I put the rifle back in the saddle bucket and swung onto old Bess. All this time he stood there looking.

"Cut it out," I said to Bess. "It's all over. I'm not going to kill him."

He let us ride about ten yards closer before he turned and trotted off and went into a patch of quakers. They have a beautiful motion when they trot. Down the trail about a mile and a half I rode onto two hunters. It was Bill Sidley with Frank Colp. Frank had a buckskin shirt on like an Indian. They'd been trailing that moose all day. He'd travelled, they said.

"He's right ahead," I told them. "I tried to herd him back to you."

"What sort of head has he?"

"He's got a good head." And I told them what it was like.

"Come on, let's go," Bill said.

For about four miles after that I would see the bull's trail every once in a while in the snow. They have a track shaped like the ace of hearts. I had seen fourteen head of game that day and before I got to the ranch I shot five more grouse with the pistol. At the ranch I got warm and read the mail and drank a whiskey sour before supper. It was a cold, sharp night, after a little thaw that day, and you could hear the coyotes starting to howl. The boys came in late. They hadn't got the moose. He had come out of the timber again near where the hunters were camped on the river and they started shooting at him out of range and he got by them and down into the lower country.

It was fine at the ranch then, at the end of October, and I didn't want to leave. Most of the game had pulled out but it was very pleasant and a good time of year. But I thought I had to go. So we started out and there was a blizzard. It lasted all the way across Nebraska and there is a special technique of driving in one that you have to learn. The trouble is to keep the windshield so you can see. You rig a candle in a can against the glass and that keeps the ice melted; for a little while. It is a technique that I haven't mastered. Well, that was last year.

This year, at the same time, we are in Paris and it is a big mistake. If you want a Paris letter full of spice and detail and funny cracks you will have to get someone else to write it. All I do is go out and get depressed and wish I were somewhere else. It is only for three weeks but it is very gloomy.

This old friend shot himself. That old friend took an overdose of something. That old friend went back to New York and jumped out, or rather fell from, a high window. That other old friend wrote her memoirs. All of the old friends have lost their money. All of the old friends are very discouraged. Few of the old friends are healthy. Me, I like it better out on the ranch, or in Piggott, Arkansas, in the fall, or in Key West, and very much better, say, at the Dry Tortugas.

The painters are about the gloomiest. It seems that people buy modern paintings in good times for snobbism and as gilt-edged securities. In bad times they do not buy them at all. One dealer said that he had not sold a picture by a painter who is supposed to be quite successful, and who is under contract to deliver all his work to that dealer, since 1929.

Montparnasse has been discovered by the French respectable bourgeoisie, just as Montmartre once was. So the big cafes do a pretty steady business. The only foreigners you see are Germans. The Dome is crowded with refugees from the Nazi terror and Nazis spying on the refugees.

There was a very big retrospective exhibition of Renoir. I came away from it with the feeling of having seen many too many Renoirs. There can never be enough Cezanne's or Van

Gogh's but I believe there were plenty of Renoirs before the old man died, all very fine, but plenty.

Food is as good as ever and very expensive. Because they could not sell it the vintners have not been bottling much champagne these last few years and there is good still champagne, that is natural champagne wine to which nothing has been added and which has not been processed in bottling to make it sparkle, on draft at the Café Regence for nine francs a wooden pitcher. This is the café where Napoleon used to play chess when he was the First Consul. They have the table that he used to play on in the café. For a while, during the boom, chess players were not encouraged at the Regence because they were not great consumers. But they are glad to see them again now.

Marcel Thil, bald, shuffling, seemingly muscle-bound and very durable, is still middleweight champion of the world to the French. He doesn't want to go to the States to fight and I doubt if anyone could get a decision over him in Paris without knocking him out. He is a good fighter, but slowing up, and is smart to stay in France, where he is a great drawing card, rather than take a chance on what might be handed to him in the way of decisions in America. French fighters have always had bad luck in America.

Carpentier was long past the top of his form when he went over and not big enough for good heavyweights who were at the top of their form. Charles Ledoux was very popular in America and was a great little fighter; one of the best in-fighters that I have ever seen, but his career was interrupted by the war.

Eugene Criqui went out to Australia after the war a big bantamweight, his face horribly mutilated by a wound. He was not a heavy hitter but a good, sound workman. He came back a full-sized featherweight with a terrific punch in his right hand. I believe he could hit nearly as hard for his size as Charley White, the great Chicago left hook artist. Charley White, for me, could hit the hardest for his size of any man I ever saw in the ring.

Criqui knocked out Johnny Kilbane for the featherweight championship but signed a contract to fight Johnny Dundee within forty-five days, I believe, if he won. Dundee broke the metal apparatus that the plastic surgeons had made in Criqui's face instead of a jaw in the first round and Criqui, smashed, cut, bleeding, took a sickening beating for fifteen rounds while he hunted Dundee's jaw with that right hand. No one could ever hit Dundee squarely on the button with a right hand except Willie Jackson and he only did it once. Anyway Criqui lost his title the first time he defended it and before he had made any money from it.

André Routis had much the same style as Ledoux but was never the hitter Ledoux was in his prime. He won the featherweight championship in America from Canzoneri and made money in a number of overweight fights until he lost his title to Bat Battalino who turned out to be managed by the same outfit that was handling Routis. Routis came back from America with a certain amount of money, without his title and with his eyes permanently injured.

Kid Francis, who fought in the States as an Italian, was a French featherweight from Marseilles. As a fighter he ranks with Routis and Ledoux.

Emile Pladner had one great year as flyweight champion but he was too easy to hit. Sparrow Robertson nicknamed him Spider for no good reason. He was a chunky kid, as unspiderlike as could be. When he outgrew the flyweight class the heavy hitters in the class above found where the alley was and Pladner was soon finished.

The French have had some great fighters; those mentioned are only a few of the lot who fought in America, but Thil is smart not to go over. He is very smart not to go over. It is a different business over there, a very different business. Europeans are as unsophisticated in what goes on behind the scenes in sport as we once were, and may be still, about what goes on behind the scenes in politics.

What really makes you feel badly here though is not any of the things I mentioned earlier. People must be expected to kill themselves when they lose their money, I suppose, and drunkards get bad livers, and legendary people usually end by writing their memoirs. What makes you feel bad is the perfectly calm way everyone speaks about the next war. It is accepted and taken for granted. All right. Europe has always had wars. But we can keep out of this next one. And the only way to keep out of it is not to go in it; not for any reason. There will be plenty of good reasons. *But we must keep out of it.* If kids want to go to see what war is like, or for the love of any nation, let them go as individuals. Anyone has a right to go who wants to. But we, as a country, have no business in it and we must keep out.

Paris is very beautiful this fall. It was a fine place to be quite young in and it is a necessary part of a man's education. We all loved it once and we lie if we say we didn't. But she is like a mistress who does not grow old and she has other lovers now. She was old to start with but we did not know it then. We thought she was just older than we were, and that was attractive then. So when we did not love her any more we held it against her. But that was wrong because she is always the same age and she always has new lovers.

But me, I now love something else. And if I fight, I fight for something else. That seems to be about all for today.

A.D. in Africa:
A Tanganyika Letter

➤ *Esquire* · APRIL, 1934

To WRITE this sort of thing you need a typewriter. To describe, to narrate, to make funny cracks you need a typewriter. To fake along, to stall, to make light reading, to write a good piece, you need luck, two or more drinks and a typewriter. Gentlemen, there is no typewriter.

The air-mail leaves tomorrow night. Your amœbic dysentery correspondent is in bed, fully injected with emetine, having flown four hundred miles to Nairobi via Arusha from where the outfit is camped on the Serenea river on the far side of the Serengeti plain. Cause of flight, a. d. Cause of a. d. unknown. Symptoms of a. d. run from weakly insidious through spectacular to phenomenal. I believe the record is held by a Mr. Mc-Donald with 232 movements in the twenty-four hours although many old a. d. men claim the McDonald record was never properly audited.

According to Dr. Anderson the difficulty about a. d. is to diagnose it. My own diagnosis was certainly faulty. Leaning against a tree two days ago shooting flighting sand-grouse as they came into a water hole near camp after ten days of what Dr. Anderson says was a. d. all the time, I became convinced that though an unbeliever I had been chosen as the one to bear our Lord Buddha when he should be born again on earth. While flattered at this, and wondering how much Buddha at that age would resemble Gertrude Stein, I found the imminence of the event made it difficult to take high incoming birds and finally compromised by reclining against the tree and only accepting crossing shots. This, the coming-of-Buddha symptom, Dr. Anderson describes as prolapsus.

Anyway, no matter how you get it, it is very easily cured. You feel the good effects of the emetine within six hours and the remedy, continued, kills the amœba the way quinine kills the malarial parasite. Three days from now we'll fly back to join the outfit in the country to the south of Ngocongoro where we are going to hunt greater Kuda. But, as stated, there is no type-writer; they won't let you drink with this; and if the reader finds this letter more dysenteric than the usual flow, lay it to the combination of circumstances.

The general run of this highland country is the finest I have ever seen. When there has been·rain the plains roll green against the blue hills the way the western end of Nebraska lifts as you approach Wyoming when it has gone too long without rain. It is a brown land like Wyoming and Montana but with greater roll and distance. Much of the upland bush country that you hunt through looks exactly like an abandoned New England orchard until you top a hill and see the orchard runs on for fifty miles. Nothing that I have ever read has given any idea of the beauty of the country or the still remaining quantity of game.

On the Serengeti we struck the great migration of the wilde-beeste. Where they were grazing the plain was green after a nine months' drought and it was black with the bison shaped antelope as far as you could see in all directions during a full day in the truck. The Game Department of Tanganyika esti-mates the herd at three million. Following them and living on the fringe of the herd were the lions, the spotted hyenas and the jackals.

Going out at sunrise every morning we would locate lions by the vultures circling above a kill. Approaching you would see the jackals trotting away and hyenas going off in that drag belly obscene gallop, looking back as they ran. If the birds were on the ground you knew the lions were gone.

Sometimes we met them in the open plain on their way toward a gully or shallow water course to lie up for the day. Sometimes we saw them on a high knoll in the plain with the herd grazing not half a mile away, lying sleepy and contemptuous looking over the country. More often we saw them under the shade of a tree or saw their great round heads lift up out of the grass of a shallow donga as they heard the noise of the truck. In two weeks and three days in lion country we saw 84 lions and lionesses. Of these twenty were maned lions.

We shot the twenty-third, the forty-seventh, the sixty-fourth and the seventy-ninth. All were shot on foot, three were killed in bush country to the west of the Serengeti and one on the plain itself. Three were full black maned lions and one was a lioness. She was in heat and when the big lion she was with was hit and had gotten into cover the lioness took up her position outside the thick bush. She wanted to charge and it was impossible to go after the lion without killing her first. I broke her neck with a 220 grain .30-06 solid at thirty yards.

At this point Dr. Anderson just came in and administered another injection of emetine and offered the information that when you take emetine you can't think coherently. So this may be a good place to knock off. Had been feeling that too for some time.

In the next letter I will attempt to discuss whether lion shooting in Tanganyika is a sport or not; go into the difference between lion and leopard hunting, have a few remarks on the buffalo and try to get in a lot of facts. This letter has been pretty well emetined.

As far as bag goes, if anyone is interested, we have good heads of Eland, Waterbuck, Grant Robertsi and other gazelles. A fine roan antelope, two big leopard, and excellent, if not record, impalla; also the limit all around on cheetah. They are much too nice an animal to shoot and I will never kill another.

On the other hand we shot thirty-five hyena out of the lot that follow the wildebeeste migration to keep after the cows that are about to calve and wish we had ammunition to kill a hundred.

In three days we start out for rhino, buffalo again, lesser and greater Kudu, and sable antelope.

Dr. Anderson, a little emetine please.

Nairobi, January 18, 1934

Shootism versus Sport:
The Second Tanganyika Letter

➤ *Esquire* · JUNE, 1934

THERE are two ways to murder a lion. One is to shoot him
from a motor car, the other, to shoot him at night with a flash-
light from a platform or the shelter of a thorn boma, or blind,
as he comes to feed on a bait placed by the shootist or his guide.
(Tourists who shoot in Africa are called shootists to distinguish
them from sportsmen.) These two ways to murder lion rank,
as sport, with dynamiting trout or harpooning swordfish. Yet
many men who go to Africa and return to think of themselves
as sportsmen and big game hunters, have killed lions from motor
cars or from blinds.

The Serengeti plain is the great lion country of present day
Africa and the Serengeti is a motor car proposition. The dis-
tances between water are too great for it to have been reached
and hunted in the old foot safari days, and that was what pre-
served it. The game migrations, which are determined by the
food which is produced by an often casual and unpredictable
rainfall, are movements over hundreds of miles, and you may
drive seventy-five or a hundred miles over a brown, dry, parched,
dusty waste without seeing a head of game, to come suddenly
onto a rise of green horizon broken and edged with the black
of wildebeeste as far as you can see. It is because of these dis-
tances that you must use the motor car in hunting the Serengeti, since your camp must be on a water hole and the game
may be over half a day's march away on the plain.

Now a lion, when you locate him in the morning after he has
fed, will have only one idea if he sees a man, to get away into
cover where the man will not trouble him. Until he is wounded,

that lion will not be dangerous unless you come on him unexpectedly, so closely that you startle him, or unless he is on a kill and does not want to leave it.

If you approach the lion in a motor car, the lion will not see you. His eyes can only distinguish the outline or silhouette of objects, and, because it is illegal to shoot from a motor car, this object means nothing to him. If anything, since the practice of shooting a zebra and dragging it on a rope behind the motor car as a bait for lion in order to take photographs, the motor car may seem a friendly object. For a man to shoot at a lion from the protection of a motor car, where the lion cannot even see what it is that is attacking him, is not only illegal but is a cowardly way to assassinate one of the finest of all game animals.

But supposing, unexpectedly, as you are crossing the country, you see a lion and a lioness say a hundred yards from the car. They are under a thorn tree and a hundred yards behind them is a deep donga, or dry, reed-filled water course, that winds across the plain for perhaps ten miles and gives perfect cover in the daytime to all the beasts of prey that follow the game herds.

You sight the lions from the car; you look the male over and decide he is shootable. You have never killed a lion. You are allowed to kill only two lions on the Serengeti and you want a lion with a full mane, as black as possible. The white hunter says quietly:

"I believe I'd take him. We might beat him but he's a damned fine lion."

You look at the lion under the tree. He looks very close, very calm, very, very big and proudly beautiful. The lioness has flattened down on the yellow grass and is swinging her tail parallel to the ground.

"All right," says the white hunter.

You step out of the car from beside the driver on the side away from the lion, and the white hunter gets out on the same side from the seat behind you.

"Better sit down," he says. You both sit down and the car

drives away. As the car starts to move off you have a very different feeling about lions than you have ever had when you saw them from the motor car.

As the end of the car is past, you see that the lioness has risen and is standing so that you cannot see the lion clearly.

"Can't see him," you whisper. As you say it you see that the lions have seen you. He has turned away and is trotting off and she is still standing, the tail swinging wide.

"He'll be in the donga," the white hunter says.

You stand up to shoot and the lioness turns. The lion stops and looks back. You see his great head swing toward you, his mouth wide open and his mane blowing in the wind. You hold on his shoulder, start to flinch, correct, hold your breath and squeeze off. You don't hear the gun go off but you hear a crack like the sound of a policeman's club on a rioter's head and the lion is down.

"You've got him. Watch the lioness."

She has flattened down facing you so that you see her head, the ears back, the long yellow of her is flat out along the ground and her tail is now flailing straight up and down.

"I think she's going to come," the white hunter says. "If she comes, sit down to shoot."

"Should I bust her?" you say.

"No. Maybe she won't come. Wait till she starts to come."

You stand still and see her and beyond her the bulk of the big lion, on his side now, and finally she turns slowly and goes off and out of sight into the donga.

"In the old days," the white hunter said, "the rule was to shoot the lioness first. Damned sensible rule."

The two of you walk toward the lion with your guns ready. The car comes up and the gunbearers join you. One of them throws a stone at the lion. He doesn't move. You lower the guns and go up to him.

"You got him in the neck," the white hunter says. "Damned good shooting." There is blood coming from the thick hair of his mane where the camel flies are crawling. You regret the camel flies.

"It was a lucky one," you say.

You say nothing about having squeezed off from his shoulder, and then, suddenly, a strain is over and people are shaking your hand.

"Better keep an eye out for the old lady," the white hunter says. "Don't wander over too far that way."

You are looking at the dead lion; at his wide head and the dark shag of his mane and the long, smooth, yellow sheathed body, the muscles still twitching and running minutely under the skin. He is a fine hide and all that but he was a damned wonderful looking animal when he was alive—it was a shame he should always have had the camel flies, you think.

All right. That is the nearest to a sporting way to use a motor car after lion. Once you are on the ground and the car is gone, lion hunting is the same as it always was. If you wound the lion in any but a vital spot he will make for the shelter of the donga and then you will have to go after him. At the start, if you can shoot carefully and accurately and know where to shoot, the odds are ten to one in your favor against anything untoward happening, provided you do not have to take a running shot at first. If you wound the lion and he gets into cover it is even money you will be mauled when you go in after him. A lion can still cover one hundred yards so fast toward you that there is barely time for two aimed shots before he is on you. After he has the first bullet, there is no nervous shock to further wounds, and you have to kill him stone dead or he will keep coming.

If you shoot as you should on the Serengeti, having the car drive off as you get out, the chances are that the first shot will be a moving shot, as the lions will move off when they see the man on foot. That means that unless you are a good or a very lucky shot there will be a wounded lion and a possible charge. So do not let anyone tell you that lion shooting, if you hunt big maned lions, who, being super-fine trophies, will obviously have been hunted before and be adept at saving their hides, is no longer a sporting show. It will be exactly as dangerous as you choose to make it. The only way the danger can be removed or mitigated is by your ability to shoot, and that is as it should be. You are out to kill a lion, on foot and cleanly, not to be mauled. But you will be more of a sportsman to come back from Africa without a lion than to shoot one from the protection of a motor car, or from a blind at night when the lion is blinded by a light and cannot see his assailant.

Notes on Dangerous Game:
The Third Tanganyika Letter

➤ *Esquire* · JULY, 1934

IN the ethics of shooting dangerous game is the premise that the trouble you shoot yourself into you must be prepared to shoot yourself out of. Since a man making his first African shoot will have a white hunter, as a non-native guide is called, to counsel him and aid him when he is after dangerous animals, and since the white hunter has the responsibility of protecting him no matter what trouble he gets into, the shooter should do exactly what the white hunter tells him to do.

If you make a fool of yourself all that you get is mauled but the white hunter who has a client wounded or killed loses, or seriously impairs, his livelihood. So when the white hunter begins to trust you and let you take chances, that is a mark of confidence and you should not abuse it. For any good man would rather take chances any day with his life than his livelihood and that is the main point about professionals that amateurs seem never to appreciate.

There are two white hunters in Africa who not only have never had a client mauled—there are many such, but these two have never been mauled themselves; and there are very few of these. It is true that Philip Percival had a buffalo die with his head in the now ample Percival lap, and that Baron von Blixen, if there were any justice for elephants, would have been trampled to death at least twice. But the point is that they do not get mauled and that their clients get record heads, record tusks and super lions year after year. They simply happen to be super hunters and super shots. (*There are too many supers in these last two sentences. Re-write them yourselves lads and see*

167

how easy it is to do better than Papa. Thank you. Exhilarating feeling, isn't it?)

Both mask their phenomenal skill under a pose of nervous incapacity which serves as an effective insulation and cover for their truly great pride in the reserve of deadliness that they live by. (*All right now, better that one. Getting harder, what? Not too hard you say? Good. Perhaps you're right.*) Blix, who can shoot partridges flying with a .450 No. 2 Express rifle will say, "I use the hair trigger because my hand is always shaking so, what?" Or, stopping a charging rhino at ten yards, remarking apologetically to his client who happened to have his rifle already started back to camp by the gunbearer, "I could not let him come forever, what?"

(*You see, this is where Papa scores. Just as you learn to better one of those awful sentences, with too many supers or too many verys in it and you think he's gone wa-wa on you, you find that it is the thing he is writing about that is interesting. Not the way it's written. Any of you lads can go out there and write twice as good a piece, what?*)

Philip, who swears by the .450 No. 2 as the only, or at least lightest, stopper for a man to use on animals that will "come," killed all his own lions with a .256 Mannlicher when he had only his own life to look after. I have seen him, careful, cautious, as wary about procedure as Saleri, Marcial Lalanda, or any of the old masters of chance controlling, light up like a schoolboy at the approach of vacation, when all the safe and sane methods were finally exhausted or rendered impractical and there was no choice but to go in after him as he went in after them in the old days before it was a matter of the safety of the client. (*Excuse me, Mr. P. You see I do this for a living. We all have to do a lot of things for a living. But we're still drinking their whiskey, aren't we?*)

Many people want not to shoot but to have shot dangerous game. These people, regardless of their means, usually make the African shoot only once, and their white hunter usually fires as many or more shots than his client does. A very good standard by which to judge your real effectiveness against buffalo, rhino, elephant, lion and leopard is to keep track of how many times your white hunter shot on the safari. (*You shot twice, Mr. P. Correct me if I'm wrong. Once at that leopard's mate when she broke back and you spun her over like a rabbit, and the other time when we caught the bull in the open and had two down and the third bull with four solids in him going at that same gallop, all one solid piece, the neck a part of the shoulders, dusty black and the horns blacker, the head not tossing in the gallop. You figured he would make the bush so you shot and the gallop changed into a long slide forward on his nose.*)

Philip Percival ranks leopard as more dangerous than lion for these reasons. They are nearly always met unexpectedly, usually when you are hunting impala or buck. They usually give you only a running shot which means more of a chance of wounding than killing. They will charge nine times out of ten when wounded, and they come so fast that no man can be sure of stopping them with a rifle. They use their claws, both fore and hind when mauling and make for the face so that the eyes are endangered, whereas the lion grabs with the claws and bites, usually for the arm, shoulders or thigh. The most effective stopper for a leopard is a shotgun and you should not fire until the animal is within ten yards. It does not matter what size shot is used at that range. Birdshot is even more effective than buck-shot as it hangs together to blow a solid hole. (*Mr. P. took the top of the head off one once with a load of number sevens and the leopard came right on by and on for fifteen yards. Didn't know he was dead it seems. Tripped on a blade of grass or something finally.*)

Personally, so far, and it is from a very minute quantity of experience indeed—the killing of four of them—I cannot see the buffalo as comparing in dangerous possibilities to either lion or leopard. We twice saw lion catch and kill wildebeeste. This is a very rare thing. Philip Percival had seen lion kill only once before in all his years of hunting. It was while he was out with Mr. Prentice Gray, who recorded the occurrence, I believe.

The sight of that speed, that unbelievable smooth rush the lioness made to close the gap between herself and the fast galloping, though ungainly, antelope made me see what a charge from a slightly wounded lion could be if allowed to get under way. The buffalo, on the other hand, seemed unbelievably slow compared to a Spanish fighting bull, and I see no reason why a man who could wait for him as he came could not be sure of blowing the front of his head in if he let him get close and shot carefully with a heavy enough rifle. Certainly a tunnel in thick bush, or high reeds, or any dense cover can make the wounded buffalo dangerous, but that is a case of circumstances rather than the animal, and in the same circumstances a lion would be much more deadly. In the open a lion or leopard is a hundred times more dangerous.

The buffalo has courage, vindictiveness and an incredible ability to absorb punishment but I believe that in the bull ring he would be more like the big truck that comes charging in during the intermission to water the dusty sand than like the light hoofed, quick whirling, fast charging fighting bull.

Of course, he is not an animal of the open and you must take him where you find him and follow him where he goes, and he goes into bad places, but the point was to compare the inherent danger in the actual animals on an equal terrain—not in the peculiar circumstances under which he must be dealt with. (*There won't be any more asides you will be glad to hear. Am going to write Mr. P. a letter instead. The asides were put in when I read this over on the boat. Got to missing him.*)

To me, also, and the experience it must be again stated is profoundly limited, the rhino is a joke. He may be a bad joke, too, but his atrociously poor eyesight gives the hunter an advantage over him that his bulk, his really remarkable speed and agility, and his sometimes idiotic pugnacity cannot overcome unless aided by advantage of terrain. Many times the rhino will have this advantage which will usually consist in encountering him on one of the paths or tunnels he has made through otherwise impossible tall grass and bush, and then he is as dangerous as a vindictive, horned, locomotive. He is, too, very fast. I be-

lieve he is faster than a buffalo. But fundamentally, to me, he
seems a dangerous practical joke let loose by nature and armed
with a horn which the Chinese pay high prices for to grind up
and use as an aphrodisiac, and the pursuit of which by white
and native hunters has made him shy and furtive in his habits
and driven him from the plains to the broken hills and high
mountain forests—where he can grow his horn and browse in
peace, and where, incidentally, he is much better hunting.

Elephant I have never shot so I cannot write of them even
to give the questionable impressions of the greenhorn. We plan
to go out again to Kenya for six months next year to try to get
a really good one, to hunt buffalo and rhino, and to see how far
wrong first impressions of these were, and to try to get a good
bull sable. Meantime, I know nothing about elephant from
personal experience, and since notes on dangerous game by a
man who has never hunted elephant are like campaign impressions of a bloke who has never seen a major engagement, that
is the sort of notes these notes will have to be.

*(There turns out to be one more of these. One night when
we were eating supper at Mombasa after fishing, A. V. and Mr.
P. and I were talking about writing these letters and I suggested
Alfred write one about hunting elephant with Blix before he
started to write on racing. I was writing on rhino and buffalo,
etc., I said. Mr. P., who was on his first deep sea fishing trip,
didn't say much, but the next day we got into a big school of
large dolphin and caught about 15 before the lousy boat broke
down. Mr. P. got so excited that his legs shook, he screwed the
reel brake backwards until it stuck, he had dolphin jumping
into, out of, and over the boat. Sometimes he jerked the bait
out of their mouths; occasionally he let them swallow it, but
always he had a dolphin jumping on his line.*

"How do you like it, Pop?" I asked him.

*"God," he said, "I haven't had so much fun since the day you
shot the buffalo." Then, a little later, "I'm going to write an
article on it for Esquire. Call it Dolphin Fishing by One Who
Knows.")*

Out in the Stream:
A Cuban Letter

➤ *Esquire* · AUGUST, 1934

THE sun on the water is the toughest part of fishing the north coast of Cuba for marlin in July and August. Havana is cooler than most northern cities in those months because the northeast trades get up about ten o'clock in the forenoon and blow until four or five o'clock the next morning, and the northeast trade is a cool and pleasant wind, but out on the water even with a breeze, the sun gives you something to remember him by. You can avoid it by going to the eastward with the current in the morning, fishing with the boat headed into the sun, and then coming back against the current in the afternoon with the sun at your back again as you troll, but sometimes all the fish will be in the short stretch between Havana and Cojimar and there is nothing to do but work back and forth in and out of the sun and take it. I do not believe it is very bad for the eyes if you wear glasses with Crookes lenses. My eyes were much better after a hundred days in the gulf than they were when we started. But it gives you a schnozzle like some rare and unattractive tropical vegetable and in the evening the sun slants up off the water like molten lead and comes up under the long visor of one of those down east swordfishing caps and broils as it works·toward that sun's ideal of a nose, the monumental proboscis of J. P. Morgan the elder.

You have a lot of time to think out in the gulf and you can touch the schnozzle with a little coconut oil with the left hand while the right holds the big reel and watch the bait bounce and the two teasers dip and dive and zig in and out in the wake and still have time to speculate on higher and lower things. Yes, you say, but why do they have to work into the sun? Why can't they work in and out, north and south instead of east and west?

It would be fine if you could but when the breeze gets up out of the northeast and blows against the current it makes a big sea and you cannot work in the trough of it but have to go either with it or against it.

Of course you may not ask that question at all. You may be bored blind with the whole thing and be waiting for the action to begin or the conversation to start. Gentlemen, I'd like to oblige you but this is one of those instructive ones. This is one of those contemplative pieces of the sort that Izaak Walton used to write (I'll bet you never read him either. You know what a classic is, don't you? A book that everyone mentions and no one reads) except that the charm, and quaintness and the literary value of Walton are omitted. Are they omitted intentionally? Ah, reader, thank you. Thank you and that's mighty white of you.

Well, here we have Piscator, as Walton puts it, sitting on a chair which, with the heat, has given him that unattractive condition called fisherman's seat, holding now in his hand a cold bottle of Hatuey beer, and trying to peer past his monumental schnozzle and out over the sea which is doing considerable rising and falling. The boat has been headed into the sun and if a fish comes now Piscator can see him. He can see the slicing wake of a fin, if he cuts toward the bait, or the rising and lowering sickle of a tail if he is travelling, or if he comes from behind he can see the bulk of him under water, great blue pectorals widespread like the wings of some huge, underwater bird, and the stripes around him like purple bands around a brown barrel, and then the sudden upthrust waggle of a bill. He can see the marlin's mouth open as the bill comes out of the water and see him slice off to the side and go down with the bait, sometimes to swim deep down with the boat so that the line seems slack and Piscator cannot come up against him solidly to hook him. Then when he is hooked he makes a sweeping turn, the drag screwed down, the line zings out and he breaks water, the drag loosed now, to go off jumping, throwing water like a speedboat, in those long, loping, rhythmic, pounding leaps of twenty feet and more in length.

To see that happen, to feel that fish in his rod, to feel that power and that great rush, to be a connected part of it and then to dominate it and master it and bring that fish to gaff, alone and with no one else touching rod, reel or leader, is something worth waiting many days for, sun and all, and as said, while you wait there is plenty of time to think. A good part of the things you think about are not put into a magazine printed on shiny paper and designed to go through the mails. Some they can put you in jail for if you write and others are simply no one's business but a great part of the time you think about fish.

Why does the south wind stop all fish biting off the north coast of Cuba while it makes them bite off the Florida keys?

Why will a mako shark not eat a hooked or dead marlin or swordfish when all other sharks will?

Is there a connection between the mako and the swordfish just as the wahoo, or peto, seems to be a connecting link between the kingfish and the sailfish and marlin?

What makes intelligence and courage in a fish like the mako who will refuse to pull, when hooked, unless you pull on him; who will deliberately charge a fisherman in a boat (I have a moving picture of this); who seems to be thinking while you are fighting him and will try different tactics to escape and come to the top of the water and rest during the fight; and who will swim around and round a hooked marlin and never hit him? The mako is a strange fish. His skin is not like a shark, his eye is not like a shark, his fins are more like a broadbill swordfish than a shark and his smell is sweet and not sharky. Only his mouth, full of those curved-in teeth that give him his Cuban name of *dentuso,* is a shark's mouth. And he has shark's gills.

What use is the sailfish's sail to that fish? Why should this fish which seems to be an unsuccessful model, an earlier and more fantastic model for the marlin, thin where the marlin is rounded, weak where the marlin is strong, provided with insufficient pectoral fins and too small a tail for its size, have survived? There must be a good reason for the sail. What is it?

Why do marlin always travel from east to west against the current and where do they go after they reach Cape San Antonio at the western end of Cuba? Is there a counter current hundreds of fathoms below the surface current and do they return working against that? Or do they make a circle through the Caribbean?

Why in the years of great abundance of marlin off the California coast are the fish equally plentiful off Cuba? Is it possible that marlin, the same fish, follow the warm currents of all the oceans, or that they have certain circuits that they make? They are caught in New Zealand, Tahiti, Honolulu, the Indian ocean, off Japan, off the west coast of South America, off the west coast of Mexico and as far north on the west coast of the United States as California. This year there were many small marlin taken off Miami, and the big ones appear off Bimini just across the gulf stream several months before they run in Cuba. Last summer they caught striped marlin as far north as Montauk Point off Long Island.

Are not the white marlin, the striped marlin and the black marlin all sexual and age variations of the same fish?

For me, with what data I have been able to get so far, they are all one fish. This may be wrong and I would be glad to have any one disprove the theory as what we want is knowledge, not the pride of proving something to be true. So far I believe that the white marlin, the common marlin caught off Miami and Palm Beach, whose top limit in weight is from 125 to 150 lbs., are the young fish of both sexes. These fish when caught have either a very faint stripe which shows in the water but disappears when the fish is taken from the sea or no stripe at all. The smallest I have even seen weighed twenty-three pounds. At a certain weight, around seventy pounds and over, the male fish begin to have very pronounced and fairly wide stripes which show brightly in the water but fade when the fish dies and disappear an hour or so after death. These fish are invariably well rounded, obviously maturing marlin, are always males, and are splendid leapers and fighters in the style of the striped marlin. I believe they are the adolescent males of the marlin.

The striped marlin is characterized by his small head, heavily rounded body, rapier-like spear, and by the broad lavender stripes that, starting immediately behind the gills, encircle his body at irregular intervals all the way back to his tail. These stripes do not fade much after the fish is dead and will come up brightly hours after the fish has been caught if water is thrown over him.

All varieties of marlin breed off the Cuban coast and as the roe brings from forty cents to a dollar and a quarter a pound in the Havana market all fish are carefully opened for roe. Market fishermen say that all the striped marlin are males. On the other hand they claim all the black marlin are females.

But what is the intermediate stage in the development of the female of the white marlin from the handsome, gleaming, well proportioned though rather large headed fish that it is as we know it at a hundred pounds, before it becomes the huge, ugly headed, thick billed, bulky, dark purple, coarse fleshed, comparatively ugly fish that has been called the black marlin?

I believe that its mature life is passed as what we call the silver marlin. This is a handsome, silvery marlin, unstriped, reaching a thousand pounds or more in weight and a terrific leaper and fighter. The market fishermen claim these fish are always females.

That leaves one type of marlin unaccounted for; the so-called blue marlin. I do not know whether these are a color variation stemming from the white, whether they are both male and female, or whether they are a separate species. This summer may show.

We have caught and examined some ninety-one marlin in the last two years and will need to catch and examine several hundred more before any conclusions can be drawn with even a pretense of accuracy. And all the fish should be examined by a scientist who should note the details of each fish.

The trouble is that to study them you have to catch them and catching them is a fairly full time job although it allows plenty of time for thinking.

It really should be subsidized too, because, by the time you buy gas in Havana at thirty cents a gallon to run twelve hours a day for a hundred days a year, get up at daylight every morning, sleep on your belly half the time because of what the fish do to your back—pay a man to gaff—another to be at the wheel, buy bait, reels at two hundred and fifty dollars apiece, six hundred yards of thirty-six thread line at a time, good rods, hooks and leaders, and try to do this out of the money you fenangle out of publishers and editors, you are too exhausted physically and financially to sit up nights counting the number of rays in the fins and putting a calipers on the ventral spikes with four hundred water front Cubans wanting to know why the fish isn't being cut up and distributed. Instead you are sitting in the stern of the boat, feeling pretty good and having a drink while the fish is being butchered out. You can't do everything.

All the people I know with enough wealth to subsidize anything are either busy studying how to get more wealth, or horses, or what is wrong with themselves with psychoanalysts, or horses, or how not to lose what wealth they have, or horses, or the moving picture business, or horses or all of these things together, and, possibly, horses. Also I freely admit that I would fish for marlin with great enjoyment even if it were of no scientific value at all and you cannot expect anyone to subsidize anything that anybody has a swell time out of. As a matter of fact I suppose we are lucky to be able to fish for them without being put in jail. This time next year they may have gotten out a law against it.

Curiosity, I suppose, is what makes you fish as much as anything and here is a very curious thing. This time last year we caught a striped marlin with a roe in it. It wasn't much of a roe it is true. It was the sort of a roe you would expect to find in certain moving picture actresses if they had roe, or in many actors. Examining it carefully it looked about like the sort of roe an interior decorator would have if he decided to declare himself and roe out. But it was a roe and the first one any of the commercial fishermen had ever seen in a striped marlin.

Until we saw this roe, and I wish I could describe it to you without getting too medical, all striped marlin were supposed to be males. All right then. Was this striped marlin how shall we put it or, as I had believed for a long time, do all marlin, white, striped, silver, etc. end their lives as black marlin, becoming females in the process? The jewfish becomes a female in the last of its life no matter how it starts and I believe the marlin does the same thing. The real black marlin are all old fish. You can see it in the quality of the flesh, the coarseness of the bill, and, above all in fighting them, in the way they live. Certainly they grow to nearly a ton in weight. But to me they are all old fish, all represent the last stages of the marlin, and they are all females.

Now you prove me wrong.

Old Newsman Writes:
A Letter from Cuba

➤ *Esquire* · DECEMBER, 1934

YOUR correspondent is an old newspaper man. That makes us all just one big family. But the bad luck for the customers is that your correspondent was a working newspaper man and as such used to envy the way columnists were allowed to write about themselves. When the papers would come over your correspondent would read a long blob-blobs by his then favorite columnist on the columnist himself, his child, what he thought and how he thought it, while on this same day your correspondent's output would be something on this order: KEMAL INSWARDS UNBURNED SMYRNA GUILTY GREEKS, sending it at three dollars a word Eastern Cable urgent to appear as, copyrighted by Monumental News Service, "Mustapha Kemal in an exclusive interview today with the correspondent of the Monumental News Service denied vehemently that the Turkish forces had any part in the burning of Smyrna. The city, Kemal stated, was fired by incendiaries in the troops of the Greek rear guard before the first Turkish patrols entered the city."

I don't know what was on the mind of the good grey baggy-pants of the columns when he used to write those I, me, my pieces but I am sure he had his troubles even before he took over the world's troubles and, anyway, it has been interesting to watch his progress from an herbivorous (out-doors, the spring, baseball, an occasional half-read book) columnist to a carnivorous (riots, violence, disaster, and revolution) columnist. But personal columnists, and this is getting to read a little like a column, are jackals and no jackal has been known to live on grass once he had learned about meat—no matter who killed the meat for him. Winchell kills his own meat and so do a few others. But they have news in their columns and are the most working of working newspaper men. So let us return to the ex-favorite who projects his personality rather than goes for the facts.

Things were in just as bad shape, and worse, as far as vileness, injustice and rottenness are concerned, in 1921, '22 and '23 as they are now but our then favorite columnist did not get around as much in those days or else he didn't read the papers. Or else we had to go broke at home before anybody would take the rest of the world seriously.

The trouble with our former favorite is that he started his education too late. There is no time for him, now, to learn what a man should know before he will die. It is not enough to have a big heart, a pretty good head, a charm of personality, baggy pants, and a facility with a typewriter to know how the world is run and who is making the assists, the put-outs and the errors and who are merely the players and who are the owners. Our favorite will never know because he started too late and because he cannot think coldly with his head.

For instance the world was much closer to revolution in the years after the war than it is now. In those days we who believed in it looked for it at any time, expected it, hoped for it—for it was the logical thing. But everywhere it came it was aborted. For a long time I could not understand it but finally I figured it out. If you study history you will see that there can never be a Communist revolution without, first, a complete military debacle. You have to see what happens in a military debacle to understand this. It is something so utterly complete in its disillusion about the system that has put them into this, in its destruction and purging away of all the existing standards, faiths and loyalties, when the war is being fought by a conscript army, that it is the necessary catharsis before revolution. No country was ever riper for revolution than Italy after the war but the revolution was doomed to fail because her defeat was not complete; because after Caporetto she fought and won in

June and July of 1918 on the Piave. From the Piave, by way of the Banca Commerciale, the Credito Italiano, the merchants of Milan who wanted the prosperous socialist co-operative societies and the socialist municipal government of that city smashed, came fascism.

It is too long a story to go into here but our present literary revolutionary mouthpieces ought to study a little contemporary history. But no history is written honestly. You have to keep in touch with it at the time and you can depend on just as much as you have actually seen and followed. And these boys started too late. Because it isn't all in Marx nor in Engels, a lot of things have happened since then.

What the boys need, to play the races successfully, is past performances. They also need to have known horses for a long time, and to be able to tell them in the early morning around sun-up with no numbers, no colors, with blankets on them, and to be able to clock them, then, as they go by in the half-light and, thus, know what times they are capable of making.

If the men who write editorials for the New Republic and The Monthly Review, say, had to take an examination on what they actually know about the mechanics, theory, past performance and practice of actual revolution, as it is made, not as it is hoped for, I doubt if any one of them would have one hundredth part of the knowledge of his subject that the average sensible follower of the horses has of the animals.

France was whipped and ready for revolution in 1917 after the failure of the Chemin des Dames offensive. Regiments revolted and marched on Paris. Clemenceau came into power when practically every politician and all the sane people of the country were secretly negotiating or hoping for a peace and by shooting or frightening out of the country all his old political enemies, refusing to negotiate a peace, executing God knows how many soldiers who died without publicity tied to stakes before the firing squads at Vincennes, and holding on without fighting until the American effort arrived, had his troops fighting again by July of 1918. Because they ended up as winners, revolution was doomed in France and anybody who saw, on Clemenceau's orders, the Garde Republicaine, with their shining breastplates, their horse-hair plumes, and those high-chested, big-hoofed, well-shod horses, charge and ride down the parade of mutilated war veterans who were confident the Old Man would never do anything to them, his poilus that he loved, and saw the slashing sabers, the start of the gallop then, the smashed wheel chairs, men scattered on the streets unable to run, the broken crutches, the blood and brains on the cobble-stones, the iron-shod hooves striking sparks from the stones but making a different sound when they rode over legless, armless men, while the crowd ran; nobody who saw that could be expected to think something new was happening when Hoover had the troops disperse the bonus army.

Germany was never defeated in a military debacle. There was never any Sedan such as prepared the way for the Commune. There was no final complete bankruptcy of faith in what the war was fought for. U.S. troops took Sedan but the Army was retreating orderly. Germany had simply failed to win in the spring and summer but the army was still intact and there was a peace made before there was a defeat of the kind that makes revolution. True, there was a revolution but it was conditioned and held in check by the way in which the war had ended and those who had never accepted a military defeat hated those who had and started to do away with the ablest of them by the vilest program of assassination the world has ever known. They started, immediately after the war, by killing Karl Liebknecht and Rosa Luxemburg, and they killed on, steadily eliminating revolutionary and liberal alike by an unvarying process of intelligent assassination. Walther Rathenau was a different and better man than Roehm, the pervert, but the same men and the same system murdered both.

Spain got a revolution that corresponded exactly to the extent of her military debacle at Annual and those who were responsible for that terrible butchery lost their jobs and their thrones. But when they tried to extend that revolution three weeks ago the mass of the people were not ready for it and they did not want it.

Neither Austria nor Hungary were ever really defeated in the war in the sense that France was defeated in 1870. The war wore out before anyone won it with them and what has happened in both countries has reflected that. Too many people still believe in the State and war is the health of the state. You will see that finally it will become necessary for the health of the so-called communist state in Russia. But the penalty for losing a war badly enough, completely and finally enough, is the destruction of the state. Make a note of this, Baggy-pants.

Now a writer can make himself a nice career while he is alive by espousing a political cause, working for it, making a profession of believing in it, and if it wins he will be very well placed. All politics is a matter of working hard without reward, or with a living wage for a time, in the hope of booty later. A man can be a Fascist or a Communist and if his outfit gets in he can get to be an ambassador or have a million copies of his books printed by the Government or any of the other rewards the boys dream about. Because the literary revolution boys are all ambitious. I have been living for some time where revolutions have gotten past the parlor or publishers' tea and light picketing stage and I know. A lot of my friends have gotten excellent jobs and some others are in jail. But none of this will help the writer as a writer unless he finds something new to add to human knowledge while he is writing. Otherwise he will stink like any other writer when they bury him; except, since he has had political affiliations, they will send more flowers at the time and later he will stink a little more.

The hardest thing in the world to do is to write straight honest prose on human beings. First you have to know the subject; then you have to know how to write. Both take a lifetime to learn and anybody is cheating who takes politics as a way out. It is too easy. All the outs are too easy and the thing itself is too hard to do. But you have to do it and every time you do it well, those human beings and that subject are done and your field is that much more limited. Of course the boys are all wishing you luck and that helps a lot. (Watch how they wish you luck after the first one.) But don't let them suck you in to start writing about the proletariat, if you don't come from the proletariat, just to please the recently politically enlightened critics. In a little while these critics will be something else. I've seen them be a lot of things and none of them was pretty. Write about what you know and write truly and tell them all where they can place it. They are all really very newly converted and very frightened, really, and when Moscow tells them what I am telling you, then they will believe it. Books should be about the people you know, that you love and hate, not about the people you study up about. If you write them truly they will have all the economic implications a book can hold.

In the meantime, since it is Christmas, if you want to read a book by a man who knows exactly what he is writing about and has written it marvelously well, read Appointment in Samarra by John O'Hara.

Then when you have more time read another book called War and Peace by Tolstoi and see how you will have to skip the big Political Thought passages, that he undoubtedly thought were the best things in the book when he wrote it, because they are no longer either true or important, if they ever were more than topical, and see how true and lasting and important the people and the action are. Do not let them deceive you about what a book should be because of what is in the fashion now. All good books are alike in that they are truer than if they had really happened and after you are finished reading one you will feel that all that happened to you and afterwards it all belongs to you; the good and the bad, the ecstasy, the remorse and sorrow, the people and the places and how the weather was. If you can get so that you can give that to people, then you are a writer. Because that is the hardest thing of all to do. If, after that, you want to abandon your trade and get into politics, go ahead, but it is a sign that you are afraid to go on and do the other, because it is getting too hard and you have to do it alone and so you want to do something where you can have friends and well wishers, and be part of a company engaged in doing something worth doing instead of working all your life at something that will only be worth doing if you do it better than it has ever been done.

You must be prepared to work always without applause. When you are excited about something is when the first draft is done. But no one can see it until you have gone over it again and again until you have communicated the emotion, the sights and the sounds to the reader, and by the time you have completed this the words, sometimes, will not make sense to you as you read them, so many times have you re-read them. By the time the book comes out you will have started something else and it is all behind you and you do not want to hear about it. But you do, you read it in covers and you see all the places that now you can do nothing about. All the critics who could not make their reputations by discovering you are hoping to make them by predicting hopefully your approaching impotence, failure and general drying up of natural juices. Not a one will wish you luck or hope that you will keep on writing unless you have political affiliations in which case these will rally around and speak of you and Homer, Balzac, Zola and Link Steffens. You are just as well off without these reviews. Finally, in some other place, some other time when you can't work and feel like hell you will pick up the book and look in it and start to read and go on and in a little while say to your wife, "Why this stuff is bloody marvelous."

And she will say, "Darling, I always told you it was." Or maybe she doesn't hear you and says, "What did you say?" and you do not repeat the remark.

But if the book is good, is about something that you know, and is truly written and reading it over you see that this is so you can let the boys yip and the noise will have that pleasant sound coyotes make on a very cold night when they are out in the snow and you are in your own cabin that you have built or paid for with your work.

Remembering Shooting-Flying:
A Key West Letter

➤ *Esquire* · FEBRUARY, 1935

THERE is a heavy norther blowing; the gulf is too rough to fish and there is no shooting now. When you are through work it is nearly dark and you can ride out on the boulevard by the sea and throw clay targets with a hand trap against this gale and they will dip and jump and rise into strange angles like a jack-snipe in the wind. Or you can throw them out with the gale behind them and they will go like a teal over the water. Or you can get down below the sea wall and have some one throw them out high over your head riding the wind, but if you puff one into black dust you can not pretend it was an old cock pheasant unless you are a better pretender than I am. The trouble is there isn't any thud, nor is there the line of bare trees, nor are you standing on a wet, leaf-strewn road, nor do you hear the beaters, nor the racket when a cock gets up and, as he tops the trees, you are on him, then ahead of him, and at the shot he turns over and there is that thump when he lands. Shooting driven pheasants is worth whatever you pay for it.

But when you cannot shoot you can remember shooting and I would rather stay home, now, this afternoon and write about it than go out and sail clay saucers in the wind, trying to break them and wishing they were what they're not.

When you have been lucky in your life you find that just about the time the best of the books run out (and I would rather read again for the first time *Anna Karenina, Far Away and Long Ago, Buddenbrooks, Wuthering Heights, Madame Bovary, War and Peace, A Sportsman's Sketches, The Brothers Karamazov, Hail and Farewell, Huckleberry Finn, Winesburg, Ohio, La*

Reine Margot, La Maison Tellier, Le Rouge et le Noire, La Chartreuse de Parme, Dubliners, Yeats's *Autobiographies* and a few others than have an assured income of a million dollars a year) you have a lot of damned fine things that you can remember. Then when the time is over in which you have done the things that you can now remember, and while you are doing other things, you find that you can read the books again and, always, there are a few, a very few, good new ones. Last year there was *La Condition Humaine* by André Malraux. It was translated, I do not know how well, as *Man's Fate,* and sometimes it is as good as Stendhal and that is something no prose writer has been in France for over fifty years.

But this is supposed to be about shooting, not about books, although some of the best shooting I remember was in Tolstoi and I have often wondered how the snipe fly in Russia now and whether shooting pheasants is counter-revolutionary. When you have loved three things all your life, from the earliest you can remember; to fish. to shoot and, later, to read; and when, all your life, the necessity to write has been your master, you learn to remember and, when you think back you remember more fishing and shooting and reading than anything else and that is a pleasure.

You can remember the first snipe you ever hit walking on the prairie with your father. How the jacksnipe rose with a jump and you hit him on the second swerve and had to wade out into a slough after him and brought him in wet, holding him by the bill, as proud as a bird dog, and you can remember all the snipe since in many places. You can remember the miracle it seemed when you hit your first pheasant when he roared up from under your feet to top a sweet briar thicket and fell with his wings pounding and you had to wait till after dark to bring him into town because they were protected, and you can feel the bulk of him still inside your shirt with his long tail up under your armpit, walking in to town in the dark along the dirt road that is now North Avenue where the gypsy wagons used to camp when there was prairie out to the Des Plaines river where Wallace Evans had a game farm and the big woods ran along the river where the Indian mounds were.

I came by there five years ago and where I shot that pheasant there was a hot dog place and filling station and the north prairie, where we hunted snipe in the spring and skated on the sloughs when they froze in the winter, was all a subdivision of mean houses, and in the town, the house where I was born was gone and they had cut down the oak trees and built an apartment house close out against the street. So I was glad I went away from there as soon as I did. Because when you like to shoot and fish you have to move often and always further out and it doesn't make any difference what they do when you are gone.

The first covey of partridges I ever saw, they were ruffed grouse but we called them partridges up there, was with my father and an Indian named Simon Green and we came on them dusting and feeding in the sun beside the grist mill on Horton's Creek in Michigan. They looked as big as turkeys to me and I was so excited with the whirr of the wings that I missed both shots I had, while my father, shooting an old lever action Winchester pump, killed five out of the covey and I can remember the Indian picking them up and laughing. He was an old fat Indian, a great admirer of my father, and when I look back at that shooting I am a great admirer of my father too. He was a beautiful shot, one of the fastest I have ever seen; but he was too nervous to be a great money shot.

Then I remember shooting quail with him when I do not think I could have been more than ten years old, and he was showing me off, having me shoot pigeons that were flying around a barn, and some way I broke the hammer spring in my single barrel 20 gauge. and the only gun down there at my Uncle's place in Southern Illinois that no one was shooting was a big old L. C. Smith double that weighed, probably, about nine pounds. I could not hit anything with it and it kicked me so it made my nose bleed. I was afraid to shoot it and I got awfully tired carrying it and my father had left me standing in a thickety patch of timber while he was working out the singles from a covey we had scattered. There was a red bird up in a tree and then I looked down and under the tree was a quail, freshly dead. I picked it up and it was still warm. My father had evidently hit it when the covey went up with a stray pellet and it had flown this far and dropped. I looked around to see nobody was in sight and then, laying the quail down by my feet, shut both my eyes and pulled the trigger on that old double barrel. It kicked me against the tree and when I opened it up I found it had doubled and fired both barrels at once and my ears were ringing and my nose was bleeding. But I picked the quail up, reloaded the gun, wiped my nose and set out to find my father. I was sick of not hitting any.

"Did you get one, Ernie?"

I held it up.

"It's a cock," he said. "See his white throat? It's a beauty."

But I had a lump in my stomach that felt like a baseball from lying to him and that night I remember crying with my head under the patchwork quilt after he was asleep because I had lied to him. If he would have waked up I would have told him, I think. But he was tired and sleeping heavily. I never told him.

So I won't think any more about that but I remember now how I broke the spring in the 20 gauge. It was from snapping the hammer on an empty chamber practicing swinging on the pigeons after they wouldn't let me shoot any more. And some older boys came along the road when I was carrying the pigeons from the barn to the house and one of them said I didn't shoot those pigeons. I called him a liar and the smaller of the two whipped hell out of me. That was an unlucky trip.

On a day as cold as this you can remember duck shooting in the blind, hearing their wings go whichy-chu-chu-chu in the dark before daylight. That is the first thing I remember of ducks; the whistly, silk tearing sound the fast wingbeats make; just as what you remember first of geese is how slow they seem to go when they are traveling, and yet they are moving so fast that the first one you ever killed was two behind the one you shot at, and all that night you kept waking up and remembering how he folded up and fell. While the woodcock is an easy bird to hit, with a soft flight like an owl, and if you do miss him he will probably pitch down and give you another shot. But what a bird to eat flambé with armagnac cooked in his own juice and butter, a little mustard added to make a sauce, with two strips of bacon and pommes soufflé and Corton, Pommard, Beaune, or Chambertin to drink.

Now it is colder still and we found ptarmigan in the rocks on a high plain above and to the left of the glacier by the Madelener-haus in the Vorarlberg with it blowing a blizzard and the next day we followed a fox track all day on skis and saw where he had caught a ptarmigan underneath the snow. We never saw the fox.

There were chamois up in that country too and black cock in the woods below the timber-line and big hares that you found sometimes at night when we were coming home along the road. We ate them jugged and drank Tyroler wine. And why, today, remember misses?

There were lots of partridges outside of Constantinople and we used to have them roasted and start the meal with a bowl of caviar, the kind you never will be able to afford again, pale grey, the grains as big as buck shot and a little vodka with it, and then the partridges, not overdone, so that when you cut them there was the juice, drinking Caucasus burgundy, and serving French fried potatoes with them and then a salad with roquefort dressing and another bottle of what was the number of that wine? They all had numbers. Sixty-one I think it was.

And did you ever see the quick, smooth-lifting, reaching flight the lesser bustard has, or make a double on them, right and left, or shoot at flighting sand grouse coming to water early in the morning and see the great variety of shots they give and hear the cackling sound they make when flighting, a little like the noise of prairie chickens on the plains when they go off, fast beat of wings and soar, fast beat of wings and soar stiff-winged, and see a coyote watching you a long way out of range and see an antelope turn and stare and lift his head when he hears the shotgun thud? Sand grouse, of course, fly nothing like a prairie chicken. They have a cutting, swooping flight like pigeons but they make that grouse-like cackle, and with the lesser bustard and the teal, there is no bird to beat them for pan, the griddle or the oven.

So you recall a curlew that came in along the beach one time in a storm when you were shooting plover, and jumping teal along a water course that cut a plain on a different continent, and having a hyena come out of the grass when you were trying to stalk up on a pool and see him turn and look at ten yards and let him have it with the shotgun in his ugly face, and standing, to your waist in water, whistling a flock of golden plover back, and then, back in the winter woods, shooting ruffed grouse along a trout stream where only an otter fished now, and all the places and the different flights of birds, jumping three mallards now, down where the beavers cut away the cottonwoods, and seeing the drake tower, white-breasted, green-headed, climbing and get above him and splash him in the old Clark's Fork, walking along the bank watching him until he floated onto a pebbly bar.

Then there are sage hens, wild as hawks that time, the biggest grouse of all, getting up out of range, and out of range, until you came around an alfalfa stack and four whirred up one after the other at your feet almost and, later walking home, in your hunting coat they seemed to weigh a ton.

I think they all were made to shoot because if they were not why did they give them that whirr of wings that moves you suddenly more than any love of country? Why did they make them all so good to eat and why did they make the ones with silent flight like wood-cock, snipe, and lesser bustard, better eating even than the rest?

Why does the curlew have that voice, and who thought up the plover's call, which takes the place of noise of wings, to give us that catharsis wing shooting has given to men since they stopped flying hawks and took to fowling pieces? I think that they were made to shoot and some of us were made to shoot them and if that is not so well, never say we did not tell you that we liked it.

The Sights of Whitehead Street:
A Key West Letter

➤ *Esquire* · APRIL, 1935

THE house at present occupied by your correspondent is listed as number eighteen in a compilation of the forty-eight things for a tourist to see in Key West. So there will be no difficulty in a tourist finding it or any other of the sights of the city, a map has been prepared by the local F. E. R. A. authorities to be presented to each arriving visitor. Your correspondent is a modest and retiring chap with no desire to compete with the Sponge Lofts (number 13 of the sights), the Turtle Crawl (number 3 on the map), the Ice Factory (number 4), the Tropical Open Air Aquarium containing the 627 pound jewfish (number 9), or the Monroe County Courthouse (number 14). The ambition of your correspondent does not even run to competition with Typical Old House (number 12), the Ley M. E. Church, South (number 37), or Abandoned Cigar Factory (number 35). Yet there your correspondent is at number 18 between Johnson's Tropical Grove (number 17) and Lighthouse and Aviaries (number 19). This is all very flattering to the easily bloated ego of your correspondent but very hard on production.

To discourage visitors while he is at work your correspondent has hired an aged negro who appears to be the victim of an odd disease resembling leprosy who meets visitors at the gate and says, "I'se Mr. Hemingway and I'se crazy about you." Of course a visitor who really knows much about leprosy is not at all terrified by this aged negro and after examining him in a cursory fashion dismisses him as an imposter and demands to be introduced into the presence of his master. But tourists with a limited knowledge of leprosy are often easily discouraged and can be seen running down the street toward Fort Taylor (number 16) with the aged negro hobbling after them on his crutches shouting out to them tales of how he caught gigantic marlin and sailfish and details of his sporting exploits with animals whose names he has a lamentable habit of confusing. Lately the poor old chap has taken to telling such visitors as will listen stories for which your correspondent can really, in no way, be responsible.

The other afternoon sitting on the verandah enjoying a cheroot your correspondent heard the old fellow regaling a group of rather horror stricken tourists with a tale of how he wrote a book which he insisted on calling "De Call to Arms." In some odd way he had confused the plot with that of another best seller, Uncle Tom's Cabin, and his description of how he wrote the passage where Missy Catherine Barkley pursues the Italian army with blood hounds over the ice would have been mirth provoking if it had not been so realistic. One of his rather reluctant audience asked him why he always wrote in the first person and the old man seemed stumped for a moment but finally answered, "No sir. You're wrong, sir. I don't write in the first person. I don't fool with no person at all. I write direct on the typewriter."

"But were you really in Italy during the war, Mr. Hemingway? Or was the background of your best seller purely imaginative?"

This always sets the old man off for he loves to talk about Italy which he describes as the place where "he first get that leppacy disease," but his audience rarely stay to hear the end of that story and drawing deeply on my cheroot I enjoyed seeing them get a good bit of exercise as they strung out along Whitehead Street toward the Cable House (number 22) with the old man making not bad time after them on the not un-gruesome remains of his legs.

On the old man's day off or on national holidays visitors will sometimes get into the house itself. Since his home has been listed as an official attraction your correspondent feels that he owes it to the F. E. R. A. to give such visitors their money's worth. Such a visitor was Mr. Questioner, a prominent business man and fellow member of the Player's Club who honored us with his visit lately. Your correspondent had just finished a hard day's work and was feeling rather fatigued when the door opened and looking up he saw Mr. Questioner.

"Why, hello Questioner, old pal," you say.

"I just dropped in," said Questioner. "Saw the door was open and noticed you sitting there reading. Not fishing today?"

"No. Been working."

"Ha. Ha. Call that working. What do they pay you for those things?"

"Oh it varies. Sometimes a dollar a word. Sometimes seventy-five cents. Sometimes you bid them up to two dollars when you have something on them. Of course the stuff the kids do is a little cheaper."

"I didn't know your children wrote."

"Well, of course, there's only one of them really writes. That's the oldest boy, Bumby. The others just dictate."

"And you can sell their stuff as yours?"

"Every word of it. Of course you have to touch up the punctuation a bit."

"It's a regular business," says Questioner, very interested now. "I had no idea there was that much money in it. What does the little boys' stuff bring?"

"We get about three for a quarter for the eldest boy. The others are in proportion."

"Even at that it's money."

"Gad yes," you say. "If. you can keep the little bastids at work."

"Is it hard?"

"It's not easy. When you over-beat them they write such damned sad stuff there's no market for it until you get down around a dime a word. And I want to keep their standards up."

"My word, yes," said Questioner. "Tell me more about it. I had no idea this writing business was so interesting. What do you mean when you 'have something on' an editor?"

"It's rather like the old badger game," you explain. "Of course we have to give quite a cut to the police though. So there's not the money in it there used to be. Say an editor comes down, a married editor, we get him off to one of those—well you know—or we just surprise him in his room sometime and then of course the price goes up. But there's really no money in that anymore. The N. R. A. has practically put a stop to it."

"They've tried to stop everything," said Questioner.

"Johnson cracked down on us about the kids," you say. "Tried to call it child labour, and the oldest boy over ten. I had to go to Washington on it. 'Listen, Hugh,' I said to him. 'It's no skin off the ants of conscience in my pants what you do to Richberg. But the little boy works, see?' Then I walked out on him. We got the little fellow up to around ten thousand words a day after that but about half of it was sad and we had to take a loss on that."

"Even at that," said Questioner, "It's money."

"It's money, yes. But is isn't real money."

"I'd like to see them working."

"We work them nights," you tell him. "It's not so good for the eyes but they can concentrate better. Then in the morning I can go over their stuff."

"You don't mind putting it all out under your name?"

"No, of course not. The name's sort of like a trade-mark. The second rate stuff we sell under other names. You've probably seen some of it around. There was quite a lot of it around at one time. Now there's not so much. We marketed it under too many names and it killed the market."

"Don't you write any yourself anymore?"

"Just a little to keep it going. The boys are doing fine and I'm proud of the boys. If they live I'm going to turn the business over to them. I'll never forget how proud I was when young Patrick came in with the finished manuscript of Death In The Afternoon. He had done the whole thing from a single inspiration. Damned odd story. He saw a negro funeral going by of the Sons and Daughters of Rewarded Sorrow, a sort of insurance agency that's quite popular down here, and as it was the afternoon at the time that gave him his title. The little chap went right ahead and dictated the whole thing straight off to his nurse in less than a week."

"Damned amazing," said Questioner. "I'd like to get in on something like that."

"I said to him, 'Pat there's a picture in this if we can get some moron to buy it.' And do you know what the little fellow answered? 'Daddy let Williams who cleans out the garage buy it. I heard you call him a black moron when he threw away the beer bottles you wanted to return to Mr. Josie.' Shows you how up to snuff they are."

"Did Williams buy it?"

"Yes. He's out on the coast now. He's trying to sell it to Jock Whitney for Technicolor. Of course Williams is colored himself."

"Do you ever write any stories about negroes?"

"Well we've tried to avoid it on account of the instability of the southern market but this year we're about ready to shoot the works."

"What do you mean about instability?"

"Well you just get a character popularized and he makes some mistake and they lynch him. But we're avoiding that by using genuine negro dialect with certified white characters, many of them daughters of the Confederacy. What do you think of it?"

"I'm for it. Tell me some more about it."

"Well we're going to write an epic. They're working on it now day and night. Bumby has the historical sense, Pat does the dialogue and Gregory does plot. You see we've got a new angle. It's an epic about the Civil War but the trouble with most epics is they weren't long enough but what somebody would be able to read the epic and pass the word it was lousy. We figure to run to three thousand pages. If it nets a million we're going to send Gregory to school, he's always crying to go to school, and let Pat open up an office on the coast. That's all he keeps talking about. 'Daddy when can I go out to the coast?' until I get so I can't listen to it. So I said to him today, 'Finish the epic and if it goes over as it should you can go to the coast.' He claims he wants to see Donald Ogden Stewart. Funny isn't it? I said to him, 'I'll go with you Pat. Because I want to see Dotty Parker. I really do.' But he says, 'No Daddy I want to go to the coast alone to open up our office and I want to see Stewart. Alone.' What do you suppose has got into a hard-working kid like that? What does he want to see Stewart about? Maybe an old debt or something like that. Kids are funny that way. Now I forgot anything we owed Stewart years ago."

"You know, I think I ought to go," Mr. Questioner said, and there is a new respect in his tone. "You may be busy."

"Never too busy to see you, Questioner old sod. Come by any time when we've knocked off. Nathaniel can always get you a quick one."

"Goodbye Hoggelway," says Questioner. "You don't know how interesting this is to me."

"Details of a man's work are always interesting."

"Goodbye and thank you so much."

"Goodbye."

Questioner is gone and you call Nathaniel.

Nathaniel: "Yes, Mr. Emmings."

You: "Nathaniel, make a practice of locking the front door at all times."

Nathaniel: "Yes sir. It wasn't my fault Mr. Questioner got in this time."

You: "I understand, Nathaniel. But make a practice of locking it, Nathaniel. If one strains the imagination so late in the day, one is always liable to rupture it. Yes, thank you Nathaniel. Yes, another."

On Being Shot Again:
A Gulf Stream Letter

➤ *Esquire* · JUNE, 1935

IF you ever have to shoot a horse stand so close to him that you cannot miss and shoot him in the forehead at the exact point where a line drawn from his left ear to his right eye and another line drawn from his right ear to his left eyes would intersect. A bullet there from a .22 caliber pistol will kill him instantly and without pain and all of him will race all the rest of him to the ground and he will never move except to stiffen his legs out so he falls like a tree.

If you ever have to shoot a shark shoot him anywhere along a straight line down the center of his head, flat, running from the tip of his nose to a foot behind his eyes. If you can, with your eye, intersect this line with a line running between his eyes and can hit that place it will kill him dead. A .22 will kill him as dead as a .45. But never think he may not move plenty afterwards simply because you know he is dead. He will have no more ideas after you hit him there, but he is capable of much undirected movement. What paralyzes him is clubbing him over the head.

If you want to kill any large animal instantly you shoot it in the brain if you know where that shot is and can call it. If you want to kill it, but it does not make any difference whether it moves after the shot, you can shoot for the heart. But if you want to stop any large animal you should always shoot for the bone. The best bone to break is the neck or any part of the spinal column; then the shoulders. A heavy four-legged animal can move with a broken leg but a broken shoulder will break him down and anchor him.

Your correspondent's mind has been turned to shooting and he is inspired to offer this information on account of just having shot himself in the calves of both legs. This difficult maneuver to perform with a single bullet was not undertaken as an experiment in ballistics but was quite casual. Your correspondent was once criticized in a letter by a reader of this magazine for not being a casual enough traveller. Trying to become more casual, your correspondent finally ends up by shooting himself through both legs with one hand while gaffing a shark with the other. This is as far as he will go in pleasing a reader. If the reader wants to break your correspondent down by smashing a large bone, or drop him cold with a well directed brain shot, or watch him race for the ice box with a bullet through the heart the reader will have to do the shooting himself.

We had left Key West early in the morning and were about twenty miles out in the Gulf Stream trolling to the eastward along a heavy, dark current of stream en route to Bimini in the Bahama Islands. The wind was in the south, blowing across the current; it was moderately rough fishing, but it was a pretty day. We had sighted a green turtle scudding under the surface and were rigging a harpoon to strike him, planning to salt him down in a keg, a layer of meat, a layer of salt, for meat for the trip, when Dos hooked a very large dolphin. While he played the dolphin we lost sight of the turtle.

Another dolphin hit Henry Strater, President of The Maine Tuna Club, hereinafter referred to as the President, and while the President was working on him a while a school of dolphin showed green in the water and from below them a large black shark of the type we call *galanos* on the Cuban coast came up to cut the surface of the water behind the President's dolphin which went into the air wildly. He kept in the air, wildly, the shark going half out of water after him. The President worked on him with Presidential skill and intelligence, giving him a free spool to run away from the shark, and on the slack he threw the hook.

The dolphin were still around the stern and while Dos took motion pictures we put another bait on the President's hook and he slacked out to a dolphin and was still slacking to this or another dolphin when the shark had taken the bait in to what Old Bread, the wheelsman, referred to in other terms as the outlet of his colon.

With the President hooked into this shark and sweating heavily your correspondent slacked out from a gigantic new 14/0 reel with a lot of discarded line on it (we had been testing the reel for capacity and to see how the new VomHofe drag worked and had not put a good line on it yet) and a very large *galano* swung up to the bait, turned and started off with it, popping the old line. "Fornicate the illegitimate," said your correspondent and slacked out another bait on the same line. The *galano* with a length of double line streaming out of his mouth like one whisker on a catfish turned and took this bait too and, when your correspondent came back on him, popped the old line again. At this your correspondent again addressed the *galano* in the third person and slacked out a third bait on the President's heavy tackle. This bait the *galano* swam around several times before taking; evidently he was tickled by the two lengths of double line which now streamed in catfishlike uncatfishivity (your correspondent has been reading, and admiring, *Pylon* by Mr. William Faulkner), but finally swallowed the bait and started off, bending the President's heavy hickory with the pull of the new thirty-nine thread line while your correspondent addressed the *galano*, saying, "All right you illegitimate, let's see you pull, you illegitimate."

For a few minutes your correspondent and the President sweated, each busy with his own shark (the President's was on a light outfit so he had to go easy with him), then your correspondent's came alongside, and while Saca, the cook, took hold of the leader your correspondent gaffed the *galano* and holding

him with the big gaff shot him in the top of the head with the
.22 caliber Colt automatic pistol shooting a greased, hollow-
point, long rifle bullet. Dos was up on top of the boat, forward,
taking some pictures of the shark going into a flurry and your
correspondent was watching for a chance to shoot him again to
quiet him enough so we could bring him up on the stern to
club him into a state where we could cut the hooks out when
the gaff broke with a loud crack, the shaft striking your correspondent across the right hand, and, looking down, your correspondent saw that he was shot through the calf of the left leg.

"I'll be of unsavoury parentage," remarked your correspondent. "I'm shot."

There was no pain and no discomfort; only a small hole about
three inches below the knee-cap, another ragged hole bigger
than your thumb, and a number of small lacerations on the
calves of both legs. Your correspondent went over and sat down.
The crack of the gaff shaft breaking and the report of the pistol
had been at the same instant and no one else had heard the
pistol go off. I could not see how there could have been more
than one shot then. But where did the other wounds come from?
Could I have pulled the trigger twice or three times without
knowing it the way former mistresses did in the testimony re-
garding Love Nest Killings. Hell no, thought your correspondent. But where did all the holes come from then?

"Get the iodine, Bread."

"What did it, Cap?"

"I got shot when the gaff broke."

All this time the President was working hard on his *galano*.

"I can't figure it," I said. "There's a regular wound from a
bullet that has mushroomed, but what in hell is all the little
stuff? Look and see if you can find a hole in the cockpit where
I was standing, or a bullet."

"Do you want a drink, Cap?" Bread asked.

"Later on."

"There ain't no bullet, Cap," Saca said. "Nowhere there
at all."

"It's in there then. We've got to hook the hell up and go in."

"We got to pick up the dinghy, Cap," Bread said. "That we turned loose when you hung the sharks."

"Jeez Hem that's a hell of a note," Dos said. "We better go in."

"We better cut Mike loose," I said.

Saca went back to tell the President who was still working on the *galano*. The Pres. cut his line and came up to where I was sitting. "Hell, kid, I didn't know you were shot," he said. "I thought you were kidding. I felt some splatters hit my shoes. I thought you were joking. I wouldn't have kept on with the damned shark."

Your correspondent stood up and went back to the stern. There, on the top of the brass strip on top of the combing, slanted a little inside, was the starry splash the bullet had made when it ricocheted. That explained the fragments. The body of the bullet was in my left calf evidently. There was absolutely no pain at all. That is why your correspondent wrote at the head of this letter that if you want to stop large animals you should shoot for bone.

We boiled some water, scrubbed with an antiseptic soap, poured the holes all full of iodine while running into Key West. Your correspondent has to report that he made an equally skillful shot on his lunch into a bucket while running in, that Doctor Warren in Key West removed the fragments, probed, had an X-ray made, decided not to remove the large piece of bullet which was about three or four inches into the calf, and that his judgment was vindicated by the wound keeping clean and not infecting and that the trip was delayed only six days. The next of these letters will be from Bimini. Your correspondent hopes to keep them informative and casual.

One thing I am willing to state definitely now, in spite of all the literature on the subject that you have ever read, is that sailfish do not tap a bait to kill it. They take hold of a bait, more or less gingerly, between their lower jaw and the bill. Their lower jaw is movable and their upper jaw is fixed and is elongated into the bill or rostrum. What is mistaken for a tap is when the fish takes hold of the bait lightly and pulls on it tentatively. When the fish comes at the bait from directly behind it in order to take it in his mouth he must push his bill out of water to bring the bait within seizing range of the lower jaw. This is an awkward position to swim in and the fish's bill wobbles from side to side with the effort. While it is wobbling it might tap the leader or the bait even. But it would be accidental rather than a tap given to kill the bait.

If sailfish tap the bait rather than take it how would they be caught on baits fished from outriggers as they are fished on the charter boats at Miami and Palm Beach? The baited line is held by a wooden clothespin and the fish *must take hold of it to pull it loose.*

I came to consider the possibility of sailfish not tapping through watching more than four hundred marlin swordfish hit a bait without tapping it in spite of all I had read about them tapping. This winter I began to think about the question of whether sailfish tapped or not and we all watched their swimming action in the water very closely and also watched the way they hit. All this winter I did not see a single sailfish tap a bait; and on one day we hooked nine. Now I believe they never tap a bait to kill it any more than a marlin does.

One other thing we have found out this winter and spring. Large fish, marlin, big dolphin and sailfish, hang about the turtles, both green and loggerhead, that you see scudding, floating, or feeding in the Gulf Stream.

Always pass a bait close to a turtle when you see one out there. I believe the large fish hang around to feed on the small fish that congregate in the shade and the shelter of the turtle; exactly as they will congregate around your own boat if you are broke down or drifting in the stream.

Blue marlin also turned up this winter off Key West. One was caught and three others were hooked and broke away. We raised five during the winter; had strikes from two, and failed to hook either one. They surged at the strip bait, then followed for awhile and went down. Two were raised just outside the reef in about twelve fathoms of water. The other three were out better than ten miles in the stream.

On the way to Bimini we want to troll well out toward the axis of the Gulf Stream and see what we can raise. There is a lot of very fine looking current out there with a world of flying fish in it, that we have had to cross going back and forth to Cuba and you cannot tell what we may hit. Your correspondent plans not to hit himself in the leg.

Notes on the Next War:
A Serious Topical Letter

➤ *Esquire* · SEPTEMBER, 1935

NOT this August, nor this September; you have this year to do in what you like. Not next August, nor next September; that is still too soon; they are still too prosperous from the way things pick up when armament factories start at near capacity; they never fight as long as money can still be made without. So you can fish that summer and shoot that fall or do whatever you do, go home at nights, sleep with your wife, go to the ball game, make a bet, take a drink when you want to, or enjoy whatever liberties are left for anyone who has a dollar or a dime. But the year after that or the year after that they fight. Then what happens to you?

First you make a lot of money; maybe. There is a chance now that you make nothing; that it will be the government that makes it all. That is what, in the last analysis, taking the profits out of war means. If you are on relief you will be drafted into this great profitless work and you will be a slave from that day.

If there is a general European war we will be brought in if propaganda (think of how the radio will be used for this), greed, and the desire to increase the impaired health of the state can swing us in. Every move that is made now to deprive the people of their decision on all matters through their elected representatives and to delegate those powers to the executive brings us that much nearer war.

It removes the only possible check. No one man nor group of men incapable of fighting or exempt from fighting should in any way be given the power, no matter how gradually it is given them, to put this country or any country into war.

The first panacea for a mismanaged nation is inflation of the currency; the second is war. Both bring a temporary prosperity; both bring a permanent ruin. But both are the refuge of political and economic opportunists.

No European country is our friend nor has been since the last war and no country but one's own is worth fighting for. Never again should this country be put into a European war through mistaken idealism, through propaganda, through the desire to back our creditors, or through the wish of anyone through war, notoriously the health of the state, to make a going concern out of a mismanaged one.

Now let us examine the present set-up and see what chance there is of avoiding war.

No nations, anymore, pay their debts. There is no longer even a pretense of honesty between nations or of the nation toward the individual. Finland pays us still; but she is a new country and will learn better. We were a new country once and we learned better. Now when a country does not pay its debts you cannot take its word on anything. So we may discard any treaties or declarations of intentions by any countries which do not coincide completely and entirely with the immediate and most cynical national aims of those countries.

A few years ago, in the late summer, Italy and France mobilized along their border to fight over Italy's desire for colonial expansion in North Africa. All references to this mobilization were censored out of cables and radiograms. Correspondents who mentioned it in mailed stories were threatened with expulsion. That difference has now been settled by Mussolini's shift of ambition to East Africa where he has obviously made a deal with the French to abandon his North African plans in return for France allowing him to make war on a free sovereign state under the protection of membership in the League of Nations.

Italy is a country of patriots and whenever things are going badly at home, business bad, oppression and taxation too great, Mussolini has only to rattle the saber against a foreign country to make his patriots forget their dissatisfaction at home in their flaming zeal to be at the throats of the enemy. By the same system, early in his rule, when his personal popularity waned and the opposition was strengthened, an attempted assassination of the Duce would be arranged which would put the populace in such a frenzy of hysterical love for their nearly lost leader that they would stand for anything and patriotically vote the utmost repressive measures against the opposition.

Mussolini plays on their admirable patriotic hysteria as a violinist on his instrument but when France and Jugo-Slavia were the possible enemy he could never really give them the full Paganini because he did not want war with those countries; only the threat of war. He still remembers Caporetto, where Italy lost 320,000 men in killed, wounded and missing, of which amount 265,000 were missing, although he has trained a generation of young Italians who believe Italy to be an invincible military power.

Now he is setting out to make war on a feudal country, whose soldiers fight barefooted and with the formations of the desert and the middle ages; he plans to use planes against a people who have none and machine guns, flame projectors, gas, and modern artillery against bows and arrows, spears, and native cavalry armed with carbines. Certainly the stage is as nearly set as it ever can be for an Italian victory and such a victory as will keep Italians' minds off things at home for a long time. The only flaw is that Abyssinia has a small nucleus of trained, well armed troops.

France is glad to see him fight. In the first place anyone who fights may be beaten; Italy's Black Caporetto, her second greatest military debacle, was administered by these same Ethiopians at Adowa when fourteen thousand Italian troops were killed or driven from the field by a force which Mussolini now describes as 100,000 Ethiopians. Certainly it is unfair to ask fourteen thousand troops to fight one hundred thousand but the essence of war is not to confront your force of fourteen thousand with a hundred thousand of anything. Actually the Italians lost more than 4500 white and 2000 native troops, killed and wounded. Sixteen hundred Italians were taken prisoners. The Abyssinians admitted losing 3000 men.

The French remember Adowa and less possibly though more recently, Baer and Braddock (who knows but what Owney Madden may have bought a piece of the Ethiopians?), and they know that anybody who fights may be beaten. Dysentery, fever, the sun, bad transport, many things can defeat an army. There are also a number of tropical diseases which can only become epidemic when given the opportunity afforded by an invading army of men unused to the climate and possessing no immunity against them. Anyone who fights near the equator can be beaten by the mere difficulty of keeping an army in the field.

Then France feels that if Italy wins or loses, the war will cost her so much that she will be in no position to make trouble in Europe. Italy has never been a serious problem unless she has allies, because she has no coal and no iron. No nation can make war without coal and iron. Lately Italy has tried to overcome this by building up an enormous air-force and it is her air-force that makes her the threat she is in Europe today.

England is glad to see Italy fight Ethiopia. First she may be whipped which, they figure, will teach her a lesson and lengthen the peace of Europe. Secondly if she wins that removes the annoyance of Abyssinian raids along the northern frontier province of Kenya and gives some one else the responsibility of suppressing the perennial Abyssinian slave trade across to Arabia. Next England must undoubtedly have an arrangement with the possible victor about the water power project in northeastern Ethiopia which she has long coveted for the watering of the Sudan. It is only logical that Anthony Eden should have arranged about that when he was in Rome recently. Lastly she knows that anything Italy finds and brings out of Ethiopia must come through the Suez Canal or, taking the long way around, the straits of Gibraltar, while if Japan had been· permitted to penetrate into

Ethiopia and thus gain a foothold in Africa what she took would go direct to Japan and in time of necessity there would be no control over it.

Germany is glad to have Mussolini try to gobble Ethiopia. Any change in the African status quo provides an opening for her soon-to-be-made demands for return of her African colonial possessions. This return, if made, will probably delay war for a long time. Germany, under Hitler, wants war, a war of revenge, wants it fervently, patriotically and almost religiously. France hopes that it will come before Germany is too strong. But the people of France do not want war.

There is the great danger and the great difference. France is a country and Great Britain is several countries but Italy is a man, Mussolini, and Germany is a man, Hitler. A man has ambitions, a man rules until he gets into economic trouble; he tries to get out of this trouble by war. A country never wants war until a man through the power of propaganda convinces it. Propaganda is stronger now than it has ever been before. Its agencies have been mechanized, multiplied and controlled until in a state ruled by any one man truth can never be presented.

War is no longer made by simply analysed economic forces if it ever was. War is made or planned now by individual men, demagogues and dictators who play on the patriotism of their people to mislead them into a belief in the great fallacy of war when all their vaunted reforms have failed to satisfy the people they misrule. And we in America should see that no man is ever given, no matter how gradually or how noble and excellent the man, the power to put this country into a war which is now being prepared and brought closer each day with all the premeditation of a long planned murder. For when you give power to an executive you do not know who will be filling that position when the time of crisis comes.

They wrote in the old days that it is sweet and fitting to die for one's country. But in modern war there is nothing sweet nor fitting in your dying. You will die like a dog for no good reason. Hit in the head you will die quickly and cleanly even sweetly and fittingly except for the white blinding flash that never stops, unless perhaps it is only the frontal bone or your optic nerve that is smashed, or your jaw carried away, or your nose and cheek bones gone so you can still think but you have no face to talk with. But if you are not hit in the head you will be hit in the chest, and choke in it, or in the lower belly, and feel it all slip and slide loosely as you open, to spill out when you try to get up, it's not supposed to be so painful but they always scream with it, it's the idea I suppose, or have the flash, the slamming clang of high explosive on a hard road and find your legs are gone above the knee, or maybe just below the knee, or maybe just a foot gone and watch the white bone sticking through your puttee, or watch them take a boot off with your foot a mush inside it, or feel an arm flop and learn how a bone feels grating, or you will burn, choke and vomit, or be blown to hell a dozen ways, without sweetness or fittingness; but none of this means anything. No catalogue of horrors ever kept men from war. Before the war you always think that it's not you that dies. But you will die, brother, if you go to it long enough.

The only way to combat the murder that is war is to show the dirty combinations that make it and the criminals and swine that hope for it and the idiotic way they run it when they get it so that an honest man will distrust it as he would a racket and refuse to be enslaved into it.

If war was fought by those who wanted to fight it and knew what they were doing and liked it, or even understood it, then it would be defensible. But those who want to go to the war, the élite, are killed off in the first months and the rest of the war is fought by men who are enslaved into the bearing of arms and are taught to be more afraid of sure death from their officers if they run than possible death if they stay in the line or attack. Eventually their steadily increasing terror overcomes them, given the proper amount of bombardment and a given intensity of fire, and they all run and, if they get far enough out of hand, for that army it is over. Was there any allied army which did not, sooner or later, run during the last war? There is not room here to list them.

No one wins a modern war because it is fought to such a point that everyone must lose. The troops that are fighting at the end are incapable of winning. It is only a question of which government rots the first or which side can get in a new ally with fresh troops. Sometimes the allies are useful. Sometimes they are Rumania.

In a modern war there is no Victory. The allies won the war but the regiments that marched in triumph were not the men who fought the war. The men who fought the war were dead. More than seven million of them were dead and it is the murder of over seven million more that an ex-corporal in the German army and an ex-aviator and former morphine addict drunk with personal and military ambition and fogged in a blood-stained murk of misty patriotism look forward hysterically to today. Hitler wants war in Europe as soon as he can get it. He is an ex-corporal and he will not have to fight in this one; only to make the speeches. He himself has nothing to lose by making war and everything to gain.

Mussolini is an ex-corporal, too, but he is also an ex-anarchist, a great opportunist, and a realist. He wants no war in Europe. He will bluff in Europe but he never means to fight there. He can still remember what the war was like himself and how he left it after being wounded in an accident with an Italian trench mortar and went back to newspaper work. He does not want to fight in Europe because he knows that anyone who fights may lose, unless of course one can arrange to fight Rumania, and the first dictator who provokes a war and loses it puts a stop to dictators, and their sons, for a long time.

Because the development of his regime calls for a war he chooses Africa as the place to fight and the only surviving free African state as his opponent. The Abyssinians unfortunately are Christians so it cannot be a Holy war. But while he is making Ethiopia Fit for Fiats he can, of course, suppress slavery on paper, and doubtless in the Italian War College, it looks like a foolproof, quick and ideal campaign. But it may be that a regime and a whole system of government will fall because of this foolproof war in less than three years.

A German colonel named Von Lettow-Vorbeck with an original force of 5000 troops, only two hundred and fifty of whom were whites, fought 130,000 allied troops for a period of over four years in Tanganyika and Portuguese Africa and caused the expenditure of 72,000,000 pounds sterling. At the end of the war he was still at large carrying on guerrilla warfare.

If the Abyssinians choose to fight on in guerrilla warfare rather than make peace Italy may find that Ethiopia will be an unhealing wound in her side that will drain away her money, her youth and her food supplies and return men broken in health and disgusted with suffering and the government that sent them to suffer with promises of glory. It is the disillusioned soldiers who overthrow a regime.

It may be that this war in Africa will prolong the temporary peace in Europe. In the meantime something may happen to Hitler. But of the hell broth that is brewing in Europe we have no need to drink. Europe has always fought, the intervals of peace are only Armistices. We were fools to be sucked in once on a European war and we should never be sucked in again.

Monologue to the Maestro:
A High Seas Letter

➤ *Esquire* · OCTOBER, 1935

ABOUT a year and a half ago a young man came to the front door of the house in Key West and said that he had hitch-hiked down from upper Minnesota to ask your correspondent a few questions about writing. Arrived that day from Cuba, having to see some good friends off on the train in an hour, and to write some letters in the meantime, your correspondent, both flattered and appalled at the prospect of the questioning, told the young man to come around the next afternoon. He was a tall, very serious young man with very big feet and hands and a porcupine hair-cut.

It seemed that all his life he had wanted to be a writer. Brought up on a farm he had gone through high school and the University of Minnesota, had worked as a newspaper man, a rough carpenter, a harvest hand, a day laborer, and had bummed his way across America twice. He wanted to be a writer and he had good stories to write. He told them very badly but you could see that there was something there if he could get it out. He was so entirely serious about writing that it seemed that seriousness would overcome all obstacles. He had lived by himself for a year in a cabin he had built in North Dakota and written all that year. He did not show me anything that he had written then. It was all bad, he said.

I thought, perhaps, that this was modesty until he showed me a piece he had published in one of the Minneapolis papers. It was abominably written. Still, I thought, many other people write badly at the start and this boy is so extremely serious that he must have something; real seriousness in regard to writing being one of the two absolute necessities. The other, unfortunately, is talent.

Besides writing this young man had one other obsession. He had always wanted to go to sea. So, to shorten this account, we gave him a job as night watchman on the boat which furnished him a place to sleep and work and gave him two or three hours' work each day at cleaning up and a half of each day free to do his writing. To fulfill his desire to go to sea, we promised to take him to Cuba when we went across.

He was an excellent night watchman and worked hard on the boat and at his writing but at sea he was a calamity; slow where he should be agile, seeming sometimes to have four feet instead of two feet and two hands, nervous under excitement, and with an incurable tendency toward sea-sickness and a peasant reluctance to take orders. Yet he was always willing and hard working if given plenty of time to work in.

We called him the Maestro because he played the violin, this name was eventually shortened to the Mice, and a big breeze would so effectually slow up his co-ordination that your correspondent once remarked to him, "Mice, you certainly must be going to be a hell of a good writer because you certainly aren't worth a damn at anything else."

On the other hand his writing improved steadily. He may yet be a writer. But your correspondent, who sometimes has an evil temper, is never going to ship another hand who is an aspirant writer; nor go through another summer off the Cuban or any other coast accompanied by questions and answers on the practice of letters. If any more aspirant writers come on board the Pilar let them be females, let them be very beautiful, and let them bring champagne.

Your correspondent takes the practice of letters, as distinct from the writing of these monthly letters, very seriously; but dislikes intensely talking about it with almost anyone alive. Having had to mouth about many aspects of it during a period of one hundred and ten days with the good old Maestro, during much of which time your correspondent had to conquer an urge to throw a bottle at the Mice whenever he would open his mouth and pronounce the word writing, he hereby presents some of these mouthings written down.

If they can deter anyone from writing he should be deterred. If they can be of use to anyone your correspondent is pleased. If they bore you there are plenty of pictures in the magazine that you may turn to.

Your correspondent's excuse for presenting them is that some of the information contained would have been worth fifty cents to him when he was twenty-one.

Mice: What do you mean by good writing as opposed to bad writing?

Your correspondent: Good writing is true writing. If a man is making a story up it will be true in proportion to the amount of knowledge of life that he has and how conscientious he is; so that when he makes something up it is as it would truly be. If he doesn't know how many people work in their minds and actions his luck may save him for a while, or he may write fantasy. But if he continues to write about what he does not know about he will find himself faking. After he fakes a few times he cannot write honestly any more.

Mice: Then what about imagination?

Y.C.: Nobody knows a damned thing about it except that it is what we get for nothing. It may be racial experience. I think that is quite possible. It is the one thing beside honesty that a good writer must have. The more he learns from experience the more truly he can imagine. If he gets so he can imagine truly enough people will think that the things he relates all really happened and that he is just reporting.

Mice: Where will it differ from reporting?

Y.C.: If it was reporting they would not remember it. When you describe something that has happened that day the timeliness makes people see it in their own imaginations. A month later that element of time is gone and your account would be flat and they would not see it in their minds nor remember it. But if you make it up instead of describe it you can make it round and whole and solid and give it life. You create it, for good or bad. It is made; not described. It is just as true as the extent of your ability to make it and the knowledge you put into it. Do you follow me?

Mice: Not always.

Y.C. (crabbily): Well for chrisake let's talk about something else then.

Mice (undeterred): Tell me some more about the mechanics of writing.

Y.C.: What do you mean? Like pencil or typewriter? For chrisake.

Mice: Yes.

Y.C.: Listen. When you start to write you get all the kick and the reader gets none. So you might as well use a typewriter because it is that much easier and you enjoy it that much more. After you learn to write your whole object is to convey everything, every sensation, sight, feeling, place and emotion to the reader. To do this you have to work over what you write. If you write with a pencil you get three different sights at it to see if the reader is getting what you want him to. First when you read it over; then when it is typed you get another chance to improve it, and again in the proof. Writing it first in pencil gives you one-third more chance to improve it. That is .333 which is a damned good average for a hitter. It also keeps it fluid longer so that you can better it easier.

Mice: How much should you write a day?

Y.C.: The best way is always to stop when you are going good and when you know what will happen next. If you do that every day when you are writing a novel you will never be stuck. That is the most valuable thing I can tell you so try to remember it.

Mice: All right.

Y.C.: Always stop while you are going good and don't think about it or worry about it until you start to write the next day. That way your subconscious will work on it all the time. But if you think about it consciously or worry about it you will kill it and your brain will be tired before you start. Once you are into the novel it is as cowardly to worry about whether you can go on the next day as to worry about having to go into inevitable action. You *have* to go on. So there is no sense to worry. You have to learn that to write a novel. The hard part about a novel is to finish it.

Mice: How can you learn not to worry?

Y.C.: By not thinking about it. As soon as you start to think about it stop it. Think about something else. You have to learn that.

Mice: How much do you read over every day before you start to write?

Y.C.: The best way is to read it all every day from the start, correcting as you go along, then go on from where you stopped the day before. When it gets so long that you can't do this every day read back two or three chapters each day; then each week read it all from the start. That's how you make it all of one piece. And remember to stop while you are still going good. That keeps it moving instead of having it die whenever you go on and write yourself out. When you do that you find that the next day you are pooped and can't go on.

Mice: Do you do the same on a story?

Y.C.: Yes, only sometimes you can write a story in a day.

Mice: Do you know what is going to happen when you write a story?

Y.C.: Almost never. I start to make it up and have happen what would have to happen as it goes along.

Mice: That isn't the way they teach you to write in college.

Y.C.: I don't know about that. I never went to college. If any sonofabitch could write he wouldn't have to teach writing in college.

Mice: You're teaching me.

Y.C.: I'm crazy. Besides this is a boat, not a college.

Mice: What books should a writer have to read?

Y.C.: He should have read everything so he knows what he has to beat.

Mice: He can't have read everything.

Y.C.: I don't say what he can. I say what he should. Of course he can't.

Mice: Well what books are necessary?

Y.C.: He should have read *War and Peace* and *Anna Karenina* by Tolstoi, *Midshipman Easy, Frank Mildmay* and *Peter Simple* by Captain Marryat, *Madame Bovary* and *L'Education Sentimentale* by Flaubert, *Buddenbrooks* by Thomas Mann, Joyce's *Dubliners, Portrait of the Artist* and *Ulysses, Tom Jones* and *Joseph Andrews* by Fielding, *Le Rouge et le Noir* and *La Chartreuse de Parme* by Stendhal, *The Brothers Karamazov* and any two other Dostoevskis, *Huckleberry Finn* by Mark Twain, *The Open Boat* and *The Blue Hotel* by Stephen Crane, *Hail and Farewell* by George Moore, Yeats's *Autobiographies*, all the good De Maupassant, all the good Kipling, all of Turgenev, *Far Away and Long Ago* by W. H. Hudson, Henry James's short stories, especially *Madame de Mauves*, and *The Turn of the Screw, The Portrait of a Lady, The American*—

Mice: I can't write them down that fast. How many more are there?

Y.C.: I'll give you the rest another day. There are about three times that many.

Mice: Should a writer have read all of those?

Y.C.: All of those and plenty more. Otherwise he doesn't know what he has to beat.

Mice: What do you mean "has to beat"?

Y.C.: Listen. There is no use writing anything that has been written before unless you can beat it. What a writer in our time has to do is write what hasn't been written before or beat dead men at what they have done. The only way he can tell how he is going is to compete with dead men. Most live writers do not exist. Their fame is created by critics who always need a genius of the season, someone they understand completely and feel safe in praising, but when these fabricated geniuses are dead they will not exist. The only people for a serious writer to compete with are the dead that he knows are good. It is like a miler running against the clock rather than simply trying to beat whoever is in the race with him. Unless he runs against time he will never know what he is capable of attaining.

Mice: But reading all the good writers might discourage you.

Y.C.: Then you ought to be discouraged.

Mice: What is the best early training for a writer?

Y.C.: An unhappy childhood.

Mice: Do you think Thomas Mann is a great writer?

Y.C.: He would be a great writer if he had never written another thing than *Buddenbrooks*.

Mice: How can a writer train himself?

Y.C.: Watch what happens today. If we get into a fish see exactly what it is that everyone does. If you get a kick out of it while he is jumping remember back until you see exactly what the action was that gave you the emotion. Whether it was the rising of the line from the water and the way it tightened like a fiddle string until drops started from it, or the way he smashed and threw water when he jumped. Remember what the noises were and what was said. Find what gave you the emotion; what the action was that gave you the excitement. Then write it down making it clear so the reader will see it too and have the same feeling that you had. That's a five finger exercise.

Mice: All right.

Y.C.: Then get in somebody else's head for a change. If I bawl you out try to figure what I'm thinking about as well as how you feel about it. If Carlos curses Juan think what both their sides of it are. Don't just think who is right. As a man things are as they should or shouldn't be. As a man you know who is right and who is wrong. You have to make decisions and enforce them. As a writer you should not judge. You should understand.

Mice: All right.

Y.C.: Listen *now*. When people talk listen completely. Don't be thinking what you're going to say. Most people never listen. Nor do they observe. You should be able to go into a room and when you come out know everything that you saw there and not only that. If that room gave you any feeling you should know exactly what it was that gave you that feeling. Try that for practice. When you're in town stand outside the theatre and see how the people differ in the way they get out of taxis or motor cars. There are a thousand ways to practice. And always think of other people.

Mice: Do you think I will be a writer?

Y.C.: How the hell should I know? Maybe you have no talent. Maybe you can't feel for other people. You've got some good stories if you can write them.

Mice: How can I tell?

Y.C.: Write. If you work at it five years and you find you're no good you can just as well shoot yourself then as now.

Mice: I wouldn't shoot myself.

Y.C.: Come around then and I'll shoot you.

Mice: Thanks.

Y.C.: Perfectly welcome, Mice. Now should we talk about something else?

Mice: What else?

Y.C.: Anything else, Mice, old timer, anything else at all.

Mice: All right. But—

Y.C.: No but. Finish. Talk about writing finish. No more. All gone for today. Store all close up. Boss he go home.

Mice: All right then. But tomorrow I've got some things to ask you.

Y.C.: I'll bet you'll have fun writing after you know just how it's done.

Mice: What do you mean?

Y.C.: You know. Fun. Good times. Jolly. Dashing off an old masterpiece.

Mice: Tell me—

Y.C.: Stop it.

Mice: All right. But tomorrow—

Y.C.: Yes. All right. Sure. But tomorrow.

The Malady of Power:
A Second Serious Letter

➤ *Esquire* · NOVEMBER, 1935

IF you tell it to them once they think it is marvelous. When you tell it to them again they say, "We heard that before somewhere. Where do you suppose he got that from?" If you tell it to them a third time they are bored to death and they won't listen to it. It may be truer every time. But they get tired of hearing it.

So this month we wrap it all up in a series of anecdotes so that perhaps you will not taste the castor-oil in the chop suey sandwich. But having read the President's reported statement to a group of Representatives that he could, if he would, put the U.S. into war in ten days, this one is still about the next war.

In the old days, when your correspondent was a working newspaper man, he had a friend named Bill Ryall, then a European correspondent for the Manchester *Guardian*. This Ryall had a white, lantern-jawed face of the sort that is supposed to haunt you if seen suddenly in a London fog, but on a bright windy day in Paris meeting him on the boulevard wearing a long fur-collared great coat he had the never-far-from-tragic look of a ham Shakespearean actor. None of us thought of him as a genius then and I do not think he thought of himself as one either, being too busy, too intelligent, and, then, too sardonic to go in for being a genius in a city where they were a nickel a dozen and it was much more distinguished to be hard working. He was a South African and had been very badly blown up in the war while commanding infantry. Afterwards he had gotten into the intelligence service and at the time of the peace conference he had been a sort of pay-off man for the disbursing of certain sums spent by the British to subsidize and influence certain individuals and certain organs of the French press. He talked very frankly about this and as I was a kid then he told me many things that were the beginning of whatever education I received in international politics. Later Ryall wrote under the name of William Bolitho, went to New York, became a genius, and worked at it until he died. You may have read his *Murder For Profit,* his *Twelve Against The Gods,* or some of the pieces he wrote in the old N.Y. *World.* I never saw him after he became Bolitho, but when he was Ryall he was a wonderful guy. He may have been even finer when he was Bolitho but I do not see how it would be possible. I think sometimes being a genius in that hick town must have bored him very much. But I never saw him to ask him.

In the fall I am remembering we were all covering the Lausanne Conference and Ryall, a man named Hamilton, and myself used to eat together nearly every night. The weather was very pleasant in Lausanne that fall and the conference was split up into two main parts; one was the enormous, spreading Beau-Rivage Hotel down on the bank of the Lake of Geneva where the British and the Italians were and the other was the very red plush Palace Hotel up in the town where the French and the Turks were lodged. To get from one to the other you took a steep little funicular railway, you walked up a steep stairway, or you wound your way up the terraced roads in very expensive taxis. The sessions of the conference itself were secret and your official news came in hand-outs or press conferences with the spokesmen for each country and, since each country was anxious to present its version of what had happened before credence was given to any other country's account, these press conferences followed in rapid succession and you had to step very fast to get them all in.

Your correspondent at that time was running a twenty-four hour wire service for an afternoon and morning news service

under two different names and was accustomed to file his last
dispatch around three a.m. and leave something with the
concierge to open the wire with in the morning at seven. Then
at eight-thirty your correspondent would wake, read the papers,
interview his tipsters, have breakfast in bed and during breakfast file another powerful piece. He would be slipping back into
sleep when the telephone would ring and there would be the
ruddy, well tubbed, cheerful, outdoor voice of G. Ward Price,
the Best Dressed Newspaper Man of the Ages, the Monocled
Prince of the Press, The Inheritor of the Tradition of William
Harding Davis and one of the best newspaper men of his time,
and it's still his time if you read his recent interview with Mussolini for the Rothermere papers, saying, "What about a spot
of exercise?"

"No," your correspondent would reply and hang up the re-
ceiver. The phone would immediately ring again and Ward
would say, "Come on. I'm off to the gym."

Always a moral coward, your correspondent would dress,
cursing, and reach the gym, slightly bleary-eyed, just in time to
see Ward finishing a quick turn with the pulleys and getting
ready for a go at the heavy bag.

"You're a lazy mucker," he would say. "Come on. Get the
gloves on."

After this, with pauses for rest during which your correspondent would lie on his back and breathe heavily while Ward
did exercises or shadow boxed about the ring, the very debonair,
handsomely built, tall, one hundred and eighty pound, perfectly conditioned Price would stick the finest left hand I've
ever seen out of the professional ring into your correspondent's
puss for a period of a half an hour. He had very good foot work,
he stayed way behind that left jab and popped it into you like
a piston and you couldn't hit him with a sackful of confetti. I
mean I couldn't.

"Wasn't that a marvelous work-out," Ward would say after
we had showered and before he selected a fresh monocle.
"Doesn't that set you up for all day?"

Your correspondent with a headache composed of one part yesterday noon's Martinis, one part last night's before-dinner whiskey-and-sodas, two parts last night's brandies until three o'clock this morning, and eight hundred and seventy-three parts Ward Price's bloody left hand would try to say something very open air and sporting, like, "Oh rugger ruddy bloody," and fall to wondering when the people who paid him to send news dispatches would begin to discover he was getting punch drunk.

So in the evening we were all having dinner and your correspondent was all but crying into his Chianti.

"What's the matter with you?" asked Ryall. "You're a jovial cove tonight."

"You don't have to box that goddamned Ward Price every morning after working all night and have him knock your ruddy can off so you can't even think until eleven o'clock."

"A.M. or P.M.?" asked Ryall, always a stickler for accuracy.

"Go to hell," said your correspondent.

"Why do you do it?"

"God knows. I suppose because he would think I was yellow if I stopped."

"Why don't you knock him out?"

"How am I going to knock him out if I can't hit him?"

"Force the pace, corner him, make him slug and knock him out."

"Force the pace! I can't even step along with him a minute before my wind is gone."

"Train," said Ryall. "We'll train you."

Training consisted of running between the lakeside press conferences and those in the hotel up in the steep town (if your correspondent got there too late the trainers would cover him on the news), in drinking nothing after dinner, and in the practice of celibacy. On the fifth day of this regime when your correspondent protested that he would rather have his head pushed off by Ward the rest of his life than run up those ungodly stairs once more Ryall looked your correspondent over in the manner of a man appraising a fifth prize hog and said, "All right. I suppose you're as fit as we'll ever get you. Fight him tomorrow."

For any details of what happened when we put the gloves on that next morning you will have to consult Mr. Ward Price. He could fight as well as box and your correspondent is no reliable witness on how it went nor any man to give you a blow-by-blow account. I do know that afterwards I felt much worse than I had felt every other morning when he had only hit me with his left. When he stopped to fight you could hit him all right. But brother he could hit you right back.

At noon that day I was back down at the Beau-Rivage bar in Ouchy waiting for the British press conference to be called. Ryall came in.

"You see," he said.

"I guess I can see," I said. "I haven't really tried yet. I'm going to try later in the day."

"Now you see."

"What?"

"What training will do. The value of roadwork, of celibacy and abstinence from brandy."

"Do I look like an advertisement for all those things?"

"Ward's got two broken ribs," he said, in the manner he always had of imparting a mystery. "He showed me the X-ray plates. He's just come from the doctor's."

"Honest to God?"

"If you want to put it that way," he said. "Now you see what training will do? You need never box him again. Come and have a drink you big oaf. There's Hamilton and Lawrence."

That was the conference where Ismet Pasha was guarded by a bodyguard who always went around with pistols showing and the leader of the bodyguard was a very tough looking citizen with four pistols plainly visible through his too tight fitting clothes and I was selected by lot in the Palace bar one night to present him with an explosive cigar. He took it very graciously and offered me a cigarette in exchange the while I was trying to fade away and when the cigar went off he pulled all four pistols at once.

That too was the conference at which a young Foreign Office secretary put through a call to the Beau-Rivage Palace to speak with Lord Curzon and said, "I say, is the Imperial Buggah in?"

And lived through hearing those clear cool tones answer, "*This* is the Imperial Buggah speaking."

That was the conference, too, that Curzon wrecked when everything was settled by a manifestation of that strange malady that Ryall claimed afflicts men in power. Everything had been settled and the Turks were ready to sign when they asked Curzon, in charge of British negotiations, to a dinner. Curzon refused, and the language of his refusal got back to the Turkish delegation. He had said, it was reported, "My duty compels me to treat with them at this conference. But there is nothing in my duty that compels me to sit at table with ignorant Anatolian peasants." His malady of greatness compelled him to say that when he was bringing to a successful termination an arduous task; and the saying of it upset all he had done, so that his work had to be finished by another man, and England never got as good terms from the Turks again.

It was one night when Hamilton and Ryall and I were dining together that Ryall brought out this theory that power affected all men holding it in a certain definite way. Ryall said that you could see the symptoms of this effect on any man, sooner or later, and he gave us many examples of it.

In Wilson, of course, he could trace it very clearly and he said that it followed a course almost like a disease and that you could chart it.

I remember saying, "What about Clemenceau?" for Clemenceau was one of my great heroes then and Ryall said you could not trace it as clearly in him because he had led an extremely active life physically and that oftentimes that kept a man from showing the usual effects of the malady of power. But he said that if I had known Clemenceau better I would never have admired him as I did. That Clemenceau had abused his power when he was a middle aged man and that then he was a great bully and had killed men unnecessarily in duels; that later, when he came in power as an old man during the war, he had all his old political opponents jailed, shot or banished; branding them all as traitors. It was this that made so many politicians hate him, so that when they went out to Versailles to elect a President of France after the war and Clemenceau was sure he would be elected for his services to France they elected Deschanel in order to humiliate the man they all had feared as the Tiger.

It was Ryall's theory that a politician or a patriot as soon as given a supreme position in a state, unless he was without ambition and had not sought the office, always began to show the symptoms of what power was doing to him. He said you could see it very clearly in all the men of the French Revolution, too, and it was because our forefathers in America knew how power affected men that they had limited the term of the executive.

Ryall said one of the first symptoms of the malady of power was suspicion of the man's associates, then came great touchiness on all matters, inability to receive criticism, belief that he was indispensable, and that nothing had ever been done rightly until he came into power and that nothing would ever be done rightly again unless he stayed in power. He said that the better and more disinterested the man, the quicker this attacked him. He said that a man who was dishonest would last much longer because his dishonesty made him either cynical or humble in a way, and that protected him.

That night I remember him quoting the example of a Lord of the British Admiralty who had been getting steadily more advanced in the malady of power. It had become impossible for almost anyone to work with him and the final smash came at a meeting at which they were discussing how to get a better class of cadets for the navy. This admiral had hammered on a table with his fist and said, "Gentlemen if you do not know where to get them, by God I will make them for you!"

Since that evening your correspondent has studied various politicians, statesmen and patriots in the light of Bill Ryall's theory and he believes that the fate of our country for the next hundred years or so depends on the extent of Franklin D. Roosevelt's ambition. If he is ambitious only to serve his country, as

Cleveland was, we, and our children, and their children will be very fortunate. If he is ambitious personally, to leave a great name, or to eclipse the luster of the name he bears, which was made famous by another man, we will be out of luck because the sensational improvements that can be made legally in the country in time of peace are being rapidly exhausted.

War is coming in Europe as surely as winter follows fall. If we want to stay out now is the time to decide to stay out. Now, before the propaganda starts. Now is the time to make it impossible for any one man, or any hundred men, or any thousand men, to put us in a war in ten days—in a war they will not have to fight.

In the next ten years there will be much fighting, there will be opportunities for the United States to again swing the balance of power in Europe; she will again have a chance to save civilization; she will have a chance to fight another war to end war.

Whoever heads the nation will have a chance to be the greatest man in the world for a short time—and the nation can hold the sack once the excitement is over. For the next ten years we need a man without ambition, a man who hates war and knows that no good ever comes of it, and a man who has proved his beliefs by adhering to them. All candidates will need to be measured against these requirements.

Wings Always over Africa:
An Ornithological Letter

➤ *Esquire* · JANUARY, 1936

A RECENT dispatch from Port Said reported the passing in one week of six ships with 9,476 wounded and sick Italian soldiers returning through the Suez Canal from the field of honor in Ethiopia. The dispatch did not give the names of any of these soldiers nor the names of the cities or villages that they left to go fight in Africa. Nor did it state that they were being sent to one of the Italian island hospital concentration camps where the sick and wounded are being delivered in order that their return to Italy shall not depress the morale of their relatives who sent them off. Italian morale is as easily depressed as it is elevated and any one who has ever seen an Italian laborer threatening or attempting to kill a physician who attends his dying child in the event of the child's death will appreciate the wisdom of Mussolini in not allowing the citizens of his corporate state to see the eggs broken in the making of his imperial omelet.

The principal expression that one recalls as hearing from the lips, mouths, or throats of wounded Italians was the words, *"Mamma mia! Oh mamma mia!"* and this admirable filial devotion in times of physical suffering could be counted on to receive reciprocation if the mother of the wounded or sick soldier were allowed to see him. There can only be a certain amount of *mamma mia*-ing in an army and have that army hold together and Mussolini is to be congratulated on keeping it one sided.

An Italian soldier can be so fired by propaganda that he will go to battle wanting only to die for Il Duce and convinced that it is better to live one day as a lion than a hundred years as a sheep and, hit in the buttocks, the fleshy part of the thigh, or the calf of the leg, all comparatively painless wounds, he is capable of uttering the most noble sentiments and of saying, "Duce! I salute you Duce! I am happy to die for you, Oh Duce!"

But hit in the belly, or if the bullet breaks bone, or if it happens to hit a nerve he will say, "*Oh Mamma mia!*" and the Duce will be far from his thoughts. Malaria and dysentery are even less capable of arousing patriotic fervor and jaundice, as I recall it, which gives a man the sensation of having been kicked in the vicinity of the interstitial glands, produces almost no patriotic fervor at all.

There is an aspect of war in Africa which Il Duce will do well to keep censored out of his newspapers and that is the part played in it by birds. In all of the territory of Ethiopia where the Italians are fighting there are five birds which prey upon the dead and wounded. These are the black and white crow which flies near to the ground and probably depends on its sense of smell to find a wounded man or a body; the ordinary buzzard which is never far from the ground and may hunt by both sight and smell; the red faced small vulture looking rather like our turkey buzzard, which flies fairly high and hunts by sight; the huge, obscene looking bare necked vulture which circles almost out of sight and falls like a whishing feathered projectile when a carcass or a fallen man is sighted and comes hopping and waddling forward to peck at anything that is alive or dead provided it is defenceless; and the great, ugly, marabou stork that wheels out of sight, high above the highest vultures, and wheels down when he sees the vultures dropping. There are only five main varieties of these birds but five hundred of them will come to a single wounded man when he lies in the open.

What happens to a man, once he is dead, is of little matter, but the carrion birds of Africa will hit a wounded man, lying in the open, as quickly as they will a dead man. I have seen them leave nothing of a zebra but the bones and a greasy black

circle covered with feathers twenty minutes from the time the
animal was killed provided the belly skin was slit open so they
could get an opening. That same night the hyenas would so
crack and devour the bones that in the morning you could not
see where the zebra had been except for a black, oily looking
blotch on the plain. Since a dead man is smaller and has no thick
hide to protect him they will deal with him much quicker.
There is no need in Africa to bury your dead for sanitary
reasons.

But it is not the fact that a dead soldier may end up in a
vulture's stomach that Il Duce needs to conceal from his troops,
but the way that the vultures and the marabous have with the
wounded. The first thing an Italian soldier should be told is
to roll over on his face if he is hit and cannot keep moving.
There is a man alive today who did not know that rule during
the fighting of the last war in German East Africa. While he
was unconscious the vultures got his eyes and he woke in the
stabbing blinding pain with the stinking, feathered shuffle over
him and, beating at them, rolled onto his face in time to save
half of it. They were pecking his clothing away to get at his
kidneys when the stretcher bearers came up and drove them off.
If you ever want to see how long it takes them to come to a live
man lie down under a tree, perfectly still, and watch them, first
circling so high they look as small as specks, then coming, dropping in concentric circles, then plummeting down in a whish
of rushing wings to deal with you. You sit up and the ring jumps
back raising their wings. But what about if you could not sit up?

So far the Ethiopians have not fought. They have retreated
and let the Italians advance. Because Ethiopia has always been
a country of strong, rival feudal chieftains the Italians have been
able to buy over certain of these chiefs who have ambitions of
their own or feuds with the Negus. In all the reports it reads
as though Italy were occupying the country almost without a
struggle. But Italy needs to win a battle to be in a position to
negotiate with the powers for an approval of her retaining her
captured territory and, perhaps, being given a protectorate over

all Ethiopia. And the Ethiopians, as this is written, have steadily refused battle.

Each day the Italian lines of communication become longer, each day it costs her no one knows how many million of lira to keep her army in the field, and each day there are the sick being taken down to the ships for evacuation. Once Ethiopia has retreated far enough so that they can wage a guerrilla warfare on the Italian lines of communication, and never fight a battle at all, Italy is beaten. The Ethiopians may be too proud, or too conceited to do this and they may risk everything in a big battle and lose. There is always a possibility that they can win although everything is against them there.

Once they become used to planes and learn to scatter and fire on the planes as the Riffians did in North Africa one of Italy's greatest assets will be nullified. Bombing planes must have towns for targets, machine gunning planes must have a concentration of troops. Scattered troops are more dangerous to the plane than the plane is to them. If the Ethiopians can hold on until the next rainy season comes Italian tanks and motorized transport will be useless. It seems doubtful that Italy can get enough money to fight through until the next rains are over. Remember the Ethiopians live in Ethiopia and eat only one meal a day, while every Italian in the field needs a gigantic and expensive transport organization to keep him there and feed him the food he is used to. If Italy wins one battle she will negotiate for peace.

Mussolini's generals have wisely employed Somali and Danakil troops as the spear head of the Italian advance and a great part of the regularity of their advance must be credited to their wise mistrust of European infantry in Africa and their sound appreciation of the lesson learnt from the last war, that to fight that close to the equator, and win, you must use black troops. If, once they have advanced far enough, a great battle is precipitated they will have to use Italian troops in the fighting since they have not enough trained askaris to fight on any large scale. This is what they are evidently seeking to avoid and what the

Ethiopians hope for. They whipped the Italians once and they are confident that they can whip them again. Italy is hoping for a fool proof battle to be fought with black infantry, tanks, machine guns, modern artillery and planes. Ethiopia is hoping to get an Italian army into such a trap as Adowa was in 1896. In the meantime the Ethiopians are retreating and stalling and the Italians are advancing, using up their askaris, gaining many untrustworthy allies, and spending all their available money to keep their army in the field.

As I see it now the next move will be for Italy to come to a confidential agreement with the powers to let her alone and remove the sanctions because of the danger of what she will present as "bolshevism" in Italy if she loses. Countries with a democratic regime of government may sometimes unite to prevent a dictator carrying out an imperialistic scheme of conquest, once those countries have consolidated their own imperialistic holdings, but let the dictator squeal that bolshevism is coming if he is allowed to be defeated or go broke and this dictator will receive the same consideration that he once had when he was a hero to the Rothermere press in England because of the myth that Mussolini saved Italy from going red. Italy was kept from going red when the workers took over the factories in Turin and not one radical group would co-operate with any other radical group. It was kept from going red by the accident that the workers seized the artificially built up war-baby metallurgical industries at the moment when they were about to go broke. Mussolini, the cleverest opportunist in modern history, rode in on the wave of disgust that followed the farcical failure of the Italian radicals to co-operate or to use their great asset, Italy's defeat at Caporetto, intelligently.

I can remember in the old days how the mothers and fathers used to lean out of windows, or from the front of wine shops, blacksmith shops or the door of a cobbler's when soldiers passed and shout, "*Abasso gli ufficiali!*" "Down with the officers!" because they saw the officers as those who kept the foot soldiers fighting when they had come to know the war would bring them no good. Then those who were officers and believed that war could only be ended by fighting that war through and winning it were bitter at the hatred that all working people bore them. Many officers hated war then as since you can hate nothing; not tyranny, not injustice, not murder, not brutality, not the corruption of the human soul; for war has the essence of all of these blended together and is strengthened by its various parts until it is stronger than any of the evils it is composed of can ever be. The only people who ever loved war for long were profiteers, generals, staff officers and whores. They all had the best and finest times of their lives and most of them made the most money they had ever made. Of course there are exceptions; there are and were generals who hated war and there are whores who did not do well out of the last war. But these excellent and generous people are exceptions.

There are many people in Italy who remember the last war as it was; not as they have been taught to believe it was. Many of these people have been beaten because they opened their mouths some were killed, others are in prison on the Lipari islands, and some have left the country. It is a dangerous thing in a dictatorship to have a long memory. You should learn to live for the great deeds of the day. As long as any dictator controls his press there will always be great daily deeds to live for. In America as we get premonitions of dictatorship you can see in the newspapers how marvelous everything is every day in the achievements of government and looking back note how lousy is the result of any given year or period of years of governmental activity. No dictatorship can last, really, except by force and that is why no dictator or potential dictator can afford to go through any period of unpopularity which will at once force him to the use of force to stay in power. A successful dictator uses clubs and has constant newspaper triumphs. An unsuccessful dictator gets scared, shoots too many of his own people, and goes out as soon as his army or police switch on him. If he shoots too many he gets shot himself, usually, even while his regime stands. But this is not about dictators but about certain ornithological aspects of African war.

Certainly no knowledge of the past war will help boys from the little steep-hilled towns of the Abruzzi where the snow comes early on the tops of the mountains, nor those who worked in garages, or machine shops, in Milano or Bologna or Firenze, or rode their bicycles in road races on the white dust-powdered roads of Lombardy, nor those who played football for their factory teams in Spezia or Torino, nor mowed the high mountain meadows of the Dolomites and guided ski-ers in the winter, or would have been burning charcoal in the woods above Piombino, or maybe sweeping out a trattoria in Vicenza, or would have gone to North or South America in the old days. They will feel the deadly heat and know the shadeless land; they will have the diseases that never cure, that make the bones ache and a young man old and turn the bowels to water, and when there is a battle, finally, they will hear the whish of wings when the birds come down and I hope when they are hit someone will have told them to roll over on their faces so they can say, *"Mamma mia!"* with their mouths against the earth they came from.

Mussolini's sons are in the air where there are no enemy planes to shoot them down. But poor men's sons all over Italy are foot soldiers, as poor men's sons all over the world are always foot soldiers. And me, I wish the foot soldiers luck; but I wish they could learn who is their enemy—and why.

On the Blue Water:
A Gulf Stream Letter

Esquire · APRIL, 1936

CERTAINLY there is no hunting like the hunting of man and
those who have hunted armed men long enough and liked it,
never really care for anything else thereafter. You will meet
them doing various things with resolve, but their interest rarely
holds because after the other thing ordinary life is as flat as the
taste of wine when the taste buds have been burned off your
tongue. Wine, when your tongue has been burned clean with
lye and water, feels like puddle water in your mouth, while
mustard feels like axle-grease, and you can smell crisp, fried
bacon, but when you taste it, there is only a feeling of crinkly
lard.

You can learn about this matter of the tongue by coming into
the kitchen of a villa on the Riviera late at night and taking a
drink from what should be a bottle of Evian water and which
turns out to be *Eau de Javel,* a concentrated lye product used
for cleaning sinks. The taste buds on your tongue, if burned
off by *Eau de Javel,* will begin to function again after about a
week. At what rate other things regenerate one does not know,
since you lose track of friends and the things one could learn in
a week were mostly learned a long time ago.

The other night I was talking with a good friend to whom all
hunting is dull except elephant hunting. To him there is no
sport in anything unless there is great danger and, if the danger
is not enough, he will increase it for his own satisfaction. A
hunting companion of his had told me how this friend was not
satisfied with the risks of ordinary elephant hunting but would,
if possible, have the elephants driven, or turned, so he could

take them head-on, so it was a choice of killing them with the difficult frontal shot as they came, trumpeting, with their ears spread, or having them run over him. This is to elephant hunting what the German cult of suicide climbing is to ordinary mountaineering, and I suppose it is, in a way, an attempt to approximate the old hunting of the armed man who is hunting you.

This friend was speaking of elephant hunting and urging me to hunt elephant, as he said that once you took it up no other hunting would mean anything to you. I was arguing that I enjoyed all hunting and shooting, any sort I could get, and had no desire to wipe this capacity for enjoyment out with the *Eeu de Javel* of the old elephant coming straight at you with his trunk up and his ears spread.

"Of course you like that big fishing too," he said rather sadly. "Frankly, I can't see where the excitement is in that."

"You'd think it was marvelous if the fish shot at you with Tommy guns or jumped back and forth through the cockpit with swords on the ends of their noses."

"Don't be silly," he said. "But frankly I don't see where the thrill is."

"Look at so and so," I said. "He's an elephant hunter and this last year he's gone fishing for big fish and he's goofy about it. He must get a kick out of it or he wouldn't do it."

"Yes," my friend said. "There must be something about it but I can't see it. Tell me where you get a thrill out of it."

"I'll try to write it in a piece sometime," I told him.

"I wish you would," he said. "Because you people are sensible on other subjects. Moderately sensible I mean."

"I'll write it."

In the first place, the Gulf Stream and the other great ocean currents are the last wild country there is left. Once you are out of sight of land and of the other boats you are more alone than you can ever be hunting and the sea is the same as it has been since before men ever went on it in boats. In a season fishing you will see it oily flat as the becalmed galleons saw it while they drifted to the westward; white-capped with a fresh breeze as they saw it running with the trades; and in high, rolling blue hills, the tops blowing off them like snow as they were punished by it, so that sometimes you will see three great hills of water with your fish jumping from the top of the farthest one and if you tried to make a turn to go with him without picking your chance, one of those breaking crests would roar down in on you with a thousand tons of water and you would hunt no more elephants, Richard, my lad.

There is no danger from the fish, but anyone who goes on the sea the year around in a small power boat does not seek danger. You may be absolutely sure that in a year you will have it without seeking, so you try always to avoid it all you can.

Because the Gulf Stream is an unexploited country, only the very fringe of it ever being fished, and then only at a dozen places in thousands of miles of current, no one knows what fish live in it, or how great size they reach or what age, or even what kinds of fish and animals live in it at different depths. When you are drifting, out of sight of land, fishing four lines, sixty, eighty, one hundred and one hundred fifty fathoms down, in water that is seven hundred fathoms deep you never know what may take the small tuna that you use for bait, and every time the line starts to run off the reel, slowly first, then with a scream of the click as the rod bends and you feel it double and the huge weight of the friction of the line rushing through that depth of water while you pump and reel, pump and reel, pump and reel, trying to get the belly out of the line before the fish jumps, there is always a thrill that needs no danger to make it real. It may be a marlin that will jump high and clear off to your right and then go off in a series of leaps, throwing a splash like a speedboat in a sea as you shout for the boat to turn with him watching the line melting off the reel before the boat can get around. Or it may be a broadbill that will show wagging his great broadsword. Or it may be some fish that you will never see at all that will head straight out to the northwest like a submerged submarine and never show and at the end of five hours the angler has a straightened-out hook. There is always a feeling of excitement when a fish takes hold when you are drifting deep.

In hunting you know what you are after and the top you can get is an elephant. But who can say what you will hook sometime when drifting in a hundred and fifty fathoms in the Gulf Stream? There are probably marlin and swordfish to which the fish we have seen caught are pygmies; and every time a fish takes the bait drifting you have a feeling perhaps you are hooked to one of these.

Carlos, our Cuban mate, who is fifty-three years old and has been fishing for marlin since he went in the bow of a skiff with his father when he was seven, was fishing drifting deep one time when he hooked a white marlin. The fish jumped twice and then sounded and when he sounded suddenly Carlos felt a great weight and he could not hold the line which went out and down and down irresistibly until the fish had taken out over a hundred and fifty fathoms. Carlos says it felt as heavy and solid as though he were hooked to the bottom of the sea. Then suddenly the strain was loosened but he could feel the weight of his original fish and pulled it up stone dead. Some toothless fish like a swordfish or marlin had closed his jaws across the middle of the eighty pound white marlin and squeezed it and held it so that every bit of the insides of the fish had been crushed out while the huge fish moved off with the eighty-pound fish in its mouth. Finally it let go. What size of a fish would that be? I thought it might be a giant squid but Carlos said there were no sucker marks on the fish and that it showed plainly the shape of the marlin's mouth where he had crushed it.

Another time an old man fishing alone in a skiff out of Cabañas hooked a great marlin that, on the heavy sashcord handline, pulled the skiff far out to sea. Two days later the old man was picked up by fishermen sixty miles to the eastward, the head and forward part of the marlin lashed alongside. What was left of the fish, less than half, weighed eight hundred pounds. The old man had stayed with him a day, a night, a day and another night while the fish swam deep and pulled the boat. When he had come up the old man had pulled the boat up on him and harpooned him. Lashed alongside the sharks had hit him and the old man had fought them out alone in the Gulf Stream in a skiff, clubbing them, stabbing at them, lunging at them with an oar until he was exhausted and the sharks had eaten all that they could hold. He was crying in the boat when the fishermen picked him up, half crazy from his loss, and the sharks were still circling the boat.

But what is the excitement in catching them from a launch? It comes from the fact that they are strange and wild things of unbelievable speed and power and a beauty, in the water and leaping, that is indescribable, which you would never see if you did not fish for them, and to which you are suddenly harnessed so that you feel their speed, their force and their savage power as intimately as if you were riding a bucking horse. For half an hour, an hour, or five hours, you are fastened to the fish as much as he is fastened to you and you tame him and break him the way a wild horse is broken and finally lead him to the boat. For pride and because the fish is worth plenty of money in the Havana market, you gaff him at the boat and bring him on board, but the having him in the boat isn't the excitement; it is while you are fighting him that is the fun.

If the fish is hooked in the bony part of the mouth I am sure the hook hurts him no more than the harness hurts the angler. A large fish when he is hooked often does not feel the hook at all and will swim toward the boat, unconcerned, to take another bait. At other times he will swim away deep, completely un-conscious of the hook, and it is when he feels himself held and pressure exerted to turn him, that he knows something is wrong and starts to make his fight. Unless he is hooked where it hurts he makes his fight not against the pain of the hook, but against being captured and if, when he is out of sight, you figure what he is doing, in what direction he is pulling when deep down, and why, you can convince him and bring him to the boat by the same system you break a wild horse. It is not necessary to kill him, or even completely exhaust him to bring him to the boat.

To kill a fish that fights deep you pull against the direction he wants to go until he is worn out and dies. It takes hours and when the fish dies the sharks are liable to get him before the angler can raise him to the top. To catch such a fish quickly you figure, by trying to hold him absolutely, which direction he is working (a sounding fish is going in the direction the line slants in the water when you have put enough pressure on the drag so the line would break if you held it any tighter); then get ahead of him on that direction and he can be brought to the boat without killing him. You do not tow him or pull him with the motor boat; you use the engine to shift your position just as you would walk up or down stream with a salmon. A fish is caught most surely from a small boat such as a dory since the angler can shut down on his drag and simply let the fish pull the boat. Towing the boat will kill him in time. But the most satisfaction is to dominate and convince the fish and bring him intact in everything but spirit to the boat as rapidly as possible.

"Very instructive," says the friend. "But where does the thrill come in?"

The thrill comes when you are standing at the wheel drinking a cold bottle of beer and watching the outriggers jump the baits so they look like small live tuna leaping along and then behind one you see a long dark shadow wing up and then a big spear thrust out followed by an eye and head and dorsal fin and the tuna jumps with the wave and he's missed it.

"Marlin," Carlos yells from the top of the house and stamps his feet up and down, the signal that a fish is raised. He swarms down to the wheel and you go back to where the rod rests in its socket and there comes the shadow again, fast as the shadow of a plane moving over the water, and the spear, head, fin and shoulders smash out of water and you hear the click the closepin makes as the line pulls out and the long bight of line whishes through the water as the fish turns and as you hold the rod, you feel it double and the butt kicks you in the belly as you come back hard and feel his weight, as you strike him again and again, and again.

Then the heavy rod arc-ing out toward the fish, and the reel in a hand-saw zinging scream, the marlin leaps clear and long, silver in the sun long, round as a hogshead and banded with lavender stripes and, when he goes into the water, it throws a column of spray like a shell lighting.

Then he comes out again, and the spray roars, and again, then the line feels slack and out he bursts headed across and in, then jumps wildly twice more seeming to hang high and stiff in the air before falling to throw the column of water and you can see the hook in the corner of his jaw.

Then in a series of jumps like a greyhound he heads to the northwest and standing up, you follow him in the boat, the line taut as a banjo string and little drops coming from it until you finally get the belly of it clear of that friction against the water and have a straight pull out toward the fish.

And all the time Carlos is shouting, "Oh, God the bread of my children! Oh look at the bread of my children! Joseph and Mary look at the bread of my children jump! There it goes the bread of my children! He'll never stop the bread the bread the bread of my children!"

This striped marlin jumped, in a straight line to the northwest, fifty-three times, and every time he went out it was a sight to make your heart stand still. Then he sounded and I said to Carlos, "Get me the harness. Now I've got to pull him up the bread of your children."

"I couldn't stand to see it," he says. "Like a filled pocketbook jumping. He can't go down deep now. He's caught too much air jumping."

"Like a race horse over obstacles," Julio says. "Is the harness all right? Do you want water?"

"No." Then kidding Carlos, "What's this about the bread of your children?"

"He always says that," says Julio. "You should hear him curse me when we would lose one in the skiff."

"What will the bread of your children weigh?" I ask with mouth dry, the harness taut across shoulders, the rod a flexible prolongation of the sinew pulling ache of arms, the sweat salty in my eyes.

"Four hundred and fifty," says Carlos.

"Never," says Julio.

"Thou and thy never," says Carlos. "The fish of another always weighs nothing to thee."

"Three seventy-five," Julio raises his estimate. "Not a pound more."

Carlos says something unprintable and Julio comes up to four hundred.

The fish is nearly whipped now and the dead ache is out of raising him, and then, while lifting, I feel something slip. It holds for an instant and then the line is slack.

"He's gone," I say and unbuckle the harness.

"The bread of your children," Julio says to Carlos.

"Yes," Carlos says. "Yes. Joke and no joke yes. *El pan de mis hijos.* Three hundred and fifty pounds at ten cents a pound. How many days does a man work for that in the winter? How cold is it at three o'clock in the morning on all those days? And the fog and the rain in a norther. Every time he jumps the hook cutting the hole a little bigger in his jaw. Ay how he could jump. How he could jump!"

"The bread of your children," says Julio.

"Don't talk about that any more," said Carlos.

No it is not elephant hunting. But we get a kick out of it. When you have a family and children, your family, or my family, or the family of Carlos, you do not have to look for danger. There is always plenty of danger when you have a family.

And after a while the danger of others is the only danger and there is no end to it nor any pleasure in it nor does it help to think about it.

But there is great pleasure in being on the sea, in the unknown wild suddenness of a great fish; in his life and death which he lives for you in an hour while your strength is harnessed to his; and there is satisfaction in conquering this thing which rules the sea it lives in.

Then in the morning of the day after you have caught a good fish, when the man who carried him to the market in a hand-cart brings the long roll of heavy silver dollars wrapped in a newspaper on board it is very satisfactory money. It really feels like money.

"There's the bread of your children," you say to Carlos.

"In the time of the dance of the millions," he says, "a fish like that was worth two hundred dollars. Now it is thirty. On the other hand a fisherman never starves. The sea is very rich."

"And the fisherman always poor."

"No. Look at you. You are rich."

"Like hell," you say. "And the longer I fish the poorer I'll be. I'll end up fishing with you for the market in a dinghy."

"That I never believe," says Carlos devoutly. "But look. That fishing in a dinghy is very interesting. You would like it."

"I'll look forward to it," you say.

"What we need for prosperity is a war," Carlos says. "In the time of the war with Spain and in the last war the fishermen were actually rich."

"All right," you say. "If we have a war you get the dinghy ready."

There She Breaches!
or Moby Dick off the Morro

➤ *Esquire* · MAY, 1936

IT was a clear, cool day in October and we were drifting about three miles off Cabañas Fortress to the eastward of Havana. Inside of us were two or three skiffs also drifting for marlin, and further in toward shore we could see the calm surface of the Gulf Stream leap in sharp, minute splashes and hear the ta-ta-ta-tat of the machine guns firing on the rifle range, the limits of which were marked with red flags that showed on the white-walled green headland with the brown barracks behind it.

"Once," said Carlos, who was sitting in the stern holding a line wrapped around each of his big toes, "we had a very big fish on close in to the Morro and those things began to splash all around us."

"What did you do?" asked Lopez Mendez.

"Made the fish fast and dove overboard and only put our noses out until we drifted clear."

"You've got a small nose," said Lopez Mendez. "There's no danger of being shot in a nose that size. But what if a fish strikes now and takes both your toes off? What do you do if a fish strikes now?"

"Watch," said Carlos and pulling on the end of the line that ran to the rod tip he tripped the bight that ran around his toe so it was free. "You can release it from the toe instantly, no matter how hard it is pulling below. It's a trick. We go to sleep with a line on our toe that way drifting in a skiff and turn it loose the instant the pull wakes us."

"Everything's a trick," Lopez Mendez said. "Life is a very difficult trick to learn."

"No," said Carlos. "No Señor. Life is a combat. But you have to know lots of tricks to make a living. You have a good trick in painting."

"Give me the trick of Enrique," I said, in Spanish. "How do you feel this morning, Enrique?"

"Marvelous," said Enrique who was dark, good looking, an aviator, a captain of artillery, and a good amateur matador and was living in Havana with his cousin, Lopez Mendez, the painter, between revolutions in Venezuela where they both came from. "I always feel good." He grinned, furrowing the stubble of his beard that showed an hour after shaving.

"Last night," said Lopez Mendez, who is very thin and distinguished looking, "Enrique ate only a straw hat and three candles."

"I don't care for eating straw hats," said Enrique. "But if some one proposes it, naturally I will eat them."

"He eats them very well," said Lopez Mendez.

"I don't like them though," said Enrique. "I can never raise any enthusiasm for a straw hat."

"What is he saying?" said the Maestro Arnold, from Minnesota, so called because he played the violin and who was on the boat as a photographer; as a very bad photographer.

"He is telling about eating a straw hat," I said.

"Why in God's name does he eat a straw hat?" asked the Maestro.

"Listen Maestro," said Lopez Mendez. "In Venezuela we have many great eaters. Late in the evening when a man wishes to perform an unusual feat of courage and show his disdain for consequences he will eat unusual and inedible objects."

"You're kidding me," said the Maestro.

"No. I swear to God Enrique ate a straw hat last night."

"Yes," said Enrique modestly.

"The night before that he ate all the flowers off the table and several candles at the house of the secretary to the embassy."

"It was nothing," said Enrique. "A candle is nothing. Only

the wicks are difficult. Now I go to prepare the spaghetti. Where is Bolo?"

"He's up in the bow," I said, "watching a line. Mice, go up in the bow and watch that line so Bolo can help Enrique get the spaghetti started."

"Let me get a big straw hat for the sun," said the Maestro.

"Don't let Enrique eat it," said Lopez Mendez.

"No," said Enrique. "There is no danger. No one has ever eaten a straw hat in the daytime."

So we drifted like that all morning, and, in the fall, the small birds that are going south are deadly tired sometimes as they near the coast of Cuba where the hawks come out to meet them, and the birds light on the boat to rest and sometimes we would have as many as twenty on board at a time in the cabin, on the deck, perched on the fishing chairs or resting on the floor of the cockpit. Their great fatigue makes them so tame that you can pick them up and they show no fear at all. There were three warblers and a thrush in the cockpit when Enrique poked his head out to get some air from working in the galley and Lopez Mendez said, "Don't let him see the birds. He would eat them."

"No," said Enrique. "I am a great lover of birds. In about half an hour the spaghetti will be ready."

"Let's have vermouth then," I said. "Tell Bolo to bring out the bottles."

We had the tall glasses with mixed French and Italian vermouth (two parts of French to one of Italian, with a dash of bitters and a lemon peel, fill glass with ice, stir and serve) in our hands and I was just raising mine when Carlos shouted *"Que canonazo!* Oh, what a cannon shot!"

"Where?"

"Way out there. To the eastward. Like the spout from a twelve inch shell."

We were at least four miles off shore by now and where Carlos pointed was another three miles to the eastward.

"They've got no guns that will shoot out there, man," I said.

"I know it. I know it. God save us it must have been a fish. But what a fish to throw a spray as high as that!"

"Watch and see if it jumps again," I said. "We can get up the lines and run out there. What do you think it could be?"

"Only a broadbill would jump like_ that and crash to make a spout of water like that in the middle of the day. It must be a huge broadbill."

"We better start to get the lines in and get out there," I said. "Give me that one."

I started reeling in the hundred and twenty fathom deep line and was grinding and pumping away when Carlos shouted again. "There it is! There is is! My God but close! Hey! No! It's a whale blowing!"

I could see the spout, high, pluming out from a narrow stem like a geyser, about a mile off our starboard bow.

"Get the lines in," I yelled. "Bolo! Get the other line in. Enrique! Come on, kid. It's a whale!"

"Is it true?" asked Enrique. "An actual whale?"

"Yes! Yes! Yes!" said Lopez Mendez. "Look there! Look."

"We'll eat him," said Enrique. "What do you want me to do?"

"Reel in the rest of that line."

I started both engines and they were still reeling in on the lines with the whole tuna baits dragging in the wake as I headed the *Pilar* out to the north to intercept the whale on the course he was making to the westward. Carlos had the box with the harpoon gun in it out in the cockpit and was going over its contents. We had about twenty feet of wire cable and plenty of good light harpoon line but we knew that sort of line would never hold and Carlos said he was going to make the wire fast directly to our three-inch hurricane hawser. We sent Bolo to clear everything out of the forward cockpit and make one end of the hundred fathom hawser fast to our six new, clean, white, cloth-covered cork, regulation life jackets and then coil the hawser on top of them. On the end of the hawser he made the wire cable fast and I turned the wheel over to him and went

into the forward cockpit with Bolo, putting a blank cartridge
in the harpoon gun, fitting a dowling into the shank of the
harpoon that was fastened onto the wire cable that led to the
hawser and shoving the dowling down into the barrel of the
sawed off old Springfield musket that served as harpoon gun
and pressing it tight against the cartridge.

I knew the harpoon gun would never carry out the weight of
the hawser and that the effective range could only be the length
of the wire cable, but I knew no reason why we could not get
close enough to get the harpoon in solidly. The trouble was
that neither did I know anything about whales.

We planned, shouting back to the wheel and to the top of the
house where Lopez Mendez sat with the 6.5 mannlicher, Enrique
with a handful of extra sticks, the ramrod and a Mauser pistol
and the Maestro with the big Graflex, when the whale was harpooned to let the hawser all go out, toss over the packet of life
belts as he sounded, and whenever he came up to blow we would
locate him by the life belts, pick them up, and stay with him,
letting the life belts go over whenever we could not hold the
hawser, and whenever the whale showed putting solids from the
mannlicher into him and eventually being able to finish him
with the killing lance. Then we were going to get a rope around
his flukes, make a hole in him and pump him full of air with
the air mattress pump. Every time I would get a new bright idea
like that about the mattress pump I would shout it back and
Enrique would cheer and wave the pistol. Carlos kept shouting,
"A whale is worth a fortune in La Habana! a whale is worth
a capital for life."

"God bless the whale!" Enrique would shout.

"Death to the whale!" yelled Lopez Mendez.

The Maestro was shaking with excitement.

There, a little way ahead, was the whale. He was very impressive. He would swim a little way under water then his broad
head would come out and he would go along with the slanted
top of his back out, seemingly unconcerned, but when we
speeded up the engine to come up on him close enough to fire

the harpoon into him he would submerge. We tried coming up on him from the back, but he would go down each time before we were in range. Then we tried coming up on him from an angle, but down he would go again to be out of sight, only to reappear ahead of us, varying his course very little. Time after time we came within thirty feet of him only to have him go down. The speeding up of the motors seemed to frighten him and put him down and only by speeding up the motors could we come up on him. He was about forty feet long and as we came up close to him we could see the indentations along the side of his blunt head running back toward the body, as though someone had made them by rubbing a finger in warm wax. Again and again we were so close to him you could have hit him with a beer bottle, but I knew for the harpoon to hold we must be almost touching him with the boat when we fired.

"Shoot! For God's sake shoot!" Bolo screamed, pulling on his hair with one hand and holding the hawser high in the air with the other.

"Shoot!" yelled Carlos.

When I would pass up the shot they both held their heads in their hands.

"It's no use to shoot unless it's close enough," I yelled back. "The gun can't carry the weight of that hawser."

Carlos shook his head. "In my life I have only seen three whales off Habana. A whale is worth a fortune. For God's sake shoot!"

The next time we came close and they began yelling to shoot, I said "All right. I'll show you what I mean," and fired when we were not quite thirty feet from the whale and he had lowered his head to sound. The blackpowder roared, the wire shot out, came taut with the weight of the hawser, and the dart was short. The whale went down and this time he came up a long way ahead and it was hard to see him in the sun.

"You see now?" I yelled back. Carlos nodded, now understanding. Then there came a shout from the top of the house.

"Look there! Look there!" Lopez Mendez was pointing and,

as we looked astern to the eastward, there were spouts rising almost as far as you could see. It looked like a small geyser basin in Yellowstone Park. There were at least ten whales blowing at once and while we watched more than twenty showed; some close, some far out, some far to the east. Some spouts were high, thin plumes spreading on top. Others were low, squat, wide.

While we had been chasing the single whale the whole school had been moving up behind us.

"This can't be," said Bolo. "This can't be."

"Come on," I said. "We'll try one from the side."

I yelled to Carlos and we headed out toward where two very big ones showed. We came close and put them both down without getting into range. This time I noticed a dark cloud like cuttlefish ink in the water as the two whales sounded.

"Did you see that?" I yelled.

They had all seen it.

"Maybe they've been eating squid," Carlos said. "Look! There's another close."

We were within two feet of effective range when this whale went down, his great flukes rising out of the water and then sinking in that slow slant.

Standing up on the deck I looked behind us. We were in the middle of the school now and the school was moving steadily to the westward against the current. Straight astern, less than a half a mile away, there were three whales, one of them, the center one, the biggest we had seen, coming directly toward us, and three of them moving steadily to the west into the sun.

"Listen," I said to Carlos, "turn her around and head for that center whale. Steer directly for him head to head. Keep the motors exactly as they are now until I raise my hand. When I raise my hand open them both wide. When I shoot cut your motors and throw out the clutch. Understand."

"Si señor," said Carlos. "Now we'll get one."

As we came up on them they were down once, a little under water, then coming as straight as submarines, the squared off rather tubular looking heads and the rising hump of the back awash like submarines running partly submerged. They held their course and I could feel Bolo trembling with excitement as he held the hawser above his head.

"For God's sake don't get tangled in that," I said. "Throw it when I shoot and step back clear."

"It's all clear," he said.

Then not forty feet ahead was the great, dark, side-furrowed, dully shiny head and the huge bulk much longer than our boat and, fixing on it, not seeing where the other two had gone, I raised my hand and as the boat lurched forward with the two motors wide open, leaned down over the bow and almost touched that head as I fired the gun into it as it slanted down. There was the noise, the white cloud of blackpowder smoke, a drenching spout of evil-smelling something that went all over us, over the deck, the windshield and the top of the house, and the hurricane hawser was going over the bow so fast it seemed almost to smoke. Then it was slack. We pulled it in and the harpoon was all right. But it had pulled out. I found out later that you do not harpoon sperm whales in the head. Not even with a cannon. There is too much bone.

Anyway we followed the school into the sun as they worked to westward until they were almost at Mariel and we could never get another shot. They would never let us come as close as we had before we struck the big whale. The speeding up of the rhythm of the propeller beating seemed to put them down.

We headed back toward Havana finally and we saw one old lone whale dark grey and huge and travelling by himself, but he would not let us get near him. At about four-thirty we ate the spaghetti Enrique had cooked and discussed whether we had good pictures of them. The Maestro was certain he had marvelous pictures. But the next day when we got the prints they were uniformly lousy. Most of them were taken into the sun; in some he had moved the camera in excitement; in others he shot when the whales were too far away, and he had a series of masterly shots of the holes they would leave in the water when they went down. Later he had whale spout on his lens and produced some shots that looked like waterfall pictures from the inside. The only good picture was one Lopez Mendez had snapped with his little camera before the Mice took it away from him when his Graflex film ran out, and this the Havana paper, to whom Lopez Mendez gave ·it to prove he was not a liar, never returned. The Maestro was depressed by the pictures but not as much as we were. We all knew his failure with the camera would make liars out of us for the rest of our lives.

When something like that happens nobody believes you. They certainly don't believe you when they see the vague pictures which were published in the rotogravure section of the *Diario de la Marina* in Havana. I had no reason to believe there were sperm whales off Havana and it was hard for me to believe it myself. If you choose not to believe it, that is perfectly all right with me. But this fall in New York I went around to the Museum of Natural History and on the charts of the old whaling voyages there found that sperm whales had been regularly taken off Havana in the old days. Where these were headed for I don't know but it seems logical that they were heading for the Caribbean and then south. The day we saw them was October tenth, 1934 and the big one we struck was close to fifty feet long.

That night in the restaurant there were some people who did not believe Enrique either. This distressed him so that he was forced to eat the labels off several beer bottles. This feat being received with some incredulity, he ate a calendar off the wall and devoured a small croton plant that stood by the table. Having his public now well in hand, he ate the complete rotogravure section of the *Diario de la Marina* and offered to eat the table. Nobody believed he would not try.

He was getting rather sullen at someone making fun of the whales so Lopez Mendez got him to come home and, riding upstairs in the elevator, he ate the card of a doctor who advertised himself as a specialist in the curing of certain diseases. Lopez Mendez thought that this last was pure bravado and that Enrique was really slowing up, but Enrique on entering the bedroom saw a caricature of Mussolini on very heavy pasteboard. To prove he was in form, he ate this with no difficulty, simply remarking as he swallowed the last bit that it was *muy pesado.* "Very heavy." After this he took a small drink from a bottle of Eau de Cologne and went happily off to sleep.

In the morning he came down to the boat and when Lopez Mendez was describing the gastronomic feats of the night before I again asked Enrique how he felt.

"Marvelous," he said. "I always feel marvelous."

You don't need to believe this either. But I swear to God it is true. In the interests of science it must be added that Enrique looked slightly pale.

Carlos was the most bitter about the photographs. He had seen only three whales off Havana in all his life and here we ran into twenty and did not even get a decent picture. But as he said, lamenting the loss of a possible life's capital and eternal fame on the waterfront, "Certainly one must be properly prepared for whales. Then, undoubtedly, there is a trick to it. There must be a trick for whales as well as for everything else, but we had never had the opportunity of learning it. But imagine if we had brought that whale into Habana harbor. Picture yourself that!"

"Maybe we'll get another one sometime," I said.

"We must learn the trick of them," he said. "There is certainly a way of getting them. You must find out about them."

"I'll study up on them," I said. But the more I learn about them the luckier I think we were that the harpoon pulled out. I think that a sperm whale might have made several very interesting moves before he permitted us to employ the mattress pump.

THREE

➤ *Spanish Civil War, 1937-1939*

The First Glimpses of War

➤ *NANA Dispatch* · MARCH 18, 1937

VALENCIA, SPAIN.—As our Air Force plane from Toulouse flew down over the business section of Barcelona, the streets were empty. It looked as quiet as downtown New York on a Sunday morning.

The plane hit smoothly on a concrete runway and roared around to a stop before a little building, where, chilled through by our trip over the edge of the snow-covered Pyrenees, we warmed our hands around bowls of coffee and milk while three pistol-armed, leather jacketed guards joked outside. There we learned why Barcelona looked so momentarily quiet.

A trimotor bomber had just come over, with two pursuit planes as escort, and had dropped its load of bombs on the town, killing seven and wounding thirty-four. Only by a half-hour had we missed flying into the dog-fight in which the Insurgent planes were driven off by Government pursuit ships. Personally, I didn't mind. We were a trimotor job ourselves, and there might have been confusion.

Flying low down the coast toward Alicante, along white beaches, past gray-castled towns or with the sea curling against rocky headlands, there was no sign of war. Trains were moving, cattle were plowing the fields, fishing boats were setting out and factory chimneys were belching smoke.

Then, above Tarragona, all the passengers were crowded over on the landside of the ship, watching through the narrow windows the careened hulk of a freighter, visibly damaged by shellfire, which had driven ashore to beach her cargo. She lay aground, looking against the sand in that clear water like a whale with smokestacks that had come to the beach to die.

257

We passed the rich, flat, dark-green fields of Valencia spotted with white houses, the busy port and the great, yellow, sprawling town. We crossed rice marshes, and up over a wild mountain chain where we had an eagle's view of civilization, and down, ear-crackingly, to the bright blue sea and the palm-lined, African-looking shoreline of Alicante.

The plane roared on toward Morocco, while I rattled into Alicante from the airport in a ramshackle bus. I arrived in the midst of a celebration that packed the beautiful sea promenade, lined with date palms, and filled the streets with a milling crowd.

Recruits between the ages of twenty-one and twenty-six were being called up, and they, their girls and their families were celebrating their enlistment and the victory over Italian regular troops on the Guadalajara front. Walking four abreast, arms linked, they were singing, shouting, playing accordions and guitars. Pleasure boats in Alicante harbor were packed with couples holding hands, taking their last rides together, but ashore, where long lines formed in front of jammed recruiting stations, the atmosphere was one of wild celebration.

All along the coast to Valencia, we passed through celebrating crowds that reminded me more of the old days of ferias and fiestas than of war. It was only the convalescent wounded, limping along in heavy, shoddy militia uniforms, who made war seem real.

Food, meat especially, was being rationed at Alicante, but, in small towns between, I saw butcher shops open and meat being sold with no lines formed outside. Our driver resolved to get himself a good steak on the way home.

Coming into Valencia in the dark through miles of orange groves in bloom, the smell of orange blossoms, heavy and strong even through the dust of the road, made it seem to this half-asleep correspondent like a wedding. But, even half asleep, watching the lights out through the dust, you knew it wasn't an Italian wedding they were celebrating.

Shelling of Madrid

➤ *NANA Dispatch* · APRIL 11, 1937

MADRID.—At the front, a mile and a quarter away, the noise came as a heavy coughing grunt from the green pine-studded hillside opposite. There was only a gray wisp of smoke to mark the Insurgent battery position. Then came the high inrushing sound, like the ripping of a bale of silk. It was all going well over into the town, so, out there, nobody cared.

But in the town, where all the streets were full of Sunday crowds, the shells came with the sudden flash that a short circuit makes and then the roaring crash of granite-dust. During the morning, twenty-two shells came into Madrid.

They killed an old woman returning home from market, dropping her in a huddled black heap of clothing, with one leg, suddenly detached, whirling against the wall of an adjoining house.

They killed three people in another square, who lay like so many torn bundles of old clothing in the dust and rubble when the fragments of the "155" had burst against the curbing.

A motor car coming along the street stopped suddenly and swerved after the bright flash and roar and the driver lurched out, his scalp hanging down over his eyes, to sit down on the sidewalk with his hand against his face, the blood making a smooth sheen down over his chin.

Three times one of the tallest buildings was hit. Its shelling is legitimate, since it is a known means of communication and a landmark, but the shelling that traversed the streets seeking the Sunday promenaders was not military.

When it was over, I went back out again to our observation

259

post, only ten minutes away by foot, in a ruined house and watched the third day of the battle where government forces are trying to complete an encircling movement to cut the neck of the Insurgent salient thrust into Madrid last November. The apex of this salient is the clinical hospital in University City and if the government can complete the pincers-like movement from the Tremadura road to the Coruña road this whole salient will be cut off.

A hill with a ruined church—ruined before our eyes two days ago by spouting shell bursts—is now three roofless walls. Two big houses on the hill below and three smaller houses to their left, all fortified by the Insurgent forces, hold up the government advance.

Yesterday I watched an attack against these positions where government tanks, working like deadly, intelligent beetles, destroyed machine gun posts in the thick underbrush while government artillery shelled the buildings and Insurgent trenches. We watched until dark but the infantry never advanced for an assault on these strong points.

But today, after fifteen minutes of the heaviest artillery fire, which with direct hit after direct hit, hid the five houses in one rolling cloud of white and orange smoky dust, I watched the infantry attack.

Behind a chalky-showing line of newly dug trenches, the men lay. Suddenly, one ran, bent low, to the rear. A half dozen followed and I saw one fall. Then four of these returned, and, bent forward like men walking along a dock in a heavy rain, the irregular line went forward. Some flopped to take cover. Others went down suddenly to stay as part of the view, a dark blue spot on the brown field. Then they were in the underbrush and out of sight and the tanks were moving ahead and shooting at the windows of the houses.

Below a sunken road there was a sudden flame and something burned yellow, with a black oily smoke rising. It burned for forty minutes, the flame mounting and then dying to mount again suddenly, and, finally, there was an explosion. Probably it was a tank. You couldn't see nor be sure because it was under the road, but other tanks passed it and, shifting to its right, went on firing into the houses and the machine gun posts in the trees. One at a time, men ran past the flame and into the woods along the slope close by the houses.

The machine gun and rifle fire made one solid crackling whisper in the air 'and then we saw another tank coming up with a moving shadow behind it that the glasses showed to be a solid square of men. It stopped and lurched and turned to the right, where the other foot soldiers had run one at a time bent double and where we had seen two fall. It passed into the woods and out of sight, its followers intact.

Then there was a great shelling again and we watched for the assault while the light failed and you could see nothing through the glasses but the plaster-shattered smoke of the houses where the shells were bursting. Government troops were within fifty yards of the houses when it was too dark to see. The outcome of the offensive designed to free Madrid from fascist pressure depends on the results of tonight's and tomorrow's action.

A New Kind of War

➤ *NANA Dispatch* · APRIL 14, 1937

MADRID.—The window of the hotel is open and, as you lie in bed, you hear the firing in the front line seventeen blocks away. There is a rifle fire all night long. The rifles go tacrong, capong, craang, tacrong, and then a machine gun opens up. It has a bigger calibre and is much louder, rong, cararong, rong, rong. Then there is the incoming boom of a trench mortar shell and a burst of machine gun fire. You lie and listen to it and it is a great thing to be in bed with your feet stretched out gradually warming the cold foot of the bed and not out there in University City or Carabanchel. A man is singing hard-voiced in the street below and three drunks are arguing when you fall asleep.

In the morning, before your call comes from the desk, the roaring burst of a high explosive shell wakes you and you go to the window and look out to see a man, his head down, his coat collar up, sprinting desperately across the paved square. There is the acrid smell of high explosive you hoped you'd never smell again, and, in a bathrobe and bedroom slippers, you hurry down the marble stairs and almost into a middle-aged woman, wounded in the abdomen, who is being helped into the hotel entrance by two men in blue workmen's smocks. She has her two hands crossed below her big, old-style Spanish bosom and from between her fingers the blood is spurting in a thin stream. On the corner, twenty yards away, is a heap of rubble, smashed cement and thrown up dirt, a single dead man, his torn clothes dusty, and a great hole in the sidewalk from which the gas from a broken main is rising, looking like a heat mirage in the cold morning air.

"How many dead?" you ask a policeman.

"Only one," he says. "It went through the sidewalk and burst below. If it would have burst on the solid stone of the road there might have been fifty."

A policeman covers the top of the trunk, from which the head is missing; they send for someone to repair the gas main and you go in to breakfast. A charwoman, her eyes red, is scrubbing the blood off the marble floor of the corridor. The dead man wasn't you nor anyone you know and everyone is very hungry in the morning after a cold night and a long day the day before up at the Guadalajara front.

"Did you see him?" asked someone else at breakfast.

"Sure," you say.

"That's where we pass a dozen times a day. Right on that corner." Someone makes a joke about missing teeth and someone else says not to make that joke. And everyone has the feeling that characterizes war. It wasn't me, see? It wasn't me.

The Italian dead up on the Guadalajara front weren't you, although Italian dead, because of where you had spent your boyhood, always seemed, still, like our dead. No. You went to the front early in the morning in a miserable little car with a more miserable little chauffeur who suffered visibly the closer he came to the fighting. But at night, sometimes late, without lights, with the big trucks roaring past, you came on back to sleep in a bed with sheets in a good hotel, paying a dollar a day for the best rooms on the front. The smaller rooms in the back, on the side away from the shelling, were considerably more expensive. After the shell that lit on the sidewalk in front of the hotel you got a beautiful double corner room on that side, twice the size of the one you had had, for less than a dollar. It wasn't me they killed. See? No. Not me. It wasn't me anymore.

Then, in a hospital given by the American Friends of Spanish Democracy, located out behind the Morata front along the road to Valencia, they said, "Raven*wants to see you."

"Do I know him?"

"I don't think so," they said, "but he wants to see you."

*J. Robert Raven

"Where is he?"

"Upstairs."

In the room upstairs they are giving a blood transfusion to a man with a very gray face who lay on a cot with his arm out, looking away from the gurgling bottle and moaning in a very impersonal way. He moaned mechanically and at regular intervals and it did not seem to be him that made the sound. His lips did not move.

"Where's Raven?" I asked.

"I'm here," said Raven.

The voice came from a high mound covered by a shoddy gray blanket. There were two arms crossed on the top of the mound and at one end there was something that had been a face, but now was a yellow scabby area with a wide bandage cross where the eyes had been.

"Who is it?" asked Raven. He didn't have lips, but he talked pretty well without them and with a pleasant voice.

"Hemingway," I said. "I came up to see how you were doing."

"My face was pretty bad," he said. "It got sort of burned from the grenade, but it's peeled a couple of times and it's doing better."

"It looks swell," I said. "It's doing fine."

I wasn't looking at it when I spoke.

"How are things in America?" he asked. "What do they think of us over there?"

"Sentiment's changed a lot," I said. "They're beginning to realize the government is going to win this war."

"Do you think so?"

"Sure," I said.

"I'm awfully glad," he said. "You know, I wouldn't mind any of this if I could just watch what was going on. I don't mind the pain, you know. It never seemed important really. But I was always awfully interested in things and I really wouldn't mind the pain at all if I could just sort of follow things intelligently. I could even be some use. You know, I didn't mind the war at all. I did all right in the war. I got hit once before and I was back and rejoined the battalion in two weeks. I couldn't stand to be away. Then I got this."

He had put his hand in mine. It was not a worker's hand. There were no callouses and the nails on the long, spatulate fingers were smooth and rounded.

"How did you get it?" I asked.

"Well, there were some troops that were routed and we went over to sort of reform them and we did and then we had quite a fight with the fascists and we beat them. It was quite a bad fight, you know, but we beat them and then someone threw this grenade at me."

Holding his hand and hearing him tell it, I did not believe a word of it. What was left of him did not sound like the wreckage of a soldier somehow. I did not know how he had been wounded, but the story did not sound right. It was the sort of way everyone would like to have been wounded. But I wanted him to think I believed it.

"Where did you come from?" I asked.

"From Pittsburgh. I went to the University there."

"What did you do before you joined up here?"

"I was a social worker," he said. Then I knew it couldn't be true and I wondered how he had really been so frightfully wounded and I didn't care. In the war that I had known, men often lied about the manner of their wounding. Not at first; but later. I'd lied a little myself in my time. Especially late in the evening. But I was glad he thought I believed it, and we talked about books, he wanted to be a writer, and I told him about what happened north of Guadalajara and promised to bring some things from Madrid next time we got out that way. I hoped maybe I could get a radio.

"They tell me Dos Passos and Sinclair Lewis are coming over, too," he said.

"Yes," I said. "And when they come I'll bring them up to see you."

"Gee, that will be great," he said. "You don't know what that will mean to me."

"I'll bring them," I said.

"Will they be here pretty soon?"

"Just as soon as they come I'll bring them."

"Good boy, Ernest," he said. "You don't mind if I call you Ernest, do you?"

The voice came very clear and gentle from that face that looked like some hill that had been fought over in muddy weather and then baked in the sun.

"Hell, no," I said. "Please. Listen, old-timer, you're going to be fine. You'll be a lot of good, you know. You can talk on the radio."

"Maybe," he said. "You'll be back?"

"Sure," I said. "Absolutely."

"Goodbye, Ernest," he said.

"Goodbye," I told him.

Downstairs they told me he'd lost both eyes as well as his face and was also badly wounded all through the legs and in the feet.

"He's lost some toes, too," the doctor said, "but he doesn't know that."

"I wonder if he'll ever know it."

"Oh, sure he will," the doctor said. "He's going to get well."

And it still isn't you that gets hit but it is your countryman now. Your countryman from Pennsylvania, where once we fought at Gettysburg.

Then, walking along the road, with his left arm in an airplane splint, walking with the gamecock walk of the professional British soldier that neither ten years of militant party work nor the projecting metal wings of the splint could destroy, I met Raven's commanding officer, Jock Cunningham, who had three fresh rifle wounds through his upper left arm (I looked at them, one was septic) and another rifle bullet under his shoulder blade that had entered his left chest, passed through, and lodged there. He told me, in military terms, the history of the attempt to rally retiring troops on his battalion's right flank, of his bombing raid down a trench which was held at one end by the fascists and at the other end by the government troops, of the taking of this trench and, with six men and a Lewis gun, cutting off a group of some eighty fascists from their own lines, and of the final desperate defense of their impossible position his six men put up until the government troops came up and, attacking, straightened out the line again. He told it clearly, completely convincingly, and with a strong Glasgow accent. He had deep, piercing eyes sheltered like an eagle's, and, hearing him talk, you could tell the sort of soldier he was. For what he had done he would have had a V.C. in the last war. In this war there are no decorations. Wounds are the only decorations and they do not award wound stripes.

"Raven was in the same show," he said. "I didn't know he'd been hit. Ay, he's a good mon. He got his after I got mine. The fascists we'd cut off were very good troops. They never fired a useless shot when we were in that bad spot. They waited in the dark there until they had us located and then opened with volley fire. That's how I got four in the same place."

We talked for a while and he told me many things. They were all important, but nothing was as important as what Jay Raven, the social worker from Pittsburgh with no military training, had told me was true. This is a strange new kind of war where you learn just as much as you are able to believe.

The Chauffeurs of Madrid

➤ *NANA Dispatch* · MAY 22, 1937

WE had a lot of different chauffeurs in Madrid. The first one was named Tomás, was four feet eleven inches high and looked like a particularly unattractive, very mature dwarf out of Velásquez put into a suit of blue dungarees. He had several front teeth missing and seethed with patriotic sentiments. He also loved Scotch whisky.

We drove up from Valencia with Tomás and, as we sighted Madrid rising like a great white fortress across the plain from Alcalá de Henares, Tomás said, through missing teeth, "Long live Madrid, the Capital of my Soul!"

"And of my heart," I said, having had a couple myself. It had been a long cold ride.

"Hurray!" shouted Tomás and abandoned the wheel temporarily in order to clap me on the back. We just missed a lorry full of troops and a staff car.

"I am a man of sentiment," said Tomás.

"Me, too," I said, "but hang on to that wheel."

"Of the noblest sentiment," said Tomás.

"No doubt of it, comrade," I said, "but just try to watch where you are driving."

"You can place all confidence in me," said Tomás.

But the next day we were stalled on a muddy road up near Brihuega by a tank, which had lurched around a little too far on a hairpin bend, and held up six other tanks behind it. Three rebel planes sighted the tanks and decided to bomb them. The bombs hit the wet hillside above us, lifting mud geysers in sudden, clustered, bumping shocks. Nothing hit us and the planes went on over their own lines. In the field glasses, standing by the car, I could see the little Fiat fighter planes that protected the bombers, very shining looking, hanging up in the sun. We thought some more bombers were coming and everybody got away from there as fast as possible. But no more came.

Next morning Tomás couldn't get the car to start. And every day when anything of that sort happened, from then on, no matter how well the car had run coming home at night, Tomás never could start her in the morning. The way he felt about the front became sort of pitiful, finally, along with his size, his patriotism, and his general inefficiency, and we sent him back to Valencia, with a note to the press department thanking them for Tomás, a man of the noblest sentiments and the finest intentions; but could they send us something just a little braver.

So they sent one with a note certifying him as the bravest chauffeur in the whole department. I don't know what his name was because I never saw him. Sid Franklin (the Brooklyn bullfighter), who bought us all our food, cooked breakfasts, typed articles, wangled petrol, wangled cars, wangled chauffeurs, and covered Madrid and all its gossip like a human dictaphone, evidently instructed this chauffeur very strongly. Sid put forty liters of petrol in the car, and petrol was the correspondents' main problem, being harder to obtain than Chanel's and Molyneux's perfumes or Bols gin, took the chauffeur's name and address, and told him to hold himself ready to roll whenever he was called. We were expecting an attack.

Until we called him he was free to do whatever he wanted. But he must leave word at all times where we could reach him. We did not want to use up the precious petrol riding around Madrid in the car. We all felt good now, because we had transport.

The chauffeur was to check in at the hotel the next night at seven-thirty to see if there were any new orders. He didn't come and we called up his rooming house. He had left that same morning for Valencia with the car and the forty liters of petrol. He is in jail in Valencia now. I hope he likes it.

Then we got David. David was an Anarchist boy from a little town near Toledo. He used language that was so utterly and inconceivably foul that half the time you could not believe what your ears were hearing. Being with David has changed my whole conception of profanity.

He was absolutely brave and he had only one real defect as a chauffeur. He couldn't drive a car. He was like a horse which has only two gaits; walking and running away. David could sneak along, in second speed, and hit practically no one in the streets, due to his clearing a swathe ahead of him with his vocabulary. He could also drive with the car wide open, hanging to the wheel, in a sort of fatalism that was, however, never tinged with despair.

We solved the problem by driving for David ourselves. He liked this and it gave him a chance to work with his vocabulary. His vocabulary was terrific.

He liked the war and he thought shelling was beautiful. "Look at that! Olé! That's the stuff to give the unmentionable, unspeakable, absolutely unutterables," he would say in delight. "Come on, let's get closer!" He was watching his first battle in the Casa del Campo and it was like a super-fireworks show to him. The spouting clouds of stone and plaster dust that pulsed up as the Government shells landed on a house the Moors held with machine guns and the great, tremendous, slither automatic rifles, machine guns and rapid fire combine into at the moment of the assault moved David very deeply. "Ayee! Ayee!" he said. "That's war. That's really war!"

He liked the tearing rush of the incomers just as much as the crack and the chu-chu-chu-ing air-parting rustle of sound that came from the battery which was firing over our heads on to the rebel positions.

"Olé," said David as a 75 burst a little way down the street. "Listen," I said. "Those are the bad ones. Those are the ones that kill us."

"That's of no importance," David said. "Listen to that unspeakable unmentionable noise."

Well, I went back to the hotel, finally, to write a dispatch and we sent David around to a place near the Plaza Mayor to get some petrol. I had almost finished the dispatch when in came David.

"Come and look at the car," he said. "It's full of blood. It's a terrible thing." He was pretty shaky. He had a dark face and his lips trembled.

"What was it?"

"A shell hit a line of women waiting to buy food. It killed seven. I took three to the hospital."

"Good boy."

"But you can't imagine it," he said. "It's terrible. I did not know there were such things."

"Listen, David," I said. "You're a brave boy. You must remember that. But all day you have been being brave about noises. What you see now is what those noises do. Now you must be brave about the noises knowing what they can do."

"Yes, man," he said. "But it is a terrible thing just the same to see."

David was brave, though. I don't think he ever thought it was quite as beautiful again as he did that first day; but he never shirked any of it. On the other hand he never learned to drive a car. But he was a good, if fairly useless, kid and I loved to hear his awful language. The only thing that developed in David was his vocabulary. He went off to the village where the motion picture outfit was making a film and, after having one more particularly useless chauffeur that there is no point in going into, we got Hipolito. Hipolito is the point of this story.

Hipolito was not much taller than Tomás, but he looked carved out of a granite block. He walked with a roll, putting his feet down flat at each stride; and he had an automatic pistol so big it came halfway down his leg. He always said "Salud" with a rising inflection as though it were something you said to hounds. Good hounds that knew their business. He knew motors, he could drive and if you told him to show up at six a.m., he was there at ten minutes before the hour.

He had fought at the taking of Montana barracks in the first days of the war and he had never been a member of any political party. He was a trade union man for the last twenty years in the Socialist Union, the U.G.T. He said, when I asked him what he believed in, that he believed in the Republic.

He was our chauffeur in Madrid and at the front during a nineteen-day bombardment of the capital that was almost too bad to write anything about. All the time he was as solid as the rock he looked to be cut from, as sound as a good bell and as regular and accurate as a railway man's watch. He made you realize why Franco never took Madrid when he had the chance.

Hipolito and the others like him would have fought from street to street, and house to house, as long as any one of them was left alive; and the last ones left would have burned the town. They are tough and they are efficient. They are the Spaniards that once conquered the Western World. They are not romantic like the Anarchists and they are not afraid to die. Only they never mention it. The Anarchists talk a little bit too much about it, the way the Italians do.

On the day we had over 300 shells come into Madrid so the main streets were a glass-strewn, brick-dust powdered, smoking shambles, Hipólito had the car parked in the lee of a building in a narrow street beside the hotel. It looked like a good safe place and after he had sat around the room while I was working until he was thoroughly bored, he said he'd go down and sit in the car. He hadn't been gone ten minutes when a six-inch shell hit the hotel just at the junction of the main floor and the sidewalk. It went deep in out of sight and didn't explode. If it had burst, there would not have been enough left of Hipolito and the car to take a picture of. They were about fifteen feet away from where the shell hit. I looked out of the window, saw he was all right, and then went downstairs.

"How are you?" I was fairly average breathless.

"Fine," he said.

"Put the car further down the street."

"Don't be foolish," he said. "Another one wouldn't drop there in a thousand years. Besides it didn't explode."

"Put it farther along the street.

"What's the matter with you?" he asked. "You getting windy?"

"You've got to be sensible."

"Go ahead and do your work," he said. "Don't worry about me."

The details of that day are a little confused because after nineteen days of heavy shelling some of the days get merged into others; but at one o'clock the shelling stopped and we decided to go to the Hotel Gran Via, about six blocks down, to get some lunch. I was going to walk by a very tortuous and extremely safe way I had worked out utilizing the angles of least danger, when Hipolito said, "Where are you going?"

"To eat."

"Get in the car."

"You're crazy."

"Come on, we'll drive down the Gran Via. It's stopped. They are eating their lunch too."

Four of us got into the car and drove down the Gran Via. It was solid with broken glass. There were great holes all down the sidewalks. Buildings were smashed and we had to walk around a heap of rubble and a smashed stone cornice to get into the hotel. There was not a living person on either side of the street, which had been, always, Madrid's Fifth Avenue and Broadway combined. There were many dead. We were the only motor car.

Hipolito put the car up a side street and we all ate together. We were still eating when Hipolito finished and went up to the car. There was some more shelling sounding, in the hotel basement, like muffled blasting, and when we finished the lunch of bean soup, paper thin sliced sausage and an orange, we went upstairs, the streets were full of smoke and clouds of dust. There was new smashed cement work all over the sidewalk. I looked around a corner for the car. There was rubble scattered all down

273

that street from a new shell that had hit just overhead. I saw the car. It was covered with dust and rubble.

"My God," I said, "they've got Hipolito."

He was lying with his head back in the driver's seat. I went up to him feeling very badly. I had got very fond of Hipolito.

Hipolito was asleep.

"I thought you were dead," I said. He woke and wiped a yawn on the back of his hand.

"Qué va, hombre," he said. "I am always accustomed to sleep after lunch if I have time."

"We are going to Chicote's Bar," I said.

"Have they got good coffee there?"

"Excellent."

"Come on," he said. "Let's go."

I tried to give him some money when I left Madrid.

"I don't want anything from you," he said.

"No," I said. "Take it. Go on. Buy something for the family."

"No," he said. "Listen, we had a good time, didn't we?"

You can bet on Franco, or Mussolini, or Hitler, if you want. But my money goes on Hipolito.

A Brush with Death

➤ *NANA Dispatch* · SEPTEMBER 30, 1937

MADRID.—They say you never hear the one that hits you. That's
true of bullets, because, if you hear them, they are already past.
But your correspondent heard the last shell that hit this hotel.
He heard it start from the battery, then come with a whistling
incoming roar like a subway train to crash against the cornice
and shower the room with broken glass and plaster. And while
the glass still tinkled down and you listened for the next one
to start, you realized that now finally you were back in Madrid.

Madrid is quiet now. Aragon is the active front. There's little
fighting around Madrid except mining, counter-mining, trench
raiding, trench mortar strafing and sniping, in a stalemate of
constant siege warfare going on in Carabanchel, Usera and
University City.

These cities are shelled very little. Some days there is no shelling and the weather is beautiful and the streets are crowded. The
shops are full of clothing, jewelry stores, camera shops, picture
dealers and antiquarians are all open and the bars are crowded.

Beer is scarce and whisky is almost unobtainable. Store windows are full of Spanish imitations of all cordials, whiskies and
vermouths. These are not recommended for internal use, although I am employing something called Milords Ecosses
Whisky on my face after shaving. It smarts a little, but I feel
very hygenic. I believe it would be possible to cure athlete's
foot with it, but one must be very careful not to spill it on one's
clothes because it eats wool.

The crowds are cheerful and the sandbag-fronted cinemas are
crowded every afternoon. The nearer one gets to the front, the

more cheerful and optimistic the people are. At the front itself, optimism reaches such a point that your correspondent, very much against his good judgment, was induced to go swimming in a small river forming a no-man's land on the Cuenca front the day before yesterday.

The river was a fast-flowing stream, very chilly and completely dominated by Fascist positions, which made me even chillier. I became so chilly at the idea of swimming in the river at all under the circumstances that, when I actually entered the water, it felt rather pleasant. But it felt even pleasanter when I got out of the water and behind a tree.

At that moment, a government officer who was a member of the optimistic swimming party shot a water snake with his pistol, hitting it on the third shot. This brought a reprimand from another not so completely optimistic officer member who asked what he wanted to do with that shooting—get machine guns turned on us?

We shot no more snakes that day, but I saw three trout in the stream which would weigh over four pounds apiece; heavy, solid, deep-sided ones that rolled up to take the grasshoppers I threw them, making swirls in the water as deep as though you had dropped a paving stone into the stream. All along the stream, where no road ever led until the war, you see trout; small ones in the shallows and the biggest kind in the pools and in the shadow of the bank. It's a river worth fighting for, but just a little cold for swimming.

At this moment, a shell has just alighted on a house up the street from the hotel where I am typing this. A little boy is crying in the street. A militiaman has picked him up and is comforting him. There was no one killed on our street, and the people who started to run slow down and grin nervously. The one who never started to run at all looks at the others in a very superior way, and the town we are living in now is called Madrid.

The Fall of Teruel

➤ *NANA Dispatch* · DECEMBER 23, 1937

TERUEL FRONT.—We lay on top of a ridge with a line of Spanish infantry under heavy machine gun and rifle fire. It was so heavy that if you had lifted your head out of the gravel you would have dug your chin into one of the little unseen things that made the stream of kissing, whisper sounds that flowed over you after the pop-pop-pop of the machine guns on the next ridge beyond would have lifted the top of your head off. You knew this because you had seen it happen.

On our left, an attack was starting. The men, bent double, their bayonets fixed, were advancing in the awkward first gallop that steadies into the heavy climb of an uphill assault. Two men were hit and left the line. One had the surprised look of a man first wounded who does not realize the thing can do this damage and not hurt. The others knew he had it very bad. All I wanted was a spade to make a little mound to get my head under. But there weren't any spades within crawling distance.

On our right was the great yellow mass of the Mansueto, the natural battleship-shaped fortress that defends Teruel. Behind us the Spanish government artillery were firing, and, after the crack, came the noise like tearing silk and then the sudden spouting black geysers of high explosive shells pounding at the earth-scarred fortifications of Mansueto.

We had come down through the pass on the Sagunto road to within nine kilometers of Teruel and had left our car. Then we walked along the road to kilometer six and there was the front line. We had stayed there a little while, but it was in a hollow and you couldn't see well. We climbed a ridge to see and were machine-gunned. Below us an officer was killed and they brought him back slowly, heavily and laid him gray-faced on a stretcher. When they bring the dead back on stretchers, the attack has not yet started.

The amount of fire we were drawing being incommensurate with the view, we broke for the ridge where the advanced positions of the center were. In a little while it was not a nice place to be either, although the view was splendid. The soldier I was lying next to was having trouble with his rifle. It jammed after every shot and I showed him how to knock the bolt open with a rock. Then suddenly we heard cheering run along the line and across the next ridge we could see the Fascists running from their first line.

They ran in the leaping, plunging gait that is not panic but a retreat, and to cover that retreat their further machine gun posts slithered our ridge with fire. I wished very strongly for the space, and then up the ridge we saw government troops advancing steadily. It went on like that all day and by nighttime we were six kilometers beyond where the first attack had started.

During the day we watched government troops scale the heights of Mansueto. We saw the armored cars go with troops to attack a fortified farmhouse a hundred yards from us, the cars lying alongside the house and whang, whang, whanging into the windows while the infantry ducked into it with hand grenades. We lay during this in the doubtful lee of a grass-stuffed hummock and the Fascists threw eighty-millimeter trench mortars behind us on the road and in the field, they coming with a sudden whushing drop and cracking burst. One landed in the wave of an attack and one man ran out of the seeming center of the smoke in a half-circle, first naturally, wildly back, then checked and went forward to catch up with the line. Another lay where the smoke was settling.

No smoke blew that day. After the Arctic cold, the blizzard and the gale that blew for five days, this was Indian summer weather and shell bursts flowered straight up and slowly sank. And all day long the troops attacked, held, attacked again. As

278

we had come along the road, the troops waiting in the ditch, mistaking us for high staff officers because there is nothing so distinguished as civilian clothes at the front, would shout, "Look at them up there on the hill. When do we attack? Tell us when we can go."

We sat behind trees, comfortable thick trees, and saw twigs clipped from their drooping lower branches. We watched the Fascist planes head for us and hunted shelter in a soil-eroded gulch only to watch them turn and circle to bomb the government lines near Concud. But all day long we moved forward with the steady merciless advance the government troops were making. Up the hillsides, across the railway, capturing the tunnel, all up and over the Mansueto, down the road around the bend from kilometer two and finally up the last slopes to the town, whose seven church steeples and neatly geometrical houses showed sharp against the setting sun.

The late evening sky had been full of government planes, the chasers seeming to turn and dart like swallows, and, while we watched their delicate precision through our glasses, hoping to see an air fight, two trucks came noising up and stopped, dropping their tailboards to discharge a company of kids who acted as though they were going to a football game. It was only when you saw their belts with sixteen bomb pouches and the two sacks each wore that you realized what they were, "dynamiters."

The captain said, "These are very good. You watch when they attack the town." So, in the short afterglow of the setting sun, with all around the town the flashing of the guns, yellower than trolley sparks but as sudden, we saw these kids deploy a hundred yards from us, and, covered by a curtain of machine gun and automatic rifle fire, slip quietly up the last slope to the town's edge. They hesitated a moment behind a wall, then came the red and black flash and roar of the bombs, and over the wall and into the town they went.

"How would it be to follow them into the town?" I asked the colonel. "Excellent," he said, "a marvelous project." We started down the road, but now it was getting dark. Two officers came up, checking on scattered units, and we told them we would stay with them because, in the dark, people might shoot hastily and the countersign had not yet arrived. In the pleasant autumn falling dusk, we walked the road downhill and into Teruel. It was a peaceful feeling night and all the noises seemed incongruous.

Then in the road was a dead officer who had led a company in the final assault. The company had gone on and this was the phase where the dead did not rate stretchers, so we lifted him, still limp and warm, to the side of the road and left him with his serious waxen face where tanks would not bother him now nor anything else and went on into town.

In town, the population all embraced us, gave us wine, asked us if we didn't know their brother, uncle or cousin in Barcelona, and it was all very fine. We had never received the surrender of a town before and we were the only civilians in the place. I wonder who they thought we were. Tom Delmer, London newspaper correspondent, looks like a bishop, Herbert L. Matthews, of the New York Times, like Savonarola, and I like, say, Wallace Beery three years back, so they must have thought the new regime would be, say, complicated.

But they said we were what they had been waiting for. They said they had stayed in the cellars and caves when the offer from the government came to evacuate because the Fascists would not let them leave. Also they said the government did not bomb the town, only military objectives. They said this, not me.

After reading in papers just received in Madrid from New York, still in the car, about General Franco giving the government five days to surrender before starting the final triumphal offensive, it seemed just a little incongruous that we should be walking into Teruel, that great rebel strongpoint from which they were to drive to the sea.

The Flight of Refugees

➤ *NANA Dispatch* · APRIL 3, 1938

BARCELONA.—It was a lovely false spring day when we started for the front this morning. Last night, coming in to Barcelona, it had been gray, foggy, dirty and sad, but today it was bright and warm, and pink almond blossoms colored the gray hills and brightened the dusty green rows of olive trees.

Then, outside of Reus, on a straight smooth highway with olive orchards on each side, the chauffeur from the rumble seat shouted, "Planes, planes!" and, rubber screeching, we stopped the car under a tree.

"They're right over us," the chauffeur said, and, as this correspondent dove head-forward into a ditch, he looked up sideways, watching a monoplane come down and wing over and then evidently decide a single car was not worth turning his eight machine guns loose on.

But, as we watched, came a sudden egg-dropping explosion of bombs, and, ahead, Reus, silhouetted against hills a half mile away, disappeared in a brick-dust-colored cloud of smoke. We made our way through the town, the main street blocked by broken houses and a smashed water main, and, stopping, tried to get a policeman to shoot a wounded horse, but the owner thought it was still possibly worth saving and we went on up toward the mountain pass that leads to the little Catalan city of Falset.

That was how the day started, but no one yet alive can say how it will end. For soon we began passing carts loaded with refugees. An old woman was driving one, crying and sobbing while she swung a whip. She was the only woman I saw crying all day. There were eight children following another cart and one little boy pushed on a wheel as they came up a difficult grade. Bedding, sewing machines, blankets, cooking utensils and mattresses wrapped in mats, sacks of grain for the horses and mules were piled in the carts and goats and sheep were tethered to the tailboards. There was no panic, they were just plodding along.

On a mule piled high with bedding rode a woman holding a still freshly red-faced baby that could not have been two days old. The mother's head swung steadily up and down with the motion of the beast she rode, and the baby's jet-black hair was drifted gray with the dust. A man led the mule forward, looking back over his shoulder and then looking forward at the road.

"When was the baby born?" I asked him, as our car swung alongside. "Yesterday," he said proudly, and the car was past. But all these people, no matter where else they looked as they walked or rode, all looked up to watch the sky.

Then we began to see soldiers straggling along. Some carried their rifles by the muzzles, some had no arms. At first there were only a few troops, then finally there was a steady stream, with whole units intact. Then there were troops in trucks, troops marching, trucks with guns, with tanks, with anti-tank guns and anti-aircraft guns, and always a line of people walking.

As we went on, the road choked and swelled with this migration, until, finally, it was not just the road, but streaming alongside the road by all the old paths for driving cattle came the civilian population and the troops. There was no panic at all, only a steady movement, and many of the people seemed cheerful. But perhaps it was the day. The day was so lovely that it seemed ridiculous that anyone should ever die.

Then we began seeing people that we knew, officers you had met before, soldiers from New York and Chicago who told how the enemy had broken through and taken Gandesa, that the Americans were fighting and holding the bridge at Mora across the Ebro River and that they were covering this retreat and holding the bridgehead across the river and still holding the town.

Suddenly, the stream of troops thinned and then there was a big influx again, and the road was so choked that the car could not move ahead. You could see them shelling Mora on the river and hear the pounding thud of the guns. Then there came a flock of sheep to clog the road, with shepherds trying to drive them out of the way of the trucks and tanks. Still the planes did not come.

Somewhere ahead, the bridge was still being held, but it was impossible to go any further with the car against that moving dust-swamped tide. So we turned the car back toward Tarragona and Barcelona and rode through it all again. The woman with the new-born baby had it wrapped in a shawl and held tight against her now. You could not see the dusty head because she held it tight under the shawl as she swung with the walking gait of the mule. Her husband led the mule, but he looked at the road now and did not answer when he waved. People still looked up at the sky as they retreated. But they were very weary now. The planes had not yet come, but there was still time for them and they were overdue.

Bombing of Tortosa

➤ *NANA Dispatch* · APRIL 15, 1938

TORTOSA, SPAIN.—Ahead of us, fifteen Heinkel light bombers, protected by Messerschmidt pursuit planes, swung 'round and 'round in a slow circle, like vultures waiting for an animal to die. Each time they passed over a certain point, there was the thud of bombs. As they swung over the bare hillside, keeping their steady formation, every third ship would dive, its guns spitting. They kept that up for forty-five minutes unmolested and what they were diving and bombing on was a company of infantry making a last stand on the hillside and bare ridge at noon on this hot spring day to defend the Barcelona-Valencia road.

Above us in the high cloudless sky, fleet after fleet of bombers roared over Tortosa. When they dropped the sudden thunder of their loads, the little city on the Ebro disappeared in a yellow mounting cloud of dust. The dust never settled, as more bombers came, and, finally, it hung like a yellow fog all down the Ebro valley. The big Savoia-Marchetti bombers shone white and silvery in the sun, and, as one group hammered over, another came.

Ahead of us all this time, the Heinkels were circling and diving with the mechanical monotony of movement of a quiet afternoon at a six-day bike race. And, under them, a company of men lay behind rocks in hastily dug fox holes and in simple folds of the ground, trying to hold up the advance of an army.

At midnight, the government communique admitted there was fighting around San Mateo and La Jana, which meant the last big defensive position, La Tancada, a steep rocky hill defending the road to the sea from Morella to Vinaroz, had been turned or taken.

At 4 o'clock in the morning, driving into a full moon that lighted the rocky Catalan hills, the jutting cypresses and weirdly chopped trunks of the plane trees, we headed for the front. By daylight, we passed the old Roman walls of Tarragona, and, by the time the sun was warming, we were meeting the first groups of refugees.

Later, we met troops who told of the break-through and that two columns were advancing on Vinaroz, a third on Ulldecona and a fourth from Lacenia toward La Galera in the direction of Santa Barbara, which is only thirteen kilometers from Tortosa. It was a four-fingered push toward the sea by General Aranda's column of Navarrese troops and Moors, and officers reported it had already taken Calig and San Jorge, the last two towns on the two roads from San Mateo toward the sea.

At 1 o'clock this afternoon, the road was still open, but all signs pointed toward its being cut or brought under artillery fire by tonight or as soon as Aranda's troops could bring up their guns. Meantime, from where this correspondent was talking in Ulldecona with a staff officer, his maps spread out on a stone wall, he could hear the firing of the machine guns.

The staff officer was talking coolly, carefully and with great politeness while Aranda's troops were advancing past San Rafael, with only one ridge left between them and us. He was a very brave and competent soldier and was ordering up his armored cars, but our car wasn't armored, so we decided to return past Santa Barbara. It was a nice little town, but it would have been better except that Tortosa was still spouting clouds of smoke as the bombers unloaded.

There were many reasons impelling us to get by Tortosa toward Barcelona, including life, liberty and the pursuit of happiness. So when the car arrived at Tortosa and a guard said the bombers had blown up the bridge and that we couldn't go through, it was something that we had worried about for so long and so many times it made almost no impression except a feeling that "now it has really happened."

"You can try the little bridge that they are fixing with some planks," the guard said.

The chauffeur jumped the car forward, threaded through a line of trucks, past bomb holes into which two trucks could drop out of sight in the still freshly scorched earth and the acrid high explosive smell, and on to the little bridge. Ahead was a mule cart.

"You can't go there," the guard shouted to the peasant leading the cart, heavily laden with grain, household goods, cooking pots, a jug of wine, and all the mule could haul with difficulty. But the mule had no reverse and the bridge was blocked. So your correspondent pushed on the wheels, the peasant hauled on the mule's head and the cart rolled slowly forward, followed by the car, the narrow ironshod cart-wheels smashing the too-light new crossroads that kids were nailing down in a rush to get the frail bridge ready for traffic.

The boys were working, hammering, nailing and sawing as fast and hard as a good crew on a vessel in distress at sea. And, on our right, one section of the great iron bridge across the Ebro had slumped down into the stream and another gaped missing. The mass bombing of forty-eight bombers, using bombs, judging from the holes they made and the way they flung houses into rubble across the road, which must have been between 300 and 450 pounds apiece, had got the Tortosa bridge at last. In the town, a gasoline truck was burning. Driving through the street was like mountaineering in the craters of the moon. The railroad bridge still stands and a pontoon bridge undoubtedly will be built, but it is a bad night for the west bank of the Ebro.

Tortosa Calmly Awaits Assault

➤ *NANA Dispatch* · APRIL 18, 1938

EBRO DELTA, SPAIN.—The irrigation ditch was full of this year's crop of frogs. As you splashed forward, they scattered, jumping wildly. A line of boys lay behind a railroad track, each having dug himself a little shelter in the gravel below the rails, and their bayonets pointed above the shiny rails that would be rusty soon. On all their faces was the look of men—boys become men in one afternoon—who are awaiting combat.

Across the river, the enemy had just taken the bridgehead and the last troops had swum across the river after the pontoon bridge was blown up. Shells were coming in now from the little town of Amposta, across the river, and registering aimlessly in the open country and along the road. You'd hear the double boom of the guns, then the whirling cloth-ripping incoming rush and dirt would fountain brownly up among the grapevines.

War had the pointless and dangerless dumbness that it has when guns first come into action, before there is proper observation and the shooting is accurately controlled, and your correspondent walked down along the railway track to find a place to watch what Franco's men were doing across the river.

Sometimes in war there is a deadliness which makes all walking upright within a certain range either foolishness or bravado. But there are other times, before things really start, when it's like the old days when you walked around in the bull ring just before the fight.

Up the Tortosa road, planes were diving and machine-gunning. German planes are absolutely methodical, though. They do their job, and, if you are a part of their job, you're out of luck. If you are not included in their job, you can go very close to them and watch them as you can watch lions feeding. If their orders are to strafe the road on their way home, you will get it. Otherwise, when they are finished with their job on their particular objective, they go off like bank clerks, flying home.

Up toward Tortosa, things looked quite deadly already from the way the planes were acting. But down here on the delta, the artillery were still only warming up like baseball pitchers lobbing them over in the bull pen. You crossed a stretch of road that in another day would be worth your life to sprint across, and headed for a white house that stood above a canal that paralleled the Ebro and dominated all the yellow town across the river where the Fascists were preparing their attack.

The doors were all locked and you couldn't get up to the roof, but from the hard-trod path along the canal you could watch men slipping down through the trees to the high green bank across the river. Government artillery was registering on the town, sending sudden spoutings of stone-dust from the houses and the church tower, where evidently there was an observation post. Still, there was no sensation of danger.

For three days you had been on the other side of the river while General Aranda's troops had been advancing and the feeling of danger, of suddenly running onto cavalry or tanks or armored cars, was something as valid as the dust you breathed or the rain that settled the dust finally and beat on your face in the open car. Now there was contact finally between the two armies and there would be a battle to hold the Ebro, but, after the uncertainty, the contact came as a relief.

Now, as you watched, you saw another man come slipping through the green trees on the other bank, and then three more. Then, suddenly, as they were out of sight, came the sharp, sudden, close clatter of machine guns. With that sound, all the walking around, all the dress-rehearsal quality of before the battle, was gone. The boys who had dug shelters for their heads behind the railway bank were right, and, from now on, theirs was the business. From where you stood, you could see them, well protected, waiting stolidly. Tomorrow it would be their turn. You watched the sharp slant of bayonets angling above the rails.

Artillery was picking up a little now. Two came in at a fairly useful place, and, as the smoke blew away ahead and settled through the trees, you picked an armful of spring onions from a field beside the trail that led to the main Tortosa road. They were the first onions of this spring and, peeling, one found they were plump and white and not too strong. The Ebro delta has a fine rich land, and, where the onions grow, tomorrow there will be a battle.

A Program for U.S. Realism

➤ *Ken* · AUGUST 11, 1938

QUESTION: What is War?

Answer: War is an act of violence intended to compel our opponent to fulfill our will.

Question: What is the primary aim of war?

Answer: The primary aim of war is to disarm the enemy.

Question: What are the necessary steps to achieve this?

Answer: First; the military power must be destroyed, that is, reduced to such a state that it will not be able to carry on the war. Second; the country must be conquered. For out of the country a new military force may be formed. Third; the will of the enemy must be subdued.

Question: Are there any ways of imposing our will on the enemy without fulfilling these three conditions?

Answer: Yes. There is invasion, that is the occupation of the enemy's territory, not with a view to keeping it, but in order to levy contributions on it, or to devastate it.

Question: Can a country which remains on the defensive hope to win a war?

Answer: Yes. This negative intention, which constitutes the principle of the pure defensive, is also the natural means of overcoming the enemy by the duration of the combat, that is of wearing him out. If then, the negative purpose, that is the concentration of all the means into a state of pure resistance, affords a superiority in the contest, and if this advantage is sufficient to balance whatever superiority in numbers the adversary may have, then the mere duration of the contest will suffice gradually to bring the loss of force on the part of the adversary to a point *at which the political object can no longer be an equivalent,* a point at which, therefore, he must give up the contest. We see then that this class of means, the wearing out of the enemy, includes the great number of cases in which the weaker resists the stronger.

Frederick the Great, during the Seven Years' War, was never strong enough to overthrow the Austrian monarchy. If he had tried to do so after the fashion of Charles the 12th, he would inevitably have had to succumb himself. But after his skillful application of the system of husbanding his resources had shown the powers allied against him, through a seven years' struggle, that the actual expenditure of strength far exceeded what they had at first anticipated, they made peace.

The answers are all by Clausewitz, who knew the answers very well. They make dry, hard reading, but there is so much nonsense written, thought and spoken about war that it is necessary to go back to the old Einstein of battles to see the military precedent by which the Spanish Republic continues to fight. If you study those two paragraphs by Clausewitz on the power of the defensive, you will see why there will be war in Spain for a long time.

There has been war in Spain, now, for two years. There has been war in China for a year. War is due in Europe by next summer at the latest.

It nearly came on May 21. It is possible that it will come now, in August. Or it may be delayed until next summer. But it is coming.

Now what is war again? We say war is murder, that it is inexcusable, that it is indefensible, that no objective can justify an offensive war. But what does Clausewitz say? He calls war "a continuation of state policy by other means."

Just when will this new war come? You may be sure that every detail of the starting of it is planned now. But just when is it coming?

"If two parties have armed themselves for strife, then a feeling of animosity must have moved them to it. As long now as they continue armed, that is, do not come to terms of peace, this feeling must exist. And it can only be brought to a standstill by either side by one single motive alone, which is, *that he waits for a more favorable moment for action.*

That is Clausewitz again.

"The Statesman, who, knowing his instrument to be ready, and seeing war inevitable, hesitates to strike first, is guilty of a crime against his country."

That is by Von Der Goltz. And that is something to read over.

There is a great demand now by Mr. Neville Chamberlain and the mouthpieces of his policy in our state department, that we should be realists.

Why not be realists? Not Chamberlain realists, who are merely the exponents of a stop-gap British policy which will be scrapped as soon as the British are armed, but American realists.

There is going to be war in Europe. What are we going to do about it as realists?

First, we want to stay out of it. We have nothing to gain in a European war except the temporary prosperity it will bring.

One way to stay out is to have nothing to do with it, not sell war materials to either side. And if you do that the British and the pro-British state department boys will be pulling you into it just the same; only it will not be for sordid ends, it will be on the highest and noblest humanitarian grounds. The other side will be working on us too; but the British are the most skillful and the most plausible.

The Germans have a genius for irritating people, for offending nations and for supplying pretexts. The Hohenzollerns were bad enough, but the Nazis will be worse, and where there was one *Lusitania* the last time you can figure on half a dozen this time. You can't expect the savages that bombed Guernica and the civilian population of Barcelona to resist a crack at the *Normandie* and the *Queen Mary*. So when war comes Americans will have to try American ships for a change. Or else make up their minds to fight for the French Line and for Cunard.

No. If you are going to be a realist you have to make up your mind beforehand whether you are going to go to war or not. There will be plenty of pretexts to get us in. And there is going to be a war.

So let us make up our minds to stay out. But why stay out and go broke? If we are realists why not sell to both sides, anything they want, anything we can manufacture? But sell it all for cash. Nothing should be sold for credit, so that we will be dragged in to help one side win so they can pay us what they owe us, and then go through the whole farce of war debts again.

There is going to be a war in Europe. Why not make something out of it if we are realists? But all sales should be for cash and the cash should be gold.

Then, to ensure our not being dragged in, nothing should be shipped to any belligerent country in American ships. Nor should any American ships carry war materials. Let the belligerent countries who can buy, send their own ships, pay cash for what they buy, and then, if their ships are sunk, it is their lookout. The more that are sunk the better.

At that point we sell them ships, also for cash; good, fast-built, cheap bottoms such as we turned out during the last war. All these we sell and build for cash. Cash down with the order; the ship the property of the country that buys it from the minute that the keels are laid.

Then when the Gestapo lads sabotage and burn ship-yards we do not go to war about that either. We are insured, see. The more sabotage the better. And if their liners are sunk too, we will build them some others too; for cash.

Let the gentlemen of Europe fight and, if they pay cash, see how long it will last. Why not be realists, Mr. Chamberlain? Why not be realists? Or don't you want to play?

Fresh Air on an Inside Story

➤ *Ken* · SEPTEMBER 22, 1938

I MET this citizen in the Florida Hotel in Madrid in the end
of April of last year. It was a late afternoon and he had arrived
from Valencia the evening before. He had spent the day in his
room writing an article. This man was tall, with watery eyes,
and strips of blond hair pasted carefully across a flat-topped
bald head.

"How does Madrid seem?" I asked him.

"There is a terror here," said this journalist. "There is evidence of it wherever you go. Thousands of bodies are being
found."

"When did you get here?" I asked him.

"Last night."

"Where did you see the bodies?"

"They are around everywhere," he said. "You see them in the
early morning."

"Were you out early this morning?"

"No."

"Did you see any bodies?"

"No," he said. "But I know they are there."

"What evidence of terror have you seen?"

"Oh, it's there," he said. "You can't deny it's there."

"What evidence have you seen yourself?"

"I haven't had time to see it myself but I know it is there."

"Listen," I said. "You get in here last night. You haven't even
been out in the town and you tell us who are living here and
working here that there is a terror."

294

"You can't deny there is a terror," said this expert. "Everywhere you see evidences of it."

"I thought you said you hadn't seen any evidences."

"They are everywhere," said the great man.

I then told him that there were half a dozen of us newspaper men who were living and working in Madrid whose business it was, if there was a terror, to discover it and report it. That I had friends in Seguridad that I had known from the old days and could trust, and that I knew that three people had been shot for espionage that month. I had been invited to witness an execution but had been away at the front and had waited four weeks for there to be another. That people had been shot during the early days of the rebellion by the so-called "uncontrollables" but that for months Madrid had been as safe and well policed and free from any terror as any capital in Europe. Any people shot or taken for rides were turned in at the morgue and he could check for himself as all journalists had done.

"Don't try to deny there is a terror," he said. "You know there is a terror."

Now he was a correspondent for a truly great newspaper and I had a lot of respect for it so I did not sock him. Besides if one should take a poke at a guy like that it would only furnish evidence that there was a terror. Also the meeting was in the room of an American woman journalist and I think, but cannot be positive on this, that he was wearing glasses.

The American woman journalist was leaving the country and, that same day, he gave her a sealed envelope to take out. You do not give people sealed envelopes to take out of a country in wartime, but this stout fellow assured the American girl the envelope contained only a carbon of an already censored dispatch of his from the Teruel front which he was mailing to his office as a duplicate in order to make sure of its safe arrival.

Next day the American girl mentioned that she was taking out this letter for him.

"It isn't sealed, is it?" I asked her.

"Yes."

"Better let me take it over to Censorship for you as I go by, then, so you won't get in any trouble over it."

"What trouble could I get into? It's only a carbon of a dispatch that's already censored."

"Did he show it to you?"

"No. But he told me."

"Never trust a man who slicks hair over a bald head," I said.

"The Nazis have a price of £20,000 on his head," she said. "He must be all right."

Well, at Censorship it turned out that the alleged carbon of a dispatch from Teruel was not a carbon of a dispatch but an article which stated, "There is a terror here in Madrid. Thousands of bodies are found, etc." It was a dandy. It made liars out of every honest correspondent in Madrid. And this guy had written it without stirring from his hotel the first day he arrived. The only ugly thing was that the girl to whom he had entrusted it could, under the rules of war, have been shot as a spy if it had been found among her papers when she was leaving the country. The dispatch was a lie and he had given it to a girl who trusted him to take out of the country.

That night at the Gran Via restaurant I told the story to a number of hard-working, non-political, straight-shooting correspondents who risked their lives daily working in Madrid and who had been denying there was a terror in Madrid ever since the government had taken control of the situation and stopped all terror.

They were pretty sore about this outsider who was going to come into Madrid, make liars out of all of them, and expose one of the most popular correspondents to an espionage charge for carrying out his faked dispatch.

"Let's go over and ask him if the Nazis really put a price of £20,000 on his head," someone said. "Somebody should denounce him for what he has done. He ought to be shot and if we knew where to send the head it could be shipped in dry ice."

"It wouldn't be a nice looking head but I'd be glad to carry it myself in a rucksack," I offered. "I haven't seen £20,000 since 1929."

"I'll ask him," said a well-known Chicago reporter.

He went over to the man's table, spoke to him very quietly and then came back.

We all kept looking at the man. He was white as the under half of an unsold flounder at 11 o'clock in the morning just before the fish market shuts.

"He says there isn't any reward for his head," said the Chicago reporter in his faintly rhythmical voice. "He says that was just something one of his editors made up."

So that is how one journalist escaped starting a one man terror in Madrid.

If a censorship does not permit a newspaper man to write the truth the correspondent can try to beat the censorship under penalty of expulsion if caught. Or he can go outside the country and write uncensored dispatches. But this citizen on a flying trip was going to let someone else take all his risk while he received credit as a fearless exposer. The remarkable story at that time was that there was no terror in Madrid. But that was too dull for him.

It would have interested his newspaper though because oddly enough it happened to be a newspaper that has been interested for a long time in the truth.

The Clark's Fork Valley, Wyoming

➤ *Vogue* · FEBRUARY, 1939

AT the end of summer, the big trout would be out in the centre of the stream; they were leaving the pools along the upper part of the river and dropping down to spend the winter in the deep water of the canyon. It was wonderful fly-fishing then in the first weeks of September. The native trout were sleek, shining, and heavy, and nearly all of them leaped when they took the fly. If you fished two flies, you would often have two big trout on and the need to handle them very delicately in that heavy current.

The nights were cold, and, if you woke in the night, you would hear the coyotes. But you did not want to get out on the stream too early in the day because the nights were so cold they chilled the water, and the sun had to be on the river until almost noon before the trout would start to feed.

You could ride in the morning, or sit in front of the cabin, lazy in the sun, and look across the valley where the hay was cut so the meadows were cropped brown and smooth to the line of quaking aspens along the river, now turning yellow in the fall. And on the hills rising beyond, the sage was silvery grey.

Up the river were the two peaks of Pilot and Index, where we would hunt mountain-sheep later in the month, and you sat in the sun and marvelled at the formal, clean-lined shape mountains can have at a distance, so that you remember them in the shapes they show from far away, and not as the broken rockslides you crossed, the jagged edges you pulled up by, and the narrow shelves you sweated along, afraid to look down, to round that peak that looked so smooth and geometrical. You climbed around it to come out on a clear space to look down to where an old ram and three young rams were feeding in the juniper bushes in a high, grassy pocket cupped against the broken rock of the peak.

The old ram was purple-grey, his rump was white, and when he raised his head you saw the great heavy curl of his horns. It was the white of his rump that had betrayed him to you in the green of the junipers when you had lain in the lee of a rock, out of the wind, three miles away, looking carefully at every yard of the high country through a pair of good Zeiss glasses.

Now as you sat in front of the cabin, you remembered that down-hill shot and the young rams standing, their heads turned, staring at him, waiting for him to get up. They could not see you on that high ledge, nor wind you, and the shot made no more impression on them than a boulder falling.

You remembered the year we had built a cabin at the head of Timber Creek, and the big grizzly that tore it open every time we were away. The snow came late that year, and this bear would not hibernate, but spent his autumn tearing open cabins and ruining a trap-line. But he was so smart you never saw him in the day. Then you remembered coming on the three grizzlies in the high country at the head of Crandall Creek. You heard a crash of timber and thought it was a cow elk bolting, and then there they were, in the broken shadow, running with an easy, lurching smoothness, the afternoon sun making their coats a soft, bristling silver.

You remembered elk bugling in the fall, the bull so close you could see his chest muscles swell as he lifted his head, and still not see his head in the thick timber; but hear that deep, high mounting whistle and the answer from across another valley. You thought of all the heads you had turned down and refused to shoot, and you were pleased about every one of them.

You remembered the children learning to ride; how they did with different horses; and how they loved the country. You remembered how this country had looked when you first came into it, and the year you had to stay four months after you had brought the first car ever to come in for the swamp roads to freeze solid enough to get the car out. You could remember all the hunting and all the fishing and the riding in the summer sun and the dust of the pack-train, the silent riding in the hills in the sharp cold of fall going up after the cattle on the high range, finding them wild as deer and as quiet, only bawling noisily when they were all herded together being forced along down into the lower country.

Then there was the winter; the trees bare now, the snow blowing so you could not see, the saddle wet, then frozen as you came down-hill, breaking a trail through the snow, trying to keep your legs moving, and the sharp, warming taste of whiskey when you hit the ranch and changed your clothes in front of the big open fireplace. It's a good country.

FOUR

➤ *World War II*

Hemingway Interviewed
by Ralph Ingersoll

➤ *PM* · JUNE 9, 1941

THIS interview with Ernest Hemingway was recorded in his hotel apartment a few days after he returned to New York from the Far East in 1941. Mr. Ingersoll, the editor of the now defunct newspaper *PM*, had commissioned Hemingway to go to the Far East to see for himself whether or not war with Japan was inevitable. This interview served as an introduction to Hemingway's series of articles. It was corrected and revised by Hemingway after having been transcribed and hence might be called an authenticated interview.

ERNEST Hemingway left for China in January. He had never been in the Orient before. He went to see for himself—how Chiang Kai-shek's war against Japan was going; how much truth there was to the reports that the Chinese position was menaced by threat of civil war; what would be the effect of the then imminent Russo-Japanese pact and—most important of all—what was our own position in the Orient. What was our position both as a leading anti-Fascist power and as a nation of 130,000,000 people with vital trade interests in other parts of the world—or were they vital?—and if they were vital, were they menaced?

Hemingway wanted to find out for himself, and for you and for me, what pattern of events might lead us into war with Japan—what alternate sequence of circumstances might possibly keep Japan in her place in the Pacific without us having to fight her.

Most people know Ernest Hemingway as America's No. 1 novelist. His reputation as a novelist is so great in fact that it overshadows two other reputations, either one of which gives him international recognition.

Long before he was a novelist, Ernest Hemingway was a noted war correspondent. He covered the fighting in the Mediterranean in the last war, the whole of the Spanish war—in which the present war was fought in miniature.

Of sufficient stature to be distinct from his reputation as a war correspondent is his reputation as a military expert. He is a student of war in its totality—everything about war, from machine gun emplacements to tactics and maneuvers to civilian morale and industrial organization for war. These things he has studied for 20 years.

So when Ernest Hemingway went to China he went as no casual visitor but as a student and an expert—he went with a reputation which made it possible for him to visit fronts that had not been visited by foreign journalists until now, and to talk with people who are running the war in the Orient on a unique basis.

When Ernest Hemingway went to the Orient, *PM* made this agreement with him: that if action broke out he was to remain there and cover the war by cable, but if no action broke out, he was to make notes as he went but not to write until he finished his study—until all the returns were in and he had time and the perspective to analyze everything he had seen and heard, and render a report of more lasting value than day-to-day correspondence.

This is the report that will be published here beginning tomorrow.

In the meantime, I have talked with Mr. Hemingway about his trip. Here is where he went and what he did and what he saw—the background from which his report is drawn:

Ernest Hemingway went to China with his wife, Martha Gellhorn. Mrs. Hemingway carried credentials as correspondent for *Collier's,* where her articles have already begun appearing. The two flew to Hong Kong by Pan American Clipper.

Hemingway stayed a month in Hong Kong, where he could

talk not only with the Chinese but with their opposition. The Japanese come in and out of Hong Kong quite freely—in fact, they celebrated the Emperor's birthday in their frock coats and with a formal toast. The British naval and military intelligence is there—and our own naval and military intelligence. The local Communist opposition is there and so are the Chinese pacifists who play Japan's game.

We asked Hemingway what it was like in Hong Kong. He said that danger had hung over the place so long it had become absolutely commonplace. People had completely adjusted themselves to the tension. He said that the city was very gay. The stabilizing element in any British colony are the British womenfolk, who keep life on a formal basis. But they had been evacuated and in general morale was high and morals low.

"There are at least 500 Chinese millionaires living in Hong Kong—too much war in the interior, too much terrorism in Shanghai to suit a millionaire. The presence of the 500 millionaires has brought about another concentration—of beautiful girls from all parts of China. The 500 millionaires own them all. The situation among the less beautiful girls is very bad because it is the British position that prostitution does not exist there, and therefore its control is no problem. This leaves about 50,000 prostitutes in Hong Kong. Their swarming over the streets at night is a war-time characteristic.

How many troops there are in Hong Kong is, of course, a military secret. Hemingway knows the exact number. That is the type of censorship *PM* does not try to beat. But Hemingway reports Hong Kong is "excellently defended.

"In case of attack Hong Kong's problem would be food. There are 1,500,000 people there now and they would have to be fed."

He continued: "Even more serious would be the sewage disposal problem—for in Hong Kong there are neither flush toilets nor drains. Sewage is disposed of by night soil coolies who collect and sell it to farmers. In case of a blackout sewage will be dumped in the streets and a cholera epidemic would be inevitable. This is known because two nights of practice blackout did produce a cholera epidemic.

"At present, however," Hemingway continued, "the food is plentiful and good, and there are some of the finest restaurants in the world in Hong Kong—both European and Chinese. There's also horse racing, cricket, rugby, association football."

After Hemingway had been in Hong Kong a month, he and Mrs. Hemingway flew to NamYung by Chinese air line. This flight took him over the Japanese lines. From NamYung, the Hemingways drove to Shaikwan, headquarters of the 7th War Zone.

The Chinese front is divided into eight war zones. Hemingway chose the 7th because he "wanted to make an intensive study of what a typical Chinese war zone was like, and the 7th has, ultimately, the greatest offensive potentiality."

Here he studied the complete organization of a Chinese war zone from headquarters through the army corps, divisions, brigades, regiments and down to the forward echelons.

The army Hemingway visited is a Kuomintang army. That is, it is part of the regular Chinese Army and not part of the Chinese Communist Army. The Chinese Communist armies have welcomed journalists and there has been much written about them. But this is the first time an American journalist has done extensive work at the front with the regular Chinese Army.

We asked Hemingway about this situation. He said:

"There are 300 divisions in the Chinese Army, 200 of which are first-class divisions and 100 secondary divisions. There are 10,000 regular troops in each division. Out of these 300 divisions three are Communist divisions. The area that the Communist divisions hold is an extremely important one and they have done marvelous fighting. But the 297 other divisions, occupying about the same amount of terrain per division, have not been visited at all before. Whereas the Communists have welcomed correspondents, there has been very strict censorship on the regular Chinese Army. Passes have been impossible to get, and correspondents have not been allowed into the forward echelons at all."

Hemingway said he went to see the regular Chinese Army because the Communist troops have already been excellently described by people like Edgar Snow, Agnes Smedley and others.

News of the Kuomintang army is important not simply because it has received no publicity but because the Kuomintang comprises the bulk of the troops on which we, in America, must depend to keep the Japanese divisions occupied in China while we are preparing to defend the Pacific.

Hemingway spent a month at the front, living with the troops, going everywhere with them. He traveled down the river by sampan first, then on horseback, and finally on foot. There were 12 days during a wet spell when he and Mrs. Hemingway never had dry clothes to put on.

They also discovered such delicacies as snake wine and bird wine. Hemingway described snake wine as "a special rice wine with a number of small snakes coiled up at the bottom of the bottle. The snakes are dead," he said. "They are there for medicinal purposes. Bird wine is also rice wine, but at the bottom of its bottle there are several dead cuckoos."

Hemingway liked the snake wine better. He says it cures falling hair and he is going to have some bottled for his friends.

After a month at the front, the Hemingways went back overland by sampan, car and train to Kweilin. This trip had not been planned, but everywhere they had gone for two months they had been told Kweilin was the most beautiful place in China. And they reported that it is the most beautiful place they saw. "There are thousands of miniature mountains there which look like a huge mountain range but are only 300 feet high. Many of the lovely imaginative scenes you see in Chinese prints and paintings, and think are made up out of an artist's imagination, are really almost photographic likenesses of Kweilin. There is also a famous cave there which is now used for an air raid shelter. It holds 30,000 people."

To get from there to Chungking they arranged to be picked

up by a freight plane which was carrying bank notes to the capital. The plane was a Douglas DC-3—the kind that flies on most of our air lines here—and all the other seats were occupied by shipments of bank notes.

All the air lines in China are owned by a company called the CNAC, or China National Aviation Corp. The Chinese Government owns 51 per cent and our own Pan American Airways owns 49 per cent and does the operating. Hemingway said:

"They used DC-2's and 3's and old Condor biplanes which can only fly on short hauls where the mountains are under 7000 feet high. There are passenger flights from Hong Kong to Chungking three times a week, for instance. But the idea of buying tickets on them is an academic one—for the waiting list is months long and only priority counts."

When it did not look as if the priority was coming through in time, Hemingway chartered a Vultee single-motored low-wing monoplane. But then the priority came through.

By the time the Hemingways got to Chungking they had learned a good deal about China. They spent some time with Chiang Kai-shek and in an all-afternoon interview, Mme. Chiang Kai-shek did the interpreting. But Hemingway reports that when the talk was on military subjects the Generalissimo understood military terms in English. He saw and got to know China's Minister of Finance, Dr. Kung, the Minister of Education, the Minister of Communications, the Minister of War, as well as various generals and the General Staff.

"Chungking," he reports, "had not been bombed seriously from August 25 until May 3—there is no bombing in Chungking during the winter because of low visibility."

He found the hotels in Chungking excellent—the food plentiful and the water hot. Everywhere he went in China, in fact, he found food sold without restrictions—even in the villages. At no time, he reports, did he see any of the signs you see when the war is being lost for lack of food. At no time did he see anything like the conditions he saw in Spain.

"But," he said, "the food in China is expensive. Moreover,

China is such a huge country that there are sections where the food situation gets bad locally—when due to a local drought a crop has failed. And communications are so bad that it is difficult to ship in food from other parts of the country. Such a condition prevails at present in South Shansi province and in other parts of the northern provinces. On the whole, the food situation this year is very good."

We asked Hemingway what people meant when they came back and said the economic situation in China was "very bad."

He said: "When people come into China from America and see signs of a monetary inflation there, they think everything is going to pot, whereas the situation is actually very good, considering China is in the fourth year of war. The inflation there is no worse than occurs in any other country that fights for four years. In the fourth year of the last war no European country was in better shape."

He felt that "China has to make some radical currency reforms—but principally to prevent the Japanese from buying up their money. The Japanese sell their own money short and buy Chinese money—now that America is backing China's money," he said. "I don't think this will be hard to control. My personal opinion is that eventually China will have to adjust its currency on a rice standard. Rice is the gold of China and only a currency based on a rice standard will prevent the kind of inflation in which people are not able to buy food."

The first time the Hemingways were in Chungking they stayed about eight days, constantly talking with people. Hemingway dined, lunched and breakfasted with Government people.

At the end of the eight days he flew up to Chengtu to visit the Chinese military academy—where Chiang Kai-shek trains his officers and cadets. And he inspected the flying schools and the new airdromes that are being constructed in this district. Here again, as a guest of the military academy, he had an opportunity to study the whole Chinese military system.

"The military academy," he said, "is in full swing. It was set up by the German General Alexander Von Faulkenhausen, and its professors are German-trained Chinese."

Hemingway flew back from the Chinese West Point to Chungking and then took another plane south over the Burma Road. He saw the trucks passing up and down the road.

We asked him whether reports that the Road was all banged up were true. He said: "Some of the bridges were out, but the Chinese have a very efficient ferry system to replace them. The Road is being bombed regularly—Kunming practically every day—but the bombing of bridges is not effective, partly because of the ferries and partly because they rebuild the bridges so quickly."

Hemingway said: "The control organization of the China section of the Burma Road is now in the charge of a committee which includes Dr. Harry Baker, formerly head of the American Red Cross in China. If Dr. Baker is not hamstrung by his fellow committee members he will be able to put through many traffic reforms."

From Lashio, which, you will see by the map, is far up on the Burma Road route, Hemingway went to Mandalay by car and then down to Rangoon by train. All along this route he studied the Burma Road problem, and gave us this picture of it:

"The first part of the problem is getting materials from the coast up to the beginning of the Road. Here there are two methods of transportation available. One is via the Burma railway, the other is via the river. So far most of the material has gone up over the railway which is Burmese owned and very jealous of river traffic. The river traffic is transported by an organization called the Irrawaddy Flotilla, which belongs to a Scottish-owned company.

"The Irrawaddy is navigable as far as Bhamo. You should look at the map here because Bhamo is becoming very important. At Bhamo a connecting road is being completed through to the Burma Road. You will see that not only does it cut off a good part of the Burma Road—and a difficult and mountainous part—but it permits goods to be transported up from the coast all the way by river. In effect this new route—from Rangoon to Bhamo by water and from Bhamo by short cut to well up on the Burma Road—constitutes a cut-off which is almost impossible for the Japanese to damage.

"The old route," he continued, "by rail from Lashio to Kunming, remains available, and shippers can also use the river up from Rangoon to Mandalay to Lashio.

"This makes two ways in.

"A third way," he went on, "is now being developed. This way uses first water and then rail to a place called Myitkyina—pronounced Michina—which, if you are interested in the Burma Road problem, you should locate for yourself on the map. Because you will see that by using Myitkyina as a railhead, a 200-mile air shuttle service from Myitkyina to Tali cuts off 509 miles of the Burma Road and leaves only 197 miles to travel to Kunming.

"This 197 miles—from Tali to Kunming—is downhill and there are no bridges and gorges which the Japanese can turn into bottlenecks by bombing. On a 200-mile hop the freight planes will not have to refuel in China at all.

"Thus," Hemingway explained, "the Chinese have what amounts to three alternate routes of supply from the south, not counting the constant bootlegging of supplies in from the whole China Coast."

Hemingway studied this traffic and says it is of enormous extent. He does not write about it in detail because he does not want to give information to the Japanese.

Now, remembering that the overland route into Russia is still open and that the Chinese are still getting supplies from Russia—as Hemingway explains in one of his articles—one realizes for the first time just what an enormous problem the Japanese have in interrupting Chinese communications.

"If the Japanese interruptions on the Road were as one, the interruptions due to inefficiency, graft and red tape would be as five. That is, take the whole route from Rangoon into Chungking—inefficiency, graft and red tape cause five times as much trouble as Japanese bombings. This is the problem which Dr. Baker has to solve."

We were startled by this figure and asked Hemingway to tell us more about it. He said:

"All projects in China move very quickly until money is involved. The Chinese have been doing business for many centuries and when things are a business matter to them they move very slowly. The Generalissimo can order something done— something in which money doesn't enter—and it is done practically, immediately. But the minute it becomes a financial thing it slows right up. No one person is responsible for this. It is the age-old Chinese custom of squeeze.

"There have been cases of truck drivers selling their gasoline, which they were hauling over the Burma Road, to private concerns. There have been cases of dumping whole loads to carry passengers. I saw with my own eyes tires being thrown off trucks loaded with them—evidently to be picked up by confederates later.

"There's no efficient policing of the Road. Of course every load should be checked as it goes in, and all the way through, and as it comes out. That is what Dr. Baker's Commission has to fix. After they opened the Road things ran wild for a while. Some people, operating transportation companies from outside of China, had no efficient control of their organizations on the Road. Now the Generalissimo realizes the importance of this. Something is being done about it."

Hemingway told us that the situation in Burma doesn't make things any better. He said: "Burma is a land of complete and utter red tape. Everything there is slowed up as much as it can be. If a military attaché comes to Rangoon to get a load of food to take back up to Kunming, it takes him two days in Rangoon just to clear through red tape. It is worse than France was before the fall. It is entirely administered by the Burmese, who combine the worst features of the Hindu Babu and the French pre-fall functionary. On the other hand, the British in Burma, not the Burmese, were efficient and uniformly helpful. Censorship was realistic and intelligent."

We asked Hemingway what it was like visiting romantic-sounding places like Mandalay and Rangoon. He said Rangoon was an English colonial city, "96 degrees at night and 103 degrees in the day, in the hot months when we were there. The flying fish were not playing. Kipling was talking about a place further down—Moulmein, below Rangoon, near the mouth of the river."

Hemingway went all the way down to Rangoon and stayed there for about a week. Then he flew back via Lashio and Kunming to Hong Kong and stayed there again for a week before leaving for America. Mrs. Hemingway continued on to Batavia and the Dutch East Indies while Hemingway worked between Clippers in Manila. She rejoined him on the next Clipper.

As this is being written Mr. Hemingway is completing his last piece for *PM*. We asked him a few final questions: What about the Chinese arsenals? If, by any mischance, the supply routes were cut, could they go on fighting?

He said: "I visited arsenals near Chungking and saw that they were manufacturing small arms and small arms ammunition, and were very self-sufficient. Moreover, much material can come right through Japanese lines. The guerrillas had been running trucks through the Japanese lines by completely dismantling them—into the smallest possible pieces—and carrying them by hand. An American motor company representative in Hong Kong was delivering trucks through the Japanese lines to Free China making a $450 service charge for delivery." Hemingway has more news of the latest developments in guerrilla fighting.

News from the Orient has been confusing and contradictory to most people. Russia supposedly offers the hand of friendship to Japan—and at the same time continues to ship supplies to China.

America gives China a $100,000,000 credit—and at the same time sells oil to China's enemy. What's it all about?

Hemingway told us. He traced for us the probable consequences of each move we were making, and each Japanese move.

He showed us how Russia was playing a devious hand in this

gigantic game of Chinese checkers which anybody might win.

Must America fight Japan? Hemingway told us why it's a matter of timing. As far as America is concerned, time itself is fighting on our side. As for Japan, time is running out on her —and no one, not even the Japanese, knows when the last strategic moment will have come. Or whether she should extricate herself from China at any price before challenging us. If Britain should fall it would be the signal for Japan aggressively to pursue her conquests in new directions. And this may well mean war with the U.S.A.

If England grows stronger and America is able to keep the fleet in the Pacific, war between the United States and Japan may never occur. And further, Hemingway tells us, we may thus beat Japan without ever firing a gun.

No one interview such as this, however—no one article—can give you the full impact, can piece together the complete pattern of this tremendously significant picture.

Russo-Japanese Pact

➤ *PM* · JUNE 10, 1941

HONG KONG.—On the day the Japanese-Soviet neutrality pact was signed in Moscow, Dr. H. H. Kung, who is both Prime Minister and Minister of Finance for his brother-in-law, Generalissimo Chiang Kai-shek, was dining with Soviet Ambassador Paniushkin in Chungking.

"We hear that a pact is going to be signed," the Chinese statesman said.

"Yes," the Soviet Ambassador answered. "That is true."

"What will be the effect of such a pact on Russian aid to China?"

"None," answered the Soviet Ambassador.

"Will you withdraw any troops from the Manchukuo frontier?"

"We will reinforce our divisions there," the Soviet Ambassador said, and the head of the Soviet military advisers in China, a Lieutenant General, nodded agreement.

At the time that incident happened I did not care to write it because diplomats rarely impart bad news over the dinner table and it was possible that very different news might come out of Moscow. But since then I have heard directly from both Dr. Kung and Mme. Chiang Kai-shek that Russian aid is continuing to arrive and that no Soviet staff officers, aviation instructors, or military advisers have been withdrawn from the Generalissimo's army.

My wife and I had lunched with Mme. Chiang Kai-shek the day the pact was announced and during the conversation she said, "But how will we know whether they will really withdraw aid or not?"

"If they are going to withdraw aid," I told her, remembering how it had happened in Spain, "the first move will be to withdraw the military advisers, the instructors and the staff officers. As long as they stay on, it means the aid will continue."

Last week a letter from Mme. Chiang Kai-shek contained these three paragraphs:

"I am fulfilling my promise to inform you of the Generalissimo's reaction to the neutrality pact between the USSR and Japan.

"The Generalissimo declares that this pact will not have the slightest effect on China's determination to continue national resistance. We began it single-handedly and if necessary, we shall end it the same way. What other nations, friendly or otherwise, may or may not do, will not influence. We will fight on until victory is won. Outer Mongolia and Manchuria are parts of China and the people of these regions themselves feel that they are indissolubly linked with the National Government, which recognizes no alienation of territory, and does not intend to, whatever happens.

"So far there is no indication that the USSR will withdraw its advisers from China, or will cease supplying us with war materials."

Soviet Russia has given China more aid than any other country has supplied. She has provided planes, pilots, trucks, some artillery, gasoline, military instructors and staff officers who act as military advisers. She has lent Chiang Kai-shek's government something over the equivalent of 200,000,000 U.S. dollars.

Most of this huge loan was attained on a barter basis and has been repaid in tea, wolfram (tungsten ore) and other products. The Russians drove a hard bargain when the barter terms were made and at present the Chinese have a difficult time buying the tea at prices agreed on with Russia. But they are still making deliveries.

Feeling between Chinese Communists and the Central Government is so bitter on both sides that I was amazed at first to find Soviet staff officers still serving in an advisory capacity with Chiang Kai-shek's armies and Soviet aid to China still coming in steadily. While I was at the front with Chinese Central Army troops I encountered Soviet staff officers and I saw new Russian planes which had come in; both bombardment and pursuit. In the officers' club where I lived at Chengtu in Northern Szechwan Province the room numbers on all the rooms were in Russian and various delicacies we had for breakfasts, including cocoa and tinned butter, had come by way of Vladivostok and Chita.

This Vladivostok route was using the Trans-Siberian Railroad to haul freight to Chita. From Chita to Urga, all transport was by truck and bus. From Urga to Ninghsia, camel caravans carried the freight to the Chinese roadhead where it was loaded onto trucks again for the haul to Chungking and Chengtu.

No visitors are allowed to see the Russian military advisers, instructors and pilot instructors, but I had run into three Russian staff officers out at the front on an impassable muddy road where all transport was stalled. So I greeted one of them whom I knew with, "How are you doing, Tovarich?" It was evidently decided after that encounter that there was very little point in concealing from me the Russians' presence and from then on the subject was always discussed very frankly. Consequently, I had a good chance to compare the Chinese field staff and general officers' opinions on the various foreign military advisers they had fought under.

Almost unanimously they ranked the Germans first as soldiers and staff officers and the Russians second. Their complaint against the Russians was that they rarely worked out any offensive action on a large or small scale in sufficient force.

To simplify the explanation to the utmost, using men in terms of money: if a position was purchasable for 50 cents, the Russians would try to take it for a dime. They would fail at that and finally have to pay $1.15 for it because there no longer was any element of surprise. On the other hand, if a position was worth 50 cents, the Germans would smack it with $1.50. After it was taken you would often find that only a quarter out of the $1.50 had been spent.

Chinese generals, if they are convinced that you know what you are talking about, are extraordinarily frank, straight talking, intelligent and articulate. I have spent some time on various British maneuvers. The atmosphere at the Chinese front with the men who had fought the war lords for five years, the Communists for 10 and the Japanese for nearly four was as different from that of a British staff as the locker room of the Green Bay Packers professional football team would be from even such a good prep school as Choate.

One Chinese general asked me what the British in Hong Kong thought of them. We were a couple of days riding together after the opening formal politenesses. We had drunk numerous cups of rice wine and worked late over the map.

"Does the General really want to know what they said?"

"Yes, truly."

"The General will not be offended?"

"Of course not."

" 'Well, we don't think very much of the Chinese, you know.' " I tried to reproduce it. " 'Johnny's all right and a very good fellow and all that. But he's absolutely hopeless on the offensive, you know. We have absolutely no confidence in him ever taking the offensive. Truly none. No. Too bad. We can't count on Johnny.' "

"Johnny?" asked the General.

"John Chinaman," I said.

"Very interesting," the General said. "Very interesting."

Then he went on, "We have no artillery to speak of, you know. No planes. Or very few. You know that, of course. Do you think the British would go on the offensive without artillery or aerial support anywhere? Any time?

"No," he interrupted me. "Let me tell you a Chinese story. A new Chinese story. Not an old Chinese story. Do you know why the British staff officer wears a single glass in his eye?"

"No," I said.

"Ho," he said. "It is a very new Chinese story. He wears a single glass in his eye so he will not see more than he can understand."

"I will tell that officer when I see him," I said.

"Very good," he said. "Tell him it is a little message from Johnny."

Rubber Supplies
in Dutch East Indies

➤ *PM* · JUNE 11, 1941

RANGOON.—One thing is as plain in the present Far Eastern situation as the rusty corrugated iron roof that bakes under the heavy metallic Burmese sun outside the hotel window as I write this. That is that an American traveling in the East studying the strategical, economic and political situation must distinguish between the pretexts for the war we are arming for out here and the basic causes of this possible war.

If we fight Japan the pretext for fighting will be that Japan has attacked the Philippines, or the Dutch East Indies or British Malaya.

But the real reason for fighting Japan will be that if she moves south in the Pacific she will be attacking the control of the world supply of rubber. Four-fifths of the world's rubber supply comes from the area Japan would be moving into and it would take at least seven years to build up rubber production anywhere else to replace the area Japan would control if she could take Singapore.

No American who drives a car, talks on a telephone, plays golf, or rides in a plane, or a train, or a bus can continue to do these things for long if our supply of rubber is cut off.

Another basic reason for opposing a southern move by Japan is that by going south Japan would gain control of necessities the U.S.A. needs to carry on industry and defend herself in war. Almost all the quinine in the world comes from Java in the Dutch East Indies. Quinine, in the area where U.S. military and naval forces will have to operate to defend the Western Hemisphere from Nazi aggression in the event of a Nazi victory over England, is as important as ammunition.

Tin, tungsten for machine tools, antimony for babbitt metal, tung oil with its myriad uses, manila hemp for rope for the Navy and merchant marine, chromium and manganese, necessities for rearmament, all of these are strategic materials necessary for the U.S.A. to conduct a war with, which Japan would control if she moved south successfully.

If the U.S.A. fights Japan it will be to keep her from depriving us of those necessities. But the principal reason it would be necessary to oppose her would be to keep our supply of rubber. Deprived of rubber the U.S.A. could never build or maintain the mechanized army that it is the first necessity to construct for national defense.

Military strategy is inseparable from economic strategy and since it is to Germany's interest that America and England both be deprived of the necessities they get from the South China Sea area, Germany has steadily urged and pushed Japan toward that area. Germany also wishes to divert every possible American and British naval unit from the Atlantic to the Pacific to oppose Japan while Germany makes her effort against England. Germany wishes to keep the bulk of the U.S. Fleet in the Pacific and to contain as many Empire divisions, ships and planes, in the Pacific area as she can. The Japanese threat against Singapore, periodically emphasized, accomplishes this.

But Japan has to move south, whether Germany wants her to or not, for another reason. Japan has not enough iron to manufacture armament and munitions. She has not enough oil to refine gasoline for her planes or to fuel her battleships. At this moment Japan is dependent on the U.S.A., Great Britain and the Dutch East Indies for the gasoline and oil that is vital for her to make war, and a great part of her iron ore comes from the Philippines.

Japan has built up a reserve supply of gasoline and oil to last her air force and Navy for one year of war. If the U.S.A. and Great Britain shut off her gasoline and oil she would be forced to move south toward oil at once or else begin exhausting her war reserve.

Naturally, she would not move the day the gasoline and oil

supply was cut off. It takes time to organize such a move. But she would have to start putting that movement into action and consuming her reserve the minute her gasoline and oil supply was cut off.

The U.S.A. and Great Britain, therefore, have a great strategical advantage over Japan. They can force her to move toward oil whenever they want. They can also, by continuing to supply Japan with gasoline and oil in progressively decreasing amounts, because of their own necessities for conserving this fuel for national defense requirements, force a decrease in the Japanese reserve of war fuel without precipitating action on Japan's part.

Japan Must Conquer China

➤ *PM* · JUNE 13, 1941

RANGOON.—The U.S.A. and Great Britain, if they are to protect their rubber, tungsten, tin, and other war essentials, must first decide at what point they will oppose Japan's southern move.

Already Japan has moved bodily into Indo-China and penetrated politically into Thailand on her way to Singapore. But there is no oil in those countries.

The first oil that Japan can reach by sea, without attacking the main British and Dutch defenses in Singapore, Sumatra and Java, is in Borneo. It is likely that she will try everything short of war to get this oil at Tarakan and Balikpapan from the Dutch. No one knows yet what she will offer. But when Japan goes south for oil is the moment the U.S.A. and Great Britain will have to oppose her if they are to avoid another Munich where Germany was given everything in Czechoslovakia she needed to overrun the Low Countries and France.

Japan without iron and oil—her only oil supply of her own is from Sakhalin Island which she shares with Russia—is as vulnerable, economically, as Italy. Deprived of oil she cannot fight longer than a year. But if she reaches oil in Borneo and controls the iron of the Philippines she will be reinforced to a much greater degree than Germany was by the gift of Czechoslovakia.

The longer the U.S.A. is allowed to rearm, to fortify Dutch Harbor in Alaska, to fortify Midway, Wake and Guam Islands to provide air bases for the great bombers that will then be able to fly the Clipper routes to objectives in the Pacific, the more does Japan's southern move become increasingly perilous.

Last year it was perfectly possible for Japan to move to oil and to control of the world's rubber supply. Last year was when Japan had her great chance to become a world power by attacking Malaya before its defenses were organized. This year, with the Empire and Dutch defenses organized, it would be gravely dangerous for Japan to try to go south. In another two years when our own preparations are completed Japan can be absolutely destroyed if she tries it.

Japan could not move southward when it was easy, because out of the 52 divisions of her Army 37 were engaged in China, nine were in Manchuria and Korea, and only six available in Japan, Formosa, Hainan Island, and Hanoi in French Indo-China.

Japan had her opportunity to move south against the unprepared British and Dutch, but her good troops were tied up in her invasion of China and her very best troops were facing the Russians in Manchuria.

Now Japan has made a neutrality pact with Soviet Russia which presumably should free her divisions in Manchuria for a southern move. But does it?

It is to the interest of Russia to see Japan move south and get smacked. Soviet Russia knows, though, that the longer Japan puts off that move the more certain she is to get smacked. . . . It does not look as though she would send Japan south now in a hurry.

The only way for Japan to move south now is to conquer China, make a peace with China or have a true working agreement with Russia. Without one of these Japan must wait and prepare in order to be able to take advantage of the confused situation that might arise if Germany ever successfully invaded England.

Japan is making definite preparations for a southern move. Which of the things that are necessary for her to move south does she count on? Can she count on any of them?

U.S. Aid to China

➤ *PM* · JUNE 15, 1941

RANGOON.—There are two things you can count on in the present Far East setup. By the present I mean as of this spring and early summer with England holding out.

First: Japan has temporarily lost her chance of making a peace with China. Last year there was a big peace drive on in Chungking. It reached its high point in December. But the aid China believes she will receive from America has put off the pro-peace movement temporarily.

Second: The U.S.A. can count on holding 37 of the 52 divisions of the Japanese Army in China for six to 10 months for a little less than the price of a battleship. That is to say that for $70,000,000 to $100,000,000 the Chinese Army will keep that many Japanese troops tied up.

At the end of six to 10 months, if past performances mean anything, the U.S.A. will have to provide about the price of another battleship to keep the Japanese tied up in China for another equal period. In the meantime the U.S.A. is arming. Insurance against having to fight in the Far East until the U.S.A. has built a two-ocean navy that can destroy any Eastern enemy, and thus probably never have to fight, is cheap at that price. Always remember that a powerful enough navy imposes its will without having to fight.

Meantime, the pro-peace groups in Chungking will undoubtedly bring all the pressure they can bear on Generalissimo Chiang Kai-shek to have him attempt to disband all Chinese Communist troops. The mechanics of this would be to order the 8th Route Army troops disbanded for failure to obey military orders. If they refused to be disbanded, as they undoubtedly would, they would be attacked. Since these tactics were successful against the other Communist army, the new Fourth Army, there is every chance the Generalissimo will be urged to repeat them.

Since the U.S.A. is interested in having all political factions in China united to fight against Japan we can counteract this move by the pro-peace groups by informing the Generalissimo that the U.S. is not interested in backing a civil war in China. Grave friction between the Communist troops and the Central Government has been present for close to two years, and for a year and a half the popular front has been little more than a fiction maintained for foreign consumption.

Since the Central Government receives its principal financial backing from two powers, the U.S.A. and Soviet Russia, if those two powers both say they will not finance a civil war there will be none.

The Generalissimo wants to beat the Japanese. No one has to advise him or urge him on that score. As long as he is alive and as long as he sees any human possibility of continuing the war there will be no peace. He can continue the war as long as he is adequately financed and communications are kept open so that supplies can be brought in.

There may be lack of food, there may be riots against the high cost of living due to the rise in prices under the effects of the natural inflation consequent on nearly four years of war. There will be innumerable stories of crookedness and graft in high places and there will be many proved stories of inefficiency. But the Generalissimo will continue to fight the Japanese under any difficulties that come up as long as he is financed and the war materials that he needs can reach him.

Anyone who tries to foment civil war in China or to spread scandal saying aid to China will only be misused plays Japan's game.

At present Germany can give China nothing. She has not the

money to finance her and she cannot send her supplies. But she promises the Chinese the moon after the war.

The Generalissimo's army was trained by the Germans. Germany was a good friend to China and the Germans are liked and admired in China. If the U.S.A. finances and helps China the Generalissimo will fight on against the Japanese indefinitely. If U.S. aid should ever be relaxed or withdrawn, the temptation for the Generalissimo would be to make a temporary peace with Japan and rely on German aid to resume the fight when Germany would be in a position to give that aid.

The Generalissimo is a military leader who goes through the motions of being a statesman. This is important. Hitler is a statesman who employs military force. Mussolini is a statesman who is unable to employ military force. The Generalissimo's objectives are always military. For 10 years his objective was to destroy the Communists. He was kidnaped under Communist auspices and agreed to give up fighting the Communists and fight the Japanese. Since then his objective has been to defeat Japan. He has never given this up. I think that somewhere inside of him he has never given up the other objective either.

When you say a man is a military man and not a statesman there are all of his speeches to prove that you are wrong. But by now we know that statesmen's speeches are often not written by the statesmen.

There is much argument whether China is or is not a democracy. No country which is at war remains a democracy for long. War always brings on a temporary dictatorship. The fact that there are any vestiges of democracy in China after the length of time she has been at war proves that she is a country that we can admire very much.

The trouble between the Chinese Communists and the Central Government will be settled only when the Central Government and the Soviet Union agree on the exact boundaries and sphere of influence of what will then be Soviet China. In the meantime, the Chinese Communists will try to get as much territory as they can and the Central Government will always nurse the hope of never having to face the fact that a part of China will be Soviet. The Soviet Government backs the Generalissimo with money, planes, armament and military advisers. It backs him to fight Japan.

The Chinese Communists are more or less on their own. Russia has two horses running in China against the Japanese. Her main entry is the Generalissimo. But the Russians know that it is never a disadvantage to have two good horses in the race. At present Russia figures to win against the Japanese with the Generalissimo. She figures to place with the Chinese Communists. After this race is run it will be another and a very different race.

Japan's Position in China

➤ *PM* · JUNE 16, 1941

RANGOON.—Japan has temporarily lost her chance of making peace with China.

The second thing you can truly count on in the Far East is that Japan can never conquer China.

The simplest way to explain the present military stalemate is to point out that Japan has conquered all the flat country, where her superiority in planes, artillery and mechanized formations has given her a tremendous advantage, and she must now fight the Chinese in mountain country, much of it roadless, where the Chinese meet the Japanese on more equal terms.

The Chinese have an enormous army of 200 first-line divisions (over 2,000,000 men) who are exceedingly well armed for the type of war they are fighting now. They also have another million men in not so good divisions; they have three Communist divisions and, probably, 500,000 Communist irregulars who are trained in guerrilla warfare.

China has ample supplies of rifles, plenty of ammunition, excellent heavy and light machine guns and automatic rifles and ample supplies of ammunition manufactured in Chinese arsenals for all of these arms. Each Chinese battalion has a mortar company of six 81-millimeter mortars which are extremely accurate at 2000 yards and have an extreme range of 3000. This is not hearsay. I saw them used many times at the front and they were excellent weapons used with great skill.

This 81-millimeter mortar is the French Brandt. The Chinese can drop a shell with it on a set of diapers at 2000 yards, and in the mountains it makes up enormously for their lack of artillery. They are also building a mortar of their own of 82 millimeters copied almost exactly from the Brandt. It is practically as accurate but a couple of hundred yards shorter in its extreme range.

In the regular divisions the discipline is of the extreme Prussian model. The death penalty starts with stealing, interfering with the people, insubordination and goes on through all the usual army crimes. They also have a few innovations, such as an entire section being shot if the section leaders advance and the section cannot get its legs moving, and other advancements in the art of making a soldier know that death is certain from behind but only possible from in front.

If we take the German idea of an army as an ideal, the best Central Government troops are very close to it. They know the trade of soldiering, they travel fast, they eat little compared with European troops, they are not afraid of death, and they have the best of the inhuman qualities that make a man a good soldier.

The Chinese medical service is fairly lamentable. One of the greatest difficulties is caused by the doctors' dislike of being near the fighting. Their position is that it takes a long time and much money to produce a doctor and then it is unjust and unreasonable to expect such an expensive and rare product to be exposed to possible extermination by enemy projectiles. As a result, often by the time the Chinese wounded see a doctor it would have been kinder to have shot them where they fell. Dr. Robert Lim has done much to change this conception of the doctor's role in the war. But the Chinese medical service is still far from perfect.

The troops of the Central Government have had no publicity. The Communists have welcomed good writers and have been well written up. Three million other men have died to oppose Japan without adequate press cuttings.

Anyone who says that the troops of the Central Government armies are not a magnificently disciplined, well trained, well officered and excellently armed defensive force has never seen them at the front.

There are many things needed before they can go on the offensive on any large scale. They also face certain grave problems. But you can bet that no matter what you may hear, if the Central Government has money to pay, feed and continue to arm them they are not going to be defeated by the Japanese this year, next year, or the year after. Nor, if you want my absolute opinion, having seen the terrain, the problems involved and the troops who will do the fighting, will the Japanese ever defeat the Chinese Army unless they are sold out. So long as the U.S.A. is putting up the money to pay and arm them and the Generalissimo is in command, they will not be sold out. But if we ceased to back them or if anything ever happened to the Generalissimo, they would be sold out very quickly.

The main drawbacks to the Chinese Army's going on the offensive is its lack of a competent air force and its lack of artillery.

China's Air Needs

➤ *PM* · JUNE 17, 1941

RANGOON.—There is much difference of opinion about the Chinese air force. I have seen them fly, visited their training schools and talked with the Americans and Russians who have taught them. Some say they are fine. Some say they are terrible. No people on earth, except the Spaniards, are more conceited than the Chinese and conceit is a hard thing for a pilot. It keeps him from progressing.

Lately kids from the people are being trained as pilots instead of the gentry having a monopoly. The course of training is not adequate and there are no planes for them when they are graduated so nothing is really proved. But they are not as conceited as the type of airman who wishes to establish the fact that he is a superior being by flying and, once he can fly, wishes to go no further.

Recently the Japanese came up to one of the Chinese air fields in northern Szechwan Province with two seater long range fighters. Sixteen Chinese pursuit pilots flying the Russian E 15-3, a Russian conversion of our old Boeing P12 with a new gull wing and retractable landing gear, took off to meet them. A few days before these same Chinese pilots had impressed President Roosevelt's representative, Dr. Lauchlin Currie, with their formation flying. But when the heat was on it was a different story and the Japanese shot down 16 of 16 that went up. They broke formation and scattered and the Japanese, keeping their formation, just went around methodically accounting for the singles after the covey had been flushed.

Any real American aid to the Chinese in the air would have

to include pilots. Sending them planes keeps them happy and keeps them fighting. It will not put them in condition to take the offensive successfully.

China can resist indefinitely with the equipment it has if it is financed and the Generalissimo sees an ultimate chance of victory through Japan being involved in war with Great Britain and the U.S.A. China cannot face the Japanese in any offensive action.

There are about 4000 supposedly competent Chinese artillery officers. Most of them are holding staff commands because of the lack of guns. Many of them are German-trained and very good. Others are of doubtful ability. There are at least two Chinese offensive projects which could be undertaken successfully if they were supplied with artillery.

There is an excellent chance that Japan will not try to move south this year at all, but will try to defeat China by two great final drives. Having lost its chance to make peace with China it may realize it can never move south successfully with the bulk of its forces held in China, which cannot be crushed economically as long as it is receiving periodic financial injections from the U.S.A.

Japan's problem is to cut the main roads into China by which aid comes in from the U.S.A. and Russia. If it does not attempt a move to the south it will undoubtedly try to drive north toward Siam to cut the communications between Russia and China.

Japan's other drive must be from Laokai on the French Indo-China frontier, or somewhat east of there, north again to Kunming to cut the Burma Road. Cutting these two roads would sever the main lifelines into China from the two countries that are helping it most. They are the two moves to be expected this summer in case Japan does not move to the south. Both of them are exceedingly difficult and the Chinese have an adequate mobile reserve to oppose them.

At this moment it looks as though Japan would not move south unless there was a German move to invade England. It does not look as though a German attack on Suez would provide sufficient confusion for her to move. It looks as though Japan will not risk war with England and America until she sees a possibility of England and the U.S.A. being so occupied that they cannot oppose her adequately.

Chinese Build Air Field

➤ *PM* · JUNE 18, 1941

MANILA.—Nelson Johnson, the last U.S. Ambassador to Chungking, who lived in China so long that he talked like an elder Chinese statesman and who never took a view shorter than 3000 years, told me as we stood looking out from the new spring green of the U.S. Embassy terrace across the fast running Yangtze River to the rising bulk of the terraced, gray, bomb-spattered, fire-gutted, grim stone island that is China's war-time capital:

"China can do anything that China wants to do."

At the time this remark irritated me profoundly. Unlike Mr. Johnson, I had never seen the Great Wall and I suppose I could not think of it as something that had been built just a few days or years before. I was thinking in immediate terms: how much money it would cost to tie up how many Japanese divisions in China; what were the offensive possibilities for the Chinese Army; could friction between the Communists and the Kuomintang be reduced so they found again a common basis for fighting against Japan; how many planes were needed before China could take the offensive and who would fly them; how many pieces of artillery were absolutely necessary and how were they to be got in; and how many gunner officers were fit to handle them when and if they were got in; and about several other things.

When Mr. Johnson brought that remark up out of the depth of his learning I was moderately appalled. It did not seem to help much on the immediate solution of many grave problems. Two days later I flew up to Chengtu in north Szechwan Province where the caravans come down from Tibet and you walk past yellow and red lamas in the dust-deep streets of the old high-walled city; the dust blowing gray in clouds with the cold wind down from the snowy mountains and you have to wear a handkerchief over your face and step into a silver-beater's shop as the caravans pass. Up there in the north I found out what Mr. Johnson meant, and I saw something that made me know what it would have been like to have ridden some early morning up from the south out of the desert and seen the great camp and the work that went on when men were building on the pyramids.

It started with the Generalissimo talking about Flying Fortresses. With some of those big four-motor Boeings the Chinese could fly over Japan at an altitude where neither Japanese anti-aircraft nor pursuit could bother them and bring to Japan the horror that she had spread through China in the past four years. There were no Chinese who were qualified to be checked out on a Flying Fortress as pilots, but none of those present brought that up. That was a thing which could presumably be arranged later. Someone did point out, though, that there was not a single airfield in China which could handle a Boeing B17.

At this point in the conversation the Generalissimo made a note.

"What do they weigh?" he asked.

"Around 22 tons," someone told him with more or less accuracy.

"Not over that?" asked the Generalissimo.

"No. But I will check."

The next day the construction of the airfield began.

Chen Loh-kwan, 38-year-old engineering graduate of the University of Illinois and chief of the Engineering Department of the Aeronautical Commission, was ordered to complete an airfield ready to receive Flying Fortresses on March 30. There was an "or else" added to the order, but Chen Loh-kwan has built so many airfields in a hurry for the Generalissimo that if they ever "or elsed" him it would be probably much the simplest solution to the hundreds of thousands of problems he has solved and has to go on solving. He never worries about "or elses."

He had from January 8 to March 30 to build an airfield with a runway a mile and an eighth long by a little over 150 yards wide with a stone-filling and top dressing macadam runway five feet deep to support the giant bombers when they land or take off.

Chen Loh-kwan's task was to level a 1000-acre field without tools; first removing 1,050,000 cubic meters of earth by hand and transporting it in baskets an average distance of half a mile. He built his runway with a yard deep layer of stone, then a layer of watered earth, then another layer of stone. This stone was all hauled in baskets from the bed of a river which flowed along from half a mile to a mile away. This runway foundation was surfaced with three layers. One was a layer of boulders set in lime mortar. Above this was a layer of lime concrete. On top of it all, in a billiard-table-rolled-smooth surface, was an inch and a half of broken stone clay bound covered with one inch of coarse sand.

There is blind drainage all around the edge of the runway which will support, when I saw it, five tons of load per square foot and will handle bombers as big as the new B19.

Chen Loh-kwan built—that is he built moulds for rollers and poured them—150 three-and-a-half- to ten-ton concrete rollers to smooth off this job. They were all pulled by manpower. One of the finest things I ever saw was that manpower pulling.

He brought in water in two ditches from ten miles away to parallel the runway during the construction to save hauling water. The workers mixed all the concrete by puddling it with their feet.

Sixty thousand workers at one time were hauling the 220,000 cubic meters of gravel from eight miles along the river. Thirty-five thousand more workers were crushing stone with hand hammers. There were 5000 wheelbarrows in use at a time and 200,000 baskets slung on carrying sticks. Every carrying stick was bent to breaking point under a double load as the men worked 12-hour shifts.

The Governor of Szechwan Province provided Chen Loh-kwan with 100,000 workers. They came in bands of 800 from the 10 different counties of the province. Some had to march 15 days from their homes. They were paid on the basis that a man can cut up to a meter and a quarter of earth a day. This was adjudged to be worth 40 ounces of rice. The man working received three-fifths of this in rice and the balance in cash. It worked out to about $2.30 a day Chinese, or $1 a day Chinese and rice.

The first I saw of the workers was a cloud of dust coming down the road with a ragged, torn-clothed, horny-footed, pock-faced army marching in the blowing dust singing as they plodded with their torn flags snapping in the wind.

We passed another band that jammed a village as they sang, boasted, and bought food for the night and then we came up on a rise and saw the field.

Looking across the great, stretching earth-leveled expanse, it looked at first like some ancient battlefield with the banners waving and the clouds of dust rolling where 80,000 men were toiling. Then you could make out the long cement-whitening mile-and-an-eighth runway and the 100-man teams that were rolling it smooth as they dragged the 10-ton rollers back and forth.

Through all the dust, the clicking of breaking rock and the hammering, there was a steady undertone of singing as of surf breaking on a great barrier reef.

"What is that song?" I asked.

"It is only what they sing," the engineer told me. "It is a song they sing that makes them happy."

"What does it say?"

"It says that they work all day and all night to do this. They work all day and all night. The rock is big. They make it small. The earth was soft. They make it hard."

"Go on," I said.

"The field was uneven and they make it smooth. They make the runway smooth as metal and the rollers are light to their shoulders. The roller has no weight because all men pull it together."

338

"What do they sing now?"

"Now we have done what we can do. Now come the Flying Fortresses. Now-we-have-done-what-we-can-do! Now-come-the-Flying-Fortresses!"

"You can send somebody who can fly them," an engineer said.

He was a very practical man, used to building airfields without tools and with no false illusions.

"You see," he looked across at the wind-blowing glory of the field where the singing was beating like surf, "there are certain things that we can do ourselves."

It was close to the end of the deadline and the field would be ready on the date that had been set.

Voyage to Victory

➤ *Collier's* · JULY 22, 1944

No ONE remembers the date of the Battle of Shiloh. But the day we took Fox Green beach was the sixth of June, and the wind was blowing hard out of the northwest. As we moved in toward land in the gray early light, the 36-foot coffin-shaped steel boats took solid green sheets of water that fell on the helmeted heads of the troops packed shoulder to shoulder in the stiff, awkward, uncomfortable, lonely companionship of men going to a battle. There were cases of TNT, with rubber-tube life preservers wrapped around them to float them in the surf, stacked forward in the steel well of the LCV(P), and there were piles of bazookas and boxes of bazooka rockets encased in waterproof coverings that reminded you of the transparent raincoats college girls wear.

All this equipment, too, had the rubber-tube life preservers strapped and tied on, and the men wore these same gray rubber tubes strapped under their armpits.

As the boat rose to a sea, the green water turned white and came slamming in over the men, the guns and the cases of explosives. Ahead you could see the coast of France. The gray booms and derrick-forested bulks of the attack transports were behind now, and, over all the sea, boats were crawling forward toward France.

As the LCV(P) rose to the crest of a wave, you saw the line of low, silhouetted cruisers and the two big battlewagons lying broadside to the shore. You saw the heat-bright flashes of their guns and the brown smoke that pushed out against the wind and then blew away.

"What's your course, coxswain?" Lieutenant (jg) Robert Anderson of Roanoke, Virginia, shouted from the stern.

"Two-twenty, sir," the coxswain, Frank Currier of Saugus, Massachusetts, answered. He was a thin-faced, freckled boy with his eyes fixed on the compass.

"Then steer two-twenty, damn it!" Anderson said. "Don't steer all over the whole damn' ocean!"

"I'm steering two-twenty, sir," the coxswain said patiently.

"Well, steer it, then," Andy said. He was nervous, but the boat crew, who were making their first landing under fire, knew this officer had taken LCV(P)s in to the African landing, Sicily and Salerno, and they had confidence in him.

"Don't steer into that LCT," Andy shouted, as we roared by the ugly steel hull of a tank landing craft, her vehicles sea-lashed, her troops huddling out of the spray.

"I'm steering two-twenty," the coxswain said.

"That doesn't mean you have to run into everything on the ocean," Andy said. He was a handsome, hollow-cheeked boy with a lot of style and a sort of easy petulance. "Mr. Hemingway, will you please see if you can see what that flag is over there, with your glasses?"

I got my old miniature Zeiss glasses out of an inside pocket, where they were wrapped in a woolen sock with some tissue to clean them, and focused them on the flag. I made the flag out just before a wave drenched the glasses.

"It's green."

"Then we are in the mine-swept channel," Andy said. "That's all right. Coxswain, what's the matter with you? Can't you steer two-twenty?"

I was trying to dry my glasses, but it was hopeless the way the spray was coming in, so I wrapped them up for a try later on and watched the battleship Texas shelling the shore. She was just off on our right now and firing over us as we moved in toward the French coast, which was showing clearer all the time on what was, or was not, a course of 220 degrees, depending on whether you believed Andy or Currier the coxswain.

The low cliffs were broken by valleys. There was a town with a church spire in one of them. There was a wood that came down to the sea. There was a house on the right of one of the beaches. On all the headlands, the gorse was burning, but the northwest wind held the smoke close to the ground.

Those of our troops who were not wax-gray with seasickness, fighting it off, trying to hold onto themselves before they had to grab for the steel side of the boat, were watching the Texas with looks of surprise and happiness. Under the steel helmets they looked like pikemen of the Middle Ages to whose aid in battle had suddenly come some strange and unbelievable monster.

There would be a flash like a blast furnace from the 14-inch guns of the Texas, that would lick far out from the ship. Then the yellow-brown smoke would cloud out and, with the smoke still rolling, the concussion and the report would hit us, jarring the men's helmets. It struck your near ear like a punch with a heavy, dry glove.

Then up on the green rise of a hill that now showed clearly as we moved in would spout two tall black fountains of earth and smoke.

"Look what they're doing to those Germans," I leaned forward to hear a G.I. say above the roar of the motor. "I guess there won't be a man alive there," he said happily.

That is the only thing I remember hearing a G.I. say all that morning. They spoke to one another sometimes, but you could not hear them with the roar the 225-horsepower high-speed gray Diesel made. Mostly, though, they stood silent without speaking. I never saw anyone smile after we left the line of firing ships. They had seen the mysterious monster that was helping them, but now he was gone and they were alone again.

I found if I kept my mouth open from the time I saw the guns flash until after the concussion, it took the shock away.

I was glad when we were inside and out of the line of fire of the Texas and the Arkansas. Other ships were firing over us all day and you were never away from the sudden, slapping thud of naval gunfire. But the big guns of the Texas and Arkansas that sounded as though they were throwing whole railway trains across the sky were far away as we moved on in. They were no part of our world as we moved steadily over the gray, white-capped sea toward where, ahead of us, death was being issued in small, intimate, accurately administered packages. They were like the thunder of a storm that is passing in another county whose rain will never reach you. But they were knocking out the shore batteries, so that later the destroyers could move in almost to the shore when they had to come in to save the landing.

Now ahead of us we could see the coast in complete detail. Andy opened the silhouette map with all the beaches and their distinguishing features reproduced on it, and I got my glasses out and commenced drying and wiping them under the shelter of the skirts of my burberry. As far as you could see, there were landing craft moving in over the gray sea. The sun was under at this time, and smoke was blowing all along the coast.

The map that Andy spread on his knees was in ten folded sheets, held together with staples, and marked Appendix One to Annex A. Five different sheets were stapled together and, as I watched Andy open his map, which spread, open, twice as long as a man could reach with outstretched arms, the wind caught it, and the section of the map showing Dog White, Fox Red, Fox Green, Dog Green, Easy Red and part of Sector Charlie snapped twice gaily in the wind and blew overboard.

I had studied this map and memorized most of it, but it is one thing to have it in your memory and another thing to see it actually on paper and be able to check and be sure.

"Have you got a small chart, Andy?" I shouted. "One of those one-sheet ones with just Fox Green and Easy Red?"

"Never had one," said Andy. All this time we were approaching the coast of France, which looked increasingly hostile.

"That the only chart?" I said, close to his ear.

"Only one," said Andy, "and it disintegrated on me. A wave

hit it, and it disintegrated. What beach do you think we are opposite?"

"There's the church tower that looks like Colleville," I said. "That ought to be on Fox Green. Then there is a house like the one marked on Fox Green and the timber that runs down to the water in a straight line, like on Easy Red."

"That's right," said Andy. "But I think we're too far to the left."

"Those are the features, all right," I said. "I've got them in my head but there shouldn't be any cliffs. The cliffs start to the left of Fox Green where Fox Red beach starts. If that's true, then Fox Green has to be on our right."

"There's a control boat here somewhere," Andy said. "We'll find out what beach we're opposite."

"She can't be Fox Green if there are cliffs," I said.

"That's right," Andy said. "We'll find out from a control boat. Steer for that PC, coxswain. No, not there! Don't you see him? Get ahead of him. You'll never catch him that way."

We never did catch him, either. We slammed into the seas instead of topping them, and the boat pulled away from us. The LCV(P) was bow-heavy with the load of TNT and the weight of the three-eighth-inch steel armor, and where she should have lifted easily over the seas she banked into them and the water came in solidly.

"The hell with him!" Andy said. "We'll ask this LCI."

Landing Craft Infantry are the only amphibious operations craft that look as though they were made to go to sea. They very nearly have the lines of a ship, while the LCV(P)s look like iron bathtubs, and the LCTs like floating freight gondolas. Everywhere you could see, the ocean was covered with these craft but very few of them were headed toward shore. They would start toward the beach, then sheer off and circle back. On the beach itself, in from where we were, there were lines of what looked like tanks, but my glasses were still too wet to function.

"Where's Fox Green beach?" Andy cupped his hands and shouted up at the LCI that was surging past us, loaded with troops.

"Can't hear," someone shouted. We had no megaphone.

"What beach are we opposite?" Andy yelled.

The officer on the LCI shook his head. The other officers did not even look toward us. They were looking over their shoulders at the beach.

"Get her close alongside, coxswain," Andy said. "Come on, get in there close."

We roared up alongside the LCI, then cut down the motor as she slipped past us.

"Where's Fox Green beach?" Andy yelled, as the wind blew the words away.

"Straight in to your right," an officer shouted.

"Thanks." Andy looked astern at the other two boats and told Ed Banker, the signalman, "Get them to close up. Get them up."

Ed Banker turned around and jerked his forearm, with index finger raised, up and down. "They're closing up, sir," he said.

Looking back you could see the other heavily loaded boats climbing the waves that were green now the sun was out, and pounding down into the troughs.

"You wet all through, sir?" Ed asked me.

"All the way."

"Me, too," Ed said. "Only thing wasn't wet was my belly button. Now it's wet, too."

"This has got to be Fox Green," I said to Andy. "I recognize where the cliff stops. That's all Fox Green to the right. There is the Colleville church. There's the house on the beach. There's the Ruquet Valley on Easy Red to the right. This is Fox Green absolutely."

"We'll check when we get in closer," Andy said. "You really think it's Fox Green?"

"It has to be."

Ahead of us, the various landing craft were all acting in the same confusing manner—heading in, coming out and circling.

"There's something wrong as hell," I said to Andy. "See the tanks? They're all along the edge of the beach. They haven't gone in at all."

Just then one of the tanks flared up and started to burn with thick black smoke and yellow flame. Farther down the beach, another tank started burning. Along the line of the beach, they were crouched like big yellow toads along the high water line. As I stood up, watching, two more started to burn. The first ones were pouring out gray smoke now, and the wind was blowing it flat along the beach. As I stood up, trying to see if there was anyone in beyond the high water line of tanks, one of the burning tanks blew up with a flash in the streaming gray smoke.

"There's a boat we can check with," Andy said. "Coxswain, steer for that LC over there. Yes, that one. Put her hard over. Come on. Get over there!"

This was a black boat, fast-looking, mounting two machine guns and wallowing slowly out away from the beach, her engine almost idling.

"Can you tell us what beach this is?" Andy shouted.

"Dog White," came the answer.

"Are you sure?"

"Dog White beach," they called from the black boat.

"You checked it?" Andy called.

"It's Dog White beach," they called back from the boat, and their screw churned the water white as they slipped into speed and pulled away from us.

I was discouraged now, because ahead of us, inshore, was every landmark I had memorized on Fox Green and Easy Red beaches. The line of the cliffs that marked the left end of Fox Green beach showed clearly. Every house was where it should be. The steeple of the Colleville church showed exactly as it had in the silhouette. I had studied the charts, the silhouettes, the data on the obstacles in the water and the defenses all one morning, and I remember having asked our captain, Commander W. I. Leahy of the attack transport Dorothea M. Dix, if our attack was to be a diversion in force.

"No," he had said. "Absolutely not. What makes you ask that question?"

"Because these beaches are so highly defensible."

"The Army is going to clear the obstacles and the mines out in the first thirty minutes," Captain Leahy had told me. "They're going to cut lanes in through them for the landing craft."

I wish I could write the full story of what it means to take a transport across through a mine-swept channel; the mathematical precision of maneuver; the infinite detail and chronometrical accuracy and split-second timing of everything from the time the anchor comes up until the boats are lowered and away into the roaring, sea-churning assembly circle from which they break off into the attack wave.

The story of all the teamwork behind that has to be written, but to get all that in would take a book, and this is simply the account of how it was in a LCV(P) on the day we stormed Fox Green beach.

Right at this moment, no one seemed to know where Fox Green beach was. I was sure we were opposite it, but the patrol boat had said this was Dog White beach which should be 4.295 yards to our right, if we were where I knew we were.

"It can't be Dog White, Andy," I said. "Those are the cliffs where Fox Red starts on our left."

"The man says it's Dog White," Andy said.

In the solid-packed troops in the boat, a man with a vertical white bar painted on his helmet was looking at us and shaking his head. He had high cheekbones and a rather flat, puzzled face.

"The lieutenant says he knows it, and we're on Fox Green," Ed Banker shouted back at us. He spoke again to the lieutenant but we could not hear what they said.

Andy shouted at the lieutenant, and he nodded his helmeted head up and down.

"He says it's Fox Green," Andy said.

"Ask him where he wants to go in," I said.

Just then another small black patrol boat with several officers in it came toward us from the beach, and an officer stood up in it and megaphoned, "Are there any boats here for the seventh wave on Fox Green beach?"

There was one boat for that wave with us, and the officer shouted to them to follow their boat.

"Is this Fox Green?" Andy called to them.

"Yes. Do you see that ruined house? Fox Green beach runs for eleven hundred and thirty-five yards to the right of that ruined house."

"Can you get into the beach?"

"I can't tell you that. You will have to ask a beach control boat."

"Can't we just run in?"

"I have no authority on that. You must ask the beach control boat."

"Where is it?"

"Way out there somewhere."

"We can go in where an LCV(P) has been in or an LCI," I said. "It's bound to be clear where they run in, and we can go in under the lee of one."

"We'll look for the control boat," Andy said, and we went banging out to sea through the swarming traffic of landing craft and lighters.

"I can't find her," Andy said. "She isn't here. She ought to be in closer. We have to get the hell in. We're late now. Let's go in."

"Ask him where he is supposed to land," I said.

Andy went down and talked to the lieutenant. I could see the lieutenant's lips moving as he spoke, but could hear nothing above the engine noise.

"He wants to run straight in for that ruined house," Andy said, when he came back.

We headed in for the beach. As we came in, running fast, the black patrol boat swung over toward us again.

"Did you find the control boat?" they megaphoned.

"No!"

"What are you going to do?"

"We're going in," Andy said.

"Well, good luck to you fellows," the megaphone said. It came over, slow and solemn like an elegy. "Good luck to all of you fellows."

That included Thomas E. Nash, engineer, from Seattle with a good grin and two teeth out of it. It included Edward F. Banker, signalman, of Brooklyn, and Lacey T. Shiflet of Orange, Virginia, who would have been the gunner if we had had room for guns. It included Frank Currier, the coxswain, of Saugus, Massachusetts, and it included Andy and me. When we heard the lugubrious tone of that parting benediction we all knew how bad the beach really was.

As we came roaring in on the beach, I sat high on the stern to see what we were up against. I had the glasses dry now and I took a good look at the shore. The shore was coming toward us awfully fast, and in the glasses it was coming even faster.

On the beach on the left where there was no sheltering over-hang of shingled bank, the first, second, third, fourth and fifth waves lay where they had fallen, looking like so many heavily laden bundles on the flat pebbly stretch between the sea and the first cover. To the right, there was an open stretch where the beach exit led up a wooden valley from the sea. It was here that the Germans hoped to get something very good, and later we saw them get it.

To the right of this, two tanks were burning on the crest of the beach, the smoke now gray after the first violent black and yellow billows. Coming in I had spotted two machine-gun nests. One was firing intermittently from the ruins of the smashed house on the right of the small valley. The other was two hundred yards to the right and possibly four hundred yards in front of the beach.

The officer commanding the troops we were carrying had asked us to head directly for the beach opposite the ruined house.

"Right in there," he said. "That's where."

"Andy," I said, "that whole sector is enfiladed by machine-gun fire. I just saw them open twice on that stranded boat."

An LCV(P) was slanted drunkenly in the stakes like a lost gray steel bathtub. They were firing at the water line, and the fire was kicking up sharp spurts of water.

"That's where he says he wants to go," Andy said. "So that's where we'll take him."

"It isn't any good," I said. "I've seen both those guns open up."

"That's where he wants to go," Andy said. "Put her ahead straight in." He turned astern and signaled to the other boats, jerking his arm, with its upraised finger, up and down.

"Come on, you guys," he said, inaudible in the roar of the motor that sounded like a plane taking off. "Close up! Close up! What's the matter with you? Close up, can't you? Take her straight in, coxswain!"

At his point, we entered the beaten zone from the two machine-gun points, and I ducked my head under the sharp cracking that was going overhead. Then I dropped into the well in the stern sheets where the gunner would have been if we had any guns. The machine-gun fire was throwing water all around the boat, and an antitank shell tossed up a jet of water over us.

The lieutenant was talking, but I couldn't hear what·he said. Andy could hear him. He had his head down close to his lips.

"Get her the hell around and out of here, coxswain!" Andy called. "*Get her out of here!*"

As we swung round on our stern in a pivot and pulled out, the machine-gun fire stopped. But individual sniping shots kept cracking over or spitting into the water around us. I'd got my head up again with some difficulty and was watching the shore.

"It wasn't cleared, either," Andy said. "You could see the mines on all those stakes."

"Let's coast along and find a good place to put them ashore," I said. "If we stay outside of the machine-gun fire, I don't think they'll shoot at us with anything big because we're just an LCV(P), and they've got better targets than us."

"We'll look for a place," Andy said.

"What's he want now?" I said to Andy.

The lieutenant's lips were moving again. They moved very slowly and as though they had no connection with him or with his face.

Andy got down to listen to him. He came back into the stern. "He wants to go out to an LCI we passed that has his commanding officer on it."

"We can get him ashore farther up toward Easy Red," I said.

"He wants to see his commanding officer," Andy said. "Those people in that black boat were from his outfit."

Out a way, rolling in the sea, was a Landing Craft Infantry, and as we came alongside of her I saw a ragged shellhole through the steel plates forward of her pilothouse where an 88-mm. German shell had punched through. Blood was dripping from the shiny edges of the hole into the sea with each roll of the LCI. Her rails and hull had been befouled by seasick men, and her dead were laid forward of her pilothouse. Our lieutenant had some conversation with another officer while we rose and fell in the surge alongside the black iron hull, and then we pulled away.

Andy went forward and talked to him, then came aft again, and we sat up on the stern and watched two destroyers coming along toward us from the eastern beaches, their guns pounding away at targets on the headlands and sloping fields behind the beaches.

"He says they don't want him to go in yet; to wait," Andy said. "Let's get out of the way of this destroyer."

"How long is he going to wait?"

"He says they have no business in there now. People that should have been ahead of them haven't gone in yet. They told him to wait."

"Let's get in where we can keep track of it," I said. "Take the glasses and look at that beach, but don't tell them forward what you see."

Andy looked. He handed the glasses back to me and shook his head.

"Let's cruise along it to the right and see how it is up at that end," I said. "I'm pretty sure we can get in there when he wants to get in. You're sure they told him he shouldn't go in?"

"That's what he says."

"Talk to him and get it straight."

Andy came back. "He says they shouldn't go in now. They're supposed to clear the mines away, so the tanks can go, and he says nothing is in there to go yet. He says they told him it is all fouled up and to stay out yet awhile."

The destroyer was firing point blank at the concrete pillbox that had fired at us on the first trip into the beach, and as the guns fired you heard the bursts and saw the earth jump almost at the same time as the empty brass cases clanged back onto the steel deck. The five-inch guns of the destroyer were smashing at the ruined house at the edge of the little valley where the other machine gun had fired from.

"Let's move in now that the can has gone by and see if we can't find a good place," Andy said.

"That can punched out what was holding them up there, and you can see some infantry working up that draw now," I said to Andy. "Here, take the glasses."

Slowly, laboriously, as though they were Atlas carrying the world on their shoulders, men were working up the valley on our right. They were not firing. They were just moving slowly up the valley like a tired pack train at the end of the day, going the other way from home.

"The infantry had pushed up to the top of the ridge at the end of that valley," I shouted to the lieutenant.

"They don't want us yet," he said. "They told me clear they didn't want us yet."

"Let me take the glasses—or Hemingway," Andy said. Then he handed them back. "In there, there's somebody signaling with a yellow flag, and there's a boat in there in trouble, it looks like. Coxswain, take her straight in."

We moved in toward the beach at full speed, and Ed Banker looked around and said, "Mr. Anderson, the other boats are coming, too."

"Get them back!" Andy said. *"Get them back!"*

Banker turned around and waved the boats away. He had difficulty making them understand, but finally the wide waves they were throwing subsided and they dropped astern.

"Did you get them back?" Andy asked, without looking away from the beach where we could see a half-sunken LCV(P) foundered in the mined stakes.

"Yes, sir," Ed Banker said.

An LCI was headed straight toward us, pulling away from the beach after having circled to go in. As it passed, a man shouted with a megaphone, "There are wounded on that boat and she is sinking."

"Can you get in to her?"

The only words we heard clearly from the megaphone as the wind snatched the voice away were "machine-gun nest."

"Did they say there was or there wasn't a machine-gun nest?" Andy said.

"I couldn't hear."

"Run alongside of her again, coxswain," he said. "Run close alongside."

"Did you say there was a machine-gun nest?" he shouted.

An officer leaned over with the megaphone. "A machine-gun nest has been firing on them. They are sinking."

"Take her straight in, coxswain," Andy said.

It was difficult to make our way through the stakes that had been sunk as obstructions, because there were contact mines fastened to them that looked like large double pie plates fastened face to face. They looked as though they had been spiked to the pilings and then assembled. They were the ugly, neutral gray-yellow color that almost everything is in war.

We did not know what other stakes with mines were under us, but the ones that we could see we fended off by hand and worked our way to the sinking boat.

It was not easy to bring on board the man who had been shot through the lower abdomen, because there was no room to let the ramp down the way we were jammed in the stakes with the cross sea.

I do not know why the Germans did not fire on us unless the

destroyer had knocked the machine-gun pillbox out. Or maybe they were waiting for us to blow up with the mines. Certainly the mines had been a great amount of trouble to lay and the Germans might well have wanted to see them work. We were in the range of the antitank gun that had fired on us before, and all the time we were maneuvering and working in the stakes I was waiting for it to fire.

As we lowered the ramp the first time, while we were crowded in against the other LCV(P), but before she sank, I saw three tanks coming along the beach, barely moving, they were advancing so slowly. The Germans let them cross the open space where the valley opened onto the beach, and it was absolutely flat with a perfect field of fire. Then I saw a little fountain of water jut up, just over and beyond the lead tank. Then smoke broke out of the leading tank on the side away from us, and I saw two men dive out of the turret and land on their hands and knees on the stones of the beach. They were close enough so that I could see their faces, but no more men came out as the tank started to blaze up and burn fiercely.

By then, we had the wounded man and the survivors on board, the ramp back up, and were feeling our way out through the stakes. As we cleared the last of the stakes, and Currier opened up the engine wide as we pulled out to sea, another tank was beginning to burn.

We took the wounded boy out to the destroyer. They hoisted him aboard it in one of those metal baskets and took on the survivors. Meantime, the destroyers had run in almost to the beach and were blowing every pillbox out of the ground with their five-inch guns. I saw a piece of German about three feet long with an arm on it sail high up into the air in the fountaining of one shellburst. It reminded me of a scene in Petrouchka.

The infantry had now worked up the valley on our left and had gone on over that ridge. There was no reason for anyone to stay out now. We ran in to a good spot we had picked on the beach and put our troops and their TNT and their bazookas and their lieutenant ashore, and that was that.

The Germans were still shooting with their antitank guns, shifting them around in the valley, holding their fire until they had a target they wanted. Their mortars were still laying a plunging fire along the beaches. They had left people behind to snipe at the beaches, and when we left, finally, all these people who were firing were evidently going to stay until dark at least.

The heavily loaded ducks that had formerly sunk in the waves on their way in were now making the beach steadily. The famous thirty-minute clearing of the channels through the mined obstacles was still a myth, and now, with the high tide, it was a tough trip in with the stakes submerged.

We had six craft missing, finally, out of the twenty-four LCV(P)s that went in from the Dix, but many of the crews could have been picked up and might be on other vessels. It had been a frontal assault in broad daylight, against a mined beach defended by all the obstacles military ingenuity could devise. The beach had been defended as stubbornly and as intelligently as any troops could defend it. But every boat from the Dix had landed her troops and cargo. No boat was lost through bad seamanship. All that were lost were lost by enemy action. And we had taken the beach.

There is much that I have not written. You could write for a week and not give everyone credit for what he did on a front of 1,135 yards. Real war is never like paper war, nor do accounts of it read much the way it looks. But if you want to know how it was in an LCV(P) on D-Day when we took Fox Green beach and Easy Red beach on the sixth of June, 1944, then this is as near as I can come to it.

London Fights the Robots

➤ *Collier's* · AUGUST 19, 1944

THE Tempest is a great, gaunt airplane. It is the fastest pursuit job in the world and is as tough as a mule. It has been reported with a speed of 400 and should dive way ahead of its own noise. Where we were living, its job was to intercept the pilotless planes and shoot them down over the sea or in open country as they came in on their sputtering roar toward London.

The squadron flew from four o'clock in the morning until midnight. There were always pilots sitting ready in the cockpits to take off when the Very pistol signaled, and there were always a number of planes on permanent patrol in the air. The fastest time I clocked a plane as airborne, from the sound of the pop of the flare pistol that would arc a twin flare over toward the dispersal area from the door of the Intelligence hut, was fifty-seven seconds.

As the flare popped, you would hear the dry bark of the starting cartridge and the rising scream of the motor, and these hungry, big, long-legged birds would lurch, bounce, and scream off with the noise of two hundred circular saws hitting a mahogany log dead on the nose. They took off downwind, crosswind, any way the weather lay, and grabbed a piece of the sky and lurched up into it with the long, high legs folding up under them.

You love a lot of things if you live around them, but there isn't any woman and there isn't any horse, nor any before nor any after, that is as lovely as a great airplane, and men who love them are faithful to them even though they leave them for others. A man has only one virginity to lose in fighters, and if it is a lovely plane he loses it to, there his heart will ever be. And a P-51 can do something to a man's heart.

Mustang is a tough, good name for a bad, tough, husky, angry plane that could have been friends with Harry Greb if Greb had had an engine instead of a heart. Tempest is a sissy name out of Shakespeare, who is a great man anywhere, but they have put it onto an airplane that is sort of like a cross between Man o' War and Tallulah Bankhead in the best year either of them ever had. They were good years, too, and many a man has been taken by the bookies because he looked at a colt that had the swelling Big Red's neck had and not any of the rest of it. And there have been many husky voices since, but none that carried good across the Western ocean.

So now we have this squadron of Tempests. They were running out of terms for meteorological disturbances when they named that one. And all day long they shoot down this nameless weapon, day in and day out. The squadron leader is a fine man, tall, small-spoken the way a leopard is, with the light brown circles under his eyes and the odd purple complexion of a man whose face has been burned away, and he told the story of his exploit to me very quietly and truthfully, standing by the wooden table in the pilots' mess.

He knew it was true and I knew it was true and he was very precise in remembering exactly how it had been, because it was one of the first pilotless aircraft he had shot down, and he was very exact in details. He did not like to say anything personal but it was evidently all right to speak well of the plane. Then he told me about the other sort of shooting down. If you do not explode them in the air, you crash them.

"It is a sort of giant bubble of blast that rises from them," he said. "Bubble" had been quite a venturesome word to use, and he took confidence from it and tried a further word. "It is rather like a huge *blossoming* of air rising."

We were both embarrassed by this articulateness, and as my mind watched the giant bubble blossoming, all tension was taken away by an American flying in the same squadron, who said, "I dropped one on a greenhouse, and the glass rose straight up a million feet. What am I going to say to the guy who owns that greenhouse when we go into the pub tonight?"

"You can't just say exactly where you'll shoot them down," the squadron leader said, standing there, speaking shyly, patiently and with strange eagerness, from behind the purple mask he would always wear now for a face. "They go very fast you know."

The wing commander came in, angry, happy. He was short, with a lot of style and a tough, bad tongue. He was twenty-six, I found out later. I had seen him get out of an airplane before I knew he was the wing commander. It did not show then, nor did it show now when he talked. The only way you knew he was the wing commander was the way the other pilots said "Sir." They said "Sir" to the two squadron leaders, one of whom was a tough Belgian like a six-day bicycle racer, and the other was the shy, fine man who lived behind the destroyed face. But they gave a slightly different "Sir" to the wing commander, and the wing commander returned no change from it at all. Nor did he notice it when he pocketed it.

Censorship, in war, is a very necessary thing. It is especially necessary about aircraft because, until a new aircraft has fallen into enemy hands, no information as to the exact speeds, dimensions, characteristics or armament should be written, since all of that furnishes information the enemy wants and needs.

It is appearance, characteristics and performance that make a man love an airplane, and they, told truly, are what put the emotion into an article about one. They are all out of this article now. I hope the enemy never shoots down a Tempest, that the Tempest will never be released from the secret list, and that all I know and care about them can never be published until after the war.

All information about tactics employed in the shooting down of pilotless aircraft is out, too, along with all the conversation that would let you know how the types feel that do the shooting down. Because you cannot have the conversation without conveying the tactics. So there isn't much in this article now, except a guy loving an airplane.

It is written in tough language because this was, in the main, a tough-speaking outfit. The only exception was the squadron leader, fragments of whose conversation are given. Some outfits in the R.A.F. are very rough spoken, and some speak as gently and correctly as in the film, Target for Tonight. I like ("like" is a very mild term to employ for the emotion felt) both kinds, and sometime, if it is ever possible to write anything interesting that the censor can conscientiously pass, I would like to try to show both kinds. In the meantime you get this.

Writing under censorship is necessary and proper in time of war, and we all censor out ourselves everything we think might be of any possible interest to the enemy. But in writing about the air on the basis of trying to include color, detail and emotion, there is a certain analogy to sports writing.

It is sort of as though in the old days you had found Harry Greb having a breakfast of double orders of ham and eggs and hashed brown potatoes in bed at nine o'clock in the morning on the day he was to fight Mickey Walker. Greb, placed on the scales, weighed exactly 12 pounds over the 162 he was to make at two o'clock that afternoon. Now suppose you had seen the weight rubbed and pounded off of him and got rid of by several other means, and him carried on the scales too weak to walk and almost too weak to curse you.

Then suppose you had seen the meal he ate and seen him enter the ring weighing exactly the same weight he had left bed with that morning. Then suppose you had seen the great, crowding, smashing, take it, come in again, thumbing, butting, mean, nasty, bloody, lovely fight he made, and you had to sum up the whole business in these terms: One of our fighters named Greb whose characteristics have not been revealed was reported to have encountered an M. Walker last night. Further details will be released in due course.

If this ever seems a screwy story, remember that through the sky at all times are passing pilotless aircraft which look, in flight, rather like an ugly metal dart with a white-hot bunghole, travel at speed up to 400 miles an hour, carry, as of this writing, 2,200 pounds of explosive in their noses, make a noise like a glorified motorcycle and, at this moment, are passing overhead the place where this is written.

One of my most esteemed colleagues told me in New York that he was not returning to the European theater because anything he might write would merely be a repetition of what he had already written. At this point I am authorized to state to my esteemed colleague that the danger of repetition in a story is one of the more negligible hazards that his old co-workers are at present confronted with.

Now if you are following this piece closely—which I am not, due to a certain amount of windowpane trouble—we should be somewhere in southern England where a group of Tempest pilots have in seven days shot down their share of pilotless aircraft. Lots of people call this weapon the doodlebug, the robot bomb, the buzz bomb and other names hatched in the brains of the keener Fleet Street types, but so far nobody I have ever known who has fought him has referred to Joe Louis as Toots. So we will continue to refer to this weapon as the pilotless aircraft in this release from your pilotless-aircraft editor, and you can call it any of those quaint or coy names you wish, but only when you are alone.

The day before your pilotless-aircraft editor started studying the interception angle, he or I (I guess it is I, although sometimes it doesn't seem the right man in the right place and I have thought some of leaving the whole thing and going back to writing books in stiff covers), went out in one of forty-eight Mitchell bombers—that is, eight boxes of six bombers each—to bomb one of the sites from which the pilotless aircraft are launched.

These sites can be readily identified by the merest tyro by the quantity of old Mitchell bombers which are strewed around them and by the fact that, when you get close to them, large, black circular rings of smoke appear alongside of the vehicle you are riding in. These circular black rings of smoke are called flak, and this flak is the author of that old piece of understatement about two of our aircraft failed to return.

Well, we (that is Wing Commander Lynn, who is nice company in an airplane and who has exactly the same voice on the intercom when Kees, the bombardier, has her held in on the run and is saying, "Bombing—Bombing—Bombing—Bombing—" as though you were not on the last mile) bombed this site with proverbial pin-point accuracy. I had a nice look at the site which appeared to be a gigantic concrete construction lying on its side or its belly (depending on whether you saw it just before the run or just after it) in a woods completely surrounded by bomb craters. There were two small clouds that didn't look lonely the way the clouds were in "I wandered lonely as a cloud."

There were many rings of the black smoke in a line coming right straight alongside of us inside the box between us and where the other Mitchell on our right was going along in the air, looking just like a picture of a Mitchell in an advertisement by the manufacturers. Then, with the smoke rings forming along her side, the belly of this kite—looking just like in moving pictures—opened, pushing out against the air, and the bombs all dropped out sideways as if she were having eight long metal kittens in a hurry.

We all were doing this, although you could not see what anybody did except this one. Then we all went home just as fast as we could go home, and that is bombing. Unlike a lot of other things, the best part is afterward. I suppose it is something like going to college. It isn't so much how much you learn. It is the wonderful people you meet.

Your pilotless-aircraft editor never went to college (here we call it a university), so now he is going to the R.A.F. instead, and the main subject he is studying is trying to understand English on the radio telephone. Face to face with an Englishman, I can understand almost everything he says. I can speak, read and write Canadian clearly and have a smattering of Scottish and a few words of New Zealand. I can understand enough Australian to draw cards and order drinks and to shove my way into a bar if it is crowded. South African I dominate as a spoken tongue almost as well as I do Basque. But English over the RT is just a glorious mystery.

Close up, over the intercom in a bomber, I get most of it. When you press the button on the stick, that isolates conversation to what is said in the cockpit, so you have those long, intimate chats that go, "Wonder who that b— is that's talking," and you answer, "Don't know. Must be the same Jerry that on the night of D-Day kept saying 'Turn back. Turn Back. The operation has been canceled!' "

"Wonder how he gets on our wave length?"

You shrug your shoulders and take your thumb off the button. That close conversation I get all right, but when real Englishmen speaking English start talking to one another between one kite and another kite and back and forth from control, I just study it hard like homework, as if you had brought home somebody's calculus book and were still on plane geometry.

Actually, I cannot understand English very well yet on the ordinary telephone, so, having been indoctrinated in the Good Neighbor policy, I always say, "Yes," and just make them repeat the time the car will be around in the morning to take us to whatever field we will be starting from.

This accounts for many of the curious sorties your pilotless-aircraft correspondent goes on. He is not a man who has a perpetual urge to seek peril in the sky or to defy the laws of gravity; he is simply a man who, not understanding very well the nature of the propositions offered over the telephone due to faulty earwork, constantly finds himself involved in the destruction of these monsters in their hellish lairs or in attempts at interception in that fine, 400-mile-an-hour airplane, the Mosquito.

At present, your pilotless-aircraft editor has stopped all telephone calls of any description in order to attempt to bring the story up to date before someone proposes something so startling and so generous to your editor in the nature of an operation that he would fail in his duties to this great book to have recorded what has happened up to this time. However, before all calls were stopped, two or three rather lovely propositions were received, and I understand that there is a feeling freely expressed in some quarters that, "Ernie is yellow. With a chance to go on absolutely wizard ops, he is up in his room at that pub, doing what do you think?"

"What?" in a horrified tone.

"Writing."

"My God! The old boy's had it!"

Battle for Paris

➤ *Collier's* · SEPTEMBER 30, 1944

ON August 19th, accompanied by Private Archie Pelkey of Canton, in upstate New York, I stopped at the command post of the infantry regiment of the division in a wood just outside of Maintenon to ask for information on the front this regiment was holding. The G2 and G3 of this regiment showed me where their battalions were placed and informed me that their most advanced outpost was at a point a short distance beyond Epernon on the road to Rambouillet (23 miles southwest of Paris), where the summer residence and hunting lodge of the president of France is located. At the regimental command post I was informed there was heavy fighting outside of Rambouillet. I knew the country and the roads around Epernon, Rambouillet, Trappes and Versailles well, as I had bicycled, walked and driven a car through this part of France for many years. It is by riding a bicycle that you learn the contours of a country best, since you have to sweat up the hills and can coast down them.

Thus you remember them as they actually are, while in a motorcar only a high hill impresses you, and you have no such accurate remembrance of country you have driven through as you gain by riding a bicycle. At the outpost of the regiment we found some Frenchmen who had just come in from Rambouillet by bicycle. I was the only person at the outpost who spoke French, and they informed me that the last Germans had left Rambouillet at three o'clock that morning but that the roads into the town were mined.

I started to return to regimental headquarters with this information, but after driving a short way down the road back to Maintenon I decided it would be better to return and get the Frenchmen, so they themselves could be interrogated and give fuller information. When I reached the outpost again, I found two cars full of French guerrilla fighters, most of whom were naked to the waist. They were armed with pistols and two Sten guns they had received by parachute. They had just come from Rambouillet and their story of the German withdrawal tallied with the information other French had given.

Private Pelkey and I conducted them back to the regimental command post, driving ahead of the two cars in our jeep, where I translated their information on the town and the state of the road to the proper authorities.

We then returned to the outpost to wait for a mine-clearing detail and a reconnaissance troop that were to join us there. After waiting some time and none coming up, the French guerrilla fighters became very impatient. The obvious thing seemed to be to proceed to the first mine field and establish a guard to prevent any American vehicle which might advance from running into it.

We were proceeding toward Rambouillet when we were joined by Lieutenant Irving Krieger of East Orange, New Jersey, from the antitank company of the infantry regiment. Lieutenant Krieger was short, stocky, exceedingly tough and very cheerful. I could see the guerrillas were very favorably impressed with him and, as soon as they saw him at work finding and clearing the mines, they had complete confidence in him. When working with irregular troops you have no real discipline except that of example. As long as they believe in you they will fight if they are good elements. The minute they cease to believe in you, or in the mission to be accomplished, they disappear.

War correspondents are forbidden to command troops, and I had simply conducted these guerrilla fighters to the infantry regiment command post in order that they might give information. Anyway, it was a beautiful day that day and when we came down the smooth black road toward Rambouillet, with the big plane trees on either side and the wall of the park on our left, we saw the road block ahead.

First, there was a smashed jeep on our left. Then there were two German miniature tanks that they used as self-propelled antitank weapons. One was in the road pointing straight up the hill that we were coming down toward the felled trees of the road block. The other was on the right side of the shoulder of the road. Each one had two hundred pounds of TNT in it, and they were controlled by wires that ran back to behind the road block. If an armored column came down the road, one of these doodlebug tanks could be sent straight up the road at it. If the vehicles swerved to the right, as they would have to because of the wall on the left, the other miniature tank would be released to hit them on their flank. They looked like ugly toads squatting on the road. There was another smashed jeep just this side of the road block, and a big truck, also smashed.

Lieutenant Krieger dived into the mine field, which was laid in and around two big trees that had been felled across the road, like a boy looking for his name on the packages under a Christmas tree. Under his direction, Archie Pelkey and the guerrillas carried mines on the wall of a culvert. We learned from the French that the Germans had shot up an American reconnaissance patrol at this point. They had let the armored car, which was leading, pass the crossroads into Rambouillet, and then they opened on the truck and the two jeeps with antitank and machine-gun fire and killed seven men. The Germans then took the American mines out of the truck and laid this field.

The French had buried the Americans in the field beside the road where they had been ambushed, and while we were clearing the mine field, French women came out and put flowers on the graves and prayed over them. No reconnaissance outfit had come up yet, but Lieutenant Krieger's men had arrived and he was now in communication with the regiment by radio.

I went into the town with a patrol of French guerrillas, and we found out to what point the Germans had withdrawn and in what force they were. I gave this information to Lieutenant

Krieger and, since we knew there was no screen of any kind between us and the Germans, who had, we found later, at least ten tanks beyond the town, it was decided to relay the mine field and establish a proper guard over it to bar the road in case the Germans should return. Fortunately, at this time, a reconnaissance troop, commanded by Lieutenant Peterson of Cleveland, Ohio, came up, and our worries were over for the moment.

That night our French guerrillas ran out patrols on the main roads out from Rambouillet to screen Lieutenant Peterson's reconnaissance force, which held the center of town. It rained very hard during the night, and the French guerrillas were wet and tired in the morning. The previous afternoon they had been clothed with fatigue uniforms abandoned in the truck in which the members of the recon outfit had been killed in the ambush.

The first time we had entered the town all but two were naked from the waist up, and the populace did not greet us with any degree of fervor. The second time I went in with them, everyone was uniformed and we were cheered considerably. The third time we went through the town the men were all helmeted and we were cheered wildly, kissed extensively and heavily champagned, and we made our headquarters in the Hotel du Grand Veneur, which had an excellent wine cellar.

On the morning of the second day I returned to the infantry regiment command post to give an account of the situation in Rambouillet and the nature of the German force which was operating between Rambouillet and Versailles. Members of the French *gendarmerie* and guerrillas in gendarme uniforms had been in and out of Versailles, and reports were coming in hourly from members of the French resistance groups. We had accurate information on German tank movements, gun positions, and antiaircraft emplacements, the strength of German troops and their disposition.

This information was continually kept up to date and made more complete. The colonel commanding the infantry regiment asked me to go to divisional headquarters, where I gave an account of what was happening in Rambouillet and beyond, and more arms were obtained for the French resistance forces from stocks of captured German matériel in Chartres.

I returned to Rambouillet to find that Lieutenant Peterson had pushed his reconnaissance troop up the Versailles road a ways, and that an armored cavalry outfit had arrived in his support. It was very cheerful to see troops in town and to know that there was something between us and the Germans, since we now knew that there were three Tiger tanks among the fifteen tanks the Germans were operating in the area north of Rambouillet.

During the afternoon a great many people arrived in town. Intelligence officers, British and American, returned from missions or waiting to go on them, some newspaper correspondents, a colonel from New York who was the ranking U.S. officer present and Lieutenant Commander Lester Armor, U.S.N.R., were all in the town when the two armored reconnaissance units received orders that all missions were canceled, and were told the point to which they should withdraw.

This withdrawal left the town with no troops of any kind between it and the Germans. By this time we knew the exact force of the Germans and their tactics. They were moving their tanks out in an area between Trappes and Neauphe le Vieux and blocking the road to Versailles from Houdon. They would run their tanks onto the main road between Rambouillet and Versailles, at various points, using side roads, and they patrolled the area to the east around Chevreuse and St. Rémy-lès-Chevreuses with light tanks and cyclists.

On that night, after the U.S. Army reconnaissance units were withdrawn, the force defending Rambouillet was composed of mixed patrols of regulars and guerrillas, armed with antitank grenades and small arms. It rained hard during the night and there was a part of the night, between 2 and 6 A.M., that was the loneliest I ever spent. I do not know if you understand what it means to have troops out ahead of you and then have them withdrawn and be left with a town, a large and beautiful town, completely undamaged and full of fine people, on your hands.

There was nothing in the book issued to correspondents for their guidance through the intricacies of military affairs which dealt with this situation; so it was decided to screen the town as well as possible and, if the Germans, observing the withdrawal of the American force, advanced to make contact, to provide them with the necessary contact. This was done.

During the next days the German tanks roamed around the roads ahead of us. They took hostages in the various villages. They picked up men of the French resistance forces and shot them. They went where they pleased. But all of this time they were followed and kept track of by French guerrillas on bicycles, who came back with accurate information on their movements.

The same man could only work through the same country once unless he had a legitimate reason for moving back and forth. Otherwise the Germans would suspect him and shoot him. People who knew in what a small force we were, who had accomplished missions, were kept under arrest in order that, returning into German-held territory, they might not be forced to talk by the Germans if they were captured.

A very young Pole deserted from the German tank unit ahead of us. He buried his uniform and his submachine gun and filtered through the lines in his underwear and a pair of trousers he had found in a shelled house. He brought good information and was put to work in the kitchen of the hotel. Security was at that time in a very primitive state, since everyone who was armed was running patrols, but I can remember the colonel being considerably shocked when the cook came into the dining room which was serving as a command post and asked permission to send the prisoner out by himself to get bread from the baker. The colonel was obliged to refuse this request. Later the prisoner asked me to send him under guard to dig up his uniform and his gun so he could fight with the outfit. This request was also regretfully refused.

During this period of unorthodox warfare a German tank took a side road and came down to within three miles of town and killed a very nice policeman, who was out on patrol, and one of our local guerrillas. Everyone present at this episode dived into the ditch and commenced firing on the tank, which, having established contact, withdrew. The Germans at this period exhibited a lamentable tendency to fight entirely by the book. If they had thrown the book away they could have moved into town and been drinking the excellent wines of the Hotel du Grand Veneur and even gone so far as to take their Pole out of the kitchen and either shot him or got him back into uniform.

It was quite a strange life in the Hotel du Grand Veneur in those days. An old man you had seen a week before during the taking of Chartres, and who had ridden in the jeep as far as Epernon, had come in the last time you had seen him and said he believed there was very interesting information to be discovered in the forest in Rambouillet. This, as a correspondent, was none of your damned business. Now you picked him up on a road six miles north of town and he had complete information on a mine field and antitank emplacement on the road just past Trappes. You sent out and verified the information. It was then necessary to hold the old man under guard since he wished to go out for more information and he knew too much about our present situation to risk his being captured by the Germans. So he joined the Polish child in protective custody.

All of this should have been handled by the Counter Intelligence Corps. But we did not have any, nor did we have any Civil Affairs. I remember the colonel saying, "Ernie, if we just had some CIC or just a little Civil Affairs. Just refer all that to the French." Everything was referred to the French. Usually, though not always, it was promptly referred back to us.

During this epoch I was addressed by the guerrilla force as "Captain." This is a very low rank to have at the age of forty-five years, and so, in the presence of strangers, they would address me, usually, as "Colonel." But they were a little upset and worried by my very low rank, and one of them, whose trade for the past year had been receiving mines and blowing up German ammunition trucks and staff cars, asked confidentially, "My Captain, how is it that with your age and your undoubted long years of service and your obvious wounds (caused by hitting a static water tank·in London) you are still a captain?"

"Young man," I told him, "I have not been able to advance in rank due to the fact that I cannot read or write."

Eventually another American Army reconnaissance outfit arrived and took up position on the road to Versailles. The town was then screened and we were able to devote all of our time to running patrols into German-held territory and checking exactly on the German defensive dispositions in order that, whenever an advance on Paris should be made, the force which would make it would have accurate information to operate on.

The main highlights of this period that I remember, outside of being scared a number of times, are not publishable at this time. Sometime I would like to be able to write an account of the actions of the colonel both by day and by night. But you cannot write it yet.

This is what the alleged front was like at that time: You come down a slope of highway to a village with a gas station and a café. Ahead is a small village with a church spire on the road opposite the café. From this point you can see a long slope of highway to your rear and a long stretch of highway ahead. Two men are standing in the road with field glasses. One watches the road to the north and the other to the south.

This is necessary since the Germans are both ahead of us and behind us. Two girls are walking down the road toward the town, which is held by the Germans. They are good-looking girls, wearing red-heeled shoes. A guerrilla comes up and says, "Those girls were sleeping with the Germans when they were here. Now they are going toward the German lines and can give them information.

"Hold them," someone says.

Just then comes a shout, "A car! A car!"

"Theirs or ours?"

"Theirs!"

At this everyone scatters with rifles or submachine guns behind the café and the filling station, and several prudent citizens take refuge in the fields.

A tiny German jeep comes up the road opposite the filling station, commences firing a 20-millimeter gun. Everyone shoots at it and it wheels around and goes back up the road. It is shot at, as it disappears, by the more prudent citizens, who become very brave as it retreats. Total casualties: Two enthusiasts who have fallen with their wine-glasses in their hands in the café and have slight cuts.

The two girls, who, it turns out, speak German as well as having allegedly been fond of the Germans, are picked up out of a ditch and put in a secure location to be returned to town. One of them says that all she did was go swimming with the Germans.

"In the nude?" asks a guerrilla.

"No, Monsieur," she answers. "They were always correct." They have in their handbags many German addresses and other articles which do not endear them to the local population, and they are sent back to Rambouillet. There is no hysteria and no beating or haircutting by the local population. The Germans are much too close for that.

Two miles off to the left a German tank comes into a village where they find three guerrillas who have been checking on their movements and who are recognized by the tankmen who have seen them too many times.

One of these is a man who, when I asked him if he had actually seen the tank himself, said, "Captain, I touched it." They are shot by the Germans and their bodies are left alongside the road. An hour later a guerrilla who was in the town brings us the news. This produces a certain amount of head-shaking and makes it more difficult to send the Germans, who are being continually picked up in the woods from the units which escaped from Chartres, back to be interrogated.

An old man appears and says that his wife is covering five Germans with a pistol. This pistol had been given him the night before, when, he said, Germans were coming into his place from the forest to eat. These are not the Germans who are organized and fighting ahead but are from scattered units which are dispersed through the forest. Some of them are trying to rejoin the main German body to continue fighting. Others are anxious to surrender if they know how they can do it without being killed.

A car is sent out to pick up the five Germans the old woman is holding. "Can we kill them?" one of the patrol asks.

"Only if they are SS," a guerrilla says.

"Bring them in here, so they can be questioned and passed on to Division," I say, and the car pulls out.

The Polish kid, who had the face of Jackie Cooper when Jackie Cooper was still young, is polishing glasses in the hotel dining room, and the old man is smoking his pipe and wondering when he can be released to go on another mission.

"My Captain," the old man says, "why cannot I be allowed to perform some useful function instead of resting here in the garden of this hotel while Paris is at stake?"

"You know too much to let the Germans get hold of you," I tell him.

"The little Pole and I could make a useful mission, and I would kill him if he attempted to escape."

"He cannot make a useful mission," I said; "he can only be sent with troops."

"He says he will return in uniform and get any information that is needed."

"Let's stop the fairy stories," I said to the old man, "and since there is no one here to guard the little Pole you are responsible for him."

At this point a large amount of information came in which had to be evaluated and typed out, and it was necessary for me to leave on a patrol to St. Rémy-lès-Chevreuses. There was a report that General Le Clerc's Second French Armored Division was approaching Rambouillet on the road to Paris, and we wanted to have ready all the information on the German dispositions.

How We Came to Paris

➤ *Collier's* · OCTOBER 7, 1944

NEVER can I describe to you the emotions I felt on the arrival of the armored column of General Leclerc southeast of Paris. Having just returned from a patrol which scared the pants off of me and having been kissed by all the worst element in a town which imagined it had been liberated through our fortuitous entry, I was informed that the general himself was just down the road and anxious to see us. Accompanied by one of the big shots of the resistance movement and Colonel B, who by that time was known throughout Rambouillet as a gallant officer and a *grand seigneur* and who had held the town ever since we could remember, we advanced in some state toward the general. His greeting—unprintable—will live in my ears forever.

"Buzz off, you unspeakables," the gallant general said, in effect, in something above a whisper, and Colonel B, the resistance king and your armored-operations correspondent withdrew.

Later the G-2 of the division invited us to dinner and they operated next day on the information Colonel B had amassed for them. But for your correspondent that was the high point of the attack on Paris.

In war, my experience has been that a rude general is a nervous general. At this time I drew no such deductions but departed on another patrol where I could keep my own nervousness in one jeep and my friends could attempt to clarify the type of resistance we could encounter on the following day between Toussus le Noble and Le Christ de Saclay.

Having found out what this resistance would be, we returned to the Hotel du Grand Veneur in Rambouillet and passed a restless night. I do not remember exactly what produced this restlessness but perhaps it was the fact that the joint was too full of too many people, including, actually, at one time two military police. Or perhaps it was the fact that we had proceeded too far ahead of our supply of Vitamin B_1, and the ravages of alcohol were affecting the nerves of the hardier guerrillas who had liberated too many towns in too short a time. At any rate I was restless and I think, without exaggeration, I may truly state that those whom Colonel B and I by then referred as as "our people" were restless.

The guerrilla chief, the actual fighting head of "our people," said, "We want to take Paris. What the hell is the delay?"

"There is no delay, Chief," I answered. "All this is part of a giant operation. Have patience. Tomorrow we will take Paris."

"I hope so," the guerrilla chief said. "My wife has been expecting me there for some time. I want to get the hell into Paris to see my wife, and I see no necessity to wait for a lot of soldiers to come up."

"Be patient," I told him.

That fateful night we slept. It might be a fateful night but tomorrow would certainly be an even more fateful day. My anticipations of a really good fight on the morrow were marred by a guerrilla who entered the hotel late at night and woke me to inform me that all the Germans who could do so were pulling out of Paris. We knew there would be fighting the next day by the screen the German army had left. But I did not anticipate any heavy fighting, since we knew the German dispositions and could attack or by-pass them accordingly, and I assured our guerrillas that if they would only be patient, we would have the privilege of entering Paris with soldiers ahead of us instead of behind us.

This privilege did not appeal to them at all. But one of the big shots of the underground insisted that we do this, as he said it was only courteous to allow troops to precede and by the time we had reached Toussus le Noble, where there was a short but sharp fight, orders were given that neither newspapermen nor guerrillas were to be allowed to proceed until the column had passed.

The day we advanced on Paris it rained heavily and everyone was soaked to the skin within an hour of leaving Rambouillet. We proceeded through Chevreuse and St. Rémy-lès-Chevreuses where we had formerly run patrols and were well known to the local inhabitants, from whom we had collected information and with whom we had downed considerable quantities of armagnac to still the ever-present discontent of our guerrillas, who were very Paris-conscious at this time. In those days I had found that the production of an excellent bottle of any sort of alcoholic beverage was the only way of ending an argument.

After we had proceeded through St. Rémy-lès-Chevreuses, where we were wildly acclaimed by the local *charcutier,* or pork butcher, who had participated in previous operations and been cockeyed ever since, we made a slight error in preceding the column to a village called Courcelle. There we were informed that there were no vehicles ahead of us and, greatly to the disgust of our people who wished to proceed on what they believed to be the shortest route into Paris, we returned to St. Rémy-lès-Chevreuses to join the armored column which was proceeding toward Châteaufort. Our return was viewed with considerable alarm by the local *charcutier.* But when we explained the situation to him he acclaimed us wildly again and, downing a couple of quick ones, we advanced resolutely toward Toussus le Noble where I knew the column would have to fight.

At this point I knew there would be German opposition just ahead of us and also on our right at Le Christ de Saclay. The Germans had dug and blasted out a series of defense points between Châteaufort and Toussus le Noble and beyond the crossroads. Past the airdrome toward Buc they had 88s that commanded all that stretch of road. As we came closer to where the tanks were operating around Trappes I became increasingly apprehensive.

The French armor operated beautifully. On the road toward Toussus le Noble, where we knew there were Germans with machine guns in the wheat shocks, the tanks deployed and screened both of our flanks and we saw them rolling ahead through the cropped wheat field as though they were on maneuvers. No one saw the Germans until they came out with their hands up after the tanks had passed. It was a beautiful use of armor, that problem child of war, and it was lovely to see.

When we ran up against the seven tanks and four 88s the Germans had beyond the airfield, the French handled the fight prettily, too. Their artillery was back in another open wheat field, and when the German guns—four of which had been brought up during the night and were firing absolutely in the open—cut loose on the column, the French mechanized artillery slammed into them. You could not hear with the German shells coming in, the 20-mm. firing, and the machine-gun fire cracking overhead, but the French underground leader who had correlated the information on the German dispositions shouted in French into my ear, "The contact is beautiful. Just where we said. Beautiful."

It was much too beautiful for me, who had never been a great lover of contact anyway, and I hit the deck as an 88 shell burst alongside the road. Contact is a very noisy business and, since our column was held up at this point, the more forceful and active of the guerrillas aided in reconstructing the road which had been churned into soup by the armor. This kept their minds from the contact taking place all around us. They filled in the mudholes with bricks and tiles from a smashed house, and passed along chunks of cement and pieces of house from hand to hand. It was raining hard all this time, and by the time the contact was over, the column had two dead and five wounded, one tank burned up, and had knocked out two of the seven enemy tanks and silenced all of the 88s.

"*C'est un bel accrochage*," the underground leader said to me jubilantly.

This means something like "We have grappled with them

prettily" or "We tied into them beautifully," searching in mind for the exact meaning of *accrochage,* which is what happens when two cars lock bumpers.

I shouted, "Prettily! Prettily!"

At which a young French lieutenant, who did not have the air of having been mixed up in too many *accrochages* in his time but who, for all I know, may have participated in hundreds of them, said to me, "Who the hell are you and what are you doing here in our column?"

"I am a war correspondent, monsieur," I replied.

The lieutenant shouted: "Do not let any war correspondents proceed until the column has passed. And especially do not let this one proceed."

"Okay, my lieutenant," the M.P. said. "I will keep an eye on them."

"And none of that guerrilla rabble, either," the lieutenant ordered. "None of that is to pass until all the column has gone through."

"My lieutenant," I said, "the rabble will be removed from sight once this little *accrochage* is finished and the column has proceeded."

"What do you mean—this little *accrochage?*" he demanded, and I feared hostility might be creeping into his voice.

Since we were not to advance farther with the column, I took evasive action at this point and waded down the road to a bar. Numerous guerrillas were seated in it singing happily and passing the time of day with a lovely Spanish girl from Bilbao whom I had last met on the famous two-way, or wide-open patrol point just outside the town of Cognières. This was the town we used to take from the Germans whenever one of their vehicles pulled out of it, and they would return whenever we stepped off the road. This girl had been following wars and preceding troops since she was fifteen and she and the guerrillas were paying no attention to the *accrochage* at all.

A guerrilla chief named C said, "Have a drink of this excellent white wine." I took a long drink from the bottle and it turned out to be a highly alcoholic liqueur tasting of oranges and called Grand Marnier.

A stretcher was coming back with a wounded man on it. "Look," a guerrilla said, "these military are constantly suffering casualties. Why do they not allow us to proceed ahead in a sensible manner?"

"Okay, okay," said another guerrilla in G.I. fatigue clothes, with the brassard of the *francs-tireurs* on his sleeve. "What about the comrades who were killed yesterday on the road?"

Another said, "But today we're going into Paris."

"Let's go back and see if we can make it by Le Christ de Saclay," I said. "The law has arrived and they won't let us go on any farther until the column has passed. The roads are too muddy and torn up here. We could push the light touring cars through, but the truck might bog down and stall things."

"We can push through by a side road," the guerrilla chief named C said. "Since when do we have to follow columns?"

"I think it is best to go back as far as Châteaufort," I said. "Maybe we can go much faster that way."

On the crossroads outside Châteaufort we found Colonel B and Commander A, who had become detached from us before we had run into the *accrochage,* and told them about the beautiful contact up the road. The artillery was still firing in the open wheat field, and the two gallant officers had found some lunch in a farmhouse. French troops from the column were burning the wooden boxes that had held the shells the artillery had been blasting with, and we took off our wet clothes and dried them at the fire. German prisoners were drifting in, and an officer in the column asked us to send the guerrillas up to where a group of Germans had just surrendered in the wheat shocks. They brought them back in good military style, all the prisoners alive and well.

"This is idiotic, you know, my captain," the oldest one of the band said. "Now someone has to feed them."

The prisoners said they were office workers in Paris and had only been brought out and put in the positions at one o'clock this morning.

"Do you believe that sort of stuff?" asked the oldest guerrilla.

"It could be possible. They weren't here yesterday," I said.

"This entire military nonsense disgusts me," the oldest guerrilla said. He was forty-one and had a thin, sharp face with clear blue eyes, and a rare but fine smile. "Eleven of our group were tortured and shot by these Germans. I have been beaten and kicked by them, and they would have shot me if they knew who I was. Now we are asked to guard them carefully and respectfully."

"They are not your prisoners," I explained. "The military took them."

The rain turned to a light drifting mist and then the sky cleared. The prisoners were sent back to Rambouillet in the big German truck that the underground big shot quite rightly was anxious to get out of the column for the moment. Leaving word with the M.P. on the crossroads where the truck could rejoin us, we drove on after the column.

We caught up with the tanks on a side road this side of the main Versailles-Paris highway and moved with them down into a deeply wooded valley and out into green fields where there was an old château. We watched the tanks deploy again, like watching dogs outside a moving band of sheep. They had fought once up ahead of us while we had gone back to see if the road through Le Christ de Saclay was free, and we passed a burned-out tank and three dead Germans. One of these had been run over and flattened out in a way that left no doubt of the power of armor when properly used.

On the main Versailles-Villacoublay highway the column proceeded past the wrecked airdrome of Villacoublay to the crossroads of the Porte Clamart. Here, while the column was stopped, a Frenchman came running up and reported a small German tank on the road that led into the woods. I searched the road with my glasses but could not see anything. In the meantime, the German vehicle, which was not a tank but a lightly armored German jeep mounting a machine gun and a 20-mm. gun, made a turn in the woods and came tearing up the road, firing at the crossroads.

Everyone started shooting at it, but it wheeled and regained the woods. Archie Pelkey, my driver, got in two shots at it but could not be sure that he had hit. Two men were hit and were carried into the lee of the corner building for first aid. The guerrillas were happy now that shooting had started again.

"We have nice work ahead of us. Good work ahead of us," the guerrilla with the sharp face and the light blue eyes said. "I'm happy some of the b——s are still here."

"Do you think we will have much more chance to fight?" the guerrilla named C asked.

"Certainly," I said. "There's bound to be some of them in the town."

My own war aim at this moment was to get into Paris without being shot. Our necks had been out for a long time. Paris was going to be taken. I took cover in all the street fighting —the solidest cover available—and with someone covering the stairs behind me when we were in houses or the entrances to apartment houses.

From now on, the advance of the column was something to see. Ahead of us would be a barricade of felled trees. The tanks would pass around them or butt them around like elephants handling logs. You would see the tanks charge into a barricade of old motorcars and go smashing on ahead with a jalopy bouncing along, its smashed fenders entangled in the tracks. Armor, which can be so vulnerable and so docile in the close hedgerow country where it is a prey to antitank guns, bazookas and anyone who does not fear it, was smashing round like so many drunken elephants in a native village.

Ahead and on our left, a German ammunition dump was burning, and the varicolored antiaircraft projectiles were bursting in the continuous rattle and pop of the exploding 20-mm. stuff. The larger projectiles started to explode as the heat increased, and gave the impression of a bombardment. I couldn't locate Archie Pelkey, but later I found he had advanced on the burning munitions dump, thinking it was a fight.

"There wasn't nobody there, Papa," he said; "it was just a lot of ammunition burning."

"Don't go off by yourself," I said. "How did you know we didn't want to roll?"

"Okay, Papa. Sorry, Papa. I understand, Papa. Only, Mr. Hemingway, I went off with *Frère*—the one who is my brother —because I thought he said there was a fight."

"Oh, hell!" I said. "You've been ruined by guerrillas."

We ran through the road where the munitions dump was exploding, with Archie, who has bright red hair, six years of regular Army, four words of French, a missing front tooth, and a *Frère* in a guerrilla outfit, laughing heartily at the noise the big stuff was making as it blew.

"Sure is popping off, Papa," he shouted. His freckled face was completely happy. "They say this Paris is quite a town, Papa. You ever been into it?"

"Yeah."

We were going downhill now, and I knew that road and what we would see when we made the next turn.

"*Frère,* he was telling me something about it while the column was held up, but I couldn't make it out," Archie said. "All I could make out was it must be a hell of a place. Something about he was going to *Paname,* too. This place hasn't got anything to do with Panama, has it?"

"No, Arch," I said, "the French call it *Paname* when they love it very much."

"I see," Archie said. "*Compris.* Just like something you might call a girl that wouldn't be her right name. Right?"

"Right."

"I couldn't make out what the hell *Frère* was saying," Archie said. "I guess it's like they call me Jim. Everybody in the outfit calls me Jim, and my name is Archie."

"Maybe they like you," I said.

"They're a good outfit," Archie said. "Best outfit I ever been with. No discipline. Got to admit that. Drinking all the time. Got to admit that. But plenty fighting outfit. Nobody gives a damn if they get killed or not. *Compris?*"

"Yeah," I said. I couldn't say anything more then, because I had a funny choke in my throat and I had to clean my glasses because there now, below us, gray and always beautiful, was spread the city I love best in all the world.

The G.I. and the General

➤ *Collier's* · NOVEMBER 4, 1944

THE wheat was ripe but there was no one there to cut it now, and tank tracks led through it to where the tanks lay pushed into the hedge that topped the ridge that looked across the wooded country to the hill he would have to take tomorrow. There was no one between us and the Germans in that wooded country and on the hill. We knew they had some infantry there and between fifteen and forty tanks. But the division had advanced so fast that the division on its left had not come up, and all this country that you looked across, seeing the friendly hills, the valleys, the farmhouses with their fields and orchards, and the gray-walled, slate-roofed buildings of the town with its sharp-pointing church tower, was all one open flank. All of it was deadly.

The division has not advanced beyond its objective. It had reached its objective, the high ground we were now on, exactly when it should have. It had been doing this for day after day after day after week after month now. No one remembered separate days any more, and history, being made each day, was never noticed but only merged into a great blur of tiredness and dust, of the smell of dead cattle, the smell of earth new-broken by TNT, the grinding sound of tanks and bulldozers, the sound of automatic-rifle and machine-gun fire, the interceptive, dry tattle of German machine-pistol fire, dry as a rattler rattling; and the quick, spurting tap of the German light machine guns—and always waiting for others to come up.

It was merged in the memory of the fight up out of the deadly, low hedgerow country onto the heights and through the forest

and on down into the plain, by and through the towns, some
smashed, and some intact, and on up into the rolling farm and
forest country where we were now.

History now was old K-ration boxes, empty foxholes, the drying leaves on the branches that were cut for camouflage. It was
burned German vehicles, burned Sherman tanks, many burned
German Panthers and some burned Tigers, German dead along
the roads, in the hedges and in the orchards, German equipment
scattered everywhere, German horses roaming the fields, and
our own wounded and our dead passing back strapped two
abreast on top of the evacuation jeeps. But mostly history was
getting where we were to get on time and waiting there for
others to come up.

Now on this clear summer afternoon we stood looking across
the country where the division would fight tomorrow. It was one
of the first days of the really good weather. The sky was high
and blue, and ahead and to our left, our planes were working
on the German tanks. Tiny and silver in the sun, the P-47s
came in high in pairs of pairs and circled before peeling off to
dive-bomb. As they went down, growing big-headed and husky-
looking in the snarl of the dive, you saw the flash and the smoke
of the bombs and heard their heavy thud. Then the P-47s
climbed and circled again to come down strafing, smoke streaming gray behind them as they dived ahead of the smoke their
eight big .50s made as they hammered. There was a very bright
flash in the trees of the wooded patch the planes were diving
on, and then black smoke arose and the planes came down
strafing again and again.

"They got a Jerry tank then," one of the tank men said.
"That's one of the b—s less."

"Can you see him with your glasses?" another helmeted tank
man asked me.

I said, "The trees hide him from this side."

"They would," the tank man said. "If we used cover like those
damned Krauts, a lot more guys would get to Paris or Berlin
or wherever it is we're going."

"Home," another man said. "That's all I care about going. That's where I'm going. All those other places will be off limits anyway. We're never going in no town."

"Take it easy," another soldier said. "Take it a day at a time."

"Say, correspondent," another soldier called. "One thing I can't understand. You tell me, will you? What are you doing here if you don't have to be here? Do you do it just for the money?"

"Sure," I said. "Big money. Lots of money."

"It don't make sense to me," he said seriously. "I understand anybody doing it that has to do it. But doing it for money don't make sense. There ain't the money in the world to pay me for doing it."

A German high-explosive shell with a time fuse cracked overhead and to our right, leaving a black puff of smoke in the air.

"Those lousy Krauts shot that stuff too high," the soldier who wouldn't do it for money said.

Just then the German artillery started shelling the hill on our left where one of the battalions of the first of the three infantry regiments in the division lay above the town. The side of the hill was jumping into the air in spurting dark fountains from the multiple bursts.

"They'll shoot on us next," one of the tank men said. "They've got good observation on us here."

"Lay down under the back of the tank there if they start to shoot," the big tank man who had told the other soldier to take it a day at a time said. "That's the best place to be."

"She looks sort of heavy," I told him. "Suppose you have to start backing out in a hurry?"

"I'll holler to you," he grinned.

Our 105s opened up behind us in counterbattery fire, and the German shelling stopped. A Piper Cub was circling slowly overhead. Another was off to the right.

"They don't like to shoot when those Cubs are up," the big tank man said. "They spot the flashes, and then our artillery gives them hell or the planes go in after them."

We stayed there a while but the German artillery only opened at intervals on the hill the battalion was holding. We were not attacking.

"Let's go back and see where the rest of the combat command has got to," I said.

"Okay," said Kimbrough, who drove the captured German motorcycle we rode on. "Let's go."

We said "So long" to the tank people and went back through the wheat field and got on the motorcycle, me on the back seat, and rode out into the dust of the road that the armor had churned into thick clouds of gray powder. The sidecar held a mixed lot of armament, photographic equipment, repair equipment, miscellaneous captured German bottled goods, live hand grenades, various automatic weapons, all belonging to Corporal (now Sergeant) John Kimbrough of Little Rock, Arkansas.

It could easily have served as a showcase for an advertisement of the well-armed guerrilla's dream, and I often wondered how Kim planned to deploy himself in the event we had to take other than evasive action on those rides through territory whose possession was in doubt. Versatile though he is and much as I respect his ability to improvise, yet I was sometimes appalled at the prospect of him managing more than three submachine guns, a variety of pistols, a carbine and, once, a German light machine gun, at a time, without dispersing his fire too much. But finally I decided he must be figuring on arming the countryside as we proceeded deeper into enemy territory. And, as it turned out, this worked out very well on one occasion and was worth one whole new stripe to my far-seeing and, I then considered, slightly overarmed pal.

We headed back down the road to the town that we had taken that afternoon and I stopped in front of the café across from the church. The road was full of armor passing-in their clanking, grinding howl; the noise of one tank dying off into the rising, retching, steel-tortured approach of the next. The tanks had their turrets open, and the crews returned perfunctorily the waves the boys of the village gave each vehicle. An old Frenchman in a black felt hat, a boiled shirt, a black tie, and a dusty black suit, with a bunch of flowers in his right hand, stood on the terrace of the church above the road and saluted each tank formally with the flowers.

"Who is the man by the church?" I asked the woman who owned the café, as we stood in the doorway to let the armor pass.

"He is a little crazy," she said. "But very patriotic. He has been there ever since you came through this morning. He has eaten no lunch. Twice his family have come for him, but he remains there."

"Did he salute the Germans, too?"

"Oh, no," madame said. "He is a man of extreme patriotism, but since several years, slightly touched, you know."

At a table, three soldiers were sitting with a carafe of cider, half full, and three glasses. "That slave driver," one of them who was unshaven, tall, thin, and limber with drink, was saying. "That dirty damn' slave driver. Sixty miles back of the front and he'll kill every one of us."

"Who you talking about?" Kimbrough said to the soldier.

"That slave driver! That general!"

"How far did you say he was?" Kimbrough asked.

"Sixty miles if he's a damned inch. Sixty miles that we have died on. We're all dead. Don't he know it? Does he give a damn? That slave driver."

"Do you know how far he is back? He isn't three thousand yards back of here now," Kimbrough said. "Maybe he has gone up ahead. We passed him on the road a while back."

"Oh, you dope," the unshaven soldier said. "What the hell do you know about the war? That damn' slave driver is sixty miles back if he is an inch. And look at me! I used to sing with good bands—good, good bands. And my wife is unfaithful to me. I don't have to prove it. She told me. And there's what I believe in, right over there."

He pointed across the road above the tanks where the middle-aged Frenchman was still lifting his flowers at each tank that passed. There was a priest in black, crossing the graveyard behind the church.

"Who you believe in? That Frenchman?" another G.I. asked.

"No. I don't believe in that Frenchman," the soldier who had sung with good bands said. "I believe in what the priest represents. I believe in the Church. And my wife is unfaithful to me not once but many times. I will not let her have a divorce because *that* is what I believe in. And that is why she would not sign the papers. And that is why I am not a bombardier. I went through Bombardier School and she would not sign the papers and right this minute now she is unfaithful to me."

"He can sing, too," one of the G.I.s said to me. "I heard him sing the other night and he can sing all right."

"I cannot say I hate my wife," the soldier who had sung with good bands said. "If she is unfaithful to me now, this minute, while we are here and have just taken this town, I cannot say I hate her, although she has ruined my life and kept me from being a bombardier. But I hate the general. I hate that black-hearted slave driver."

"Let him cry," said one of the other G.I.s. "It makes him feel better."

"Listen," the third G.I. said. "He's got a domestic problem and he has his troubles. But let me tell *you* something. This is the first town I have ever been in. In the infantry we take them, and more often we by-pass them, and then when we come back they are off limits and full of MPs. So far there is not an MP in this town except the traffic at the corner. It isn't right, truly, that we never can go in a town."

"Later on—" I started to say. The soldier who had sung with many good bands cut in.

"There isn't going to be any later on," he said. "That slave driver will kill every one of us. All he is doing it for is to be famous and because he does not know that men are human."

"He hasn't any more to say about whether we are in the line than I have," Kimbrough said. "You don't know what a divisional general does, or that he gets his orders like you or I do."

"All right. You get us out of the line, then. If you know all that, then *you* get us out of the line. I want to go home. If I was at home maybe none of this would ever have happened. Maybe my wife would never have been unfaithful to me at all, ever. Anyway, I don't care about anything now. I do not care about anything at all."

"Why don't you shut up, then?" Kimbrough asked.

"I will shut up," the band singer said. "And I will not say what I think about that general who is killing me every day."

That night we got back to advanced Division Headquarters late. After leaving the G.I.s at the café in the newly taken town, we had followed the armor down to where it had been stalled by mines, a road block and antitank fire.

At Division someone said, "The general wants to see you."

"I'll wash up."

"No. Go over. He's been worrying about you."

I found him in the trailer, stretched out in an old gray woolen union suit. His face that was still handsome when he was rested was gray and drawn and endlessly tired. Only his eyes were alive and his kind, warm voice said, "I was worried about you. What made you so late?"

"We ran into some armor and I came back the long way around."

"Which way?"

I told him.

"Tell me what you saw today with the this and the that" (mentioning the names of the infantry units committed).

I told him.

"The people are very tired, Ernie," he said. "They ought to have a rest. Even one good night's rest would help. If they could have four days . . . just four days. But it's the same old story."

"You're tired yourself," I said. "Get some sleep. Don't let me keep you awake."

"There should never be tired generals," he said. "And especially there should never be sick generals. I'm not as tired as they are."

Just then the telephone rang, and he picked it up, answering with the code name for the G.O.C. of the division.

"Yes," he said. "Yes. How are you, Jim? . . . No. I have them

bedded down for the night. I want them to get some sleep . . .
No. I am attacking in the morning but I am not assaulting.
I am going to by-pass it. I don't believe in attacking towns, you
know. You ought to know that by now . . . No. I'll come in
below there . . . Yes. That's right."

He slipped off the blanketed shelf bed and over to the huge
wall map, still holding the telephone, and I watched his compact, bellyless body in the gray woolen underwear, remembering what a spit-and-polish general this had been before the division had been in action.

He went on talking into the telephone: "Jim? . . . Yes. The
only trouble you have ahead of you really is that cloverleaf-
shaped business. You'll have to work around that. Now you
know there's been some talk of something . . . Yes. I understand.
Now if this happens, and when you're up with me, you can
have all my artillery if you need it . . . Yes. Absolutely . . . That's
quite right . . . No. Of course, I mean it. I wouldn't say it otherwise . . . That's right . . . Good . . . Good night."

He hung up. His face was gray-glazed with tiredness. "That
was the division on our left. They've done very well but they
had slow going through the forest. When they come up and pass
us, we are supposed to have four days' rest. The infantry needs
it very badly. I'm very happy that they will have it."

"You ought to get some sleep now," I said.

"I have to get to work now. Keep off those lonesome roads
and watch yourself."

"Good night, sir," I said. "I'll be by early in the morning."

Everybody thought that the division was going to be pulled
out for four days, and the next day there was much talk of
showers, clubmobiles, beautiful Red Cross girls including Whitney Bourne, who had played in the movies in a picture called
Crime Without Passion, and we were all deeply moved by the
prospect, ignoring the year in which the picture had been made.
But it didn't turn out that way. There was a big German coun-
ter-attack instead and, as I write this, the division is still in the
line.

War in the Siegfried Line

➤ *Collier's* · NOVEMBER 18, 1944

A LOT of people will tell you how it was to be first into Germany and how it was to break the Siegfried Line and a lot of people will be wrong. So this will not be held up by the censor while all the claims are threshed out. We do not claim anything. No claims, see? You get it? No claims at all. Let them decide and then we will see who was in there first. I mean which outfit. Not which people.

The infantry cracked the Siegfried Line. They cracked it on a cold rainy morning when even the crows weren't flying, much less the Air Force. Two days before, on the last day before the weather broke for the bad, we had come to the end of the rat race. It had been a fine rat race from Paris up as far as Le Cateau, with bitter fighting at Landrecies that few saw and fewer still are left to remember. Then there had been the forcing of the passes of the Ardennes Forest in country like the illustrations for Grimm's Fairy Tales only a lot grimmer.

Then the rat race went on again through rolling, forested country. Sometimes we would be half an hour behind the retreating enemy's mechanized force. Sometimes we would get up to within five minutes of them. Sometimes we would overrun them and, from the point of the recon, you would hear the fifties hammering behind you and the 105-millimeter Wump guns going on the tank destroyers and the merging roar and rattle of enemy fire, and the word would come along: "Enemy tanks and half-tracks in the rear of the column. Pass the word along."

Then, suddenly the rat race was over, and we were on a high

hill, out of the forest, and all the rolling hills and forests that you saw ahead of you were Germany. There was a heavy, familiar roar from the creek valley below as the bridge was blown, and beyond the black cloud of smoke and debris that rose, you saw two enemy half-tracks tearing up the white road that led into the German hills.

Our artillery was blasting yellow-white clouds of smoke and road dust ahead of them. You watched one half-track slither sideways across the road. The other stopped on the turn of the road after trying twice to move like a wounded animal. Another shell pounded up a fountain of dust and smoke alongside the crippled half-track and when the smoke cleared, you could see the bodies on the road. That was the end of the rat race, and we came down a trail in the woods and into the ford over the river and across the slab-stoned river bed and up the far bank into Germany.

We passed the unmanned old-fashioned pillboxes that many unfortunate people were to think constituted the Siegfried Line, and got up into good high ground that night. The next day we were past the second line of concrete fortified strong points that guarded road junctions and approaches to the main Westwall, and that same night we were up on the highest of the high ground before the Westwall, ready to assault in the morning.

The weather had broken. It was cold and raining and blowing half a gale, and ahead of us was the dark forest wall of the Schnee Eifel range where the dragon lived, and behind us on the first hill behind was a German reviewing stand that had been built for high officers to occupy when they watched the maneuvers that proved that the Westwall never could be broken. We were hitting it on the point that the Germans had chosen to prove, in sham battles, that it was impregnable.

The rest of this story is told in the words of Captain Howard Blazzard of Arizona. It may give you a little idea of what happens in combat.

"That night we got L Company into that town to hold it. It was practically unoccupied. Six Jerries, and we shot them. *(This*

*was the town, or small village rather, from which the attack
started in the morning up the hill and across the level field of
fire over a cropped wheatfield, the wheat shocks stacked, to
assault the main fortifications of the Westwall which were in
the thick pine forest of the dark hill beyond.)*

"The Colonel, of Washington, D. C., got the three battalion
commanders together and the S-2 and the S-3 and planned the
break-through for in the morning. Where this break was going
to be made *(you notice the phrasing 'Going to be made,' not
'Going to be attempted')* we were supposed to have one company
of tanks and one company of T.D.s (Tank Destroyers) but they
only gave us one platoon of tanks (five). We were supposed to
have twelve T.D.s and we had only nine. You remember how
everything was then and how the gas was short and all.

"The way it was supposed to be now *(There is a great difference in combat between the way it is supposed to be and the
way it is—as great as the difference in how life is supposed to be
and how it is):* L Company, that had moved into town the night
before, was going to be on the right flank, and they were going
to make the holding attack with fire.

"K Company had started walking early, before six A.M., and
they were going to ride the tanks and the T.D.s. While they
were coming up we got the T.D.s up into town and finally by
twelve-thirty we got one platoon of tanks. Five of them. All five
of them.

"Now I Company was back so far they couldn't get up. You
remember everything that was happening that day. *(Plenty.
Plenty was happening.)* So the Colonel, he took a company away
from the First Battalion and threw them in, so he'd have three
companies to make the attack.

"That was around one o'clock. The Colonel and I went up
this left fork that was sort of drawn off on the left, to watch the
attack get started. It started fine. K Company sarted riding the
tanks and the T.D.s, and then they moved up and got just
below the crest and fanned out. Just as they should. Just as they
hit that little crest, L Company on their right opened up with

machine guns and 60-millimeter mortars and all that fire, to attract attention from K Company.

"The tanks and T.D.s got up the hill and the flak guns *(German antiaircraft guns, which fire almost as rapidly as machine guns, being used for direct fire on the ground against the attacking troops)* opened up first. The 88 which we knew was in there held its fire. When the ack-ack and the machine guns opened up, the men started to dismount from the tanks, just as they should, and they went on up and they went fine till they got out in the open on that big bare field and almost to the edge of the last field in front of the woods.

"About that time they really opened up with the 88s—the 88s and all that flak. One T.D. hit a mine over on the left by that little road, you remember, just before it goes into the woods, and the tanks began to run. Lost a T.D. and a tank and they all started backing up. You know how they are when they start backing up.

"They started coming back down across the field, dragging a few wounded and a few limping. You know how they look coming back. Then the tanks started coming back and the T.D.s coming back and the men coming back plenty. They couldn't stay in that bare field, and the ones who weren't hit started yelling for the medicos for those who were hit, and you know how that excites everybody.

"The Colonel and I were sitting by the house and we could see the fight and the way it started fine and good. We thought they'd got right through. But then this stuff starts. Then come four tankers tearing along on foot and yelling and hollering how everything was knocked out.

"Then I asked the Colonel—I'd been in the Third Battalion a long time—and I said, 'Sir, I can go out there and kick those bastards in the tail and take that place.' And he said, 'You're S-2 in a staff function and you stay where you are.' That chewed my tail out. That made me unhappy.

"We sat there another ten or fifteen minutes, and the wounded kept drifting along back, and we were just there and I thought we're going to lose this battle. Then the Colonel says, 'Let's get up there. This thing has got to move. Those chickenspits aren't going to break down this attack.'

"So we started up the hill and we passed little groups here and there—you know how they drift together—and you know how the Colonel looks, and he is carrying his forty-five and walking up that hill. There is a sort of little terrace at the top where the hill starts to come down; under the cover of that little terrace were all the tanks and the T.D.s, and K Company was lined up along in a sort of skirmish line and they were all just sort of dead, and the attack was gone.

"The Colonel came up the hill and out over this terrace where they were all lying and he said, 'Let's go get these Krauts. Let's kill these chickenspitters. Let's get up over this hill now and get this place taken.'

"He had his goddam forty-five and he shot three-four times at where the Kraut fire was coming from, and he said, 'Goddam, let's go get these Krauts! Come on! Nobody's going to stop here now!'" They were plenty cold as hell but he kept talking to them and telling them, and pretty soon he got some of them, and in fifteen minutes he got most of them moving. Once he got them moving, the Colonel and I and Smith *(Sergeant James C. Smith from Tullahoma, Tennessee),* we went on ahead of them and the attack was going again and we headed into the woods. It was bad in the woods but they went in good now.

"When we got into the woods *(The woods were close-planted fir trees, and the shell-bursts tore and smashed them, and the splinters from the tree bursts were like javelins in the half-light of the forest, and the men were shouting and calling now to take the curse off the darkness of the forest and shooting and killing Krauts and moving ahead now)* it was pretty thick for the tanks, and so they went to the outside. They were shooting into the woods, but we had to stop them now because K Company had pushed through ahead of them way into the woods.

"The Colonel and I and Smith, we went on ahead and found a hole in the timber where we could get a T.D. in. Now the attack was going good on ahead and all of a sudden we saw a

bunker right beside us, and they started shooting at us. We
decided there were Krauts in it. *(The bunker was completely
hidden by fir trees planted over it and grass growing over it
and was a subterranean fort on the Maginot Line style with
automatic ventilation, concussion-proof doors, bunks fifteen feet
underground for the men, special exit provisions so that it could
be run over and then its occupants attack the enemy from the
rear, and it held fifty SS troops whose mission was to let the
attack pass and then come out and fire on it.)*

"All there was left with us now was the Colonel, I and Smith
and Roger, this French boy who had been with us ever since
St. Poix. I never knew his last name but he was a wonderful
Frenchman. Best boy in a fight you ever saw. These Krauts in
the bunker started shooting at us. So we started walking over
toward it and we decided we'd got to get them out.

"There was an embrasure over on our side, but we couldn't
see that, the way it was all planted over. I had only one grenade
because I wasn't expecting what we were going to do. We got
over within about ten yards of the pillbox, coming in this side
of it. We couldn't see the aperture at the bottom of it. It all
looked like a wooded hillock.

"They're shooting sort of scattered all the while. The Colonel
and Smith were at the right of it. Roger was going in right toward the aperture. You couldn't see the fire.

"I yelled at Roger to get down, and right then they shot him.
I saw the goddam hole then and I threw the grenade to go in,
but you know how those apertures are beveled, and it hit and
bounced out. Smith grabbed the Frenchman by the heels and
started to drag him clear because he was still alive. In that slit
trench on the left, there was a Kraut and he stood up, and Smith
shot him with his carbine. You can tell how fast this happened
because just then the grenade went off, and we all ducked.

"Then we started to get a lot of fire from the field out in
front of the woods—the field we'd crossed to get into the woods
—and Smith said, 'Colonel, you better get down in that hole
because here come those Krauts.'

"They were firing from the wheat shocks in the field right

there in front of the woods and in that little tongue of brush. The Krauts started shooting at us from out there, which should have been our rear.

"The Colonel dropped one Kraut with his forty-five. Smith shot two with his carbine; I was in back of the pillbox and I shot the one who was in back of us across the road about fifteen yards away. I had to shoot at him three times before he stopped and then I didn't kill him good because when the T.D. came up finally he was lying right across the middle of the road and, seeing the T.D. coming up, he sort of scrounged up and tried to get out of the way, and the T.D. went over him and flattened him out.

"The rest of the Krauts sort of took off across the field and we didn't have any real trouble with that lot. Just sort of long-range fire. We know we killed three and we wounded some more that took off.

"We didn't have any more hand grenades and the bastards in the bunker wouldn't come out when we yelled at them. So the Colonel and I were waiting for them to come out, and Smith went off to the left and found a T.D. and brought it up. That was the T.D. that ran over the Kraut I had to shoot three times with that little old German pistol.

"The Krauts still wouldn't come out when talked to, so we pulled that T.D. right up to the back of that steel door we had located by now, and that old Wump gun fired about six rounds and blasted that door in, and then you ought to have heard them want to come out. You ought to have heard them yell and moan and moan and scream and yell 'Kamerad!'

"The T.D. had that old Wump gun pointed right in the door, and they started to come out, and you never saw such a mess. Every one of them was wounded in five or six different places, from pieces of concrete and steel. About eighteen good ones came out, and all the time inside there was the most piteous moaning and screaming, and there was one fellow with both his legs cut off by the steel door. I went down to see how everything was and got a suitcase with a couple of quarts of whisky in it and a couple of boxes of cigars and a pistol for the Colonel.

"One of the prisoners was in pretty good shape, not really good shape but he could travel. He was a noncom. The rest of them were lying down outside, all moaning, wounded and shot up.

"This noncom showed us where the next bunker was. By then, we knew what they looked like, and you could spot them by any sort of rise of ground. So we took the T.D. and went down the road about seventy-five yards to this second bunker—you know which one—and had this bird ask them to surrender. You ought to have seen this Kraut. He was a Wehrmacht, regular army, and he kept saying, 'Bitty. S.S.S.' He meant they were those real bad ones and they would kill him if he asked them to surrender. He yelled at them to come out, and they wouldn't come. They wouldn't answer. So we pulled the Wump gun up to the back door just like the other time and yelled to them to come out, and they wouldn't come. So we put in about ten shots from the Wump gun and then they came out—what was left of them. They were a sad and bedraggled lot. Every one of them was in awful shape.

"They were SS boys, all of them, and they got down in the road, one by one, on their knees. They expected to get shot. But we were obliged to disappoint them. There were about twelve that got out. The rest were all blown to pieces and wounded all to hell. There were legs and arms and heads scattered all over that goddamn place.

"We had so many prisoners and nobody to guard them but the Colonel and I and Smith and the Wump gun, so we sort of sat around there until things sort of clarified. After a while a medical aide came up and looked at the French boy, Roger. He was lying there all the time and when they came to dress him, he said, *'Mon colonel, je suis content.* I am happy to die on German soil.'

"They put a tag on him reading 'Free French' and I said, 'The hell with that,' and changed the tag to read 'Company L.'

"Every time I think about that Frenchman, it makes me want to get to killing Krauts again. . . ."

There is a lot more to the story. Maybe that is as much as you can take today. I could write you just what I Company did, what the other two battalions did. I could write for you, if you could take it, what happened at the third bunker and the fourth bunker and at fourteen other bunkers. They were all taken.

If you want to know something, get someone who was there to tell you. If you wish, and I can still remember, I will be glad to tell you sometime what it was like in those woods for the next ten days; about all the counterattacks and about the German artillery. It is a very, very interesting story if you can remember it. Probably it has even epic elements. Doubtless sometime you will even see it on the screen.

It probably is suitable for screen treatment, because I remember the Colonel saying, "Ernie, a lot of the time I felt as though I were at a Grade B picture and kept saying to myself, 'This is where I came in.' "

The only thing that will probably be hard to get properly in the picture is the German SS troops, their faces black from the concussion, bleeding at the nose and mouth, kneeling in the road, grabbing their stomachs, hardly able to get out of the way of the tanks, though probably the cinema will be able to make this even more realistic. But a situation like that is the fault of the engineers who, when they designed those concussion-proof doors, did not expect to have 105-mm. Wump guns come up and fire point-blank at them from behind.

That was not provided for when the specifications were laid down. And sometimes, observing such sad sights and such elaborate preparations gone wrong, I have a feeling that it really would have been better for Germany not to have started this war in the first place.

FIVE

➤ *After the Wars,*
1949-1956

The Great Blue River

➤ *Holiday* · JULY, 1949

PEOPLE ask you why you live in Cuba and you say it is because you like it. It is too complicated to explain about the early morning in the hills above Havana where every morning is cool and fresh on the hottest day in summer. There is no need to tell them that one reason you live there is because you can raise your own fighting cocks, train them on the place, and fight them anywhere that you can match them and that this is all legal.

Maybe they do not like cockfighting anyway.

You do not tell them about the strange and lovely birds that are on the farm the year around, nor about all the migratory birds that come through, nor that quail come in the early mornings to drink at the swimming pool, nor about the different types of lizards that live and hunt in the thatched arbor at the end of the pool, nor the eighteen different kinds of mangoes that grow on the long slope up to the house. You do not try to explain about our ball team—hardball, not softball—where, if you are over forty, you can have a boy run for you and still stay in the game, nor which are the boys in our town that are really the fastest on the base paths.

You do not tell them about the shooting club just down the road, where we used to shoot the big live-pigeon matches for the large money, with Winston Guest, Tommy Shevlin, Thorwald Sanchez and Pichon Aguilera, and where we used to shoot matches against the Brooklyn Dodgers when they had fine shots like Curt Davis, Billy Herman, Augie Galan and Hugh Casey. Maybe they think live-pigeon shooting is wrong. Queen Victoria did and barred it in England. Maybe they are right. Maybe it is wrong. It certainly is a miserable spectator sport. But with strong, really fast birds it is still the best participant sport for betting I know; and where we live it is legal.

You could tell them that you live in Cuba because you only have to put shoes on when you come into town, and that you can plug the bell in the party-line telephone with paper so that you won't have to answer, and that you work as well there in those cool early mornings as you ever have worked anywhere in the world. But those are professional secrets.

There are many other things you do not tell them. But when they talk to you about salmon fishing and what it costs them to fish the Restigouche, then, if they have not talked too much about how much it costs, and have talked well, or lovingly, about the salmon fishing, you tell them the biggest reason you live in Cuba is the great, deep blue river, three quarters of a mile to a mile deep and sixty to eighty miles across, that you can reach in thirty minutes from the door of your farmhouse, riding through beautiful country to get to it, that has, when the river is right, the finest fishing I have ever known.

When the Gulf Stream is running well, it is a dark blue and there are whirlpools along the edges. We fish in a forty-foot cabin cruiser with a flying bridge equipped with topside controls, oversize outriggers big enough to skip a ten-pound bait in summer, and we fish four rods.

Sometimes we keep Pilar, the fishing boat, in Havana harbor, sometimes in Cojimar, a fishing village seven miles east of Havana, with a harbor that is safe in summer and imminently unsafe in winter when there are northers or nor'westers. Pilar was built to be a fishing machine that would be a good sea boat in the heaviest kind of weather, have a minimum cruising range of five hundred miles, and sleep seven people. She carries three hundred gallons of gasoline in her tanks and one hundred and fifty gallons of water. On a long trip she can carry another hundred gallons of gas in small drums in her forward cockpit and the same extra amount of water in demijohns. She carries, when loaded full, 2400 pounds of ice.

Wheeler Shipyard, of New York, built her hull and modified it to our specifications, and we have made various changes in her since. She is a really sturdy boat, sweet in any kind of sea, and she has a very low-cut stern with a large wooden roller to bring big fish over. The flying bridge is so sturdy and so reinforced below you can fight fish from the top of the house.

Ordinarily, fishing out of Havana, we get a line out with a Japanese feather squid and a strip of pork rind on the hook, while we are still running out of the harbor. This is for tarpon, which feed around the fishing smacks anchored along the Morro Castle-Cabañas side of the channel, and for kingfish, which are often in the mouth of the main ship channel and over the bar, where the bottom fishermen catch snappers just outside the Morro.

This bait is fished on a twelve-foot No. 10 piano-wire leader from a 6/0 reel, full of fifteen-thread line and from a nine-ounce Tycoon tip. The biggest tarpon I ever caught with this rig weighed 135 pounds. We have hooked some that were much bigger but lost them to outgoing or incoming ships, to port launches, to bumboats and to the anchor chains of the fishing smacks. You can plead with or threaten launches and bumboats when you have a big fish on and they are headed so that they will cut him off. But there is nothing you can do when a big tanker, or a cargo ship, or a liner is coming down the channel. So we usually put out this line when we can see the channel is clear and nothing is coming out; or after seven o'clock in the evening when ships will usually not be entering the harbor due to the extra port charges made after that hour.

Coming out of the harbor I will be on the flying bridge steering and watching the traffic and the line that is fishing the feather astern. As you go out, seeing friends along the water front—lottery-ticket sellers you have known for years, policemen you have given fish to and who have done favors in their turn, bumboatmen who lose their earnings standing shoulder to shoulder with you in the betting pit at the jai-alai fronton, and friends passing in motorcars along the harbor and ocean boulevard who wave and you wave to but cannot recognize at that distance, although they can see the Pilar and you on her flying bridge quite clearly—your feather jig is fishing all the time.

Behind the boulevards are the parks and buildings of old Havana and on the other side you are passing the steep slopes and walls of the fortress of Cabañas, the stone weathered pink and yellow, where most of your friends have been political prisoners at one time or another; and then you pass the rocky headland of the Morro, with O'Donnell, 1844, on the tall white light tower and then, two hundred yards beyond the Morro, when the stream is running well, is the great river.

Sometimes as you leave the gray-green harbor water and Pilar's bows dip into the dark blue water a covey of flying fish will rise from under her bows and you will hear the slithering, silk-tearing noise they make when they leave the water.

If they are the usual size flying fish it does not mean so much as a sign, unless you see a man-of-war hawk working, dipping down after them if they go up again; but if they are the big three-pound, black-winged Bahian flyers that come out of the water as though they were shot out, and at the end of their soaring flight drop their tails to give the flight a new impulse and fly again and again, then it is a very good sign. Seeing the big Bahian flyers is as sure a sign as any, except seeing fish themselves.

By now, Gregorio, the mate, has gotten the meat line out. The meat line is a new trick that I'll tell about later because once it is out, and he wants to get it out fast to cover this patch of bottom before we get outside of the hundred-fathom curve, he must get outrigger baits out, since marlin will come in over this bottom any time the stream is running and the water is blue and clear.

Gregorio Fuentes has been mate on Pilar since 1938. He is fifty years old this summer and went to sea in sail from Lanzarote, one of the smaller Canary Islands, when he was four. I met him at Dry Tortugas when he was captain of a fishing smack and we were both stormbound there in a very heavy northeast gale in 1928. We went on board his smack to get some onions. We wanted to buy the onions, but he gave them to us, and some rum as well, and I remember thinking he had the cleanest ship that I had ever seen. Now after ten years I know that he would rather keep a ship clean, and paint and varnish, than he would fish. But I know, too, that he would rather fish than eat or sleep.

We had a great mate before Gregorio, named Carlos Gutierrez, but someone hired him away from me when I was away at the Spanish Civil War. It was wonderful luck to find Gregorio, and his seamanship has saved Pilar in three hurricanes. So far, knocking on wood, we have never had to put in a claim on the all-risk marine insurance policy carried on her; and Gregorio was the only man to stay on board a small craft in the October, 1944, hurricane when it blew 180 mph true, and small craft and Navy vessels were blown up onto the harbor boulevard and up onto the small hills around the harbor. He also rode out the 1948 hurricane on her.

By now, as you have cleared the harbor, Gregorio has the meat line out and is getting the outrigger baits out and, it being a good day, you are getting flying fish up and pushing to the eastward into the breeze. The first marlin you see can show within ten minutes of leaving your moorings, and so close to the Morro that you can still see the curtains on the light.

He may come behind the big, white wooden teaser that is zig-zagging and diving between the two inside lines. He may show behind an outrigger bait that is bouncing and jumping over the water. Or he may come racing from the side, slicing a wake through the dark water, as he comes for the feather.

When you see him from the flying bridge he will look first brown and then dark purple as he rises in the water, and his pectoral fins, spread wide as he comes to feed, will be a light lavender color and look like widespread wings as he drives just under the surface. He will look, in the sea, more like a huge submarine bird than a fish.

Gregorio, if he sees him first will shout, "Feesh! Feesh, Papa, feesh!"

If you see him first you leave the wheel, or turn it over to Mary, your wife, and go to the stern end of the house and say "Feesh" as calmly as possible to Gregorio, who has always seen him by then, too, and you lean over and he hands you up the rod the marlin is coming for, or, if he is after the teaser, he hands you up the rod with the feather and pork rind on.

All right, he is after the teaser and you are racing-in the feather. Gregorio is keeping the teaser, a tapering, cylindrical piece of wood two feet long, with a curve cut in its head that makes it dive and dance when towed, away from the marlin. The marlin is rushing it and trying to grab it. His bill comes out of water as he drives toward it. But Gregorio keeps it just out of his reach. If he pulled it all the way in, the fish might go down. So he is playing him as a bullfighter might play a bull, keeping the lure just out of his range, and yet never denying it to him, while you race-in the feather.

Mary is saying, "Isn't he beautiful? Oh, Papa, look at his stripes and that color and the color of his wings. Look at him!"

"I'm looking at him," you say, and you have the feather now abreast of the teaser, and Gregorio sees it and flicks the teaser clear, and the marlin sees the feather. The big thing that he chased, and that looked and acted like a crippled fish, is gone. But here is a squid, his favorite food, instead.

The marlin's bill comes clear out of water as he hits the feather and you see his open mouth and, as he hits it, you lower the rod that you have held as high as you could, so the feather goes out of sight into his mouth. You see it go in, and the mouth shuts and you see him turn, shining silver, his stripes showing as he turns.

As he turns his head you hit him, striking hard, hard and hard again, to set the hook. Then, if he starts to run instead of jumping, you hit him three or four times more to make sure, because he might just be holding feather, hook and all, tight in his jaws and running away with it, still unhooked. Then he feels the hook and jumps clear. He will jump straight up all clear of the water, shaking himself. He will jump straight and stiff as a beaked bar of silver. He will jump high and long, shedding drops of water as he comes out, and making a splash like a shell hitting when he enters the water again. And he will jump, and jump, and jump, sometimes on one side of the boat, then crossing to the other so fast you see the belly of the line whipping through the water, fast as a racing ski turn.

Sometimes he will get the leader over his shoulder (the hump on his back behind his head) and go off greyhounding over the water, jumping continuously and with such an advantage in pull, with the line in that position, that you cannot stop him, and so Mary has to back Pilar fast and then turn, gunning both motors, to chase him.

You lose plenty of line making the turn to chase him. But he is jumping against the friction of the belly of the line in the water which keeps it taut, and when, reeling, you recover that belly and have the fish now broadside, then astern again, you have control of him once more. He will sound now and circle, and then you will gradually work him closer and closer and then in to where Gregorio can gaff him, club him and take him on board.

That is the way it should go ideally; he should sound, circle, and you should work him gradually alongside or on either quarter of the stern, and then gaff him, club him and bring him on board. But it doesn't always go that way. Sometimes when he gets up to the boat he will start the whole thing all over again and head out for the northwest, jumping again as fresh, seemingly, as when he was first hooked, and you have to chase him again.

Sometimes, if he is a big striped marlin, you will get him within thirty feet of the boat and he will come no farther, swimming, with his wings spread, at whatever speed and direction you elect to move. If you don't move, he will be up and under the boat. If you move away from him, he will stay there, refusing to come in one inch, as strong a fish for his weight as any in the world and as stubborn.

(Bonefish angler, on your way! You never saw a bonefish in mile-deep water, nor up against the tackle striped marlin have to face sometimes. Nor did you know how your bonefish would act after he had jumped forty-three times clean out of water. Your bonefish is a smart fish, very conservative, very strong too. Too smart by far to jump, even if he could. I do not think he can, myself. And the only nonjumping fish that has a patent of nobility in our books is the wahoo. He *can* jump, too, if he wants to. He will do it sometimes when he takes the bait. Also, bonefish angler, your fish might be as fat and as short of wind, at four hundred pounds, as some of the overstuffed Nova Scotia tuna are. But do not shoot, bonefish angler; at four hundred pounds, your fish might be the strongest thing in the sea, the strongest fish that ever lived; so strong no one would ever want to hook into one. But tell me confidentially: would he jump . . . ? Thank you very much. I thought not.)

This dissertation has not helped you any if you have a strong, male, striped marlin on and he decides he won't be lifted any closer. Of course you could loosen up the drag and work away from him and wear him out that way. But that is the way sharks get fish. We like to fight them close to the boat and take them while they are still strong. We will gaff an absolutely green fish, one that has not been tired at all, if by any fluke we can get him close enough.

Since 1931, when I learned that was how to keep fish from being hit by sharks, I have never lost a marlin nor a tuna to a shark, no matter how shark-infested the waters fished. We try to fight them fast, but never rough. The secret is for the angler never to rest. Any time he rests the fish is resting. That gives the fish a chance to get strong again, or to get down to a greater depth; and the odds lengthen that something may close in on him.

So now, say, you have this marlin down thirty feet, pulling

as strong as a horse. All you have to do is stay with him. Play him just this side of breaking strain, but do it softly. Never jerk on him. Jerking will only hurt him or anger him. Either or both will make him pull harder. He is as strong as a horse. Treat him like a horse. Keep your maximum possible strain on him and you will convince him and bring him in. Then you gaff him, club him for kindness and for safety, and bring him on board.

You do not have to kill a horse to break him. You have to convince him, and that is what you have to do with a truly strong, big fish after the first jumps, which correspond to a wild horse's bucking, are over. To do this, you have to be in good condition.

There is tackle made now, and there are fishing guides expert in ways of cheating with it, by which anybody who can walk up three flights of stairs, carrying a quart bottle of milk in each hand, can catch game fish over five hundred pounds without even having to sweat much.

There is old-fashioned tackle with which you can catch really big fish in short time, thus ensuring they will not be attacked by sharks. But you have to be a fisherman or, at least, in very good shape to use it. But this is the tackle that will give you the greatest amount of sport with the smaller and medium-sized marlin. You don't need to be an athlete to use it. You ought to be in good condition. If you are not, two or three fish will put you in condition. Or they may make you decide marlin fishing in the Gulf Stream is not your sport.

In almost any other sport requiring strength and skill to play or practice, those practicing the sport expect to know how to play it, to have at least moderate ability and to be in some sort of condition. In big-game fishing they will come on board in ghastly shape, incapable of reeling in 500 yards of line, simply line, with no question of there being a fish on it, and yet full of confidence that they can catch a fish weighing twice or three times their weight.

They are confident because it has been done. But it was never done honestly, to my knowledge, by completely inexperienced and untrained anglers, without physical assistance from the guides, mates and boatmen, until the present winch reels, unbreakable rods and other techniques were invented which made it possible for any angler, no matter how incompetent, to catch big fish if he could hold and turn the handle of a winch.

The International Game Fish Association, under the auspices of the American Museum of Natural History, has tried to set a standard of sporting fishing and to recognize records of fish taken honestly and sportingly according to these standards. It has had considerable success in these and other fields. But as long as charter boats are extremely expensive, and both guides and their anglers want results above everything else, big-game fishing will be closer to total war against big fish than to sport. Of course, it could never be considered an equal contest unless the angler had a hook in his mouth, as well as the fish. But insistence on that might discourage the sporting fishermen entirely.

Education as to what makes a big fish legitimately caught has been slow, but it has progressed steadily. Very few guides or anglers shoot or harpoon hooked fish any more. Nor is the flying gaff much used.

The use of wire line, our meat line, is a deadly way of fishing, and no fish caught that way could possibly be entered as a sporting record. But we use it as a way of finding out at what depths fish are when they are not on the surface. It is a scientific experiment, the results are carefully noted, and what it catches are classed in our books as fish caught commercially. Its carefully recorded results will surely provide valuable information for the commercial fisherman, and its use is justified for that end. It is also a very rough, tough, punishing way to catch big fish and it puts the angler who practices it, fishing standing up, not sitting in a chair, into the condition he needs to be able to fight fish honestly with the sporting tackle that allows the fish to run, leap and sound to his fullest ability and still be caught within an hour by the angler, if the angler knows how to handle big fish.

Fighting a really big fish, fast and unaided, never resting, nor letting the fish rest, is comparable to a ten-round fight in the ring in its requirements for good physical condition. Two hours of the same, not resting, not letting the fish rest, is comparable to a twenty-round fight. Most honest and skillful anglers who lose big fish do so because the fish whips them, and they cannot hold him when he decides, toward the end of the fight, to sound and, sounding, dies.

Once the fish is dead, sharks will eat him if any are about. If he is not hit by sharks, bringing him up, dead, from a great depth is one of the most difficult phases of fishing for big fish in deep water.

We have tried to work out tackle which would give the maximum sport with the different fish, small, medium, large and oversize, at the different months of the year when they run. Since their runs overlap it has been necessary to try to have always a margin of safety in the quantity of line. In a section at the end of the article this tackle is described. It would not suit purists, or members of some light-tackle clubs; but remember we fish five months out of the year in water up to a mile deep, in a current that can make a very big sea with the trade wind blowing against it, and in waters that are occasionally infested with sharks. We could catch fish with the very lightest tackle, I believe. It would prove nothing, since others have done it, and we would break many fish off to die. Our ideal is to catch the fish with tackle that you can really pull on and which still permits the fish to jump and run as freely as possible.

Then, altogether apart from that ideal, there is the meat line. This is 800 yards of monel wire of eighty-five-pound test which, fished from an old Hardy six-inch reel and old Hardy No. 5 rod, will sink a feather jib down so that it can be trolled in thirty-five fathoms if you put enough wire out. When there are no fish on the surface at all, this goes down where they are. It catches everything: wahoo out of their season when no one has caught one on the surface for months; big grouper; huge dog snappers, red snappers, big kingfish; and it catches marlin when they are deep and not coming up at all. With it we eat, and fill the freezing unit, on days when you would not have caught a fish surface-trolling. The fight on the wire which actually tests no more than thirty-nine-thread line but is definitely wire, not line, is rugged, muscle-straining, punishing, short and anything but sweet. It is in a class with steer bulldogging, bronc riding and other ungentle sports. The largest marlin caught in 1948 on the meat line was a 210-pound striped fish. We caught him when we had fished three days on the surface and not seen a thing.

Now we are anxious to see what the meat line will dredge into during those days in August and September, when there are flat calms, and the huge fish are down deep and will not come up. When you hook a marlin on the wire he starts shaking his head, then he bangs it with his bill, then he sees if he can outpull you. Then if he can't, he finally comes up to see what is the matter. What we are anxious to find out is what happens if he ever gets the wire over his shoulder and starts to go. They can go, if they are big enough, wire and all. We plan to try to go with him. There is a chance we could make it, if Pilar makes the turn fast enough. That will be up to Mary.

The really huge fish always head out to the northwest when they make their first run. If you are ever flying across between Havana and Miami, and looking down on the blue sea, and you see something making splashes such as a horse dropped off a cliff might make, and behind these splashes a black boat with green topside and decks is chasing, leaving a white wake behind her—that will be us.

If the splashes look sizable from the height that you are flying, and they are going out to the northwest, then wish us plenty of luck. Because we will need it.

In the meantime, what we always hope for is fish feeding on the surface, up after the big flying fish, and that whoever is a guest on the boat, unless he or she has fished before, will hook something under one hundred and fifty pounds to start with. Any marlin from thirty pounds up, on proper tackle, will give a new fisherman all the excitement and all the exercise he can assimilate, and off the marlin grounds along the north Cuban coast he might raise twenty to thirty in a day, when they are running well. The most I ever caught in one day was seven. But Pepe Gomez-Mena and Martin Menocal caught twelve together in one day, and I would hate to bet that record would not be beaten by them, or by some of the fine resident and visiting sportsmen who love and know the marlin fishing of the great river that moves along Cuba's northern coast.

ERNEST HEMINGWAY'S TACKLE SPECIFICATIONS

WHITE MARLIN RUN: *April-May-Early June.*

Gear for the feather jig, fished astern, with pork-rind strip on the hook:

Rod, 9 oz. or 12 oz. tip; Reel, 6/o; 500 yards #15 thread line; 12-foot piano-wire leader #9 or #10; 8/o or 9/o O'Shaughnessy hook, or 8/o Mustad, smallest type of Japanese feather jig (white) and three-inch strip of pork rind attached. (This gives a beautiful motion in the water. Of white marlin hooked we average six out of ten on the feather compared to the baits.)

First rod (light for smaller bait) of the two outrigger rods:

Rod, 14 oz. tip; Reel, 9/o; 600 yards of #18 thread line; 14-foot piano-wire leader #10 or #11; 10/o Mustad hook.

Baits: small mullet, strip bait, boned needle fish, small cero mackerel, small or medium size flying fish, fresh squid and cut baits.

Second rod of two outriggers:

14 oz. tip; Reel, 9/o; 400 yards of #18 thread line, spliced to 150 yards of #21 thread, on the outside for when the fish is close to the boat. 14-foot piano-wire leader #11; 11/o or 12/o Mustad hook.

Baits: big cero mackerel, medium and large mullet, large strip baits, flying fish and good-sized squid.

Above rod is designed to attract any big fish that might be mixed in with the smaller run.

BIG MARLIN RUN: *July-August-September-October.*
(Fish from 250 to over 1000 pounds.)

Feather is fished same as ever, since after white marlin are

415

gone it will catch school tuna, albacore, bonito and dolphin. An extra rod is in readiness, equipped with feather jig in case schools of above fish are encountered.

Outrigger rods: Either 22 or 24 oz. tips. (The best I have found, outside of the old Hardy Hickory-Palakona bamboo #5, are those made by Frank O'Brien of Tycoon Tackle, Inc. His rods are incomparably the best I know made today.)

Reels: 12/0 or 14/0 Hardy, and two 14/0 Finor for guests. If inexperienced anglers want to catch big fish they need the advantage the Finor changeable gear ratio reel gives them.

Line: all the reels will hold without jamming of either 36 or 39 thread good Ashaway linen line. We use this line for years, testing it, discarding any rotted by the sun, and splicing on more as needed.

Leaders are 14½ foot stainless-steel cable.

Hooks: 14/0 Mustad, bent in the crook of the shank to give the point an offset hooking drive.

Baits: Albacore and bonito, whole, up to seven pounds and barracuda, whole, up to five and six pounds. These are the best. Alternative baits are large cero mackerel, squid, big mullet and yellow jacks, runners and big needlefish. Of all baits, the whole bonito and albacore have proved, with us, the best for attracting really big marlin.

The wire line has been described in the article.

The Shot

➤ *True* · APRIL, 1951

WE were finishing lunch by the swimming pool. It was a hot day for Cuba because the breeze had fallen off. But the pool was cool where the trees had made shade over it and it was cool and next to cold if you went down deep enough into it at the deep end.

I didn't see these two Negroes until they were by the table where it was set under the arbor to be in the shade. I had been watching the reflection of the bamboos and the Alamo trees in the pool and when I looked up and saw these two by the table I knew that I was slipping. They had come up a piece of dead ground but I should have seen them come around the corner of the shower house.

One was very big and tough with a face I remembered. The other was his *guardaspaldas*. That is the man who keeps you from being shot in the back. He doesn't have to be big, very big, and he is always a little behind and he turns his head like a pitcher watching a man on first with no one out. *Guardaspaldas*, it is usually shortened to that, get the same kind of neck that pitchers get and that fighter pilots are afflicted with if they stay alive if there is real fighter opposition in the air.

This man, who looked like an oversized Joe Walcott, had a letter to me. It was from himself. He was a little hot, it seemed, and he needed to go to a certain South American republic very fast. He was unjustly accused of being in the second of two cars which had killed two and wounded five in what is known as the old one-two. The first car comes by the house of friends whom they have checked are there and wish to surprise. They shoot the house up as a gesture. The friends swarm out, unhurt and bear-

417

ing arms and full of defiance, and the second car comes by with the mains and wipes them out.

This man was falsely accused, he explained to me, of being one of the mains. He had been falsely accused many times. But he claimed to be a friend of a friend of mine who was shot dead in the street with thirty-five cents in his pocket, and never a nickel stolen and no personal fortune, while he held a government post. I suppose you know, gentlemen, what that means in these times.

This friend who had been shot dead had been a beautiful backfield man on the local university team. He was a fine quarterback and he could play halfback. He was director of sports of the republic when he died. No one has ever been punished for the killing. The friend of mine was supposed to have been a little triggery; but I never heard of him killing the wrong people. Anyway, when they killed him he had thirty-five cents in his pocket, no money in any banks, and he was unarmed.

So what this man, who claimed to be his friend, and whose face I remembered, needed was $500. I told him it was two. I hope he doesn't get falsely accused of anything before he emigrates.

So with a background of this sort of shooty-shooty, I'm going to write 2,000 words about an antelope hunt where you kill one antelope that can't shook back.

There are two ways to hunt pronghorn antelope; maybe three is juster. One is to shoot the buck that has been hanging around the back pasture and who believes himself to be a member of the family. He is shot on the opening day of the season by some dude who has been enticed to Wyoming by an outfit that advertises "Antelope Guaranteed" and has scouted the country closely for guaranteeable antelope. Oftentimes he is gut-shot and makes an effort to get away with a hole in his belly or a broken leg. But he is in that pasture, gentlemen, and what a trophy his head must make.

Then they hunt them on the flats and in that broken country between Casper and Rawlins, Wyoming, with the aid of command cars, these carry more hunters; jeeps, out of which only a few can hunt; weapons carriers, plenty hunters, Jack, but just about as uncomfortable as a weapons carrier always was. But you are after antelope, men, and shots are guaranteed. These vehicles will put you in range of the ferocious beasts and your marksmanship can be proved or unproved. Hold your breath a little bit; put the peak, or the spike, or the cross hairs of the reticule low down on the shoulder and squeeze off. It's a trophy, men, if you glassed them right and took the biggest buck and didn't shoot a doe mistaking ears for horns. It is probably shot through both shoulders too and it still 'living and will try to get up, looking at you, as you come with the knife. From the eyes you can tell that the buck is thinking, "What the hell did I do to deserve this?"

Then there is the third way where you hunt them in high country on foot or on horseback and no antelope are guaranteed. The author of this article, after taking a long time to make up his mind, and admitting his guilt on all counts, believes that it is a sin to kill any non-dangerous game animal except for meat. Now, with low-temperature refrigeration, you can keep meat properly and the amount of hunters has greatly increased. It has increased to such a point that you are lucky if some character does not loose off at you or your horse at least once in any three days of shooting. There is only one answer when this starts. Loose off quick yourself, shooting low. Because antelope, deer, elk and moose never shoot back and the character who opens fire, however undeveloped he may be in a sporting way, understands this basic principle. And if you should hit the son of a bitch it is only a hunting accident anyway. Shoot back if they shoot at you.

Don't run up any white flags. They might take you for a bald eagle. Or, if you waved your red bandanna that we wear around a Stetson since shooters became really at large, they might think it was a fox maybe or even a subversive element. But so far I have never seen one return the fire when you shot back. Especially if you shoot back at where you figure their feet will be.

Of course a hunter could go into the hills with a megaphone strapped to his back, and when shot at simply shout through his megaphone, "Please cease firing, brother shooter and fellow sportsman. I am the animal that walks on two legs and pays income tax and there is no open season on us this year . . . You fooled yourself there, boy."

Or he might make it shorter and more sporting and say, "Desist, brother sportsman. It is I."

But until they issue us with the proper megaphones at the time we purchase the licenses, I figure to shoot back quick if any brother sportsman shoots at me. Because he might not even be a brother sportsman. He might be an old friend or some companion of early youth or childhood.

Now about antelope in the hills.

This was a funny hunt. Three of my kids were along and one, Jack, who is a captain of infantry in Berlin, is a fisherman; so he wanted to fish the Pahsimeroi for salmon. (No salmon.) Of the other two boys one stayed the pace all the way and the other joined Jack in Operation No Salmon.

We figured to find the big bucks high up in the draws above timberline. Somebody had spooked them. Anyway there was something wrong and for keeps wrong. They were in broken country; could see you for a mile and were nervous and watching.

We were sleeping, down on the Pahsimeroi, in the cabin of a character known as the Old-timer. This was before the days of DDT or of bug bombs and the Old-timer had been raising the more hardy insects instead of cattle. He called Taylor Williams who was then in his later fifties "Young Man" and he called me "Kid." He said, "Kid, you're going to make a rider and you can shoot pretty good and I'll be proud if you get some place."

He said, "Kid, if these are really your boys they ought to have something to drink." Then he added, "What have you got?"

We had come from Sun Valley, Idaho, and were a little softened up by the swimming pool, nights in The Ram, and the wheels of Ketchum; but the Old-timer fixed that. We rode to the top of the range where we could look over all the way into the Middle Fork of the Salmon, across the loveliest mountains that I know. We rode down the mountain, across the mountain, back across the broken ground and down into the foothills and flats. All the time there were antelope; but they watched you from a mile away and moved. Taylor was mounted on a white horse and the Old-timer started to refer to him as "The young fellow on the white horse. Scares antelope to death."

The night of the first day was Saturday and that was a big night at Goldburg where they had some sort of a mine and always a big Saturday night. The children slept in the car and Taylor Williams and I and a boy named Wild Bill, who could hit like Stan Ketchell with either hand, went to Goldburg. The Old-timer stayed home to care for his insects.

It was a rough night although I bypassed all the fights. You might have fought ten or twelve times if you weren't pacific. Taylor never fights because he does not have to anymore and I try never to fight. Wild Bill, however, who was horse wrangling for us, spotted the Sheriff's boy from one of the nearest towns who had turned King's Evidence or something corresponding to that, one time versus Wild Bill. Wild Bill asked him outside and demolished him. Wild Bill could certainly hit. Every time he hit Sheriff's boy you could hear something go. Sheriff's boy fought well; but it wasn't any courtroom. Finally Sheriff's boy went just like the things you had been hearing go. We gentled down Wild Bill and gave first aid to Sheriff's boy and drove home. The fight had, in a way, quieted down the happiness in Goldburg.

The next day was like the first day. Only now they looked back over their lovely brown shoulders at a mile and a half and then you would see the white ruff on their rumps when they would take off. We rode to the top of the range. We blocked several draws and turned them. We crisscrossed the mountain, staying in dead ground and coming up on the ridges dismounted, and crawling to the edge of high ground and glassing the country.

We rode downhill, uphill and around hill. By this time there was only Gigi, my youngest boy, who rides a horse as though his mother had dropped him into the saddle; Taylor Williams, the old Kentucky Colonel who will kill you dead at 300 yards with a borrowed rifle; the Old-timer who you had to keep to windward of, and whose scent was possibly driving the antelope out of the country; and me, on a nice mare with more brains than I had. She was an old rope horse.

So that was the second day and when we hit the shale and then the pebbles and rode over the wooden bridge and through the cottonwoods the moon was up. It was a nice night at the Old-timer's to be off-horse and hear the no-salmon fisher's stories and we had brought some lemons and made whisky sours. The Old-timer said he had never tasted a mixed drink but he would try it this once.

"How old are you, Old-timer?" I asked him.

"Son," he said, "when they killed General George Armstrong Custer on the Little Big Horn, I was getting along in years."

This was obviously impossible so I asked the Old-timer how old he thought Taylor was.

"He's a boy," he said.

"What about me?" I asked.

"You're just starting."

"What about the boys?"

"They're all false except that one was poured into a saddle and stuck there."

"Where you come from, Old-timer?"

"God knows. I forgot."

"Were you ever around Montana way?"

"Sure."

"Were you in Wyoming?"

"I was there for the Wagon Box fight when we were snaking timber to the Fort."

This was impossible so I asked him if he knew Tom Horn.

"Tom? I heard him say, standing up there before they put the hood over him; no; they didn't put any hood over Tom. What he said was, 'Gentlemen, all I want in this life is a pair of heavy shoes and a long drop. And I forgive all my enemies. Amen!' Everybody was crying but Tom never cried. He stood there looking sort of distinguished but he wanted a heavy pair of shoes and a decent drop so he wouldn't resist the rope. That's the worst thing can happen to a man, to resist the rope. I seen them hang since I was a boy and it ain't no good. Not for him that is hung nor for anybody. It's just a sort of legal vengeance."

The next day we were out at daylight with the horses saddled and our guns in the gun buckets and Wild Bill's hands sore and him sort of ashamed. We knew the Sheriff's boy couldn't really fight a lick and he remembered that in the middle of the night. It made him feel bad because he was a fighter and would have fought anybody. Besides, he broke the Sheriff's boy's jaw and we all heard it go. And he had his sore hands to remind him. He wasn't riding with us. He was just staying at the shack and corrals with break-jaw remorse.

So we start early and there is a little mist over the flat and then we start to climb in the sage.

"How does it look to you, Colonel?" I asked Taylor.

Gigi is asleep in the saddle letting the horse do the work.

"I think we've got them," Taylor said. "We haven't shot at them and this is the third day and they are getting used to us and some of the big bucks will stand. They don't know what we are now and they have curiosity and want to find out."

We did the usual; gained our altitude, worked the draws, the pockets, and the ridges and then started to move down and across.

Then we jumped a bunch that were sleeping, or feeding, in a draw and there was only one way for them to go. I got off the horse and pulled the old .30-06 out of the bucket. We hang them forward. Then I started to run for where they would have to pass. It was about 200 or 250 yards. I picked the biggest buck when they came streaming over the edge of the hump and swung ahead of him and squeezed gently and the bullet broke his neck. It was a very lucky shot.

The Old-timer said, "You no-good kid. I knew you would amount to something sometime."

Taylor said, "Do you know how far you ran and how far you shot him at? I'm going to pace it."

I didn't care, because nobody ever believes shooting stories ever, and the pleasure had been in the run and trying to hold your heart in when you swing and hold your breath, sweet and clean, and swing ahead and squeeze off lightly with the swing.

So end of antelope story.

The Christmas Gift

➤ *Look* · APRIL 20, MAY 4, 1954

I

FOR some weeks, I have been substituting for Mr. Denis Zaphiro, acting as temporary game ranger in the Emali-Laitoki-tok area of Kenya. In the emergency, which is the name we apply in understatement to an actual state of war, it was possible for me as an honorary game warden of Kenya to aid by taking this position. Unfortunately, the duties I had to perform were not in all ways pleasurable to my wife.

It was impossible, for example, to get into Nairobi and buy any form of Christmas gift, and our marital relations were frequently interfered with and almost severed by the constant minor forms of emergency which were presented. This type of emergency could consist in the arrival of one Masai who had been slightly speared about the head and face and chest by another Masai, who must then be sorted out and detained. We might be in bed when this incident arose.

The emergency could consist in the notice of the arrival of a troupe of elephants in one of the neighbouring *shambas*. This is a situation which must be carefully checked and explored, since elephants often move through a *shamba* without any evil intent and continue on their way. It is necessary to track the elephants and determine where they are going and why. This is an obligation when one is acting as a temporary game ranger.

There are other interruptions, such as a leopard which had become an habitual killer of goats. I think that he probably only killed one goat on purpose, and then with the clamor which he roused, he became more or less hysterical and killed some ten goats in succession.

But this action was not approved of by the people who owned the goats and they desired this leopard to be done away with. I had obtained by purchase—nothing is ever given in Africa—a goat which bleated wonderfully during the daytime but which remained absolutely silent at night, thus refusing to attract a leopard or leopards. At this point, Mrs. Hemingway suggested that she would like for her Christmas present, which I had not been able to obtain in Nairobi since my duties made Nairobi inaccessible, a trip by air to the Belgian Congo. Although she had been through Tanganyika to as far as Mbeya and had made a safari up the great Ruaha River, and we had visited various areas of Kenya in official and semi- or comic-official capacities, Mrs. Hemingway felt that she had not seen Africa. She wished to see the Congo.

Never have I had any desire to see the Congo myself. I wished, rather than undertaking this voyage, to remain in the Laitokitok area where we had an unfinished problem, that of the leopard, which had not returned to the *shamba* and had killed no more goats, but whose tracks were plainly visible on what we had ascertained to be his more or less weekly rounds. This leopard was in the habit of sleeping in the Kimana Swamp on the grass rather than in a tree. I saw him once in a tree, but he came out of the tree like a lizard and as it was raining and I was wearing glasses I passed up the shot. The chances are I would have wounded him and the country was no good to follow him up. He would have gone off into high papyrus.

At this time, we were hunting this leopard constantly, gazing into the trees where he often reposed in the daytime and had been seen by my native game scouts. While walking with the scouts with all of our eyes raised to the trees, I trod on an eight-foot cobra who immediately took evasive action.

This was considered an extremely comic incident by the local Wakamba present. The action of the cobra was most ignominious. He did not raise his head or put up his hood as a cobra should, but retreated into a dense piece of bush. A self-admitted great marksman, I missed this cobra twice with a pistol and after this what is known in Wakamba as the Great Snake Fight commenced. A number of rounds were fired and the cobra took evasive action into the papyrus. While desiring to remain in the area, I thought that Miss Mary, my wife, had a point in her plan for visiting the Belgian Congo (which is known to be one of the centers of civilization in Africa).

From the Laitokitok area, we proceeded in two motor vehicles, one of which belonged to my son Patrick, a resident of John's Corner, P.O. Box 6, Tanganyika. It had been cannibalized, i.e., all parts usable removed from it to reinforce a second vehicle of the same type. I drove the vehicle of my son Patrick who, unfortunately, was unable to be with us, being in the hospital in Iringa, Tanganyika, with an attack of fever. This vehicle was unable to negotiate a river due to general lack of a functioning generator which flooded, and it was pulled from the river by the vehicle of the same type which had received the vital organs of the vehicle which I was driving. After this, we proceeded to Kajiado.

From Kajiado, which at that time had no airstrip, we continued to Nairobi and took off in a Cessna 180 for the Belgian Congo, on Mrs. Hemingway's Christmas-present trip. We left Nairobi West Airport at approximately 11:30 a.m., being delayed from our usual early departure waiting for the arrival of a friend who was bearing most important information.

We took off and flew a course for Lake Magadi, where we saw the houses of various friends and the local store, and then flew toward the escarpment in order to locate Denis Zaphiro, who was reported to be camped in that area. Knowing his habits and where he would probably be, we located him at a place known as Fig Tree Camp on a small stream of clear water which comes out of the escarpment. This was the camp where Denis had been chased into the bed of the stream twice by a rhino and its location was more or less embedded in my memory. It was easy to ascertain by following the road along which the construction of a pipeline for Magadi had been interrupted by a rhino—an incident in which we had been called on to intervene. This road was also impressed in my memory, and by following it we continued to the escarpment and, after making a 40-degree turn, it was easy to locate Denis and his guest Keith Caldwell, who is certainly one of the ten best wing shots in Great Britain. Things appeared to be normal in their camp and we dropped them a message wishing them all the best in the circumstances.

We then proceeded down the Rift Valley to the point where Miss Mary, for a period of 17 days, had hunted a large black-maned lion accompanied by his friend, who was almost of equal category. We found the place where this lion had once attempted to join our group or, perhaps, only penetrate through our group in a desire to go up the escarpment. We then went up the escarpment and found where he would have been and we discussed this event at length. Where he would have been was a pleasant glade and in my opinion we could have killed him easily.

Discussing this type of event in a small plane is done in a more or less staccato manner.

I said, "You can see where the splendid beast went and where he was when we quit."

Miss Mary responded, "Okay, you and your splendid dog companions could possibly have continued and encountered the beast, but it was impossible for anybody in their right mind to go further up that escarpment."

I replied, *"Ndio,* darling" (*Ndio* meaning yes) and we called the thing off and proceeded down the Rift Valley until we encountered on the port side a small volcano which I had long been interested in.

We had a good look at this volcano, which had recently been in eruption, and then broke away from it in order to have a look at Lake Natron. This lake is very interesting for its intense color, which is produced by a sort of alga, and the presence of a large herd of buffalo. The buffalo are very black and have, in the case of the male, wide-spreading horns. These horns are quite impressive even from the air.

The lake bed was a deep pink in color; almost magenta. There was an abundance of wild fowl, including flocks of flamingos, and we identified a large number of these and then left Lake Natron to explore an extinct volcano on the west side of the escarpment. Then, having noted that from the air there is nothing to hold one's interest permanently in the crater of an extinct volcano, we proceeded to the Ngorongoro Crater, which is a rather notorious place frequently visited by tourists and heavily populated by game. On a cursory inspection of this remarkable depression, we noted several thousand wildebeest, kongoni and various types and species of antelope. No lions were observed.

Leaving the Ngorongoro Crater, we flew over the Serengeti Plains, where I showed Miss Mary the site where my previous and lovely wife Miss Pauline had killed a very fine maned lion. Mr. Marsh and I also showed Miss Mary the spot at which I killed a fair lion and killed a hyena with a shotgun while hunting duck. The hyena appeared out of the tall grass and in a way asked for his unfortunate demise.

The hyena, although a splendid actor in the motion pictures and the best performer in a film we always refer to as *The Snows of Zanuck,* and also the possessor of an extraordinary voice which one misses when in the metropolis of Nairobi, is in some ways an unpleasant character. We are all prejudiced against him at the moment, having seen him tear out the genitals of a living rhinoceros which had just been wounded by a cow elephant. Then this hyena with his mate attacked the rhino and proceeded to feed on the tusk wound that the rhino had in his left buttock.

So remembering old memories of the death of *fisi,* which is the Swahili name for hyena, we proceeded to the small town of Mwanza where we refueled the aircraft. We did not enter Mwanza itself but stayed at the airstrip since the generator had

429

evidently cut out on the aircraft and it was necessary to wind up the aircraft manually to become air-borne.

We then flew across Lake Victoria and over the Ruanda-Urundi. This is a rather desolate part of Africa and we were unable to see the sable antelope which are said to abound there, but did see one extremely aged-looking rhino who appeared to have nothing particular to do at that time of day, which was now evening, and four rather aimless-looking elephants, none of whom wore ivory over 90 pounds. After the Ruanda-Urundi, we came into a very heavily populated country where the huts were conical in shape and where quite a lot of social life appeared to be going on. We were able to observe groups of the local citizens who appeared to be enjoying themselves extraordinarily. In other words, a number appeared to be blind drunk.

We landed at a very fine airstrip at the town of Costermansville situated on Lake Kivu. There is a first-class hotel with excellent food and accommodation and a view over the lake. The lake is one of the most beautiful that I have ever seen. It is impossible to compare lakes accurately, but I would think that with its islands, broken outline, color of water, it would be certainly as beautiful as Lago Maggiore or Lago di Garda. It is certainly much more beautiful than Lago di Como and I am quite sure that it contains less dead bodies, of human beings at any rate.

In the morning, which was bright and lovely, we repaired the generator and the plane was thoroughly checked and we proceeded north flying over the Gorilla Sanctuary where Carl Akeley collected.

We then flew between two active volcanos and for a short time the air in the plane was somewhat reminiscent of the smell in a kite which has been hit by 20-millimeter antiaircraft fire. In other words, there was a strong sulphurous odor which made it necessary to open the side window vents. These volcanos were smoking to such an extent that any photographs taken would probably be worthless, so we broke off and headed in a northwest direction to observe the Ruwenzori Range which is known through my reading of *Life,* and through hearsay about the all-girl safari, as "The Mountains of the Moon."

I believe this original title came from the late Sir Rider Haggard. The "Mountains of the Moon" were unfortunately obscured by clouds as mountains so often are and we were unable to observe or photograph them. So we turned away and laid a course for Entebbe, where there was a very long and beautiful airstrip on which there was little activity due to the unfortunate grounding of the aircraft described by the British as the *Comet.*

The lack of the *Comet,* on which the social structure of Entebbe is temporarily based, was felt by all. We hoped piously that *Comets* would soon be flying again, had a drink to their early return to the airlines in the airport, and proceeded to the very excellent Lake Hotel. This is a really lovely hotel and the view over Lake Victoria is superb. By this time, I hoped that Miss Mary was beginning to lose the claustrophobia she had experienced while being confined to the Masai Reserve and the slopes of Mount Kilimanjaro.

We waited in the hotel until the mist had cleared and then went to the airport and took off for Lake Albert. Lake Albert is a very beautiful lake and there are many fishing villages along its western shore. We watched the fishermen and saw their various methods of fishing. They were using both nets and set lines which were marked by buoys made of native woods. The fishermen were using dugout canoes and when they were collecting their catch we saw one fish that appeared to be a Nile perch of at least 200 pounds.

He was a huge fish and the fishermen were rowing him rapidly to shore, being obviously very satisfied. We waved to them, dipped our wings rather, and they waved back. It was a truly splendid fish and to see him from the air made it even better.

We proceeded up the western bank of Lake Albert and then ascended the Victoria Nile to Murchison Falls. On the way, we saw many hippo and elephant along the banks and a sight which I had never seen before, mixed herds of elephant and buffalo. Everyone seemed to be getting along very well together, except one large hippo which was recently dead and was in the process of being eaten by crocodiles. The crocodiles seemed to be very confident in this area.

Formerly in Southern Tanganyika along the great Ruaha River, the only sight we ever had of a crocodile was the tip of his nostrils in the water. But there the crocodiles were being hunted heavily and were wary. These crocodiles along the Nile were on the banks and with their heads facing the shore rather than the water. They possibly expected something to come down to the water. In any event, they were present in profusion. I counted seventeen of the length of 12 feet and over (remember this is done from the air and therefore you cannot have complete accuracy—they might have been much longer), but they were extremely large crocs and they were together and under the brush or trees along the side of the river. As well as being very long, they were very broad and the plane did not disturb them at all. We began to consider that this was a fairly rough country.

Murchison Falls is very beautiful. It is a cataract which descends in various levels rather than an abrupt falls such as Niagara.

We circled these falls several times at a reasonably legal height and then after Miss Mary had taken two or three magazines full of film, which I loaded and supplied to her, we decided to return to Entebbe, where we planned to take a short break and see that the film was properly cared for. It needs to be packed with dehydrating material and sealed airtight in these latitudes. As we broke away from the falls, we encountered a flight of large birds which I identified as black and white ibis. We had seen this same flock on our way up the river. A bird of this type can easily go through the Plexiglas and could eliminate the pilot of an aircraft of this type or the co-pilot. Since the co-pilot's seat was occupied by Miss Mary, Roy Marsh dove sharply under these birds which we observed passing overhead and I had the chance to admire their black and white markings and their down-swept black bills.

At this point, having deviated through no fault of our own from our proposed course, we encountered a telegraph wire on an abandoned line. This telegraph had been abandoned when the radio network was set up and nearly all the wire had been removed for the benefit of the natives, who wore it in circular coils in their ears. This small section of the line remained, as it was inaccessible to the natives, who are more or less allergic to Murchison Falls. This might be due to the presence of the various beasts which we had observed.

The aircraft had encountered the wire with its propeller and its tail assembly. It was temporarily uncontrollable and then was so obviously damaged that it was necessary to land. There was a choice of going into what we refer to in RAF parlance as "the drink" which was directly below. However, the drink which was carefully observed and had already been scouted by Roy Marsh and myself contained too many crocodiles to make landing advisable. Also, as you know, one does not land an aircraft with nonretractable wheels in the water. Water is one of the hardest substances on which to land an aircraft and unless you can make a belly landing the ditching will not be successful. The action of the unretracted wheels when coming in contact with the water will almost inevitably precipitate the aircraft forward so that the pilot and the passengers will find themselves upside down and under water. If this water is occupied by the crocodiles this maneuver is considered by experienced defiers of the laws of gravity to be extremely inadvisable.

Roy Marsh chose the simpler and better course of swinging sharply to his left where there was solid land observable. This land was covered by heavy bush but a Cessna 180 can land at a speed of approximately 40 mph. Roy Marsh, who found that his flaps were working, laid her down very sweetly in the softest bushes which were available. These bushes were medium-sized trees. There was the usual sound of rending metal which is audible in a forced landing, but everything was intact. We observed the damage to the aircraft and to Miss Mary who had previously not participated in this sort of thing. I was unable to obtain a pulse on her for some time although at no time was she unconscious. This is a phenomenon that I would like to offer in the interest of science. When the pulse was obtained it was 155. This was verified by Roy and we decided that we would have to make our way very slowly up to the high ground to avoid the elephants who were already starting to comment audibly on our presence.

We made camp at what seemed to be an old elephant-poacher's camp since it controlled two main elephant paths and had behind it a small rise of ground topped by a steep rock up which no elephant could come. Roy and I cut grass and made a bed for Miss Mary, obtained wood for a fire and Roy went down to the aircraft at least five times in order to send the usual Mayday signal, which in aircraft parlance is equivalent to the former SOS which has become quite notorious through publicity given by sinking vessels. I talked in wild dog to Roy and he answered in straight dog baboon. The elephants commented each time we spoke and in this way Roy knew where they were and how to best avoid them. We decided that our objectives were primarily to exist. First, to care for Miss Mary, who we did not know at that time had two broken ribs which were causing her considerable pain and from which she was never complaining at any point. Secondly, to conserve our supplies, thus rationing the one bottle of water, the four bottles of Carlsberg beer and the bottle of the Grand MacNish Scotch whisky which I will recommend without any hope of recompense.

We decided that after posting the usual signals for a crashed aircraft, we might have to wait a period of several days before being recovered since the terrain was not suitable for the landing of an aircraft and no landing strip existed.

We planned to prepare an emergency landing strip where a small aircraft could land. We rationed the Carlsberg beer, which was to be consumed at the rate of one bottle each two days shared among three people. We rationed the Grand MacNish, which was to be issued one drink each evening. The water we planned to renew from the Murchison Falls where there seemed to be a plentiful supply.

Roy had a gallon tin which had contained petrol at one time but which was suitable for carrying water from the falls. This left no problem about water except that we had a lengthy discussion of the type that occurs on this kind of picnic as to whether the tin would unsolder when placed on the fire to boil the water. This discussion, along with general discussion of alternative plans, was one of our principal ways of passing the evening until there appeared a herd of some 60 elephants who, as usual, approached in perfect silence except when they spoke among themselves.

Miss Mary was sleeping well on the straw. We had covered her with my coat and my raincoat since we believed her to be in a state of shock, which she would well be entitled to be in. I was lying beside her from time to time but most of the time huddled over the fire with Roy who was sleeping in a light open shirt and shorts. We had no means of ascertaining the temperature but I am sure it was quite low as I have never been colder.

I was very much better off than Roy, however, since I had a fairly intact flannel shirt and also trousers. We had not thought we were going to be on an extended flight so we were lightly clad, since in Africa it is usually warm in an aircraft. Our conversation about the water tin was interrupted by a male elephant with quite big ivory who appeared at a distance of about 20 yards. He was evidently making his way up the elephant path to graze along the ridge when he stopped to investigate our fire. He spread his ears wide. They looked to me to be about 60 feet wide but I know from seeing elephants in the daytime that they attain no such dimensions.

He raised his trunk which appeared to me to be several hundred feet long but I also know that such dimensions are impossible. He then uttered a very strange squealing noise and gave every sign of attempting to join our group. Roy and I maintained a rigid silence, including stopping of breath, and hoped, sincerely, that the elephant would decide to proceed upon his own business.

This he decided to do. During the night, visits from curious elephants were more or less routine but the only defensive measures taken against these large beasts, who, incidently, can assume imposing proportions in the moonlight, were to maintain strict silence and to hold and rehold any sound of breathing which might be offensive to these elephants who were, really, our hosts. Anyone who broke this attempt at complete silence in the presence of our hosts the elephants was remonstrated with as gently as possible. Miss Mary passed an excellent night and while she was in considerable pain in the morning she was extremely cheerful, asked what there was for breakfast, was surprised that tea had not been served, and consumed an unrationed apple.

Roy had already left at daylight to obtain water from the Murchison Falls which in the crash of their falling water had prevented us from hearing any sound of aircraft which undoubtedly were searching the area. Several times, I thought I heard aircraft and at least once I was sure I had, but the sound of the falls, which was wind-borne toward us and varied with the intensity of the wind, made it impossible to be sure.

During the morning while Roy was away, I maintained a signal fire to show our location to any passing aircraft and in the course of this it was necessary to search for dead wood. We burned live wood, breaking the branches off and putting them on the fire to maintain smoke. It was necessary however to get good-sized pieces of dead wood to maintain the fire. At one time, it was impossible to do this because every time you broke off a branch of dead wood you would be challenged by an elephant. However, with the use of collected twigs which were put in a pile as a source of replenishment for the fire and roots which were pulled out from the immediate vicinity of the camp, we maintained a good fire and kept up sufficient smoke.

Unfortunately, we were in competition with several large

brush fires of such an extent that one of our party had confused one with the rising of the moon. At this point, I had a rare moment, I hope, of irascibility and remarked, "The beloved moon would rise in such and such a direction over that ridge or it was not our moon."

On one of these early-morning trips in search of wood, I had finally been able to get approximately 50 yards to the left of where we were camped, considering that we were facing down the ridge toward the river. The elephants were protesting any effort to obtain wood. They were browsing on the green brush and the crack of breaking dry wood annoyed them. However, by working very carefully with the wind in our favor, I had reached a tree which had very promising dry branches. At this point, hearing an elephant protesting when I broke a branch off the tree, I looked toward the sound of the protest and saw a white launch proceeding up stream on the river. During the course of this safari, we had many times seen mirages when the sun got high, and at the sight of this launch I thought first that I must check my eyesight. I called Miss Mary and told her that a launch was coming up the river. The launch by this time had disappeared behind a point. Miss Mary doubted my veracity, but in a most friendly way. I took her to the limit of the point of security against the elephants who were still talking and the launch emerged from behind the point.

It was a very beautiful launch, fairly old-fashioned in lines, and we later found that it was the vessel which had been used in the motion picture called *The African Queen,* which starred two intrepid African characters called Katharine Hepburn, who has my great admiration, and Humphrey Bogart, whom I have never yet seen at bat in real life. He, however, was most convincing in this motion picture and I regarded the sight of this launch as a most pleasurable experience.

We signaled to the launch which was making a trip which might have been made only once a month, and therefore was a most fortuitous arrival, and a group of characters commenced the arduous journey up the ridge. These characters were all Africans, one of them being of extraordinary stature, and I tried to direct their ascent in a manner in which they would not encounter the elephants. This was accomplished by keeping them on the western side of the draw.

The elephants, scenting so many people, withdrew to the vicinity of the crashed aircraft. At this point, from my observation, they seemed to disperse. They had made a complete reconnaissance of the aircraft which was later verified by a BOAC pilot, Capt. R. C. Jude, who had flown over the aircraft, and they seemed to regard the aircraft in some way as their property. Since they did no damage to it, perhaps they regarded it as their guest, much as they appeared to look on us.

Mrs. Hemingway descended from the camp with our visiting friends from the S.S. *Murchison,* alleged *African Queen;* one of the characters carried a large-caliber rifle and had the look of an extremely competent character. I thought Miss Mary was in good hands.

I remained at the camp to await Roy Marsh to whom I had given rendezvous. He was returning to the camp after obtaining water from Murchison Falls which we all regarded as a very interesting waterfall. After sighting the S.S. *Murchison,* and seeing that Miss Mary was safely embarked, I made a decision to open the Grand MacNish and make a scotch and water with the now unrationed water which was the distilled water for the battery of the plane and which was now, I considered, eminently expendable. The only difficulty in preparing this beverage was the lack of any glass or other receptacle. I therefore commenced to drink, hurriedly, a bottle of the Carlsberg beer in which, when it was empty, I planned to make a mixture of the Grand MacNish and water.

This operation was interrupted by the arrival of a group of elephants. No one of these elephants appeared to have any hostile intentions, except one which evidently had some memories of this old poacher's site. Perhaps she had lost a lover or a husband there, at any rate she was definitely hostile. She extended her ears to their full extent and approached. I took immediate evasive action by scrambling on hands and feet up the steep rock on which we had planned to make the local variation of Custer's last stand with Miss Mary.

Roy and I had planned to propel Miss Mary manually up this rock in case the elephant approached beyond the bounds of normal approach by elephants. This elephant, for some extraordinary reason, since we had been in no way molesting elephants, seemed to have taken a great dislike to me, myself, personally. She attempted to ascend the incline below the rock. Since the rock had been selected for the defense of Miss Mary, and therefore was as secure as any such rock can be, I selected a number of slabs or pieces of rock and, although I am a right-handed pitcher, commenced to throw them at her with the left hand. The right had temporarily been immobilized by a dislocation of the elbow and the shoulder. The elephant was extremely noisy in her protest at my having taken a position on this rock.

When you are throwing from the left side at the eyes of an elephant you hit the right eye if you throw a strike. I threw one strike at this elephant and then two balls. The elephant maintained an aggressive attitude and raised her trunk to what I considered an exaggerated attitude since it was very nearly touching my person; a thing about which I am extremely sensitive; and especially with the elephant. This elephant seemed to be attempting to make contact which I consider was, in the highest traditions of whatever service to which I belonged, highly undesirable. The trunk of the elephant seemed at extremely close range a rather formidable object and the thing that I noticed about it most was that there was a strong odor from the tip and that the nose of the trunk was definitely pink on the inside. It also had a curious folding arrangement on the end. I wished I were back in the Kimana Swamp with the gentle cobra. The eyes of the elephant are small, but I tried for the right eye again and missed it. I threw a strike on the left eye and when this seemed to make slight impression on the elephant, who had not ceased speaking in what seemed uncivil tones, I was able to obtain a direct hit on the mouth.

I will omit the dialogue between the elephant and myself but it was conducted, I am sure, on both sides in a rather unpleasant fashion. I can recall stating to the elephant, "Debark, you unspeakable elephant, before you are called upon to take the consequences." The elephant replied in her own language which by this time I was commencing to have a small knowledge of.

I then said, "Elephant, you die." This was a phrase which I have read in correspondents' reports of what happened with the Japanese in the late Pacific hostilities and since I was in no position to cause the death of an elephant it was much the same as the Japanese who being in no position to defend himself probably uttered the statement first.

The elephant maintained her position of, should we say, potential malevolence. Seeing that words and speeches had practically no effect on the elephant, I resumed the throwing of slates and rocks. As anyone knows, a right-handed pitcher, of which I was one of the worst, is not qualified to pitch with his left hand, but I succeeded in getting the elephant in the mouth one out of three times that she raised her trunk and addressed me in an impolite manner.

Finally, she broke off the action and rejoined the other elephants, no one of which seemed particularly interested, although they talked a good deal among themselves and several bulls had their ears spread and seemed ready to participate in case their female champion should not gain the decision. Elephants are extremely nice people and I think that this elephant who misbehaved had probably been either ill bred or at some time mistreated. It is difficult to know exactly how an elephant feels about a human being since a good number of them have been wounded in the past by unskillful or careless people. One that I know of, when killed while we were in Southern Tanganyika, had fourteen different wounds with the projectiles embedded in the flesh when his tusks were removed and the carcass butchered.

The man who killed him waited through the butchery to

find out if possible the cause of the elephant's temper. Evidently the elephant, an admirable beast who, however, can become dangerous, had become irascible through the lodging of these various projectiles in his flesh, bone and marrow; two were lodged in his skull. One could consider this to be sufficient provocation for any beast to suffer a slight loss of good temper. I do not know what had happened to this cow but it is possible that she had suffered the loss of some member of her family at the spot at which she took a dislike to me.

After the departure of the elephants who went on up the ridge, I walked down to the aircraft and from the aircraft joined Miss Mary on board the S.S. *Murchison*. There was a charming party on board, consisting of a couple who were celebrating their golden wedding and their son-in-law and daughter and a young grandson named Ian. We photographed the plane for evidence after the crash and then built a back fire in order that the Cessna would not be damaged by any of the bush fires which were burning at the time.

On the S.S. *Murchison*, we found that the son-in-law of the golden-wedding couple was Mr. McAdam, an excellent surgeon of the Protectorate. He examined Miss Mary and found that she had two broken ribs but was otherwise in quite good condition, having recovered rapidly from the shock.

When Roy Marsh came aboard the *Murchison*, and the members of the party who had gone to view the Murchison Falls returned, we slipped the lines, lifted the single anchor and started down the river for Lake Albert with Butiaba as our eventual destination. It was lovely being aboard the launch which was clean, well run and had an excellent refrigerator containing Tusker beer and several brands of ale.

No hard liquor was served, but a bottle of Gordon's gin was obtainable from the Hindu in charge of the launch who sold it for what I considered and he admitted to be a rather exorbitant sum. Under the terms of his charter, he could dispense this beverage by the drink at a fairly reasonable amount, but in Africa the average drink which is dispensed is of such a minute size that it has no comparison to the drink one pours on safari. However, still having our money in our possession at this time, we obtained a bottle of this gin which I held in reserve in case there should be any necessity for its use.

I had with us two bunches of bananas. One was exactly right and the other was slightly over-ripe. These had constituted our principal reserve when we were expecting to spend some time in the Murchison Falls area.

The trip down the river was truly delightful. On both sides of the river, you could see large male hippo and female hippo with their young and there were many crocodiles. We were also able, as we descended the river on the left bank, to observe various elephants which I had come to know personally. It was a pleasure to toast these elephants and to drink to their health in Tusker beer, the first cold beer we had tasted in some time. It was nice to see that the crocodiles had not been disturbed by the crash of the Cessna 180 and still remained on the banks and under the trees with their heads pointing toward the banks. This seemed to impress Roy Marsh whose duty it had been to obtain water from the bank of the river. The maximum number of crocodiles I counted was seventeen in one group. We saw, perhaps, five hundred.

All along the river, we encountered elephants, both solitary and in groups of six to twenty. Due to the drought which has dominated a large part of Africa for the last two years, this was probably one of the greatest concentrations of game along a water course there has ever been. Ordinarily, game are suspicious of a water course and prefer to take their water in any casual source where it may have accumulated in the rains; but due to the grass fires which were raging, the game had been concentrated along the river. They all seemed to be extremely amicable among themselves and the only incident that we saw of any being killed was the hippo which I have already mentioned.

The river empties into Lake Albert and after that it is a rather gray expanse of water but there are many birds and you can see fish rising. The launch makes about seven knots at her best and so it is possible to observe the water and the distant shore line closely. There are concentrations of lake birds, pelicans, terns and considerable flights of duck, mostly teal and what we call puddle ducks.

We were very happy on the boat and Miss Mary, after her examination, was offered the use of the bath which belonged to the golden-wedding couple. She had a good bath, rest and sleep and Roy Marsh also took a well-deserved nap while Mr. McAdam and myself discussed things in general. We came into Butiaba which is a small and rather unimpressive village on the lake shore and offers no form of accommodation except possibly a hotel for what is referred to in the Protectorate as Asiatics.

The commander of the ship was an Asiatic and had long hairs growing out of both ears. For some reason, possibly tribal, which we always respect, he had never cut these hairs and they had attained a length which was, if not enviable, certainly extraordinary. One might even say that they bristled like a hedge and gave him, possibly, his only true distinction. They grew not only from inside his ears but also from the edges of the lobes. He had demanded as a fee for carrying us, Shs. 100/—a head. Since Mr. (you call a surgeon who has attended a university in the present British language Mr. rather than Dr.) McAdam had paid for the charter and considered rescued characters could ride on a ship free at his invitation, he protested this charge.

Being conversant with maritime law, and knowing that the master of the ship was well within his rights even though an exaggerated amount of hair protruded from his ears, I paid this charge and Mr. McAdam made formal protest in writing. I explained to Mr. McAdam over a bottle of Tusker that you always paid these charges and then recovered them when you were in the right. This was subsequently proved true by the receipt of a checque for Shs.300/—from the East African Railways and Harbours, an eminently just institution which employed the skipper with the slight overgrowth of hair in and on his ears.

At Butiaba, we had the choice of spending the night on the *Murchison,* which I thought would not be too attractive to Miss

Mary since a small vessel moored alongside a quay with her sleeping accommodation below offers little ventilation, or going by motor car to Masindi. We decided to go by motor car to Masindi. However, we met a pilot who had been searching for us all day and who was anxious to take us and our effects direct to Entebbe. He had refueled his plane, a de Havilland *Rapide*, and was ready to take off. My own reaction would be to proceed to Masindi which we eventually did, by motor transport.

However, when one is invited to go upstairs in our set, known as the Fast International Sporting House Set, the suggestion is almost in the nature of a command. Capt. Reginald Cartwright, the pilot of the aircraft, made a rapid reconnaissance of the airstrip in a truck or, as we say here, a lorry. It was impossible to observe his progress on this reconnaissance due to the amount of dust raised. To me the landing strip appeared rather like the red hills of South Dakota and appeared to have large ridges shaped like a washboard along what we had to consider as the airstrip.

When in the aircraft, Captain Cartwright got into what we refer to as the driver's seat, Roy Marsh into the starboard seat, myself in the second port seat to balance the weight of Captain Cartwright who wished us to be well forward and had given an order that we should be. When we were one third of the way down the alleged airstrip, I was convinced that we would not be airborne successfully. However, we continued at the maximum rate of progress of the aircraft which was leaping from crag to crag and precipice to precipice in the manner of the wild goat. Suddenly, this object which was still described as an aircraft became violently air-borne through no fault of its own. This condition existed only for a matter of seconds after which the aircraft became violently de-air-borne and there was the usual sound, with which we were all by now familiar, of rending metal.

Unfortunately, on this second occasion flames were observed coming from the starboard engine which was burning. The right-wing tank, which was fully loaded for the considerable flight to Entebbe, had also caught fire and due to the wind these flames were coming toward the rear of the aircraft. There is very little in an aircraft which is inflammable, but as the gasoline comes out of the tank it bathes the side of the aircraft and it burns in the direction in which the wind is blowing.

At this moment when the crash of the aircraft had gone into Technicolor, I remembered the old rule that in a twin-engined aircraft you get out the same way you came in. I therefore went to the door through which we entered and found it jammed by the bending of the material of which the aircraft was constructed. I got the door open and called out to Roy Marsh, "I have it open here. Miss Mary okay?" Roy responded, "Okay, Papa, going out the front way."

I opened the door by pressure exerted by my head and left shoulder. Once the door was open I mounted the left wing of the aircraft which wing had not yet taken fire and counted Miss Mary, Roy and the pilot who had left the aircraft through an aperture through which I myself could not have emerged.

I spoke to them and they said they were okay and we all formationed well forward of the aircraft. Some people are under the impression that the aircraft burned in a sudden burst but I can testify honestly that I have never seen a kite burn more slowly. It must be a very rugged species of aircraft and she did not ignite completely until everyone was at a reasonable distance.

Roy explained to me that he had taken Miss Mary out of the aircraft by kicking out a window. He and Miss Mary are more or less of the same dimensions. Roy went first to ensure Miss Mary's exit. He then helped her out in the best traditions of any airline stewardness. I was acting as an airline stewardness at the normal exit but I had no customers. Reggie made it through a window when there was no one else in the aircraft and that is the way a *Ndege* character should comport himself.

This business of *Ndege* characters is probably quite incomprehensible to those who are not members of this outfit. *Ndege* means bird and is the African name for an aircraft. People who have to do intimately with the aircraft have certain secret feelings and much undeclared knowledge. They also have a set of ethics which are not publicly declared. If you are one, you are one. If you are not, you will be detected and exposed. The worst thing anyone can do except for stepping on an eight-foot cobra is to pretend that one is a *Ndege* character if one is not. It will, in a country where the *Ndege* is the normal form of transportation, be detected sooner or later. I could write about that, but as a much better writer than I am, the late Rudyard Kipling, said, that is another story.

Various people and several periodicals have asked me what one thinks at the hour of one's death, a rather exaggerated phrase, and what it feels like to read one's obituaries. Being a *Ndege* character, I can answer truthfully that at the moment of an aircraft crashing and/or burning, your only thoughts are of technical problems. Your past life does not rush through your brain like a cinema film and your thoughts are purely technical. Perhaps there are people whose past lives rush through their brains, but so far in my life I have never experienced this sensation.

After you have crashed and/or burned in a plane, you are usually in a state of what is loosely described as shock. On a crash-landing where the aircraft has been set down comparatively softly there is not much shock but I believe there is always some. However, if you are conditioned to this by the practice of more or less contact sports, you are familiar with the sensations and can sort them out.

In the case of an aircraft burning on takeoff, the shock is considerably greater and you cannot sort it out much at the time and so attempt to behave in a completely normal manner. This is quite easy to do and fools most people completely. For example, when an aircraft has crashed and burned, you first, automatically, listen for the ammo to go. You check with yourself as to whether she is carrying bombs, standing at a reasonable distance from the aircraft and listening for the ammo to go. At this moment, standing in such a fashion and receiving the congratulations of various over-excited Africans who were vigorously pumping my right arm which had been dislocated, I heard what there was of ammo go.

There were four small pops representing the explosion of the bottles of Carlsberg beer which had constituted our reserve. This was followed by a slightly louder pop which represented the bottle of the Grand MacNish. After this, I clearly heard a louder but still not intense explosion which I knew signified the un-opened bottle of Gordon's gin. This is sealed by a metal cap and therefore gives an explosion of greater power than that of the Grand MacNish which is only sealed by a cork and, in any event, had been half consumed. I listened for further explosions but there were none.

We then left the scene of the crash in the motor vehicle of a young policeman who had kindly consented to take us to Masindi. In this vehicle was the charming wife of this police officer and Miss Mary and myself, adjusting ourselves to the 53-mile ride which was accomplished on no liquor or any other beverage. This was the longest ride of my life and I am sure it did not seem short to Miss Mary. At one time I remarked to her, "Miss Mary, can you make it okay without our stopping at any friendly place or *dukka* for a small quick one?" It is customary to administer to *Ndege* characters one or two ounces of, preferably, bourbon, after the crash and burning of an aircraft if it has crashed or burned on what is considered a friendly airfield.

"Papa," Miss Mary replied, "I can make it if you can, but it is the hard way."

We held hands with our good hands and rode it out.

II

There had been what we describe in the parlance of the R.A.F. as the meat wagon present at the scene of our second crash. It was in charge of an African practitioner who was extremely cordial, deeply moved, but so excited that he forgot he was to administer certain first-aid treatment. After we completed our journey to Masindi and had the usual reception by former mourners and enthusiasts who had seen a kite burn for the first time in their lives, we finally went to bed.

During the night, I heard a hyena howl repeatedly and I wondered whether it was attracted by the odor of burnt flesh and hair which I could clearly smell. I checked the entrances and exits of our hotel room in a more or less mechanical manner and decided that if this more or less blessed animal wished to howl he might continue the exercise.

Miss Mary was in great pain from the broken ribs and did not sleep well. However, the howling of the beast reassured her and made her feel that she was back in the dear old days of the Kimana Swamp before she had accepted the Christmas present of this trip in the *Ndege*.

In the morning, we met the African practitioner who had been so overjoyed at our miraculous escape from the consumed *Ndege*, and he applied what I should, perhaps, out of racial understanding and friendship, not describe as home remedies. He wished to strap Miss Mary up and care for her ribs. This would doubtless have been an interesting experience for this noble practitioner but I did not approve of the action.

There is nothing you can do about broken ribs anyway, except to hope you receive them in the ninth round of a ten-round fight rather than in the first. Strapping them up only means that the plaster must be removed and even for a girl whose body is less hirsute than that of a man, the removal of plaster may be extremely painful. As an offer to science, I would like to say that the damage inflicted on the skin when the ribs are encased in plaster is, in my mature consideration, much greater than the good which is obtained by this rather questionable practice.

This rather noble African, for whom I incidentally formed a perhaps lasting affection, then clipped my skull in a most skillful manner with a pair of scissors. I do not know whether he cut tribal patterns or whether the clipping was a purely functional one. In any event, it was both effective and spectacular. He applied some form of antiseptic and a dressing which consisted of various strips of plaster which could be described as moderately sensational.

He dressed the left leg, which by this time was suppurating. He checked the amount of what we in Africa refer to as *damu,* or blood, which was flowing from all of the five classic orifices of the human body, and very kindly announced that we were fit to proceed to Entebbe. This was our objective since Miss Mary had expressed a wish to remain several weeks there in order to recuperate. We also wished to rejoin any articles of clothing or articles of value which we might have left at the hotel since I did not know if the old R.A.F. custom still existed of sacking up the kit or gear of any *Ndege* character who did not return promptly to the field where his squadron was stationed after being presumably down in enemy terrain or in what we still in our primitive ignorance continue to refer to as the drink.

Actually, the drink at this time was Gordon's gin, of which we had been able to obtain a supply in Masindi. I do not work for the Gordon's people and this is a testimonial which I offer freely and in what I hope is my right mind. This beverage is one of the sovereign antiseptics of our time. Penicillin enjoys a temporary popularity and there are some people who use sulpha. There are various other antibiotics. However, these products may prove to be only of passing worth. Gordon's product is of approved merit and can be counted on to fortify, mollify and cauterize practically all internal or external injuries. Nevertheless, what we refer to in Wakamba as *Nanyake*—members of the tribe who are not yet allowed to drink beer—should never be encouraged to employ this magic beverage since their judgment might be insecure; it might lead them into grave errors and perhaps to the commission of crimes of violence and sexual depravity which we all deplore. In other words, do not let children drink gin.

After we had been treated, we traveled by motor car from Masindi to Entebbe. This is a rather dull and dusty drive—

449

result of the continued failure of the rains in the north—and there is not much to see until you hit Kampala, the City of the Seven Hills, which is an exceedingly charming town. The journey is, however, one of some 135 miles and it affords ample time for thought and reflection.

This thought is conditioned by the fact that the so-called thinker has suffered a major concussion and therefore is not responsible for his thoughts. This type of concussion induces the type of thinking which sometimes tends toward violence. I believe this violence is a phenomenon of concussion due to the violent demise of the aircraft. In any event, it is to be deplored and I hereby disavow any responsibility for the thoughts which passed through my head, but here is what some of them were.

First, I wished that Sen. Joseph McCarthy (Republican) of Wisconsin had been with us at the crash of both aircraft. I have always had a certain curiosity, as one has about all public figures, as to how Senator McCarthy would behave in what we call the clutch. Doubtless he would be admirable but I have always had this fleeting curiosity. I wondered if without his senatorial immunity he would be vulnerable to the various beasts with whom we had been keeping company. This thought held my disordered mind for some 10 or 12 miles, I must admit with a certain degree of enjoyment.

Then with my disordered mind pursuing the same train, if it could be called a train, of thought, I wondered if there was anything wrong, if there should be anything wrong with Sen. Joseph McCarthy (Republican) of Wisconsin which a .577 solid would not cure.

Then I remembered Mr. Leonard Lyons, my very old friend, and his experience with the .577 when we tried out 20 rounds of ammunition in the proving booth in the basement of Abercrombie & Fitch in New York. It was old ammo and it was necessary to determine if it was still reliable. Mr. Lyons, who is extremely gallant, well built but a little short on weight, fired the .577 and the recoil lifted him from his feet and laid him against an iron doorway at the back of the proving ground. He dropped the .577 but it was uninjured, and for some miles I pondered happily on this incident and on other incidents that happened to me with Mr. Leonard Lyons. Mr. Lyons will probably recall them. They were all pleasant.

I then commenced to ponder, in my still disordered condition, on Mr. Toots Shor. Pondering on Mr. Shor, you may pass many miles quite happily. I remembered Mr. Shor's unfailing courtesy. Mr. Shor is supposed to be extremely rude to everyone but I doubt if we have ever exchanged an impolite phrase. I was able to reconstruct Mr. Shor's countenance in my mind, which is a considerable feat under the circumstances. Mr. Shor's countenance resembles much of the broken country unsuitable for farming that we were passing through.

At this point, I reluctantly abandoned the thought of Mr. Shor, whose place seemed far distant, and started to remember another friend of mine, Mr. Joe Russell, popularly known as Sloppy Joe, who ran a saloon which was the counterpart in Key West of the saloon and restaurant run by Mr. Shor. Mr. Joe Russell was my partner and friend for many years in many ventures. I then spent several miles remembering the manner of his death.

I then recalled in succession the great privilege it had been to be associated with Mr. George Brown of 225 West 57th Street and the now-happy remnants of my brain recalled moments with Brown which could hardly be exceeded. Coming directly south from West 57th Street, as one has often done sitting backwards in the taxi in order not to catch cold after working out with Mr. Brown, I recalled with vast pleasure Mr. Sherman Billingsley. I thought of Mr. Billingsley with whom I have many things in common and for whom I hold a benevolent affection.

Then, there being no order in which I thought of these gentlemen, due to having been hit too hard over the head, I thought of Mr. Bill Corum and what he must have looked like when he was the youngest major in the American Army. Then I thought of what Mr. Ben Finney must have looked like when he was in the Marines in the first war. I met Mr. Finney in his prime when he was the first man to run the Cresta at St. Moritz, Switzerland, the first time that he was ever in that strange vehicle which is employed in this descent. Thinking about Mr. Finney and his loyalty as a friend and how he cannot fight a lick but will always go made me very happy.

I thought, since now my brain was somewhere round 52nd and 53rd Streets, of Mr. Earl Wilson and his gentle loyalty over a period of many years. I thought of Mr. Walter Winchell and how we used to sit up late together with Damon Runyon, when Mr. Runyon was still a living man and fine companion and not yet a Fund, and I hoped that Walter and Lenny Lyons would cease feuding.

In this time, my brain had become benevolent and wished good will to all men. I thought of many other friends and of their great assets and their occasional defects. My brain refused to have anything to do with my past life, contrary to the usual reports, and continued about other people and about places and about food and good drink.

We were equipped with the product of the Messrs. Gordon and I thought about this and the pleasure it had given me in life. This started my brain to think about my past life, but I was able to break the brain away from that subject, in which a certain amount of remorse is involved, and I began to consider economic and political problems which my brain resolutely refused to handle.

At times such as this, you have certain phenomena which may be interesting. In place of one beautiful woman on the street, you see two beautiful women. Your brain seems to be something like your brother rather than a complete integrated organ. Your hearing comes and goes and sometimes you cannot hear the sound of your own voice and at other times noises become far too acute. There was a steady oozing between my skull and my left ear and I asked Miss Mary to look and see if she saw any exudence of gray matter. She said, "Papa, you know you have no brains and that must be some form of liquid that we are unfamiliar with."

Miss Mary can joke as roughly as anyone and sometimes much rougher. It is for this quality that she is considered so highly by the circle of Mr. Toots Shor. I think it would be no exaggeration to say that Miss Mary can do with a few words what Miss Maureen Connolly can do with her forehand. This in the language of our set is described as "She can murder you." Bearing my wayward brain and Miss Mary with her broken ribs, her unquestioned valor and her lovely incisive speech, we arrived at Entebbe. Up to this time, neither of us had read our obituaries, which I understand had been published in considerable amount before our arrival.

At Entebbe, we met the journalists and the interrogators. Actually, it was in the opposite order. The British equivalent of our Civil Aeronautics Administration is extremely thorough since the loss of a *Ndege* involves loss to the insurance company or to the company owning the aircraft and in order to see if any negligence can be proved on the part of the pilot the interrogation is profound and exhaustive. I had hoped to be interrogated jointly with our pilot, Roy Marsh, so I could refresh my memory which was not in absolutely perfect condition. The interrogators, whom I referred to constantly in the course of our conversation as the inquisitors, were very able men. At once seeing that I was in the worst shape of the two and therefore might commit an indiscretion during an interrogation, they chose me first. Mr. Marsh and Captain Cartwright were to come later, in that order. An interrogation is not difficult when you have a true story to tell but you must be most careful about technical details.

I believe that is one reason why people when they know they are crashing observe all such details so thoroughly. I believe that the details are observed in the mind with as great an intensity as the means of self-preservation. This is natural since any means of self-preservation which was not absolutely ethical would be detected in the interrogation and so you are doing three things.

One, you are trying to stay alive in order to keep all passengers alive, thus avoiding what are classified as "fatal crashes." The fatal crash is viewed very badly and all efforts are made to avoid it.

The second thing you are doing is to attempt to perform this in a completely ethical manner; that is, according to your own ethics.

The third thing you are doing when you crash is to do it so it will look good to the insurance company.

To have it look good to the insurance company, you must make this sort of triple play with extreme speed and accuracy and later must remember everything including in larger aircraft such things as propeller pitch. We had excellent photographs which would have borne out all our statements, but unfortunately these burned in the crash of the second aircraft. It was therefore a question of a long, both exhaustive and exhausting test of one's veracity and technical knowledge.

No one knew for several days whether he had passed this test. The Inquisitors were always kind and gentle when interrogating, as is the tradition of Scotland Yard; but on about the third day of interrogation, we began to note a certain note of cordiality rather than the regulation politeness.

After the preliminary inquiry, we met the press, rather, I met them while Miss Mary went to her room for a needed rest. I felt an urgent need to rest also but attempted to give the reporters a clear account of the two crashes with certain possibly interesting details. I reserved the details that you have been reading. At the time, I did not wish to ever write anything about the two crashes but since then I have read so many absurd accounts in our various obituaries, especially in the foreign press, that I thought it would be best to give a true and accurate account.

It was interesting while talking to the press to note that there were two of each of them where only one stood and it was odd to be talking and occasionally not hear the sound of one's own voice. It is a great relief sometimes not to hear the sound of one's own voice if one is the talkative rather than the strong, silent type. However, not hearing the sound of my voice made it much simpler to talk to people that I had not previously met.

Roy Marsh had proceeded by aircraft to Nairobi to report to his company and be inquisited a little more. He returned to Entebbe with a Cessna 170, the older brother of the 180 we had left behind at Murchison Falls. In the meantime, and almost immediately after we arrived in Entebbe, my middle son Patrick arrived, having chartered a plane in the Southern Highlands of Tanganyika and flown by way of Mwanza. He arrived as fast as any man could and had with him 14,000 shillings. This is the first time any son of mine has ever arrived without being broke or, if you did not hear from him, asking you to either get him back into the Army or get him out of jail. He thus to me becomes the hero of this story just as Miss Mary is the one and only heroine. Roy Marsh occupied the top hero billing until the arrival of Patrick with the 14,000 shillings.

Quickly reducing Patrick's capital, Roy Marsh and I took off in the Cessna for Nairobi to face the Inquisitors and left Patrick to care for Miss Mary and bring her with him on the regular airline. In Nairobi, we were very well received and met a number of extremely nice people.

It was at this point that I commenced that strange vice which I believe could become extremely destructive to one's general equilibrium and cause one, perhaps, to lose one's status as a completely well-adjusted person. I had always run as an adjusted person though various tinhorn biographers had attempted to prove otherwise.

This strange vice was the reading of one's own obituaries. Most of the obituaries I could never have written nearly as well myself. There were certain inaccuracies and many good things were said which were in no way deserved. There were, however, some rather glaring inaccuracies in the account of my unfortunate death. One in the German press stated that I had attempted to land the aircraft myself on the summit of Mount Kilimanjaro, which we call "Kibo." It seems that I was landing this aircraft accompanied by Miss Mary in an effort to approach the carcass of a dead leopard about which I had written a story in 1934. This story was called *The Snows of Kilimanjaro* and was made into a motion picture which I unfortunately was not able to sit through so I cannot tell you how it came out. Perhaps the end was that I crashed an aircraft accompanied by Miss Mary at the extreme summit of this peak, which is 19,565 or 19,567 feet high entirely according to which surveyor you believe. Maybe it rises and falls.

During our tour of duty in the Laitokitok area which is on the slopes of this mountain, we had frequently flown over its flanks perhaps as high as 15,000 feet. I would have no wish, under any circumstances, to put down a Cessna 180 on the extreme summit of Mount Kilimanjaro in my "constant efforts to court death." In the first place, it would be difficult to get the Cessna up there, impossible to put her down, and there would be a long walk home to Laitokitok.

It is much easier to walk downhill on this mountain than uphill. I had proved that assertion through having to walk some 15 miles downhill in pursuit—at one time, close pursuit—of a lion which was bothering local characters. The pursuit was most pleasant and the lion escaped. The only tragic part of this story, unlike most of the thrilling details one hears about the King of Beasts, is that we were then forced to walk 15 miles back uphill to the point from which we started. This puts you in excellent shape but in no sense resembles a few hands of canasta after dinner, especially if you have been sweating heavily, have no raincoat, and it starts to rain. However, in Laitokitok, I rubbed myself down with Messrs. Gordon's excellent product, purchased a shirt of the type which is stocked in the *dukka* (Hindu store) and sold to the local Christian converts of Laitokitok, who seem to me a uniformly worthless lot and who stood around on the corner of the street of Laitokitok wearing large tight shoes and dressed in European clothes while other people were comfortably dressed, able to lean on their spears and were either barefoot or wore comfortable sandals.

Many of these latter citizens, the spear-carrying variety, became fairly intimate friends. I joined an elderly chief of the Masai Tribe, for whom we had killed a lion which had been bothering the cattle, in splitting a bottle of Tusker beer which he offered me. Although we were a part of the Law West of the Pecos, I saw no reason not to join an elderly chief that one knew quite well in a couple of glasses of beer since he was a man of great authority in his district and, if I refused to drink with him, which could be making a grave breach of etiquette, he might drink instead some of the inferior beer produced on some of the neighbouring *shambas*.

Some of this beer is excellent and I have often sampled it. It is much healthier for those Masai who, unfortunately, have taken up the habit of drinking due to their wealth and the inactivity of the men, who do not now kill the marauding lion nor engage in war. The warriors have generally, in this area, become addicted to a beverage manufactured in South Africa and shipped into the colony, which is known as Golden Jeep sherry. This is a beverage that I would always be forced to refuse no matter by whom it was offered. As a moral force in the Masai country, I have attempted to discourage the consumption of this beverage at any cost except drinking it.

The chief and I were shortly joined by three other tribal leaders and started discussing lion hunting in general, and the lion hunt of that day on which several warriors (Morani) had been initiated into this science or sport, which is infinitely more pleasurable if the lion is chased out of the country rather than makes his bid.

I had ascertained, with the aid of my own trackers who were on the left flank, and the best tracker of the game scouts, an old ivory poacher, Arab Minor, called by his intimates Mehna, who was expiating a fairly grave sin which he had committed, what direction the lion was pursuing. We were all fairly relieved that Arab Minor was expiating this sin, which involved the consumption of Golden Jeep, by being given the honor of taking the center and staying on the track, which he was to follow as rapidly as possible while we flanked on the left. We were then to pick up the track if it turned or take the lion if he came in Arab Minor's direction. If he came in Arab Minor's direction we would kill him if it were humanly possible.

Arab Minor would also attempt to kill him whenever he saw him. With me were the three best Wakamba trackers, one with a 12-gauge shotgun, one with my big gun, the .577, one with a spear. I was carrying the Springfield 30-06 with six 220-grain Silvertip rounds. We had given the right flank to a young police officer six months out from England who had not previously hunted lion and he had with him the local Masai who were also taking up lion hunting for the first time.

For our sins, but not with evil intention, rather in the spirit of good clean fun, we hoped the lion would break to the right. He neither broke to the right nor broke to the left but continued on his way until Mehna and my people knew he had gone clean out of the country. At one time, we were quite close to him but he had been lying down and had rested. He then picked up speed, or, as I would say in *Ndege* or aircraft parlance, he poured on the coal. We determined this by the sudden depth of the tracks and the length of the bounds. He then settled into a steady trot. We followed him over a ridge, climbed the ridge and saw that there was no sight of him. We then sent Mehna, and he picked up the lion's tracks and returned to say that he was still going at speed and moving out of the country. The mission accomplished, we returned up the hill.

This hill was one which Earl Theisen, our photographer at the start of the expedition, finding difficulty with the word Kilimanjaro and forgetting the word Kibo, always referred to as "that big hill Papa made all his money from." On the way back up the slope of the big hill, the Masai suddenly became very lion-conscious. They would suddenly shout, "He's in there! He's in there!"

I, being rained on while sweating, was irascible, not as irascible as Miss Mary can get when she wishes to go into true irascibility with a fool, but still irascible. I would say, "Well, then, my beautiful Morani, why don't you go in and drive him out?"

The Masai would consult among themselves, with the Wakamba all laughing but trying not to let the Masai see them. Arab Minor, having expiated, was in an excellent mood. Knowing the lion was not there and wishing to acquire a reputation for fearlessness, I would take the spear of one of the Masai and go in and thresh the bushes and speak insultingly to Mr. or Mrs. Simba as if they were present. Of course they were not present, but after about twelve of these "That's where he is, he's in there" incidents, I began to wonder if perhaps there might not be a lion somewhere that we had not seen, in which case considerable activity would have resulted. So I then said, "Let us proceed to Laitokitok where the Wakamba can slake their thirst and the Masai can quaff a little mixed milk and blood."

I knew of course that they would hit the Golden Jeep sherry but having been irascible I now wished to be polite, so we proceeded to Laitokitok and that was the end of that lion hunt.

In the reading of our obituaries, it was incidents like that which came into my mind and I thought that perhaps a true account of the two crashes and how one felt before, during and after might be justified.

If the German obituaries were romantic and full of *Götterdämmerung* although extremely laudatory, the Italian obituaries passed them in many aspects. There were appreciations of us by people who described themselves as our only true and intimate friends and who knew the innermost contents of my heart.

Since I myself have no idea of the innermost contents of my heart and would not trust it for a minute if I did, some of these obituaries came as a surprise. Actually in regard to the innermost contents of my heart, probably a most foul place, I would rather have a good cardiograph report. However, I was touched deeply by the friendship that was displayed.

We love Italy very much and more than that we love many individual Italians. Maybe too many individual Italians. None of those we truly loved wrote obituaries. They were instead,

I believe, at Mass and many old friends would not believe that we were dead unless they saw the bodies.

The British papers I know about only through a cutting which was sent to me by a friend, and opinions seemed to be quite mixed.

What gave one most pleasure was to read in some papers, not the *Times* nor the *Observer* nor the *Guardian,* descriptions of one's habits and character and the exact circumstances under which one's death was achieved. Some of these were the work of great imaginative writers. We resolved to attempt to live up to them at some future date.

In all obituaries, or almost all, it was emphasized that I had sought death all my life. Can one imagine that if a man sought death all of his life he could not have found her before the age of 54? It is one thing to be in the proximity of death, to know more or less what she is, and it is quite another thing to seek her. She is the most easy thing to find that I know of. You can find her through a minor carelessness on a road with heavy traffic, you could find her in a full bottle of Seconal, you could find her with any type of razor blade; you could find her in your own bathtub or you could find her by not being battle-wise. There are so many ways of finding her that it is stupid to enumerate them.

If you have spent your life avoiding death as cagily as possible but, on the other hand taking no backchat from her and studying her as you would a beautiful harlot who could put you soundly to sleep forever with no problems and no necessity to work, you could be said to have studied her but you have not sought her. Because you know among one or two other things that if you sought her you would possess her and from her reputation you know that she would present you with an incurable disease. So much for the constant pursuit of death.

It is a facile theory to hold though and I can see when someone has to write an obituary in a hurry it would be a quick solution to a complicated subject. The most complicated subject that I know, since I am a man, is a man's life. I am sure that a woman's life is most complicated if she has any ethics. Lately, these have seemed, from my reading of the newspapers, a fairly lost commodity, but I know that they still exist in the people who do not spend their time in the newspapers nor in the acquiring of alimony, and I have always considered that it was easy to be a man compared to being a woman who lives by as rigid standards as men live by. No one of us lives by as rigid standards nor has as good ethics as we planned but an attempt is made.

At this point, I went to sleep and had a dream. Fortunately, I dream a great deal and the night is almost as much fun as the day. They are all nocturnal dreams, for so far I have never daydreamed, being too busy observing or having fun, and latterly reading my obituaries, a new and attractive vice.

In my nocturnal dreams, when they are not the bad kind that you get after a war where other people are killed sometimes by your fault, I am nearly always a very gay and witty person faintly addicted to the more obvious types of heroism and, with all, a most attractive type. In my nocturnal dreams, I am always between 25 or 30 years old, I am irresistible to women, dogs and, on one recent occasion, to a very beautiful lioness.

In the dream, this lioness, who became my fiancée, was one of the most delightful creatures that I have ever dreamt about. She had some of the characteristics of Miss Mary and she could become irascible. On one occasion, I recall she did an extremely perilous act. Perilous to me, that is. When I recalled the dream to Miss Mary and Denis Zaphiro at breakfast, they appeared to be appreciative of the dream, but they seemed slightly shocked. Denis invited me to share a bottle of beer with him, a thing that I almost never do at breakfast, and I sat drinking this beer and remembering with great pleasure the night I had spent with the beautiful lioness.

One of the aspects of this dream that I remember was that the lioness was killing game for me exactly as she would for a male of her own species; but instead of our having to devour the meat raw, she cooked it in a most appetizing manner. She used only butter for basting the impala chops. She braised the tenderloin and served it, on the grass, in a manner worthy of the Ritz in Paris. She asked me if I wanted any vegetables, and knowing that she herself was completely nonherbivorous, I refused in order to be polite. In any case, there were no vegetables.

This is the type of dream which I have more or less habitually so perhaps you can understand, and Freudian scholars may interpret, the following dream, which was an odd dream indeed, but my brain being in this damaged condition, I was not responsible. It was quite strange and I can remember one of the dislocated sides of my brain being surprised at the language of the characters.

In this dream, I was out, barefoot, on a moonlight night with my best and second-best spear hunting the wild-dog pack. They only hunt at first light and at dusk though they will trail through the day. But at night, they pack in together, under a tree usually, and sometimes you can get one with the spear and you might get two.

In the dream, and a few nights before in real life, I had made a very careful approach, barefoot, and bagged, or rather killed, one out of the pack of vermin. Then in the dream, I saw the Honorable Senator standing in the moonlight with his spear. I recognized him from his photographs in a news magazine.

"Hi, Senator," I said. "How are you doing?"

"What are you after?" the Senator asked sternly.

"Wild dogs," I said cheerfully, just having got a wild dog.

"I am after subversives," the Senator replied.

"Get many?" I asked.

"Thousands," he said. "Have you seen Cohn and Schine?"

"No," I answered. "Maybe they are up at Laitokitok. That's where you can get the good Golden Jeep sherry."

"They never drink," he said sternly.

"Poor chaps," I said. "We have Pepsi-Cola in camp."

"Schine isn't with me any more," the Senator said. Then he

appeared to check himself and added: "Or perhaps it's Cohn."

"Rotten luck," I said. I jammed the butt of my spear in the ground to show sympathy. In the dream, the Senator retained a grip on his spear.

Trying to make conversation, I asked, "Whatever happened to Huey Long, Senator?"

"Who?"

"Senator Long (Democrat) of Louisiana, great friend of my friend Seymour Weiss who runs the Roosevelt Hotel in N.O."

"Oh," said the Senator. He also placed the butt of his spear in the ground.

"Senator Long was a very promising man," I recalled. "Had a great following, looked as though he'd go a long way."

"A lamentable tragedy," the Senator said. He looked a trifle changed in the moonlight. "Even if he was a Democrat," he added.

At this time, due to the concussion, the dream became slightly fantastic.

"Like to take off your boots so we can sneak up on the pack?" I asked. "I marked where they went and the wind is okay to get up on them."

"This is childish sport," the Senator said. But he did not reach out to withdraw his spear from where the butt was sunk into the earth. "I am out after all enemies of the true American way of life."

"I'm after wild dogs," I said.

Then I thought perhaps I had been rude or unpatriotic or inhospitable so I said, in the dream, "If you find any subversives that aren't dead and the hyenas haven't hit them, please send over and I'll come with my trackers and the game scouts. I'm not sure they can work with Cohn and Schine but they're quite good. They can track a man or a vehicle from here to Nairobi."

"I lost Schine," the Senator said.

"Truly rotten luck," I said in the dream, being deeply moved. "How did you lose him?"

"The Army took him."

"Senator," I said in the dream, "my truest sympathy. What a fate for a professional loyal American! May I escort you to your camping place?"

At this point, I woke up horrified at the enormity of the type of dream produced by a certified concussion. Then I began to think how lovely it would be if instead of having unknown fluid running out of the juncture of my left ear and my head, which still had the slightly scorched odor, I were hunting barefoot at night alone and with my best and second-best spear. My second-best spear was given to me by Miss Roshan of the general store at Laitokitok. If this be treason make the most of it, I thought in my dreams.

As you most probably know, the night in Africa is completely different from the day. Very few people see the night without the benefit of the headlights of a car which distort it since the headlights terrify or occasionally anger the animals. After the sun has set and the fire is built in camp, the usual thing is for you to sit for a time and with your white hunter and companions discuss the events of the day and the plans for the following day.

You have a moderate amount of drinks and then bathe in a canvas tub with water which has been warmed at the cook fire. After that, you put on pajamas and mosquito boots and over them a dressing gown and go out to the fire where you have one more drink and wait for dinner to be served. After dinner, you go to bed which is covered by a mosquito net, and sleep or lie awake listening to the sound of the animals until half an hour before first light when you are roused by your personal boy bringing tea, known locally as *chai*. If you have no white hunter and consequently no need to observe rituals nor to be under anyone's discipline except your own, you are at liberty to do what you wish with the night, which is the loveliest time in Africa.

In the night, the animals are quite transformed. The lion, who is nearly always silent in the daytime, hunts by himself and from time to time coughs, grunts or roars. I have not been able yet to discover if he is communicating with his mates who are also hunting, or whether he is trying to make the game which sleeps quietly at night move and thus disclose its position. It may be that he roars much as Irishmen do in public drinking places occasionally. It may also be that he coughs from dyspepsia and grunts from irascibility due to the difficulty of procuring a meal.

The hyenas follow the lion and when he kills or when his women folk kill you can hear the talking of the hyenas among themselves. This is the time when you hear the so-called laughter of the hyena. His normal note at night is quite pleasant and I believe he gives it as communication to the other hyenas.

In hunting at night with a spear, you hear many other sounds. The wildebeest, which is a big antelope which was designed to try to look like a buffalo or bison, gives off terrifying noises in the effort to seem a dangerous beast. You can in the night, if you sight the silhouette on the ground and approach the wilde-beest, or gnu, with extreme caution, tap him on the rump with the butt end of your spear. He will spring to his feet and emit this terrifying sound. At this point, you may say, "Had you there, wildebeest, old boy."

In the night, you will see many bat-eared foxes. These are lovely animals which live in burrows and are almost never seen in broad daylight and live on insects and other small deer. This does not refer to actual deer but to the animals on which Poor Tom in *King Lear* existed. Mr. Gene Tunney, the Shakespear-ean scholar, can provide the quotation. The bat-eared fox looks like a real fox except for his ears, which are at least three times the size of those of Clark Gable, the actor, but are in no way to be compared to those of the elephant.

You will probably hear the voice of Mr. Chui, the leopard. He is about on his beat giving short coughing grunts. These are given in such a deep bass voice that they cannot be confused with the voice of the other beasts. At night if you hear Mr.

Chui on your left, you make a smart right turn. Mr. Chui is a very serious beast. He has his defects but he has great and terrible qualities as a beast.

If you hear Mr. Chui and he is working along a stream or wooded area you may mark his progress by the speech of the baboons who respond to his grunts with what I take in baboon to be imprecations, insults and warnings to all other baboons to seek the highest part of the treetops. At daylight, coming home from the night out with the spear, I have noted the tops of the fig trees along the creek loaded as though these trees bore fruit of baboons rather than figs. They had been placed in this difficult position by the passage of Mr. Chui.

Thinking about these times and about how fine the night could be when you were allowed to roam freely, I skipped further dreams and decided to think about the past.

This past was never my past life which truly bores me to think about and is often very distasteful due to the mistakes that I have made and the casualties to various human beings involved in that sad affair. I tried to think instead of other people, of the fine deeds of people and animals I have known, and I thought a long time about my dog Black Dog and what the two winters must have been when he had no master in Ketchum, Idaho, having been lost or abandoned by some summer motorist. Any small hardships we had encountered seemed to me to be dwarfed by Blackie's odyssey.

We encountered Blackie when we were living in a log cabin in Ketchum and had two deer, killed, respectively, by Mary and Patrick, hung up in the open door of the barn. There was also a string of mallard ducks hung out of the reach of cats and there were also hung up Hungarian partridges, different varieties of quail and other fine eating birds. It seeming that we were people of such evident solidarity, Blackie abandoned promiscuous begging and attached himself to us as our permanent dog. His devotion was exemplary and his appetite enormous. He slept by the fireplace and he had perfect manners.

When it came time to leave Ketchum and return to Cuba, I was faced with a grave moral problem as I did not know whether a dog bearing such a heavy coat as he had grown living in the snow could be brought to Cuba without making him suffer. But Blackie solved this problem when he saw us start packing by getting into the car and refusing to leave it unless he was lifted out. Lifted out, he would immediately leap back into the car and look at you with those eyes which are possessed only by springer spaniels and certain women.

"Black Dog," I asked him, "can you use a can opener?"

Black Dog appeared to give a negative answer, and I decided against leaving him with several cases of tinned dog food. There was also the first licensing project for dogs on in Ketchum. This was a town where a man was once not regarded as respectable unless he was accompanied by his dog. But a reform movement had set in, led by several local religionists, and gambling had been abolished and there was even a movement on foot to forbid a dog entering a public eating place with his master. Blackie had always tugged me by the trouser leg as we passed a combination gambling and eating place called the Alpine where they served the finest sizzling steak in the West. Blackie wanted me to order the giant sizzling steak and it was difficult to pass the Alpine and go to a place called the Tram where the steak while good was much smaller. We decided to make a command decision and take Blackie to Cuba.

I would have liked to have brought him to Africa but there were too many difficulties and I was afraid that he might be eaten by Mr. Chui who prefers the dog to the baboon or any other of the more toothsome things in Africa. I do not know what the culinary attraction of the dog is to Mr. Chui, but if you have a dog in areas where leopard are plentiful you will lose the dog. Mr. Chui can omit his nightly grunt and enter anywhere so quietly that he is not perceived until you feel the gentle touch of his whiskers.

This was an experience of young Denis Zaphiro last week in the camp beyond Magadi. He reached under his bed and fortunately encountering his weapon did away with Mr. Chui. The range was short and he was able to touch Mr. Chui with the muzzle of his weapon. This is the type of incident which makes the life of a game ranger an interesting one and I thought of various other incidents which I will not elaborate on because no one would believe me.

It was now getting toward morning and I got up, being careful not to wake Miss Mary, and went into the bathroom where I could put on a light and read and check the extent of bleeding from the various five orifices of the human body. Some authorities say there are seven but they include the nostrils and the ears as two each. The bleeding was no more than was to be expected. I felt quite well but rather de-primated so putting on a number of sweaters and a bush jacket and wrapping myself in a blanket I sat at the window of the hotel room to observe the early-morning traffic of Nairobi.

The native police, yawning and stretching their arms, descended from a truck carrying them to their various morning posts and moved at far from a brisk pace up the street. Natives went by going to market and later returning, the women heavily laden, the men walking beside them in admiration of their wives' strength and beauty. Many Hindus passed on financial errands. A car went by, its top covered with baskets of beautiful flowers. No spivs were yet to be seen. None of the beautiful big cars parked outside the hotel were in action. No two-pistol men were in view. Hundreds of bicycles of all types passed ridden by Africans and Asiatics. Then, yielding to my new vice, I began reading the obituaries I had not been able to finish.

When I had gotten well into the obituaries to the point of the fullest fulfillment of my new vice, Miss Mary woke up and said, "Haven't they brought the tea? And what are you reading?"

"Darling," I said, "I am observing the early-morning traffic of Nairobi and reading a number of obituaries that came last night."

"Darling," Miss Mary said, "I really wish you would not read so many of those obituaries. I think it is morbid probably. Anyway we are not dead and so it is rather an affectation. We never read other people's obituaries and I do not really see why we should read our own. Besides it could be bad for you."

"I quite agree with you," I said. "But it is becoming a vice."

"Darling," Miss Mary said, "don't you think you have enough vices already?"

"Quite," I said.

"Besides," Miss Mary said, "we are due for lunch at Government House today and I want you to be at your best."

I thought this over wondering how I could achieve my best and, in the light of my obituaries, what my best would be. However, an invitation to Government House is not to be taken lightly, and conserving my energy and leaving off the vice of reading obituaries, we prepared to proceed to Government House.

It was most pleasant, the Governor and his wife were charming, I met a brace of old friends and we returned to the hotel. I would like to say that at this point I ceased reading obituaries due to my strong and sterling character and the sound advice of my beloved wife Miss Mary, but I am afraid the sad end of this story is that I continued to read them, bootlegging them, in a sense, by reading them in the confines of either the bathroom or the toilet. I placed a blanket over the seat of the toilet so that I might sit comfortably while pursuing this, by now, illicit pastime. I would like to say, in the character which the obituaries had given me, that I then dropped them and flushed them away.

However, trying to make this an absolutely true account, I must admit that we are preserving them in two scrapbooks. One of these scrapbooks is covered with zebra hide and the other with lion skin. They are very handsome scrapbooks and since it is not easy to desert a newly acquired vice, I intend to read them at least once a year in order to keep my morale up to par when the critics have recovered their aplomb and return to the assault. Since Miss Mary and I sympathize with even the lowest forms of animal life, we will hope to die in some altogether ignominious fashion and give some of those gentlemen a break. In the meantime, we hope to have fun and to write as well as possible.

A Situation Report

➤ *Look* · SEPTEMBER 4, 1956

HAVANA

"The more books we read, the sooner we perceive that the true function of a writer is to produce a masterpiece and that no other task is of any consequence. Obvious though this should be, how few writers will admit it or, having made the admission, will be prepared to lay aside the piece of iridescent mediocrity on which they have embarked! Writers always hope that their next book is going to be their best, for they will not acknowledge that it is their present way of life which prevents them ever creating anything different or better.

"All excursions into journalism, broadcasting, propaganda and writing for the films, however grandiose, are doomed to disappointment. To put of our best into these forms is another folly, since thereby we condemn good ideas, as well as bad, to oblivion. It is in the nature of such work not to last, so it should never be undertaken. . . ."

THIS was written by Cyril Connolly in a book called *The Unquiet Grave*. It is a book which, no matter how many readers it will ever have, will never have enough.

So, rereading it and having interrupted a book that you loved and believed in on the eight hundred and fiftieth manuscript page, to work four months on the script and photography of a motion picture of another book that you believed in and loved, you know that now you will never again interrupt the work that you were born and trained to do until you die. Since in almost any week you can read the obituaries of good dead friends, this is not much of a promise. But it is one that you can keep.

The company of jerks is neither stimulating nor rewarding, so for a long time you have tried to avoid it. There are many ways to do this and you learn most of them. But the jerks and twerps, the creeps and the squares and the drips flourish and seem, with the new antibiotics, to have attained a sort of creeping immortality, while people that you care for die publicly or anonymously each month. Those that make the New York *Times* in death are gone away as far as, and are probably little happier than, those that make the Key West *Citizen*, or the Billings (Mont.) *Gazette*.

So Mary and I live here and work until visitors interrupt work so much that we have to leave. It was a nice life here for a long time, and it still is a nice life when we are left alone and we will always come back here from wherever we go. This is our home. And you do not get run out of your home; you defend it. Spain and Africa are good places, but they are being overrun. They are not too badly overrun yet and there are places that have not been ruined. But you have to find them.

The places in Wyoming, Montana and Idaho that I loved, and where we would be pulling out for now at the end of June, have all been overrun and nobody who knew them in the old days could live in them now. Those things which are necessary to develop or to rape a country ruin it for those who knew it before it was spoiled.

We have to make a break now in the fall and let the pressure and the interruptions die off. So we will go somewhere to get a change from two years in the tropics. We were going to Africa, but the rains failed there last year and nobody wants to see another drought so soon. You can always go back after it has rained. In the meantime, it is work on the book at Finca Vigia this summer. The interruption of the picture is over. There will never be any more picture work ever.

As for journalism, that writing of something that happens day by day, in which I was trained when young, and which is

not whoring when done honestly with exact reporting; there is
no more of that until this book is finished.

This is a situation report of how things go until we go back
to work tomorrow on the long book. Three other books are
finished, and this piece can tell how things go now and, after
slightly bad times, I hope it is a little cheerful. Read the last part.

No one can work every day in the hot months without going
stale. To break up the pattern of work, we fish the Gulf Stream
in the spring and summer months and in the fall. The changes
of each season show in the sea as they do on the land. There is
no monotony as long as the current is alive and moving, and
each day you never know what you will meet with.

You go out early or later, depending on the tide which pushes
the heavy blue water out or brings it close to shore. When
the current is running well and the flying fish are coming into
the air from under the bow of the *Pilar,* you have an even
chance or better to catch dolphin and small tuna and to catch
or lose white marlin.

When you have finished far enough down with the current,
you go into some beach to swim and have a drink while Gregorio, the mate, cooks lunch. In the late afternoon, you fish back
toward home against the current until sunset. The small marlin
are there in the spring and early summer and the big fish in
the summer and the fall.

This fishing is what brought you to Cuba in the old days.
Then you took a break on a book, or between books, of a hundred days or more and fished every day from sunup to sun-
down. Now, living on the hill in the country, you fish the days
you pick.

It was different in Peru where we went to try to photograph
big fish for the picture. There the wind blew day and night.
Sand blew in your room from the desert that makes the coast
and the doors banged shut with the wind.

We fished 32 days from early morning until it was too rough
to photograph and the seas ran like onrushing hills with snow

blowing off the tops. If you looked from the crest of a sea toward shore you could see the haze of the sand blowing as the wind furrowed the hills and scoured and sculptured them each day.

The sea birds huddled in the lee of the cliffs, coming out in clouds to dive wildly when a scouting bird would sight school-fish moving along the shore, and the condors ate dead pelicans on the beaches. The pelicans usually died from bursting their food pouches diving and a condor would walk backwards along the beach lifting a large dead pelican as though it weighed nothing.

The marlin were large and did not fight as the fish off Cuba do. But their weight and bulk in the heavy seas made it hard work, and a fish that you would bring to gaff in eight or twelve minutes you would let run again, holding him always in close camera range, feeling his weight through the soles of your feet, your forearms and your back, and finally when he was dead tired, have Gregorio harpoon him to try for the camera shot you needed in the picture.

It was steady punishing work each day and it was fun too because the people were nice and it was a strange new sea to learn. It was good too to be back in Cuba and on *Pilar* again.

Down in Peru, 420 miles south of the Equator, where she was working as interpreter on the main camera boat between the Spanish-speaking, Indian-blooded captain and crew and the United States-speaking cameramen, putting in a full day under arduous conditions, Miss Mary announced one evening that the first thing her husband needed in a wife was that she be durable.

Miss Mary is durable. She is also brave, charming, witty, exciting to look at, a pleasure to be with and a good wife. She is also an excellent fisherwoman, a fair wing shot, a strong swimmer, a really good cook, a good judge of wine, an excellent gardener, an amateur astronomer, a student of art, political economy, Swahili, French and Italian and can run a boat or a household in Spanish. She can also sing well with an accurate and true voice, knows more generals, admirals, air marshals, politicians and important persons than I know dead company commanders, former battalion commanders, rummies, coyotes, prairie dogs, jack rabbits, leaders of café society, saloon keepers, airplane drivers, horse players, good and bad writers and goats.

Miss Mary can also sing in Basque and is a brilliant and erratic rifle shot. She has been known to be irascible and can say in her own perfect Swahili, *"Tupa ile chupa tupu,"* which means take away that empty bottle.

When she is away, the Finca is as empty as the emptiest bottle she ever ordered removed and I live in a vacuum that is as lonely as a radio tube when the batteries are dead and there is no current to plug into.

She does not suffer fools gladly. She does not suffer them at all. She has great energy and she can stay the distance, but she also knows how to be as lazy as a cat.

There is the matter of being expatriots. It is very difficult to be an expatriot at 35 minutes by air from Key West and less than an hour, by faster plane, from Miami. I never hired out to be a patriot but regularly attend the wars in which my country participates and pay my Federal taxes. An expatriate (I looked up the spelling) is, consequently, a word I never cared for. Born in Cook County, Illinois, I early ceded the territory as a writer to Mr. Carl Sandburg, who had taken it over anyway, and to Mr. James Farrell and to Mr. Nelson Algren when they came of age. They have ruled it very well and I have no complaints.

It was possible to stake out a few claims in other places, and I am glad that not all of these have been jumped. One of these claims is here.

All you have to do to see your compatriots is to get into the car after work and go into the Floridita Bar in Havana. There are people from all of the states and from many places where you have lived. There are also Navy ships in, cruise ships, Customs and Immigration agents you have known for years, gam-

blers who are opening up or have just closed or are doing well
or badly, embassy characters, aspirant writers, firmly or poorly
established writers, senators on the town, the physicians and
surgeons who come for conventions, Lions, Elks, Moose, Shrin-
ers, American Legion members, Knights of Columbus, beauty
contest winners, characters who have gotten into a little trouble
and pass a note in by the doorman, characters who get killed
next week, characters who will be killed next year, the F.B.I.,
former F.B.I., occasionally your bank manager and two other
guys, not to mention your Cuban friends. There are also the
usual phonies who help you to keep your hand in on the
language.

One of the most enjoyable nights I remember recently at the
Floridita was when several fleet units were in with an annual
cruise of midshipmen. Miss Mary was away and I was lonesome
as a goat and felt like going on the town. Some erudite midshipmen had been by in the early afternoon to ask my views on
Ezra Pound. These views are succinct, although the subject is
complicated. Ezra, I told them, should be released from St.
Elizabeth's Hospital and be allowed to practice poetry without
let or hindrance.

At this point a group of Navy CPO's, all with the several long
hash marks of their re-enlistments, turned up to see old Ernie.
They tolerated the midshipmen but were suspicious that by
these queries about Pound and other subjects alien to them,
they might be preventing old Ernie from writing; a thing they
themselves would never do.

"Give me the word," one of the chiefs said, "and they're out
of here before they know it. Who the hell is going to bother
you while I'm alive?"

"Ernie," the chief said to me, "you got to have somebody steer
people away from you. You got to be allowed to think. I will
be your A.D.C. I will be your personal aide. I will be the man
that wears the chicken guts on his shoulders for you and I will
handle all your public relations."

"Chief," I said, "you are my pal and now you are my personal aide. Handle my public relations."

"Sir," he said, "let there be no familiarity between us even though I may sometimes speak as man to man under stress. Sir, this is the chance I have prepared myself for during long years."

"The Floridita," I said.

"You hear that, you bums?" the chief said. "Hit the bag. It's the Floridita."

On the way in, although we opened up the new Chrysler New Yorker convertible a little once, to the extent the highway permitted, the chief said, "Ernie, sir, she is a mighty nice little car except maybe that fireman red they have her painted. But from now on maybe you will wish to have a bigger car."

"A bigger car it is. Steady as you go," I warned Juan, the driver.

"Yes, sir," the chief said. "Make a note of it, Healey."

The Floridita was quite crowded, but my public relations officer evicted a number of characters from the stools in the corner in which we usually sat.

We sat and ordered and various people approached, some seeking autographs, others wishing to shake hands.

"Do you know Ernie?" asked my public relations officer. "No? You don't come from his home town or anything? Scram. He's thinking."

We were all engaged in serious literary discussion and had gone very deeply into things. Another chief joined us and he said, "The two books I like the best were. . . . No three. . . . Were *When the Rains Came, The Mooney Sixpense,* and *The Towers of Babel.*"

"Mac," I said, "I didn't write a one of them."

"He probably means the *Torrents of Spring,*" one of our chiefs said. "I liked where that no-armed Indian shot that wonderful stick of pool."

"*The Mooney Sixpense* was a good book," the new chief said defensively.

"Ernie wrote them all," my aide said. "Only he's too modest. He wrote them under a synonym. But every one of them has got the old touch. You were smart to have spotted them, chief."

Soon we were singing, very softly and surprisingly in tune, that lovely old ballad, "Meet me by the slop chutes on the old Whangpoo."

Around then, I got the eye from the naval attaché who was sitting at a table with the admiral and a couple of other people, all in civilian clothes.

I refused the eye once, but I got it again and I said, "Excuse me, gentlemen, but I have to go over and speak to a man I know pretty well who would feel I was rude if I did not come over."

"Be careful, sir," said my aide. "Do you need me, Ernie? They may be false friends."

"No," I said. "You handle this end and I'll be right back."

So I went over and sat down with my good friend and found the visiting admiral to be cordial, extremely intelligent, pleasant and good company.

We had talked for some little time when I heard a voice at shoulder height, "Ernie, what are you doing here, wasting your time with a bunch of civilians?" It was my aide and public relations officer.

The admiral stood up and said, "I'm sorry, son, but I am your admiral."

"Admiral, sir, excuse me, sir. I have never seen you before, sir, so I did not recognize you in civilian clothes."

"I understand that perfectly," the admiral said.

"Admiral, sir, may I respectfully request, sir, that Ernie be allowed to return to our group?"

"It's not necessary to make the request," the admiral said. "Mr. Hemingway had said he was overdue to return."

"Thank you, sir."

It was a very good evening. At the end the chief said, "Ernie, I hate to relinquish this job I have worked for so hard and so well over so many years."

"I feel bad too, chief," I said. "I'll never have another personal aide and public relations officer if it isn't you."

"Stand back there, you guys," the chief said. "Let Ernie get in the car. He's got to get home so he can sleep good and think right and work good tomorrow."

INDEX

Index

481

BY-LINE: ERNEST HEMINGWAY